The Future of the Profit Split Method

The Future of the Profit Split Method

Edited by

Robert Danon
Guglielmo Maisto
Vikram Chand
Gabriella Cappelleri

Wolters Kluwer

Published by:
Kluwer Law International B.V.
PO Box 316
2400 AH Alphen aan den Rijn
The Netherlands
E-mail: international-sales@wolterskluwer.com
Website: lrus.wolterskluwer.com

Sold and distributed by:
Wolters Kluwer Legal & Regulatory U.S.
7201 McKinney Circle
Frederick, MD 21704
United States of America
Email: customer.service@wolterskluwer.com

ISBN 978-94-035-2430-6

e-Book: ISBN 978-94-035-2431-3
web-PDF: ISBN 978-94-035-2432-0

Editors

Robert Danon, Professor of Law, Director, Tax Policy Center, University of Lausanne

Guglielmo Maisto, Professor of Tax Law at the Catholic University of Piacenza, Founding Partner at Maisto e Associati.

Vikram Chand, Associate Professor of Law and Program Director, Executive Program in Transfer Pricing, Tax Policy Center, University of Lausanne.

Gabriella Cappelleri, Of Counsel at Maisto e Associati.

Contributors

Paolo Valerio Barbantini, Italian Revenue Agency.

Yariv Brauner, Professor, Hugh Culverhouse Eminent Scholar Chair in Taxation, at the University of Florida.

Vikram Chand, Associate Professor of Law and Program Director, Executive Program in Transfer Pricing, Tax Policy Center, University of Lausanne.

Simone Di Vaia, Head of APA/MAP Office - Italian Revenue Agency.

Xaver Ditz, Partner/Tax Advisor at Flick Gocke Schaumburg and lecturer at the Universities of Trier, Zurich and Lausanne.

Steve Edge, Partner at Slaughter and May.

Mauro Faggion, Seconded National Expert European Commission.

Bruno Gibert, Partner at CMS Francis Lefebvre Avocats.

Andrew Hickman, Independent Consultant.

Harlow Higinbotham, Managing Director at NERA.

Joan Hortalà I Vallvé, Partner at Cuatrecasas, Barcelona.

Michael Kobetsky, Associate Professor at Melbourne Law School, University of Melbourne, Adjunct Professor at ANU College of Law, Australian National University, Global Professor of Law, Faculty of Law, New York University.

Emmanuel Llinares, Managing Director, Chair of NERA's Global Transfer Pricing Practice.

Aurelio Massimiano, Partner at Maisto e Associati.

Guglielmo Maisto, Professor of Tax Law at the Catholic University of Piacenza, Founding Partner at Maisto e Associati.

Andrea Parolini, Partner at Maisto e Associati.

Celine Pasquier, Associate at CMS Francis Lefebvre Avocats.

Amanda Platz, Associate Director at NERA.

Patrick Schmid, Research Assistant at the University of St. Gallen; Attorney-at-Law, Swiss Certified Tax Expert.

Caroline Silberztein, Partner at Baker & McKenzie A.A.R.P.I.

Vladimir Starkov, Managing Director at NERA.

Raoul Stocker, Assistant Professor at the University of St. Gallen; Partner, Bär & Karrer AG.

Alicia Tan, Associate at Farrer & Co.

Mario Tenore, Associate at Maisto e Associati.

Marco Valdonio, Partner at Maisto e Associati.

Summary of Contents

Table of Contents

Preface

As affirmed by one of the authors, 'The Revised Guidance on Profit Splits' is, to a large extent, the culmination of the OECD work on risks and intangibles in the course of the BEPS Actions 8–10 'Aligning Transfer Pricing Outcomes with Value Creation'. This work entailed three public discussions and three discussion drafts, which received over 150 comments. Although the revised guidance is controversial, these numbers highlight two aspects.

First of all, this is the culmination of the evolution of the OECD approach to the transfer pricing methods, which began with the 1979 OECD Report that recognized a general possibility to apply the so-called other methods. Indeed, in recent years, the profit split method has received considerable attention as a method to counteract BEPS issues. As affirmed by the Final Report, '[the] consultation process confirmed that transactional profit splits can offer a useful method which has the potential when properly applied, to align profits with value creation in accordance with the arm's length principle and the most appropriate method, particularly in situations where the features of the transaction make the application of other transfer pricing methodologies problematic'.

The identification of profit split methods as the method to tackle BEPS has perhaps led the OECD to expand the scope of situations in which a profit split method will effectively be regarded as the most appropriate method. However, a likely increased application of the profit split methods should not be confused with a de facto departure from the most appropriate method standard set forth by the OECD Guidelines. This standard still remains the basis of the process of selecting the transfer pricing method based on the OECD Guidelines: the profit split methods should not be considered a method to be applied when it is difficult to apply what is actually the most appropriate method.

The second aspect concerns the many issues arising from the application of this method. These issues affect several areas: the application of the OECD Guidelines and the UN Manual, as well as the relationship with the State aid and indirect taxation topics.

As observed by the OECD at the outset of the work on profit split methods, it is necessary 'to reflect on clarifying, improving, and strengthening the guidance on when it is appropriate to apply a transactional profit split method and how to do so, since experiences indicate that this method may not be straightforward for taxpayers to apply, and may not be straightforward for tax administrations to evaluate'. However, as shown by the analysis carried out in the second and following parts of this book, these aspects are still largely open: How should the different relevant factors for the application of profit split methods be considered? What is the profit to be split? What are the factors to split the profit?

Such a conclusion on the open issues related to the profit split method also emerged from the work of the EU Joint Transfer Pricing Forum, which affirms that 'The main challenge in the application of the PSM highlighted by the survey is the choice of the appropriate splitting factors, their relative weights and the valuation of the contributions, especially heterogeneous contributions (they featured in practically all of the replies as one of the main challenges in applying the profit split methods).'

As already stated, the question is whether the lack of clear guidance may entail extreme complexity for taxpayers and tax authorities alike, broad uncertainties and outcomes that are potentially not aligned with the arm's-length standard. This concern also stems from the countries' chapters of this book, which highlight the experience of countries – particularly during the tax audit phase. They all indicate a high level of uncertainty in terms of results and alignment to the international guidance in the application of the profit split methods.

Moreover, further consideration should be made in the following two possible different and extreme scenarios. If the profit split method is applied in an articulated way, additional attention should be paid to the assessments made by the European Commission on State aid. Indeed, in this scenario, the European Commission could consider the application of the profit split as 'artificial and complex'.

Instead, in the case of a simplified application of the profit split method, e.g., as proposed by the Commission Service to the Joint Transfer Pricing Forum, it is possible that a 'soft' introduction of the formulary apportionment may occur. This would create a concrete risk of a departure from the arm's-length principle that would remain, therefore, confined to the role of a mere inspiring principle within this approach. Some pressure in this direction could also come from the OECD's work on the digital economy.

In fact, the Profit Split Method (albeit a new version) is at the centre state vis-à-vis the Digital Economy Debate. Action 1 of the BEPS project, which is now Pillar I of the OECD's digital project, deals with re-allocating profits of large MNEs to market/user countries. A new/modified version of the PSM applicable on a residuary basis has been put forward as a solution. It is considered to be a new/modified version as it goes beyond the ALP. This is because the new/modified approach applies on an MNE Group basis as opposed to being applied on a separate entity basis. Moreover, it uses a pre-determined approach to determine the profits to the re-allocated as opposed to a facts and circumstances analysis that is deployed under a transactional profit split. The details of the new approach, which has been analysed towards the end of this book, have been made public in the recently released blueprint on Pillar I.

In light of the above backdrop, the application of the PSM is under the spotlight. Undoubtedly, the existing and new version will be applied widely by taxpayers and tax administrations. Considering these developments, this book undertakes an in-depth analysis of the PSM applicable within and beyond the boundaries of the ALP from a global as well as a local perspective.

We would like to thank all the contributors, many of whom lecture in the Executive Program in Transfer Pricing (EPTP) offered by the University of Lausanne (UNIL), for making this book a reality. Specifically, we would like to thank Mirko Severi (former EPTP alumnus) for coordinating and ensuring that the book gets finalized.

Prof Robert Danon
Prof Guglielmo Maisto
Prof Vikram Chand
Mrs Gabriella Cappelleri
Lausanne / Milan, October 2020

CHAPTER 1

The Rise (and Fall?) of the Profit Split Method

Guglielmo Maisto

I INTRODUCTION

This chapter is aimed at describing the rise of the profit split as one of the OECD-recognized transfer pricing methods, in order to put the recent developments in the right perspective. It is also purported to discuss how the profit split method, due to its inherent flexibility, may be used in order to allocate the profits of multinational enterprises in hard cases, such as in agency permanent establishment (hereinafter 'PE') scenarios. Finally, as an introductory chapter to this book, it briefly touches upon the various topics that are analysed in the following chapters.

The structure of the chapter follows from the above-mentioned objectives. Section II succinctly describes the evolution of the profit split method in the works of the OECD on transfer pricing. Section III discusses when and how to apply the profit split as the most appropriate method under the current OECD Guidelines. Section IV illustrates how the profit split method may be applied to agency PE cases, in particular, for the purpose of splitting under Article 7 of the OECD Model the relevant profits between the head office of the foreign company and the local PE thereof (created by the activity carried out by a local subsidiary on behalf of the foreign company).[1] Section V discusses certain open issues and, in particular, how the profit split method influences tax treaty policy and interpretation. Finally, section VI concludes, by highlighting the possible future employment of the (modified) profit split method to allocate among

1. It is obviously possible that the profit split method may be found to be also the most appropriate method to split the relevant profits between the local subsidiary and the foreign company under Art. 9 of the OECD Model. This is not, however, a case that the author will discuss in this contribution.

jurisdictions the multinational group profits generated from cross-border activities in the digital age.

II BRIEF HISTORY OF THE PROFIT SPLIT METHOD[2]

When, in 1979, the OECD published its first guidance on the allocation of profits between associated enterprises (hereinafter '1979 TP Guidelines'),[3,4] it specifically identified three transfer pricing methods. The OECD regarded those methods as applicable under a strict hierarchical order, according to which the comparable uncontrolled price (CUP) method was to be applied first, as it represented the most direct and reliable means to establish the arm's-length price of an intercompany transaction. The other two identified transfer pricing methods, i.e., the cost-plus method and the resale price method, might be applied only where the CUP could not be reliably used, due to the absence of comparable uncontrolled transactions.

However, due to the practical difficulties that both tax authorities and taxpayers faced in applying these three methods, in particular, with regard to the identification of comparable transactions and enterprises, the OECD recognized, already in the 1979 TP Guidelines, the possibility to have recourse to 'other methods'[5] in order to establish the arm's-length price of intercompany transactions. In the words of the OECD, '[t]he complexities of real life business situations may put many conceptual and practical difficulties in the way of the application of the [three identified] methods referred to above. A mixture of these methods, or other methods still, may sometimes therefore have to be used'.[6]

It is also worth mentioning that, in 1979, the OECD appeared to generally oppose to the use of formulary apportionment and profit split methods aimed at dividing the global profits of multinational enterprises among the different group entities.

On the one hand, the OECD found that those methods arbitrary and contrary to Article 9 of the (1977) OECD Model Convention were based on predetermined splitting factors. In this respect, the 1979 TP Guidelines considered that those methods would necessarily be arbitrary, tending to disregard market conditions as well as the particular circumstances of the individual enterprises and tending to ignore the

2. *See* to a further extent: BARBANTINI, s. I, in Part I of this book.
3. *See* OECD, Transfer Pricing and Multinational Enterprises (1 June 1979) OECD Publishing, Paris.
4. For a historical overview, *see*: MAISTO, Il 'Transfer Price' nel Diritto Tributario Italiano e Comparato, Chapter 1, s. 5, and also the 1992 IFA General Report in MAISTO (1992), Introduction Part a) and s. 2. *See also*: HAY/HORNER/OWENDS, Past and Present Work in the OECD on Transfer Pricing and Selected Issues, pp. 432–437; HIGINBOTHAM, The Profit Split Method: Effective Application for Precision and Administrability; HAMAEKERS, Arm's Length – How Long?, para. I; COLLIER/ANDRUS, Transfer Pricing and the Arm's Length Principle after BEPS, Chapter 2, s. C.2; LANG ET AL., Transfer Pricing in a Post BEPS World, Chapter I; KOOMEN, Transfer Pricing in the BEPS Era: Rethinking the Arm's Length Principle – Part I, para. 2.4; CHAND/WAGH, The Profit Split Method: Status Quo and Outlook in Light of the BEPS Action Plan, para. 2; AHMADOV, The 'Most Appropriate Method' as the New OECD Transfer Pricing Standard: Has the Hierarchy of Methods Been Completely Eliminated?, para. 2.1.
5. A mixture of the traditional methods and/or other methods. *See* OECD, Transfer Pricing and Multinational Enterprises (1 June 1979) OECD Publishing, Paris, Chapter I, para. 13.
6. *Id.*

management's own allocation of resources, thus producing an allocation of profits which may bear no sound relationship to the economic facts and inherently running the risk of allocating profits to an entity which is, in truth, making losses (or possibly the contrary). A number of such methods are sometimes advocated, allocating profits in some cases in proportion to the respective costs of the associated enterprises, sometimes in proportion to their respective turnovers or to their respective labour forces, or by some formula taking account of several such criteria. They are all, however, to some degree, arbitrary.[7]

On the other hand, the OECD recognized that to allocate profits by such methods in a way which reduced the arbitrariness of the results to a negligible degree would necessitate a complex analysis of the different functions of the various associated enterprises and a sophisticated weighing up of the different risks and profit opportunities in the various different stages of manufacturing, transportation, marketing and so on. The information necessary for such an assessment would not be readily available or, in many cases, may not be available at all.[8]

Thus, back in 1979, the OECD considered the possibility to apply methods aimed at dividing the profits of multinational enterprises on the basis of carefully selected splitting factors to be chosen based on functional/value chain analyses but rejected such possibility due to the practical difficulties connected to those methods and to the limits at that time existing in finding the necessary information.

The opportunity to indirectly determine the arm's-length profits of the relevant intercompany transactions through the split of the global profits of the multinational enterprise, however, was not entirely rejected. Indeed, the OECD noted that 'some regard to the total profits of the relevant MNE may ... be helpful' for the purpose of 'seeking to arrive at the arm's length price in a range of transactions', for instance, 'as a check on the assessment of the arm's length price or in specific bilateral situations where other methods give rise to serious difficulties and the two countries concerned are able to adopt a common approach and the necessary information can be made available'.[9]

The OECD continued working on the Transfer Pricing Guidelines in the following years, in particular, with a view to developing a more detailed guidance on the application of the 'other methods'. Indeed, practice had shown that the concrete application of the CUP, the cost-plus and the resale price methods often turned out to be extremely complex if not impossible, due to the difficulty to find reliable external comparables (both price comparables and gross margin comparables) and to the frequent lack of internal comparables, as many intercompany transactions were carried out exclusively within the multinational group.[10]

7. *See* OECD, Transfer Pricing and Multinational Enterprises (1 June 1979), OECD Publishing, Paris, Chapter I, para. 14.
8. *Id.*
9. *Id.*
10. *See* Barbantini, s. II of Part I of this book.

This further work led to the issue in 1995 of the new Transfer Pricing Guidelines for Multinational Enterprises and Tax Administrations (hereinafter '1995 TP Guidelines').[11] which distinguished between the traditional transaction methods (i.e., the CUP, the cost-plus and the resale price methods)[12] and the transactional profit methods.[13]Among the transactional profit methods, the OECD explicitly referred to the profit split method.[14]

Under the 1995 TP Guidelines, the three traditional methods (i.e., the CUP, the cost-plus and the resale price methods) were regarded as superior to the other methods, as they represented the most direct and reliable means to establish the arm's-length price of intercompany transactions. However, the OECD explicitly recognized the possibility to use the transactional profit methods (including the profits split method) in 'those exceptional cases in which the complexities of real life business put practical difficulties in the way of application of the traditional transaction methods', as in such cases, the 'application of the transactional profit methods may provide an approximation of transfer pricing in a manner consistent with the arm's length principle'.[15]

Once again, however, practice departed from the theoretical framework delineated by the OECD in its guidelines, as the transactional profit methods turned out to be, by far, the most used methods to establish the arm's-length price of intercompany transactions.[16] This conflict between theory and practice led the OECD to restructure the 1995 TP Guidelines with a view to supersede the hierarchical relation existing between the traditional and the transactional profit methods.

The solution adopted in the 2010 Transfer Pricing Guidelines for Multinational Enterprises and Tax Administrations (hereinafter '2010 TP Guidelines') was to attribute paramount importance, for the purpose of the selection (and the application) of the transfer pricing methods, to the functional analysis and to the availability of the information necessary to apply the relevant methods. Thus, under the 2010 TP

11. *See* OECD, Transfer Pricing Guidelines for Multinational Enterprises and Tax Administrations (June 1995), OECD Publishing, Paris. For a detailed analysis of the changes made to the 1995 OECD Guidelines *see* Torvik, Transfer Pricing and Intangibles. US and OECD Arm's Length Distribution of Operating Profits from IP Value Chain, para. 5.4 and pp. 304–305; Collier/Andrus, Transfer Pricing and the Arm's Length Principle after BEPS, Chapter 2, s. D.3; Lang et al., Transfer Pricing in a Post BEPS World, p. 12; Chand/Wagh, The Profit Split Method: Status Quo and Outlook in Light of the BEPS Action Plan, para. 2; Ahmadov, The 'Most Appropriate Method' as the New OECD Transfer Pricing Standard: Has the Hierarchy of Methods Been Completely Eliminated?, para. 2.2; Weber/van Weeghel, The 2010 OECD Updates: Model Tax Convention & Transfer Pricing Guidelines, A Critical Review, pp. 153–154.; Manganelli, Critical Analysis of Transactional Profit Methods and of Their Practical Application, pp. 207–213.
12. *See* OECD, Transfer Pricing Guidelines for Multinational Enterprises and Tax Administrations (June 1995), OECD Publishing, Paris, Chapter II.
13. These methods represented the only acceptable 'other methods' under the 1995 Guidelines. *See* OECD, Transfer Pricing Guidelines for Multinational Enterprises and Tax Administrations (June 1995), OECD Publishing, Paris, Chapter III.
14. *See id.*, Chapter III, s. B i).
15. *See id.*, Chapter III, s. B para. 3.2.
16. *See* to a greater extent: Barbantini, s. IV in Part I of this book. *See also* Ahmadov, The 'Most Appropriate Method' as the New OECD Transfer Pricing Standard: Has the Hierarchy of Methods Been Completely Eliminated?, para. 1, p. 184.

Guidelines, no method was a priori regarded as preferred to the others, while the most appropriate method to be applied had to be chosen on the basis of the outcome of the functional analysis and the existence of appropriate information at disposal.[17,18]

In the same vein, the 2010 TP Guidelines also added new guidance on how to apply the transactional profit methods (in particular, the profit split method).[19]

The 2017 TP Guidelines[20] and the 2018 OECD Revised Guidance on Profit Splits (hereinafter 'Revised Guidance on Profit Split')[21] have further emphasized the role of the comparability analysis in order to select and apply the most appropriate transfer pricing method, thus substantially confirming the 2010 approach.

III THE PROFIT SPLIT AS THE MOST APPROPRIATE METHOD

1 The Profit Split Method in a Nutshell

The profit split method, like all other OECD-compliant transfer pricing methods, is aimed at establishing an approximation of the profit allocation that independent parties would have attained in comparable circumstances. In order to achieve this result, the OECD suggests two (main) alternative approaches to the application of the profit split method, i.e., (i) the one-stage 'contribution analysis'; and (ii) the two-stage 'residual analysis'.[22]

---

17. *See* OECD, Transfer Pricing Guidelines for Multinational Enterprises and Tax Administrations (18 August 2010), OECD Publishing, Paris, Chapter II, s. I, A, http://www.oecd.org/ctp/transfer-pricing/transfer-pricing-guidelines.htm.
18. In this regard, *see* MAISTO, Chapter 12: OECD Revision of Chapters I-III and IX of the Transfer Pricing Guidelines: Some Comments on Hierarchy of Methods and Re-characterization of Actual Transactions Undertaken', in: D. WEBER/VAN WEEGHEL (eds.), The 2010 OECD Updates: Model Tax Convention and Transfer Pricing Guidelines, A Critical Review; SILBERZTEIN, Chapter 10: The 2010 Updates to the OECD Transfer Pricing Guidelines', in: WEBER/VAN WEEGHEL (eds.), *id.*; HEIMERT/MICHAELSON, Guide to International Transfer Pricing, p. 24f.; COLLIER/ANDRUS, Transfer Pricing and the Arm's Length Principle after BEPS, Chapter 2, s. E.4 and Chapter 3, s. D.; LANG ET AL., Transfer Pricing in a Post BEPS World, p. 13; JAMIL, The 'Most Appropriate Method' as the New OECD Transfer Pricing Standard: Has the Hierarchy of Methods Been Completely Eliminated?, para. 2.3.
19. *See* OECD, Transfer Pricing Guidelines for Multinational Enterprises and Tax Administrations (18 August 2010), OECD Publishing, Paris, Chapter II, part III.
20. *See* OECD, Transfer Pricing Guidelines for Multinational Enterprises and Tax Administrations (10 July 2017), OECD Publishing, Paris, https://doi.org/10.1787/tpg-2017-en. For a better understanding of the evolution of the OECD Guidelines, *see* A. HICKMAN, The BEPS Action plan and Updating the OECD Guidance on Profit Split, s. II, of Part II of this book.
21. *See* OECD, Revised Guidance on the Application of the Transactional Profit Split Method: Inclusive Framework on BEPS: Action 10, OECD/G20 Base Erosion and Profit Shifting Project (June 2018), OECD Publishing, Paris, www.oecd.org/tax/beps/revised-guidance-on-the-application-of-the-transactional-profitsplit-method-beps-action-10.pdf. To a further extent, *see* BARBANTINI, History and Evolution of the OECD Guidelines, s. VI in Part I of this book.
22. For a more detailed analysis, *see* HIGINBOTHAM/STARKOV, s. I.1, in Part II of this book. *See also*: ANGIOLILLI ET AL., Limiting Base Erosion, pp. 462–464. In addition *see* OECD, Revised Guidance on the Application of the Transactional Profit Split Method: Inclusive Framework on BEPS: Action 10, OECD/G20 Base Erosion and Profit Shifting Project (June 2018), OECD Publishing, Paris, para. C.3.1.

Under (i), the total profits from the controlled transactions are divided between the associated enterprises on the basis of external comparable data, if available. In the absence of those data, the profit split should be based on the relative value of the contributions by each of the associated enterprises participating in the controlled transactions, as determined by using information internal to the group, as a proxy for the division that independent enterprises would have achieved.[23] In order to attain this result, it is necessary either to measure the actual market value of each party's contributions or, at least, to establish their relative values. Those values, in turn, depend on the functions performed, assets used and risks assumed by each of the associated enterprises engaged in these controlled transactions.[24]

Under (ii), on the other hand, the profits attributable to contributions for which market comparables exist (generally less complex contributions) are first attributed to the party(ies) making such contributions. This first part of the analysis is carried out by applying one of the traditional transactional methods, or the transactional net margin method (hereinafter 'TNMM'). The remaining profits, i.e., those deriving from unique and valuable contributions, the shared assumption of economically significant risks (or the separate assumption of closely related risks), and/or a high level of business integration, are split between the participant parties based on the relative value of their contributions. This second part of the analysis is carried out, in substance, by applying the contribution analysis described under (i).[25]

23. *See* OECD, Revised Guidance on the Application of the Transactional Profit Split Method, (June 2018), OECD Publishing, Paris, para. C.3.1.1.
24. *See* to a further extent: Torvik, Transfer Pricing and Intangibles. US and OECD Arm's Length Distribution of Operating Profits from IP Value Chain, s. 9.3.3; Stahli, The Use of the Profit Split Method in Highly Integrated Transactions, para. 2.1; Zucchetti/Piva, Revised Guidance on the Application of the Transactional Profit Split Method: Evolution or Revolution?, para. 4.1. Moreover, with reference to the OECD, Public Discussion Draft, Revised Guidance on Profit Split (2017), *see*: Ilhan, The Use of Value Chain Analysis in a Profit Split. With reference to the 2010 OECD Transfer Pricing Guidelines, *see*: Peng, The Application of the Arm's Length Principle to the Allocation of the Joint Efficiencies within MNEs, para. 2.2.3.2; Chand/Wagh, The Profit Split Method: Status Quo and Outlook in Light of the BEPS Action Plan, para. 3.2.1. With reference to the 1995 OECD Transfer Pricing Guidelines, *see*: Gonnet, Contribution Analyses under the Profit Split Method.
25. *See* OECD, Revised Guidance on the Application of the Transactional Profit Split Method, (June 2018), OECD Publishing, Paris para. C.3.1.2. To a further extent, *see*: Ilhan, The Use of Value Chain Analysis in a Profit Split; Zucchetti/Piva, Revised Guidance on the Application of the Transactional Profit Split Method: Evolution or Revolution?. With reference to the OECD 2017 Public Discussion Draft, Revised Guidance on Profit Split: Torvik, Transfer Pricing and Intangibles. US and OECD Arm's Length Distribution of Operating Profits from IP Value Chain, s. 9.3.3. With reference to the OECD 2010 Transfer Pricing Guidelines: Peng, The Application of the Arm's Length Principle to the Allocation of the Joint Efficiencies within MNEs, para. 2.2.3.2; Chand/Wagh, The Profit Split Method: Status Quo and Outlook in Light of the BEPS Action Plan, para. 3.2.1.

2 When to Apply the Profit Split Method under the OECD TP Guidelines

The profit split method should be chosen as the most appropriate method only as a result of appropriate functional analysis and delineation of the relevant transaction.[26]

As the lack of comparables should not trigger, per se, the selection of the profit split as the most appropriate transfer pricing method, the TP Guidelines[27] provide for three autonomous indicators that should be generally employed to that end:[28]

(i) the existence of unique and valuable contributions by each party to the transaction;
(ii) a high level of integration with regard to the relevant transaction; and/or
(iii) the shared assumptions of economically significant risks, or the separate assumption of economically closely related risks, by the parties in connection to the relevant transaction.

When at least one of these indicators is met, it is likely (although not necessary) that the profit split is the most appropriate method to apply to the relevant transaction.

With regard to (i) above, the TP Guidelines provide that contributions should be regarded as unique and valuable when they are not comparable to contributions made by uncontrolled parties in comparable circumstances, and they represent a key source of actual or potential economic benefits.[29] It appears that the contribution must be both

---

26. *See* the EU JTPF, The Application of the Profit Split Method within the EU, (2019), s. 3; EU JTPF, Profit Split Method (PSM) Summary of Replies to the Survey, (2018), paras 2.2, 2.3, 2.4. In addition, *see also*: DITZ, Accurately delineating the transaction, s. I of Part I, of this book. At the JTPF meeting of 8 March 2018 a survey was conducted in order to gather information on the PSM. One of the main points of the survey regarded the situations where the PSM was applied as the most appropriate method. To have more detailed information about the result, *see*: FAGGION/DI VAIA, Reason to consider the profit split method the most appropriate method, s. III, in Part III of this book. *See also*: ZUCCHETTI/PIVA, Revised Guidance on the Application of the Transactional Profit Split Method: Evolution or Revolution?, para. 3; STAHLI, The Use of the Profit Split Method in Highly Integrated Transactions, para. 3.2; ROBILLARD, Contractual Arrangements and the Delineation of a Transaction: A Duo in Crisis Mode. With reference to the OECD 2017 Discussion Draft: ILHAN, The Use of Value Chain Analysis in a Profit Split, para. 2.3,3.
27. Unless otherwise specified, 'TP Guidelines' hereinafter refers to the 2017 TP Guidelines as amended in 2018 by the Revised Guidance on Profit Split.
28. *See* OECD, Revised Guidance on the Application of the Transactional Profit Split Method, (June 2018), OECD Publishing, Paris, paras 2.128, 2.143. *See also*, to a further extent: SILBERZTEIN, When is a Transactional Profit Split Method the Most Appropriate Method?, ss II, III, IV in Part II of this book; ZUCCHETTI/PIVA, Revised Guidance on the Application of the Transactional Profit Split Method: Evolution or Revolution?, para. 2.3. With reference to the OECD 2017 Discussion Draft, *see*: TORVIK, Transfer Pricing and Intangibles: US and OECD Arm's Length Distribution of Operating Profits from IP Value Chain, s. 9.2.3; BILANEY, The Profit Split Method: Deciphering the OECD's 2017 Discussion Draft, para. 2; CHRISTMAN/MUKHERJEE, An Analysis of the OECD's Discussion Draft on Profit Splits. With reference to the OECD 2010 Transfer Pricing Guidelines: CHAND/WAGH, 'The Profit Split Method: Status Quo and Outlook in Light of the BEPS Action Plan', para. 3; ERNIK, More Profit Split, para. 2.
29. *See* OECD, Revised Guidance on the Application of the Transactional Profit Split Method, (June 2018), OECD Publishing, Paris, s. C.2.1 para. 2.119, s. C.2.2.1, and Annex II to Chapter II examples 2,3,5.

unique and valuable[30] in order for it to satisfy the first criterion put forward by the OECD. Indeed, the TP Guidelines use 'unique and valuable contribution' as a single term and highlight that 'uniqueness' and 'value' are often linked since contributions that are a key source of economic advantage (i.e., valuable) are, for that reason, also seldom. In this respect, the OECD explicitly maintains that a contribution should be regarded as 'unique and valuable' only where: (a) it is not comparable to contributions made by uncontrolled parties in comparable circumstances; and (b) it represents a key source of actual or potential economic benefits in the business operation.[31]

In respect of (ii) above, the TP Guidelines take the view that a high degree of integration exists when the way one party to the transaction performs functions, uses assets and assumes risks is interlinked with, and cannot reliably be evaluated in isolation from, the way in which another party to the transaction performs functions, uses assets and assumes risks.[32] Thus, there is no high degree of integration where the contribution of at least one party to the transaction can be reliably evaluated by reference to comparable uncontrolled transactions.[33] The necessary and inextricable link that must exist between the activities of the two parties is emphasized by the EU Joint Transfer Pricing Forum (hereinafter 'JTPF'), according to which operations should be regarded as 'highly integrated' where two or more entities 'share and/or combine functions, assets and risks, while jointly achieve a common objective', so that 'it would not be possible to materialise such a jointly achieved objective without the participation of the other party in the transaction'.[34] As previously mentioned, the three indicators are autonomous from each other. In particular, where there is a high degree of integration, the profit split is likely to be regarded as the most appropriate method, even in the absence of unique and valuable contributions.[35]

30. For the purpose of qualifying the contribution as 'valuable', it is not important whether an economic benefit is effectively realized or not, but whether the success of the contribution is key for the success of the business operations. Thus, a contribution may still bel considered valuable to a transaction even if the potential economic benefit is not realized. *See* accordingly, EU JTPF, The Application of the Profit Split Method within the EU, (2019), para. 3.1.5.
31. *See* OECD, Revised Guidance on the Application of the Transactional Profit Split Method, (June 2018), OECD Publishing, Paris, s. C.2.2.1. *See* to a further extent, EU JTPF, The Application of the Profit Split Method within the EU, (2019), para. 3.1. *See also*: Zucchetti/Piva, Revised Guidance on the Application of the Transactional Profit Split Method: Evolution or Revolution?, para. 3.2.2 (1). With reference to the OECD 2017 Public Discussion Draft, Revised Guidance on Profit Split: Stahli, The Use of the Profit Split Method in Highly Integrated Transactions, para. 3.
32. *See* OECD, Revised Guidance on the Application of the Transactional Profit Split Method, (June 2018), OECD Publishing, Paris, para. C.2.2.2; Stahlin, The Use of the Profit Split Method in Highly Integrated Transactions.
33. *See* to a further extent, EU JTPF, The Application of the Profit Split Method within the EU, (2019), s. 3.2. *See also* Zucchetti/Piva, Revised Guidance on the Application of the Transactional Profit Split Method: Evolution or Revolution?, para. 3.2.2 (2). With reference to the OECD 2017 Discussion Draft: Lang, et al., Transfer Pricing Developments Around the World 2017, Chapter 6, s. 4.
34. *See* EU JTPF, The Application of the Profit Split Method within the EU, (2019), para 3.2.3. *See,* in this respect: OECD, Revised Guidance on the Application of the Transactional Profit Split Method, (June 2018), OECD Publishing, Paris, Annex II to Chapter II, Examples 6 and 7.
35. *See* OECD, Revised Guidance on the Application of the Transactional Profit Split Method, (June 2018), OECD Publishing, Paris, s. C.2.2.3 para. 2.140.

With regard to (iii) above, the TP Guidelines clarify that risks should be regarded as 'closely related' where the playing out of the risks of each party cannot reliably be isolated.[36] In addition, it should be mentioned that, although the existence of a unique and valuable contribution of a party to a transaction is generally linked to the assumption of risk related to that contribution by that party, the existence of unique and valuable contributions by each party to the transaction does not necessarily trigger a joint assumption of the same risk (or separate assumption of closely related risks). This supports the conclusion, which is also based on the wording of the TP Guidelines, that the shared assumption of risk should be regarded as a separate factor from the others (i.e., (i) and (ii) above).[37]

Conversely (and in general terms), the profit split should not be selected as the most appropriate transfer pricing method where one of the parties to the relevant transaction performs only simple functions, does not make unique and valuable contributions, and does not assume economically significant risks in relation to the transaction.[38]

At the same time, one should bear in mind that, if the relevant transaction can be appropriately benchmarked as sufficiently comparable transactions, and functions can be identified, it is less likely that the profit split turns out to be the most appropriate method to be applied.[39]

This holds true even where no full comparability exists, but nonetheless, the comparables that have been identified are reliable.[40,41]

---

36. *See* to a further extent, EU JTPF, The Application of the Profit Split Method within the EU, (2019), s. 3.3. *See also*: ZUCCHETTI/PIVA, Revised Guidance on the Application of the Transactional Profit Split Method: Evolution or Revolution?, para. 3.2.2 (3). With reference to the OECD 2017 Discussion Draft: TORVIK, Transfer Pricing and Intangibles: US and OECD Arm's Length Distribution of Operating Profits from IP Value Chain, s. 9.2.3.
37. *See* OECD, Revised Guidance on the Application of the Transactional Profit Split Method, (June 2018), OECD Publishing, Paris, para. 2.127, and Annex II to Chapter II, Examples 4 and 8.
38. *See* OECD, Revised Guidance on the Application of the Transactional Profit Split Method, para. 2.127.
39. *See* EU JTPF, The Application of the Profit Split Method within the EU, (2019), s. 3; OECD, Revised Guidance on the Application of the Transactional Profit Split Method, (June 2018), OECD Publishing, Paris, para. 2.143.
40. *See* to a further extent, BARBANTINI, History and Evolution of the Profit Split Method in the OECD Guidelines, s. VI and SILBERZTEIN, When is a Transactional Profit Split Method the Most Appropriate Method?, s. VI, respectively in Parts I and II of this book.
41. In this respect, the TP Guidelines make it clear that: '[a] lack of closely comparable, uncontrolled transactions which would otherwise be used to benchmark an arm's length return for the party performing the less complex functions should not per se lead to a conclusion that the transactional profit split is the most appropriate method. Depending on the facts of the case, an appropriate method using uncontrolled transactions that are sufficiently comparable, but not identical to the controlled transaction is likely to be more reliable than an inappropriate use of the transactional profit split method'. *See* OECD, Revised Guidance on the Application of the Transactional Profit Split Method, (June 2018), OECD Publishing, Paris, para. 2.128. With reference to 2010 OECD Transfer Pricing Guidelines, *see*: COLLIER/ANDRUS, Transfer Pricing and the Arm's Length Principle after BEPS, Chapter 3 s. C and Chapter 4 s. B.2.

3 How to Apply the Profit Split Method

As previously mentioned, under both the contribution analysis and the second stage of the residual analysis, the profit split method aims at dividing the total profits from the controlled transactions based on external comparables data, or, absent those data, on the relative value of the contributions by each of the associated enterprises. The purpose is to approximate the result that would have been achieved, in comparable circumstances, between independent enterprises.

As a matter of fact, the division of the relevant profits is usually made on the basis of profit-splitting factors. The TP Guidelines clearly highlight that these splitting factors should be chosen and weighted based on a careful functional and contextual analysis. In this respect, the 'determination of appropriate profit-splitting factor(s) should reflect the key contributions to value in relation to the transaction'.[42] As a result of this approach, the splitting factors may be either fixed figures (e.g., 50%–50%, 80%–20%, etc., based on evidence of similar splits achieved between independent parties in comparable transactions), or variable figures (e.g., relative values of participant's contributions, which can change from year to year). In the latter case, the TP Guidelines allow for the use of one single profit-splitting factor or for the use of weighting of multiple splitting factors.[43]

This meticulous procedure of selecting the profit-splitting factors on the basis of the results of the functional and contextual analysis is what structurally distinguishes the profit split method under the TP Guidelines from any global formulary apportionment methods, which generally operate through the application of predetermined splitting factors of the tax base.[44]

---

42. *See* OECD, Revised Guidance on the Application of the Transactional Profit Split Method, (June 2018), OECD Publishing, Paris, para. 2.169; ZUCCHETTI/PIVA, Revised Guidance on the Application of the Transactional Profit Split Method: Evolution or Revolution?, para. 3.2.1.
43. *See* OECD, Revised Guidance on the Application of the Transactional Profit Split Method, (Paris: OECD Publishing, 2018), para. 2.170, June 2018. To better analyse the topic, refer to: ILHAN, The Use of Value Chain Analysis in a Profit Split, para. 3.2; ROBILLARD, Profits in Profit-Split Methods: Hazardous Crossovers on the Way to Global Formulary Apportionment, both with reference to the OECD Transfer Pricing Guidelines (2017).
44. The use of predetermined splitting factors to compute the taxpayers' taxable base is envisaged, for instance, both in the first version of the Proposal for a Council Directive on a Common Consolidated Corporate Tax Base (CCCTB), COM(2011) 121/4 and in the second version of such proposal issued in 2016 (COM(2016) 683). In particular, such proposals provide for the consolidated tax base to be shared between the group members in each tax year on the basis of a formula for apportionment, which takes into account the level of sales, payrolls, assets and the number of employees. Another example is provided by the Italian Regional Tax on Productive Activities (IRAP). In particular, if a taxpayer carries on its activity in more than one Italian region, the taxpayer must apportion the net value of production among the regions involved. In this case, the region is indeed allocated a part of the taxpayer's base in proportion to the costs incurred by the taxpayer in respect of the personnel employed therein. *See* to a further extent, M. KOBETSKY, A Comparative Analysis of the UN and OECD Approaches on the Transactional Profit Split Method and Formulary Apportionment, s. IV, in Part IV of this book. With reference to the formulary apportionment, *see*: BLAY, Reviving Transfer Pricing Enforcement Through Formulary Apportionment, s. III; ANGIOLILLI ET AL., Limiting Base Erosion, Subtopic 4, pp. 465–466; ROBILLARD, BEPS: Is the OECD Now at the Gates of Global Formulary Apportionment?; KROPPEN/DAWID/SCHMIDTKE, Profit Split, the Future of Transfer Pricing? Arm's Length Principle and Formulary Apportionment Revised from a Theoretical and Practical Perspective, in:

In addition, with specific reference to intangibles, the TP Guidelines emphasize that particular attention should be paid to the identification of: (i) the relevant contributions of unique and valuable intangibles; (ii) the assumption and control of the related economically significant risks; and (iii) the performance of the key functions of development, enhancement, maintenance, protection, and exploitation of such intangibles.[45]

The TP Guidelines list a (short) inventory of profit-splitting factors,[46] such as those based on assets (or capital),[47] costs,[48] incremental sales, employees' compensation,[49] headcount or time spent by a coherent group of employees.[50] The list is by no means intended to be exhaustive, as other profit-splitting factors might be acceptable provided that they result in arm's-length outcomes for all parties involved in the relevant transactions.[51]

In this respect, the JTPF has recently published a study including a longer, and more detailed, non-prescriptive list of splitting factors with a brief analysis of the pros and cons of each factor, as well as the circumstances and value drivers possibly behind

---

Fundamentals of International Transfer Pricing in Law and Economics, W. Schon & K.A. Konrad (eds.) 2012; Avi-Yonah, Between Formulary Apportionment and the OECD Guidelines: A Proposal for Reconciliation, para. 3; Hellerstein, The Case for Formulary Apportionment; Sadiq, Unitary Taxation – The Case for Global Formulary Apportionment.

45. *See* OECD, Revised Guidance on the Application of the Transactional Profit Split Method, (June 2018), OECD Publishing, Paris, para. 2.178; and OECD, Transfer Pricing Guidelines for Multinational Enterprises and Tax Administrations, (10 July), OECD Publishing, Paris, para. 6.54. With reference to the OECD 2017 Transfer Pricing Guidelines: Peng/Lagarden, DEMPE Functions and the RACI Concept – More Clarity or Confusion Ahead?; Hoor, The Revised OECD Transfer Pricing Guidance on Intangibles: A Critical Analysis. With reference to the OECD 2010 Transfer Pricing Guidelines: Turley, et al., A New Dawn for the International Tax System – Evolution from Past to Future and What Role Will China Play?, Part 2 Chapter 7, s. 7.3.2; Pankiv, Post-BEPS Application of the Arm's Length Principle to Intangible Structures, paras 2.2.1 and 2.2.2.
46. *See* OECD, Revised Guidance on the Application of the Transactional Profit Split Method, (June 2018), OECD Publishing, Paris, paras 2.171–2.172. In addition, *see*: Higinbotham/Starkov, Application of the Profit Split, s. I.4, in Part II of this book. For a detailed analysis of the splitting factors, *see*: Zucchetti/Piva, Revised Guidance on the Application of the Transactional Profit Split Method: Evolution or Revolution?, para. 3.2.1.
47. For example, operating assets, fixed assets (e.g., production assets, retail assets, IT assets), intangibles).
48. For example, relative spending and/or investment in key areas such as research and development, engineering, marketing). The TP Guidelines highlight that, while costs may be a poor measure of the value of intangibles contributed, the relative costs incurred by parties may provide a reasonable proxy for the relative value of those contributions where such contributions are similar in nature (*See* OECD, Revised Guidance on the Application of the Transactional Profit Split Method, (Paris: OECD Publishing, 2018) para. 2.171.
49. Typically concerning the individuals involved in the key functions that generate value to the transaction.
50. If there is a strong and relatively consistent correlation between this and the creation of value represented by the relevant profits.
51. *See* OECD, Revised Guidance on the Application of the Transactional Profit Split Method, (June 2018), OECD Publishing, Paris, para. 2.172.

their selection.[52] This inventory is merely intended to record the most often encountered splitting factors.[53]

The splitting factors, most of which are derived from financial or management accounting, are grouped by the JTPF in the following categories:[54]

(a) *People-based factors*, such as employee compensation and/or headcount, which may be used, in particular, where people functions are key value drivers to the specific business.
(b) *Sales/volume-based factors*, often used in combination with other splitting factors, which may be used as a market measure of value realized or created in a particular jurisdiction, in particular, where the level of sales is an indicator of contribution to the overall group profits.
(c) *Asset-based factors*, which are often employed when the contributions are in the form of (intangible) assets.
(d) *Cost-based factors*, which may be used to measure the joint performance of the value-creating activities, whereby the respective contribution is reflected in the costs borne to perform those activities.
(e) *Other factors*, which, according to the JTPF, may include contribution weightings assigned based on functional analysis, external benchmarks and hedge-fund financing.

IV THE APPLICATION OF THE PROFIT SPLIT METHOD TO AGENCY PEs

1 Possible Use of the Profit Split to Allocate Profits to Agency PEs

A problematic case in which the profit split method may represent the most appropriate transfer pricing method, through which resolving an otherwise thorny issue, is that of the allocation of profits between the head office and its agency PE. This is particularly true where the agency PE comes to existence due to the activities performed, on behalf of the non-resident enterprise, by a local company of the same group acting as an intermediary, and the non-resident enterprise exercises together with the local intermediary the controlling functions over specific business risks.

In such a case, there might be a high level of integration between the head office and the PE with regard to the specific functions performed, as well as a shared assumption of economically significant risks. Depending on the circumstances, there could even be a unique and valuable contribution to the transaction by both the head

52. *See* to a further extent, EU JTPF, The Application of the Profit Split Method within the EU, (2019), Annex 3.
53. *See* EU JTPF, The Application of the Profit Split Method within the EU, (2019), s. 4.1.
54. *See id.* In addition, *see*: Zucchetti/Piva, Revised Guidance on the Application of the Transactional Profit Split Method: Evolution or Revolution?, para. 4.3; Stahli, The Use of the Profit Split Method in Highly Integrated Transactions, para. 3.4. With reference to the OECD 2017 Draft Guidance: Bilaney, The Profit Split Method: Deciphering the OECD's 2017 Discussion Draft, s. 5.

office and the PE (for instance, the joint contribution of unique and valuable intangibles). These circumstances, matched with the absence of reliable comparables, may indeed trigger the application of the profit split method.

The following subsections explore this matter.

2 Parallel Application of Article 7 and Article 9 of the OECD Model in the Case of Agency PEs

The 2018 OECD Report Additional Guidance on Attribution of Profits to Permanent Establishments[55] (hereinafter 'Report') confirms that the determination of the profits attributable to a PE resulting from the application of the 2017 version of Article 5(5) of the OECD Model should be governed by the rules of Article 7 of the Model.[56] It also highlights that where a PE is deemed to exist under Article 5(5) of the OECD Model due to the activities of an intermediary, those activities are relevant in the source State both to the intermediary (which may be a resident of that State) and to the PE. In this respect, the arm's-length reward to the intermediary for the services provided to the non-resident enterprise should be deducted from the profits attributable to the PE under Article 7 of the OECD Model.

Furthermore, the Report recognizes that where the intermediary[57] and the non-resident enterprise are associated enterprises, Article 9 of the OECD Model shall apply. The Report highlights that the order in which Article 7 and Article 9 of the OECD Model are applied should not impact on the amount of the profits over which the source State has taxing rights.[58]

The Report also stresses that any approach to the application of Articles 7 and 9 of the OECD Model to cases of agency PEs under Article 5(5) must ensure that there is no double taxation in the source State, i.e., no taxation of the same profits in the hands of the PE (under Article 7) and of the intermediary (under Article 9). This result is typically achieved through the deduction of the arm's-length remuneration paid to the intermediary from the profits attributable to the PE.

55. OECD, Additional Guidance on the Attribution of Profits to Permanent Establishments, BEPS Action 7 (22 March 2018), OECD Publishing, Paris, https://www.oecd.org/tax/transfer-pricing/additional-guidance-attribution-of-profits-to-permanent-establishments-BEPS-action-7.pdf. *See also*: Collier/Vella, Five Core Problems in the Attribution of Profits to Permanent Establishments.
56. *See*: OECD: Additional Guidance on the Attribution of Profits to Permanent Establishments, BEPS Action 7 (22 March 2018), OECD Publishing, Paris, para. 31.
57. The Report (*see* in this regard: p. 14, n. 7 of the Report) defines the term 'intermediary' as a person, whether or not an employee of the enterprise, who acts on behalf of the enterprise and is not doing so in the course of carrying on a business as an independent agent within the meaning of Art. 5(6). In the Authorised OECD Approach, this is referred to as a dependent agent enterprise.
58. *See*: OECD, Additional Guidance on the Attribution of Profits to Permanent Establishments, BEPS Action 7 (22 March 2018), OECD Publishing, Paris, para. 35.

3 Interactions Between the TP Guidelines and the Authorized OECD Approach

A Risk Management Functions Versus Significant People Functions Relevant to the Assumption and/or Management of Risks

The Report addresses the implications that the work under BEPS Actions 8–10[59] may have on the determination of the arm's-length remuneration recognized to the intermediary for the services provided to the non-resident enterprise and, consequently, on the profits attributable to the PE. In particular, with reference to the assumption of risks, the Discussion Draft highlights that, under the guidance provided by BEPS Actions 8–10, risks are to be allocated to the enterprise that actually exercises the control over the risk and has the financial capacity to assume it.[60] In turn, the control over the risk is deemed to be performed by the entity that exercises the 'risk management functions'.

These guidelines are not applicable to the relations between head offices and PEs, as there is no single part of a single enterprise that legally owns the assets, assumes the risks, possesses the capital or contracts with separate enterprises. On the contrary, these features pertain to the enterprise as a whole. In this context, the attribution of risk assumption (as well as economic ownership of assets) to a PE, under the Authorized OECD Approach (hereinafter 'AOA'),[61] is based on the notion of 'significant people functions'.[62]

Against this background, it is worth noting that the definition of 'risk management functions' under the TP Guidelines (i.e., for the purpose of Article 9 of the OECD

59. OECD, Aligning Transfer Pricing Outcomes with Value Creation, Actions 8–10: 2015 Final Reports, OECD/G20 Base Erosion and Profit Shifting Project (5 October 2015), OECD Publishing, Paris, https://doi.org/10.1787/9789264241244-en.
60. *See* OECD, Additional Guidance on the Attribution of Profits to Permanent Establishments, BEPS Action 7 (22 March 2018), OECD Publishing, Paris, para. 36.
61. For a comprehensive analysis of the AOA and of the notion of 'significant people function', *see*: COLLIER/VELLA, Five Core Problems in the Attribution of Profits to Permanent Establishments, s. 2; TORVIK, Transfer Pricing and Intangibles: US and OECD Arm's Length Distribution of Operating Profits from IP Value Chain, Chapter 17, s. 17.4.2; OOSTERHOFF, The True Importance of Significant People Functions, para. 2.2.; DROBNIK, The Attribution of Profits to a Dependent Agent PE – If the Dependent Agent Is a Commissionaire (Wholly Owned Subsidiary) of the Principal, para. 3.2; SCHWARZLER, Using the Capital Allocation Approach to Attribute Capital to a Permanent Establishment, s. 2.2. LANG, ET AL., Transfer Pricing Developments Around the World 2017, Chapter 7, s. 3; COLLIER/ANDRUS, Transfer Pricing and the Arm's Length Principle after BEPS, Chapter 7, s. A.1, Chapter 6 s. C, Chapter 8 s. D.4; HEIMERT ET AL., Guide to International Transfer Pricing, Chapter 2, s. 2.02; JOCHUM ET AL., Practical Problems in European and International Tax Law, Chapter 8, s. 8.4.3. (*see*: 8.4.3.1 stage 1, and 8.4.3.2 stage 2); EISENBEISS, BEPS Action 7: Evaluation of the Agency Permanent Establishment, s. 4.2; HUIBREGTSE, ET AL., Status of Implementation of the Authorized OECD Approach into Domestic Tax Law and Tax Treaties – Part 1, s. 5; DZIURDZ, Attribution of Profits to a Dependent Agent PE: Different Arm's Length Principles under Art. 7(2) and 9?, s. 2; VERDONER, The Concept of Dependent Agent Permanent Establishment in Transfer Pricing Theory, para. 2; KOFLER/VAN THIEL, The Authorized OECD Approach and EU Tax Law.
62. *See* OECD, Report on the Attribution of Profits to Permanent Establishments (22 July 2010), OECD Publishing, Paris, paras 21–27 and 68–71 of Part I.

Model)[63] evokes the concept of 'significant people functions relevant to the assumption and/or management (subsequent to the transfer) of risks'[64] under the AOA, which 'require active decision-making with regard to the acceptance and/or management (subsequent to the transfer) of those risks'.[65] It also appears natural, taking into account the progressive development of the OECD work on the subject in the last fifteen years,[66] to consider such concepts as being close to each other, also having regard to the fact that they are both grounded on fact-specific analyses that focus on the actual conduct of the parties in assuming and managing the risks, rather than on a formalistic analysis of the contractual framework. As a consequence, it might be argued that the concept of 'risk management functions', directly relevant for the purpose of Article 9 of the OECD Model, could be also employed as a useful tool to identify the 'significant people functions for the assumption of risk' under the AOA (which should be based on the application of the TP Guidelines 'by analogy').[67]

Indeed, the Report similarly recognizes that although it is not possible to conclude that those two concepts are aligned or can be used interchangeably for purposes of Article 7 and Article 9 of the OECD Model, 'there may be functions that would be considered both significant people functions for the attribution of risk for the purposes of the AOA and risk control functions for the purposes of Article 9'.[68]

The possible overlapping between 'significant people functions', for the purpose of Article 7, and 'risk control functions', for the purposes of Article 9, triggers the risk that the specific risk connected to the functions performed by the intermediary for the benefit of the related non-resident enterprise is attributed by the source State both to the (resident) intermediary and to the PE of the non-resident enterprise. In this respect,

---

63. *See* OECD, Transfer Pricing Guidelines for Multinational Enterprises and Tax Administrations (10 July 2017), OECD Publishing, Paris, para. 1.61, which provide that risk management 'comprises three elements: (i) the capability to make decisions to take on, lay off, or decline a risk-bearing opportunity, together with the actual performance of that decision-making function, (ii) the capability to make decisions on whether and how to respond to the risks associated with the opportunity, together with the actual performance of that decision-making function, and (iii) the capability to mitigate risk, that is the capability to take measures that affect risk outcomes, together with the actual performance of such risk mitigation'.
64. OECD, Report on the Attribution of Profits to Permanent Establishments (22 July 2010), OECD Publishing, Paris, para. 15.
65. *Id.*, para. 22.
66. OECD: Additional Guidance on the Attribution of Profits to Permanent Establishments (2018); Public Discussion Draft – BEPS Action 7 – Additional Guidance on the Attribution of Profits to Permanent Establishments (2017); Additional Guidance on the Attribution of Profits to Permanent Establishments (July 2016); Attribution of Profits to Permanent Establishments – Report (2010); Attribution of Profits to Permanent Establishments (with Addendum) – Report (2008); Attribution of Profits to Permanent Establishments – Report (2006).
67. As indicated in the OECD 2010 Report on the Attribution of Profits to Permanent Establishments (paras 54 and 55), '[o]ne issue in applying this approach is that for the purposes of Article 7, it is necessary to postulate the PE as a hypothetical enterprise that is separate from the enterprise of which it is a PE, whereas in an Article 9 case the enterprises being examined are actually legally separate. To reflect this issue, the authorised OECD approach is to apply the guidance given in the Guidelines not directly but by analogy'.
68. OECD, Public Discussion Draft, BEPS Action 7, Additional Guidance on Attribution of Profits to Permanent Establishments, (22 June – 15 September), OECD Publishing, Paris, para 40, https://www.oecd.org/tax/transfer-pricing/beps-discussion-draft-additional-guidance-attribution-of-profits-to-permanent-establishments.pdf.

the Report rightly concludes that 'when both Article 7 and Article 9 are applicable ... and the functions performed by the intermediary can qualify as significant people functions for the attribution of a specific risk to the PE and as risk control functions for the allocation of a risk under Article 9, it is important to ensure that the risk to which those functions relate is not simultaneously allocated to the intermediary[69] ... and attributed to the PE'.[70] Thus, where the specific risk is attributed to the intermediary under Article 9, that risk cannot be also attributed the non-resident enterprise (and, thus, to the PE) for the purposes of Article 7, as otherwise the profits related to the assumption of that risk would be taxed twice by the source State, i.e., in the hands of both the PE and the intermediary.[71]

Thus, the issue to be tackled is twofold. On the one hand, it is necessary to identify the relevant factors to be used for the purpose of establishing whether the specific risk should be attributed to the (resident) intermediary or to the non-resident enterprise. On the other hand, in cases where the specific risk related to the functions performed by the intermediary for the benefit of the non-resident enterprise is attributed to the latter, there is a need to establish whether, and under what conditions, the profits stemming from the performance of those functions may be attributed to the agency PE of the non-enterprise, which is deemed to exist in the source State under Article 5(5) of the OECD Model.

B Assumption of Risks

As previously mentioned, the TP Guidelines indicate that the analysis of risks assumption for transfer pricing purposes should establish whether the party contractually assuming the risk also controls it and has the financial capacity to assume it.[72] In this respect, the TP Guidelines recognize that, in cases where more than one party to the transaction has the control over a specific risk, only the enterprise which has the financial capacity to bear the risk will actually be deemed to assume it.[73] Based on the above, where, for example, the non-resident enterprise and the intermediary are associated enterprises and exercise together control over a risk (i.e., they exercise together the controlling functions – hereinafter referred to as 'Controlling Risk Functions' – over a specific risk, e.g., the risk of market development), but only the non-resident enterprise has the financial capacity to assume it; the latter will be

---

69. Subject to the conditions laid out in s. D of Chapter I of the Transfer Pricing Guidelines.
70. OECD, Public Discussion Draft, BEPS Action 7, Additional Guidance on Attribution of Profits to Permanent Establishments (22 June–15 September), OECD Publishing, Paris, para 41.
71. *See* for a deeper analysis: DROBNIK, The Attribution of Profits to a Dependent Agent PE – If the Dependent Agent Is a Commissionaire (Wholly Owned Subsidiary) of the Principal, para. 6; EISENBEISS, BEPS Action 7: Evaluation of the Agency Permanent Establishment, s. 4; HUIBREGTSE, ET AL., Status of Implementation of the Authorized OECD Approach into Domestic Tax Law and Tax Treaties – Part 1, s. 5.2.1; TRACANA, The Effect of the OECD/G20 BEPS Initiative on the Attribution of Profits to Permanent Establishments: The Special Case of Agency Permanent Establishments.
72. OECD, Transfer Pricing Guidelines for Multinational Enterprises and Tax Administrations (10 July 2017), OECD Publishing, Paris, para. 1.90.
73. *Id.*, para. 1.94.

deemed to assume the risk for transfer pricing purposes (and, consequently, it will be rewarded with an arm's-length compensation for the assumption of that risk).

When dealing with the attribution of profits to the PE, the analysis of the assumption of risks is grounded on different principles.[74] Indeed, under the AOA, on the one hand, the PE is attributed with all the functions that the intermediary undertakes for the non-resident enterprise,[75] and, on the other hand, the risks are allocated between the head office and the PE on the basis of their respective functions, as risks cannot be separated from functions.[76] As a consequence, in the above-mentioned example where the non-resident enterprise and the intermediary are associated enterprises that exercise together the control over the risk of market development, the PE of the non-resident enterprise could be attributed with the Controlling Risk Functions performed by the intermediary for the benefit of the non-resident enterprise, disregarding in this respect the analysis of the entity which has the financial capacity to bear the risk. Therefore, due to the different principles underlying the attribution of risks under Article 7 and Article 9 of the OECD Model, the risks that were exclusively attributed to the non-resident enterprise under Article 9, due to the lack of financial capacity of the intermediary, under Article 7 could be split between the head office and the PE of that enterprise *in proportion* to the division of the Controlling Risk Functions between the head office and the PE (the latter including the functions performed by the intermediary for the benefit of the enterprise). Moreover, based on the AOA,[77] the PE would be attributed with the amount of capital (which could substantially be used as a proxy of the 'financial capacity') needed to assume and support the mentioned risk.

As a result, the profits attributable to the PE would not be reduced down to zero by the deduction of the arm's-length compensation paid to the intermediary for the service it provides, since, even in the case the functions performed by the intermediary were the same as those attributed to the PE, those functions would attract to the PE an amount of risks that, under the TP Guidelines, would have been allocated exclusively to the non-resident enterprise of which the PE is part.

74. *See* OECD, Report on the Attribution of Profits to Permanent Establishments (22 July 2010), OECD Publishing, Paris, paras 68–71. In this sense, the Discussion Drat observes that '[i]n a PE context, the legal and factual position is that there is no single part of an enterprise which legally owns the assets, assumes the risks, possesses the capital or contracts with separate enterprises. The mechanism to determine the attribution of risk assumption to a PE will depend on the applicable tax treaty in a given case' (para. 15).
75. *See* OECD MTC (2014), Art. 5(5), according to which the 'enterprise shall be deemed to have a permanent establishment in that State in respect of any activities [i.e. functions] which that person [i.e. the intermediary] undertakes for the enterprise' (that wording is not going to be amended as result of the 2017 changes to the OECD MTC).
76. OECD, Report on the Attribution of Profits to Permanent Establishments (22 July 2010), OECD Publishing, Paris, para. 70.
77. OECD, Report on the Attribution of Profits to Permanent Establishments (22 July 2010), OECD Publishing, Paris, para. 71.

4 The Profit Split as the Most Appropriate Method to Allocate the Profits Between the Enterprise Head Office and the PE

Under the circumstances described in the previous section, the profit split method could represent the most appropriate method for allocating the profits between the PE and the non-resident enterprise based on the functions performed and risks assumed. Indeed, in those circumstances, there appears to exist a high level of integration between the head office and the PE with regard to the Controlling Risk Functions, as well as a shared assumption of economically significant risks by them, which is inherently consequent to the fact that the relevant risk is exclusively attributed, under Article 9 of the OECD Model, to the non-resident enterprise due to the lack of financial capacity of the intermediary, notwithstanding that the Controlling Risk Functions are inextricably performed by both the non-resident enterprise (head office) and the local intermediary (and attributed to the PE). Depending on the circumstances, there could even be a unique and valuable contribution to the transaction by both the head office and the PE (for instance, the joint contribution of unique and valuable intangibles).

Consider, for instance, the case of A Co, a company resident of State A operating in the automotive industry with a number of subsidiaries around the world. A Co develops and manufactures special industrial vehicles for the shipping of chemical products, which may be customized based on the specific safety requirements set forth by the legislation of each client's Country. B Co, a subsidiary of A Co, resident of State B, performs marketing and sales support functions solely on behalf of A Co under a service agreement concluded with the latter. Based on such agreement, B Co is responsible for promoting A Co's vehicles in State B and for tailoring the products offer by selecting for each client the specific features and components required for the vehicle to meet the local safety regulations. B Co's business contributes to the enhancement of the reputation of A Co's products in State B and entails the development of a valuable intangible represented by the know-how concerning the combinations of A Co's components that better fit local safety requirements. The fee payable by A Co to B Co is equal to a percentage of the revenues received by A Co from the sales of the industrial vehicles in State B. The effect of the arrangement between A Co and B Co is that the latter habitually plays the principal role leading to the conclusion of sales by A Co to customers in State B without A Co making any material modification to the terms and conditions negotiated by B Co.

Assume that there is a tax treaty in effect between State A and State B, which includes the 2017 version of Article 5(5) and (6) of the OECD Model. In that case, A Co would have a PE in State B under Article 5(5). Assume also that the tax treaty requires the use of the AOA and that, based on Article 9, the remuneration that A Co pays to B Co is found to be at arm's-length considering the functions performed, assets used and risks assumed by both parties to the transaction. In particular, the analysis reveals that A Co (as manufacturer) and B Co (as service provider) exercise together the Controlling Risk Functions over the risk that the customized industrial vehicles do not comply with the safety regulations of State B (hereinafter 'Product liability risk'), but since only A Co has the financial capacity to assume such risk, the latter is rewarded with an arm's-length compensation consistently with the recommendations of the TP Guidelines.[78]

Under step one of the AOA,[79] the sales of the customized industrial vehicles in State B would be deemed to be made, in substance, by the personnel of B Co on behalf of A Co. Accordingly, the PE would be hypothesized to have A Co's rights and obligations arising from the transactions between A Co and the final customers and also between A Co and B Co. Moreover, an internal dealing between the PE and the head office would be identified, namely the sale of the customized industrial vehicles from the head office to the PE. Since the personnel of B Co performs a relevant part of the significant people functions related to the assumption of the product liability risk, such risk (entirely attributed to and rewarded at the level of A Co, from a transfer pricing perspective) would be split between the PE and the head office, in proportion to the significant people functions relevant for the assumption of the product liability risk carried out, respectively, by A Co (and attributed to the head office) and B Co (and attributed to the PE of A Co).[80]

Under step two of the AOA,[81] the TP Guidelines should be applied by analogy to determine the arm's-length pricing of the internal dealing between the PE and the head office. In this case, the profit split method could represent the most appropriate method to be employed. Indeed, as previously mentioned, the PE – differently from B Co – is deemed to share with the head office economically significant risks (i.e., the product liability risks) through the significant people functions performed by B Co's personnel on its behalf, which also appear to be highly integrated with those carried out by the personnel of the head office. Additionally, both the PE (through B Co's personnel) and the head office (of A Co) contribute valuable intangible assets: indeed, the former owns the know-how necessary to customize the products to State B's market, whereas the latter possesses the brand and all the intangible assets related to the development and manufacturing of the vehicles.

The profit split method could, in this case, be applied by splitting the combined profits from the sale (not the production) of the industrial vehicles in State B, after having rewarded the routine functions performed, based on the relative value of the contributions by the PE and by the head office (i.e., by applying the residual analysis). Such relative value may be, for example, approximated by using as allocation key the salaries of the key employees performing the significant functions at A Co's head office and at B Co (and attributable to A Co's PE). As a result, the PE would necessarily be attributed with an amount of profits which is higher than the arm's-length compensation paid by A Co to B Co (and deducted by the PE). This is due to the fact that, under

78. OECD, Transfer Pricing Guidelines for Multinational Enterprises and Tax Administrations (10 July 2017), OECD Publishing, Paris, para. 1.94.
79. For a brief description of the first step of the AOA *see*: Jochum et al., Practical Problems in European and International Tax Law, Chapter 8, s. 8.4.3.1; Oosterhoff, The True Importance of Significant People Functions, s. 3.
80. I would highlight that, under the AOA, risks just follow functions.
81. For a brief description of the second step of the AOA, *see*: Jochum et al., Practical Problems in European and International Tax Law, Chapter 8, s. 8.4.3.1; Oosterhoff, The True Importance of Significant People Functions, s. 4.

the AOA, the PE is allocated with risks (i.e., part of the product liability risks) that could not be remunerated in the hands of B Co due to the above-mentioned different principles governing the attribution of risks under Article 9 of the OECD Model.

V OPEN ISSUES: HOW DOES THE PROFIT SPLIT METHOD INFLUENCE TAX TREATY POLICY AND INTERPRETATION?

1 Profit Split Versus PE Separate Entity (And Accounting) Approach

The parallel development of the OECD MC and the TP Guidelines in the last years might be read as an instance of divergent approaches taken by the OECD in respect of the attribution of profits to PEs, on the one hand, and transfer pricing, on the other hand. This is the case, in particular, where one would compare,[82] on face value, (i) the 2008/2010 revisions[83] to Article 7 of the OECD MC and its Commentaries with (ii) the emphasis put by the OECD on the profit split method in the 2017 TP Guidelines, and the Revised Guidance on Profit Split.

Indeed, the 2008/2010 revisions to Article 7 and Commentaries push the separate entity approach[84] to its utmost limits, requiring the PE to be treated as if it were a separate and independent enterprise engaged in the same or similar activities under the same or similar conditions and taking into account the functions performed, assets used and risks assumed. This, in turn, entails that the PE profits have to be determined based on separate accounts, where all the transactions intervened with other companies of the MNE and the internal dealings with the head office and the other PEs should be identified and recorded at their fair market values.[85]

On the other hand, the profit split method, in particular under the contribution analysis approach, could be seen as disregarding the separate identification and measurement of the various transactions (or internal dealings) occurring between the relevant companies of the MNE. In this respect, the TP Guidelines provide that the profit split method 'is particularly useful when the compensation to the associated

82. Which refers to the: OECD, Report on the Attribution of Profits to Permanent Establishments (22 July 2017), OECD Publishing, Paris and Report on the Attribution of Profits to Permanent Establishments (17 July 2008), OECD Publishing, Paris.
83. In this regard *see*: Burgers, OECD Commentary on Art. 7 of the OECD Model, paras: 3.8, 3.9, 3.10; Wintsch, Attribution of Profits to Permanent Establishments: The 2008 Art. 7 Versus the 2010 Art. 7 of the OECD Model Tax Convention; Vann (Editor in Chief) et al., Global Tax Treaty Commentary, para. 1.2.3.3.
84. *See* to a further extent: Vann (Editor in Chief) et al., Global Tax Treaty Commentary, para. 4.2.1; Schwarzler, Using the Capital Allocation Approach to Attribute Capital to Permanent Establishments, para. 2.2; Jochum et al., Practical Problems in European and International Tax Law, Chapter 8, s. 8.4; Huibregtse, et al., Status of Implementation of the Authorized OECD Approach into Domestic Tax Law and Tax Treaties – Part 1; Verdoner, The Concept of Dependent Agent Permanent Establishment in Transfer Pricing Theory, para. 2; De Wilde, A Step Towards Fair Corporate Taxation of Groups in the Emerging Global Market; Kofler/van Thiel, The Authorized OECD Approach and EU Tax Law, para. 1; Rosalem, The Agent Permanent Establishment Reconsidered: Application of Arts. 5,7, and 9 of the OECD Model Convention, para. 2.3.
85. *See* OECD, Report on the Attribution of Profits to Permanent Establishments *(22 July 2017), OECD Publishing, Paris,* para. 177.

enterprises can be more reliably valued by reference to the relative shares of their contributions to the profits arising in relation to the transaction(s) than by a more direct estimation of the value of those contributions'.[86]

The conclusion that the OECD is taking two different directions in respect of the attribution of profits to PEs, on the one hand, and the application of the profit split method for transfer pricing purposes, on the other hand, is, however, too far-reaching. In fact, with regard to the attribution of profits to PEs, it is the very same 2010 Report that highlights that the accounting records may be (in whole or part) disregarded if it is necessary in order to attribute to the PE its fair amount of profits based on 'the functional and factual analysis', which represents the only ultimate evidence of whether and how the internal dealings have taken place.[87]

On the other hand, the importance of accurately delineating the actual transactions taking place between related parties (and, by analogy, the internal dealings occurring between the PE and the head office) is highlighted by the OECD also in respect of the application of the profit split method. In particular, the Revised Guidance on Profit Split provides that due regard should be paid to 'the commercial and financial relations between the associated enterprises, including an analysis of what each party to the transaction does, and the context in which the controlled transactions take place'.[88] Moreover, the same TP Guidelines point out that, in cases where both parties to a transaction make unique and valuable contributions, the application of the profit split method approximates the approach that independent parties could take by effectively pricing the transaction in proportion to their respective contributions. Indeed, since in these cases the contributions by the parties are unique and valuable, there could be no reliable comparables information, even for independent parties, which might be used to price the entirety of the transaction in a more reliable way.[89] The fact that independent parties would use, in substance, a profit split method in order to price the transaction in proportion to their respective contributions gives evidence of the fact that there is no contradiction between applying the profit split method and appropriately recording the relevant transactions in the enterprise books, as independent parties are compelled to identify, value and record all transactions for the purpose of drafting their financial statements. The same conclusion, obviously, can be drawn by analogy where the profit split method is applied to intercompany transactions and for the purpose of attributing profits to PEs.

This does not mean that the application of the profit split is a straightforward exercise, nor that the profits allotted to a company (or PE) under the profit split method can be easily split between the various delineated transactions performed by that

86. *See* OECD, Revised Guidance on the Application of the Transactional Profit Split Method: Inclusive Framework on BEPS: Action 10, OECD/G20 Base Erosion and Profit Shifting Project (2018), para. 2.114.
87. *See* OECD, Report on the Attribution of Profits to Permanent Establishment (2010), para. 177. In addition, *see also* para. 181 of the same Report.
88. *See* OECD, Revised Guidance on the Application of the Transactional Profit Split Method: Inclusive Framework on BEPS: Action 10, OECD/G20 Base Erosion and Profit Shifting Project (2018), para. 2.125.
89. *See id.*, para. 2.119.

company (or PE). This practical difficulty, which does not detract from the theoretical possibility to proceed to such an allocation, arises, in particular, where the profit split is applied *ex post* (e.g., in the course of a tax audit). In such a case, the difficulty often arises from the original misidentification or improper characterization of the relevant transactions by the taxpayer and by the fact that sometimes the tax authorities, while applying the profit split method, do not precisely identify and characterize all the transactions in the course of the audit.[90]

The fact that the application of the profit split method does not necessarily entail a contextual separate characterization of the relevant underlying transactions also potentially affects the application of domestic and treaty provisions applicable to the taxation of the non-resident enterprises. This issue, with specific regard to tax treaty rules, is dealt with in the next section.

2 Does Profit Split Affect the Interpretation and Application of Other Treaty Provisions?

The profits divided between related companies (and PEs) under the profit split method should be characterized for both domestic and treaty tax purposes. The need to characterize such profits derive from: (i) the possibility that special tax rules apply to certain types of income received by resident companies (or local PEs) under domestic or treaty law;[91] and (ii) the application of income tax to domestic-source income received by non-resident companies.

In case (ii) above, the income must be appropriately characterized since it is common that, under domestic law, different types of income are subject to different sourcing rules, computation rules and tax rates. Moreover, under the applicable tax treaties, only specific types of income are taxable in the source State,[92] the general rule being exclusive taxation in the Residence State.[93]

This need is particularly evident with regard to Articles 11 and 12 of tax treaties (which allocate the primary taxing right to the source State), as these provisions depart from the general rule highlighted above. Thus, especially in the case of tax audits and MAPs, the tax and competent authorities should not only proceed to split the profits under Article 9 of the relevant tax treaty but should also characterize the profits allocated to the different companies (and PEs) for the purpose to apply the relevant domestic and treaty provisions.

---

90. With reference to other difficulties arising from the application of the PSM during a tax audit, *see*: Gibert, Administrative Approaches to Profit Split Method, s.II.2, in Part II of this book. For an overview of the French, Italian and Spanish experiences in the application of the profit split during the tax audit, *see*: Gibert, Countries Experience: Status Quo and Likely Evolutions – France, s. II.2; Massimiano/Valdonio, Countries Experience: Status Quo and Likely Evolutions – Italy, s. II.2; Vallvé, Countries Experience: Status Quo and Likely Evolutions – Spain, s. II.2, in the Part V of this book.
91. For example., patent box reduced taxation on income deriving from qualifying IPs.
92. This taxation is often subject to a cap, e.g., 10% of the gross income under Art. 11 of OECD Model-like tax treaties.
93. *See* Art. 7 (absent a PE in the source State) and Art. 21(1) of the OECD Model.

3 Profit Split, Business Integration and PEs

As highlighted in section IV, the profit split method may also be applied for the purpose of attributing profits to PEs under Article 7 of the OECD Model. In these cases, the application of the profit split is often triggered by the high level of integration between the head office and the PE with regard to the performance of key functions,[94] as well as by the shared assumption of economically significant risks.[95]

The performance of key functions (i.e., significant people functions) is the element that characterizes the PE, which gives it its shape and represents its modus operandi. Although a PE may exist even in the absence of a high level of integration of the functions performed at the level of the head office and those performed at the level of the PE, the presence of such integration and the consequential shared assumption of economically significant risks may lead to the conclusion that the profit split is indeed the most appropriate method for allocating profits under Article 7.

With regard to PEs, the relevance attributed by the OECD to the integration of business activities also emerges from the analysis of the specific anti-fragmentation rule recently added to Article 5 of the OECD Model. Under new paragraph 4.1. of that article, the exceptions provided for under paragraph 4 shall not apply to a fixed place of business that is used or maintained by an enterprise if a closely related enterprise carries on business activities at the same place or at another place in the same Contracting State and the overall activity resulting from the combination of the activities carried on by the two enterprises is not of a preparatory or auxiliary character, provided that the business activities carried on by the two enterprises constitute complementary functions that are part of a cohesive business operation.[96]

However, the business integration relevant for the purpose of applying the anti-fragmentation rule under Article 5(4.1) of the OECD Model does not coincide with the functional integration relevant for the purpose of assessing whether the profit split is the most appropriate method under Article 9 thereof. Indeed, the former merely requires that the activities performed by the different companies constitute complementary functions that are part of a cohesive business operation, while the latter also demands that the way one party to the transaction performs functions, uses assets and assumes risks is so interlinked with the way in which the other party to the transaction

94. Such as the Controlling Risk Functions.
95. Depending on the circumstances, there could even be a unique and valuable contribution to the transaction by both the head office and the PE (for instance, the joint contribution of unique and valuable intangibles).
96. *See* to a further extent: ARGINELLI, Chapter 5, PE Negative List and Fragmentation of Activities Within Groups of Companies, in: G. MAISTO, New Trends in the Definition of Permanent Establishment, EC and International Tax Law Series (IBFD) 2019. In addition, *see*: GARBARINO, Permanent Establishment and BEPS Action 7: Perspectives in Evolution; SPINOSA/CHAND, A Long-Term Solution for Taxing Digitalized Business Models: Should the Permanent Establishment Definition Be Modified to Resolve the Issue or Should the Focus Be on a Shared Taxing Rights Mechanism?, para. 2.1.2; GADŽO, Nexus Requirements for Taxation of a Non-Residents' Business Income – A Normative Evaluation in the Context of the Global Economy, Chapter 7, s. 7.3.1.3; JOCHUM ET AL., Practical Problems in European and International Tax Law, Chapter 8, s. 8.3.5.3; PLEIJSIER, The Artificial Avoidance of Permanent Establishment Status: A Reaction to the BEPS Action 7 Final Report, para. 3.

performs functions, uses assets and assumes risks that they cannot be reliably evaluated in isolation from one another.

In both cases, yet, the emphasis put by the OECD on business integration is a clear indication of the increasing awareness, by governments and tax administrations, of the fact that multinationals tend to structure more and more their business according to holistic and integrated business models, which cannot be disregarded from a substantive tax perspective. Thus, more than denoting a real treaty policy change, the emphasis on business integration seems to reveal the need to adapt the relevant tax rules to the modified business environment.

4 Profit Split, Tax Administration and Risks of Misrepresentation of Economic Reality

The profit split method may represent a convenient tool for tax authorities when dealing with the allocation of taxing rights (e.g., during unilateral, bilateral, or multilateral APAs and MAPs). Indeed, its flexibility may allow finding more easily an acceptable balance among the conflicting interests at stake. In addition, as already discussed, the application of the profit split method does not necessarily require (and, in fact, it does not always involve) the precise characterization of each transaction.

These features may lead the tax authorities to prefer dealing with each other during APAs[97] and MAPs[98] by using the profit split as a transfer pricing method, especially when comparables are not readily available. The impression, thus, is that the choice of the profit split method may be also driven by the above-mentioned reasons of opportunity, rather than being only demanded as the outcome of a thorough technical analysis of the relevant transaction(s) at stake in a specific case.

In this respect, since the TP Guidelines require the choice of the profit split method to be justified based on the factors identified in section III.2,[99] the relevant players (taxpayers and tax authorities) may tend to overemphasize the presence of unique and valuable contributions by each party to the transaction, as well as the level of business integration, both function- and risk-wise, in order to favour the recourse to the profit split method.

Thus, as it appears doubtful that the number of strictly integrated enterprises is so high, one could wonder whether this emphasis on the need to justify the use of the profit split method in the TP Guidelines is actually commendable since it seems to

97. For an analysis of the approaches to the PSM in APAs, *see*: Gibert, Administrative Approaches to Profit Split Method, s. II.3.A, in Part II of this book. For an overview of the practical application of the Italian operators' experience when liaising with the APA procedures, *see*: Massimiano/Valdonio, Countries Experience: Status Quo and Likely Evolutions – Italy, s. II.3 in Part V of this book.
98. For an analysis of the approaches to the PSM in MAPs, *see*: Gibert, Administrative Approaches to Profit Split Method, s. II.3.B in Part II of this book.
99. That is, the existence of unique and valuable contributions by each party, a high level of integration with regard to the relevant transaction, and the shared assumptions of economically significant risks, or the separate assumption of economically closely related risks.

prompt a false representation of the economic reality, rather than effectively limiting the cases where the profit split is used.

VI CONCLUSIONS

In the last ten years, the formal approach towards the application of the profit split method has changed considerably. The profit split went from being regarded as a method to be applied only in 'those exceptional cases in which the complexities of real life business put practical difficulties in the way of application of the traditional transaction methods' (under the 1995 TP Guidelines) to being recognized with a status of equal dignity as compared to the other four OECD-accepted transfer pricing methods.

Thus, starting from the 2010 TP Guidelines, the choice to apply the profit split method in any specific case has been made subject exclusively to the assessment so that, based on a careful functional and contextual analysis, it results in the most appropriate method to be used in that case. This formal change of perspective, as a matter of fact, codified the widespread practice (of both the taxpayers and the tax authorities) to have recourse to the profit split method in those common cases where the traditional methods (and the TNMM) resulted in difficulty to apply due to the lack of reliable comparables.

As a result of the further amendments brought about by the 2017 TP Guidelines and the Revised Guidance on Profit Split, it is currently generally recognized that the profit split method might be regarded as the most appropriate transfer pricing method when, in addition to the lack of reliable comparables, at least one of the following conditions is met:

(i) the existence of unique and valuable contributions by each party to the transaction;
(ii) a high level of integration with regard to the relevant transaction; or
(iii) the shared assumptions of economically significant risks, or the separate assumption of economically closely related risks, by the parties in connection to the relevant transaction.

The increasing actual use and formal recognition of the profit split method appear strictly due to its extreme flexibility, which allows it to be applied in significantly different circumstances, and to its autonomy from the mantra of comparables.[100] Indeed, as proven in section IV, it is the author's opinion that such flexibility allows the profit split method to also be effectively employed for the purpose of determining the profits attributable to agency PEs under the AOA. Indeed, within multinational groups, the presence of an agency PE is often connected with a high level of integration and the shared assumptions of economically significant risks with regard to the relevant transactions. In certain cases, the unique and valuable contributions by both the

100. These pros, however, also cause its main drawback, i.e., the lower level of reliability of the results (in terms of arm's-length prices) it leads to.

foreign enterprise and the local dependent intermediary (and thus the agency PE) can also be at stake. In these cases, the profit split method may be used to allocate the profits between the agency PE and the head office on the basis of splitting factors that approximate the allocation of functions (and risks) between the two.

Furthermore, the rise of the profit split method poses several tax-policy questions. First, it creates a tension between the need to find a workable and balanced transfer pricing solution and the requirement for the profits allotted to a company (or PE) under the profit split method to be split among the various delineated transactions performed by that company (or PE). The necessity to appropriately split and characterize the profits allocated to the relevant enterprise under the profit split method is particularly strong with regard to source taxation since it is common that, under domestic law, different types of income are subject to different sourcing rules, computation rules and tax rates.

Moreover, under the applicable tax treaties, only specific types of income are taxable in the source State, the general rule being exclusive taxation in the Residence State. In addition, the recent OECD documents on the use of the profit split method put a significant emphasis on business integration, as other recent OECD works similarly do. In all such cases, the emphasis put by the OECD on business integration is a clear indication of the increasing awareness, by governments and tax administrations, of the fact that multinationals tend to structure more and more their business according to holistic and integrated business models, which cannot be disregarded from a substantive tax perspective. In this regard, this approach reveals the need to adapt the relevant tax rules to the modified business environment.

In addition, current practice shows that the choice for the profit split method may be also triggered by reasons of opportunity (to find a workable and balanced solution), in particular in the case of APAs and MAPs, rather than being only demanded as the outcome of a thorough technical analysis of the relevant transaction(s) at stake in a specific case. In this respect, since the TP Guidelines require the choice of the profit split method to be justified based on the factors identified in section III.2, the relevant players (taxpayers and tax authorities) may tend to overemphasize the presence of unique and valuable contributions by each party to the transaction, as well as the level of business integration, both function- and risk-wise, in order to favour the recourse to the profit split method. Thus, as it appears doubtful that the number of strictly integrated enterprises is so high, one could wonder whether this emphasis on the need to justify the use of the profit split method in the TP Guidelines is actually commendable since it seems to prompt a false representation of the economic reality, rather than effectively limiting the cases where the profit split is used.

Finally, the flexibility of the profit split method allows it to be used (with certain adaptations) in unconventional contexts. This is the case, for instance, with regard to the recent OECD/G20 Inclusive Framework work on BEPS and digital economy taxation, where one of the proposed solutions for the allocation of the profits deriving from cross-border activities is represented by a *modified residual profit split method* (hereinafter 'MRPSM').[101] In this respect, the MRPSM would allocate to the jurisdictions of the customers and/or users the portion of the multinational group's non-routine profits that reflects the value created in the market jurisdictions and that is not recognized under the existing profit allocation rules. The application of the MRPSM would involve four steps:[102] (i) the establishment of the total profit to be split; (ii) the carve out of routine profits, using either current transfer pricing rules or simplified conventions; (iii) the computation of the part of the non-routine profits that should be allocated to the market jurisdictions under the new approach,[103] by using either current transfer pricing rules or simplified conventions; and (iv) the allocation of such profits among the various market jurisdictions based on specific allocation keys, such as revenues.

This extreme application of the profit split method appears to bring it closer to formulary apportionment methods, due to the possibly extensive use of predetermined allocating factors (referred to as 'simplified conventions'). It is perhaps worth keeping in mind, in this respect, what the OECD affirmed forty years ago with regard to the formulary apportionment:

> Proposals for radical reformulations of the approach to intra-group transfer pricing which would move away from the arm's-length approach towards so-called global or direct methods of profit allocation, or towards fixing transfer prices by reference to predetermined formulae for allocating profits between affiliates, are not endorsed in this report. The use of such alternatives to the arm's-length principle is incompatible in fact with Articles 7 and 9 of the OECD Model Double Taxation Convention. Such methods would necessarily be arbitrary, tending to disregard market conditions as well as the particular circumstances of the individual enterprises and tending to ignore the management's own allocation of resources, thus producing an allocation of profits which may bear no sound relationship to the economic facts and inherently running the risk of allocating profits to an entity which is in truth making losses (or possibly the contrary). A number of such methods are sometimes advocated, allocating profits in some cases in proportion to the respective costs of the associated enterprises, sometimes in proportion to their respective turnovers or to their respective labour forces, or by some formula taking account of several such criteria. They are all however to some degree arbitrary.[104]

If this path were finally taken, that would mark (at least partial) a regression of the profit split.

101. OECD/G20 Inclusive Framework on BEPS, Programme of Work to Develop a Consensus Solution to the Tax Challenges Arising from the Digitalization of the Economy, (2019), s. 1.2.
102. *See* Finley, Harter Says OECD Digital Work Should Focus on Non-Routine Returns Organization for Economic Cooperation and Development/United States.
103. That is, the part of the profits that is not recognized and allocated to the market jurisdictions under the existing profit allocation rules.
104. *See* OECD, Transfer Pricing and Multinational Enterprises (1979), Chapter I, para. 14.

SELECTED BIBLIOGRAPHY

AHMADOV JAMIL, The 'Most Appropriate Method' as the New OECD Transfer Pricing Standard: Has the Hierarchy of Methods Been Completely Eliminated?, in: 18 International Transfer Pricing Journal 3 (16 May 2011).

ANGIOLILLI LUCA, et al., Limiting Base Erosion, Series on International Tax Law (2017), M. LANG (ed).

ARGINELLI PAOLO, Chapter 5, PE Negative List and Fragmentation of Activities Within Groups of Companies, in: G. MAISTO (ed.), New Trends in the Definition of Permanent Establishment, EC and International Tax Law Series (IBFD) 2019.

AVI-YONAH REUVEN S., Between Formulary Apportionment and the OECD Guidelines: A Proposal for Reconciliation, in: World Tax Journal, 2010 (Vol. 2) No. 1.

BILANY SUNNY KISHORE, The Profit Split Method: Deciphering the OECD's 2017 Discussion Draft, in: Bulletin for International Taxation, 2017 (Vol. 7) No. 9.

BLAY PAUL A., Reviving Transfer Pricing Enforcement Through Formulary Apportionment, in: Tax Development Journal, 2017 (Vol. 7).

CHAND VIKRAM / WAGH SAGAR, The Profit Split Method: Status Quo and Outlook in Light of the BEPS Action Plan, in: International Transfer Pricing Journal, 2014 (Vol. 21) No. 6.

CHRISTMAN KENNET P. / MUKHERJEE ROMITA, An Analysis of the OECD's Discussion Draft on Profit Splits, in: 25 Transfer Pricing Report 1110 (2017).

COLLIER RICHARD / ANDRUS JOSEPH L. / J. VELLA, Five Core Problems in the Attribution of Profits to Permanent Establishments, in: World Tax Journal, 2019 (Vol. 11) No. 2.

COLLIER RICHARD / J.L. ANDRUS, Transfer Pricing and the Arm's Length Principle after BEPS, Oxford University Press (2017).

DROBNIK PIOTR, The Attribution of Profits to a Dependent Agent PE – If the Dependent Agent Is a Commissionaire (Wholly Owned Subsidiary) of the Principal, in: International Transfer Pricing Journal, May/June 2018.

DZIURDZ KASPER, Attribution of Profits to a Dependent Agent PE: Different Arm's Length Principles under Article 7(2) and 9?, in: World Tax Journal (2014).

EISENBEISS JUSTUS, BEPS Action 7: Evaluation of the Agency Permanent Establishment, in: Intertax 2016 (Vol. 44).

ERNIK DAVID, 'More Profit Split', in: 47 TM International Journal 548.

FINLEY RYAN, Harter Says OECD Digital Work Should Focus on Non-Routine Returns Organization for Economic Cooperation and Development/United States, available online at: IBFD, News Tax Analysts (2019).

GADZO STJEPAN, Nexus Requirements for Taxation of a Non-Residents' Business Income – A Normative Evaluation in the Context of the Global Economy, IBFD Doctoral Series (Vol. 41), 2018.

GARBARINO CARLO, Permanent Establishment and BEPS Action 7: Perspectives in Evolution, in: Intertax, 2019 (Vol. 47) Issue 4.

GONNET SÉBASTIEN, Contribution Analyses under the Profit Split Method, in: 6 International Tax Review 11 (2007).

HAY DIANE / HORNER FRANCIS / OWENDS JEFFREY, Past and Present Work in the OECD on Transfer Pricing and Selected Issues, in: Intertax 1994/10.

HAMAEKERS HUBERT, Arm's Length – How long? in: International Transfer Pricing Journal, March/April 2001.

HEIMERT MICHAEL / MICHAELSON T. J., Guide to International Transfer Pricing, Duff & Phelps, Eighth Edition (2018).

HELLERSTEIN WALTER, The Case for Formulary Apportionment, in: International Transfer Pricing Journal, May/June 2005.

HIGINBOTHAM HARLOW N., The Profit Split Method: Effective Application for Precision and Administrability, in: Tax Management Transfer Pricing Special Report, 1996 (Vol. 5) No. 11 Report No. 24.

HOOR OLIVER R., The Revised OECD Transfer Pricing Guidance on Intangibles: A Critical Analysis, (2018) available online at: IBFD Tax Analysts.

HUIBREGTSE STEEF, et al., Status of Implementation of the Authorized OECD Approach into Domestic Tax Law and Tax Treaties – Part 1, in: European Taxation, 2015 (Vol. 55) No. 8.

IFA General Report (1992).

ILHAN CANSU B., The Use of Value Chain Analysis in a Profit Split, in: International Transfer Pricing Journal, 2018 (Vol. 25) No. 4.

JAMIL AHMADOV, The 'Most Appropriate Method' as the New OECD Transfer Pricing Standard: Has the Hierarchy of Methods Been Completely Eliminated?, in: 18 International Transfer Pricing Journal 3 (16 May 2011).

JOCHUM HEIKE, et al., Practical Problems in European and International Tax Law, IBFD Online Books (2016).

KOFLER GEORGE / VAN THIEL SERVAAS, The Authorized OECD Approach and EU Tax Law, in: European Taxation, August 2011.

KOOMEN MIRJAM, Transfer Pricing in the BEPS Era: Rethinking the Arm's Length Principle – Part I, in: International Transfer Pricing Journal, 2015 (Vol. 22) No. 3.

KROPPEN HEINZ KLAUS / DAWID ROMAN / SCHMIDTKE RICHARD, Profit Split, the Future of Transfer Pricing? Arm's Length Principle and Formulary Apportionment Revised from a Theoretical and Practical Perspective, in: Fundamentals of International Transfer Pricing in Law and Economics, W. SCHON & K.A. KONRAD (eds.) 2012.

LANG MICHAEL et al., Transfer Pricing in a Post BEPS World, Wolters Kluwer (2016).

MAISTO GUGLIELMO, Il 'Transfer Price' nel Diritto Tributario Italiano e Comparato, Cedam (1985).

MAISTO GUGLIELMO, New Trends in the Definition of Permanent Establishment, IBFD EC and International Tax Law Series, 2019.

MANGANELLI ANDREA, Critical Analysis of Transactional Profit Methods and of Their Practical Application, in: International Transfer Pricing Journal, November/December 2000.

OOSTERHOFF DANNY, The True Importance of Significant People Functions, in: International Transfer Pricing Journal, March/April 2018.

PANKIV MARTA, Post-BEPS Application of the Arm's Length Principle to Intangible Structures, in: International Transfer Pricing Journal, November/December 2016.

PENG XUE, The Application of the Arm's Length Principle to the Allocation of the Joint Efficiencies Within MNEs, in: International Transfer Pricing Journal, 2016 (Vol. 23) No. 5.

PENG XUE / LAGARDEN MARTIN, DEMPE Functions and the RACI Concept – More Clarity or Confusion Ahead?, in: International Transfer Pricing Journal, January/February 2019.

PLEIJSIER ARTHUR, The Artificial Avoidance of Permanent Establishment Status: A Reaction to the BEPS Action 7 Final Report, International Transfer Pricing Journal, 2016 (Vol. 23) No. 6.

ROBILLARD ROBERT, 'Contractual Arrangements and the Delineation of a Transaction: A Duo in Crisis Mode', in: Intertax, 2017 (Vol. 45), issue 12.

ROBILLARD ROBERT, Profits in Profit-Split Methods: Hazardous Crossovers on the Way to Global Formulary Apportionment, available online at: IBFD, Journals Tax Analysts (2017).

ROBILLARD ROBERT, BEPS: Is the OECD Now at the Gates of Global Formulary Apportionment?, in: Intertax, 2015 (Vol. 43), Issue 6,7.

Rosalem FRANCINE BARRIEROS, The Agent Permanent Establishment Reconsidered: Application of Arts. 5,7, and 9 of the OECD Model Convention, in: International Transfer Pricing Journal, January/February 2010.

SADIQ KERRIE, Unitary Taxation – The Case for Global Formulary Apportionment, in: Bulletin for International Taxation, July 2001 (Vol. 55) No. 7.

SCHWARZLER TAMARA, Using the Capital Allocation Approach to Attribute Capital to a Permanent Establishment, in: International Transfer Pricing Journal, 2017 (Vol. 24) No. 2.

SPINOSA LISA / CHAND VIKRAM, A Long-Term Solution for Taxing Digitalized Business Models: Should the Permanent Establishment Definition Be Modified to Resolve the Issue or Should the Focus be on a Shared Taxing Rights Mechanism?, in: Intertax, 2018 (Vol. 46) Issues 6 and 7.

STAHLI LIKAS, The Use of the Profit Split Method in Highly Integrated Transactions, in: International Transfer Pricing Journal, 2018 (Vol. 25) No. 4.

TORVIK ODDLEIF, Transfer Pricing and Intangibles: US and OECD Arm's Length Distribution of Operating Profits from IP Value Chain, IBFD Doctoral Series (2018).

TRACANA DINIS, The Effect of the OECD/G20 BEPS Initiative on the Attribution of Profits to Permanent Establishments: The Special Case of Agency Permanent Establishments, in: Bulletin for International Taxation, March/April 2019.

TURLEY CONRAD et al., A New Dawn for the International Tax System – Evolution from Past to Future and What Role Will China Play?, available at: IBFD Online Books 2016.

VANN RICHARD et al., Global Tax Treaty Commentary, IBFD Online Collection.

VERDONER LOUAN, The Concept of Dependent Agent Permanent Establishment in Transfer Pricing Theory, in: International Transfer Pricing Journal, 2011 (Vol. 18) No. 2.

WEBER DENNIS / VAN WEEGHEL STEF, The 2010 OECD Updates: Model Tax Convention & Transfer Pricing Guidelines, A Critical Review, Wolters Kluwer Law & Business (2011).

DE WILDE MAARTEN F., A Step Towards Fair Corporate Taxation of Groups in the Emerging Global Market, in: Intertax, 2011 (Vol. 39) Issue 2.

WINTSCH ALEXANDRA, Attribution of Profits to Permanent Establishments: The 2008 Article 7 versus the 2010 Article 7 of the OECD Model Tax Convention, in: International Transfer Pricing Journal, September/October 2017.

ZUCCHETTI SIMONE / PIVA CATERINA, Revised Guidance on the Application of the Transactional Profit Split Method: Evolution or Revolution?, in: International Transfer Pricing Journal, 2019 (Vol. 26), No. 2.

Part I History and Evolution of the OECD Guidelines

CHAPTER 2

History and Evolution of the Profit Split Method in the OECD Guidelines

Paolo Valerio Barbantini[*]

I INTRODUCTION: SELECTING TRANSFER PRICING METHODS

The selection of the 'correct' transfer pricing method is one of the key steps of any transfer pricing analysis.

Since the publications of the first Organisation for Economic Co-operation and Development (OECD) Transfer Pricing Report in 1979 (hereinafter: '1979 OECD Report'),[1] identifying generally accepted transfer pricing methods and the conditions of their applicability in a specific case has been widely debated.

This debate led to changes and developments in the selection process recommended in the OECD Transfer Pricing Guidelines (hereinafter: '2017 OECD TPG').[2] Currently, as for any other transfer pricing methods, the transactional profit split is applicable when it is found to be the most appropriate method in a particular case.

In order to clarify what the most appropriate method standard implies and how it is applicable in the case of the transactional profit split, it is necessary to put the analysis in the right context and to have a clear understanding of the development and revision process of the OECD Transfer Pricing Guidelines from 1979 until today: in particular, the shift from a strict hierarchy to the current standard.

It is also important to take into account the latest developments following the outcome of the OECD follow-up work on the transactional profit split in the context of the (Base erosion and profit shifting) BEPS Actions 8–10.

* The views and opinions expressed in this chapter are those of the author and do not necessarily reflect any official position of the Italian Revenue Agency (Agenzia delle Entrate).

1. OECD, Transfer Pricing and Multinational Enterprises (1 June 1979), OECD Publishing, Paris.
2. OECD, OECD Transfer Pricing Guidelines for Multinational Enterprises and Tax Administrations 2017 (10 July 2017), OECD Publishing, Paris, https://doi.org/10.1787/tpg-2017-en.

II THE SELECTION PROCESS

In broad terms, the selection of a transfer pricing method is based on the application of paragraph 1 of Article 9[3] of the OECD Model Tax Convention on Income and Capital (hereinafter: 'OECD Model') under which: 'when … *conditions* are made or imposed between the two enterprises in their commercial or financial relations *which differ* from those which would be made between independent enterprises, *then any profits which would, but for those conditions, have accrued* to one of the enterprises, but, by reason of those conditions, may be included in the profits of that enterprise and taxed accordingly' [emphasis added].

The provision of this paragraph is the foundation for the comparability analysis that according to Chapter III of the 2017 OECD TPG should ordinarily follow this non-linear (but iterative) process:[4]

Table 2.1 Description of the Comparability Analysis

Steps	*Description*
1–2	Broad-based analysis of the taxpayer's circumstances
3	Accurate delineation of the transaction
4–5	Initial review of possible sources of comparable information
6	Select the most appropriate transfer pricing method
7	Identification of potential comparables
8	Comparability adjustments (where appropriate)
9	Interpretation

Indeed, Article 9 requires a comparison between the conditions made or imposed between associated enterprises with those which would be made between independent enterprises, as well as a calculation of the arm's-length profits that would have accrued

3. The arm's-length principle is not expressly defined in Art. 9 of the OECD Model, but rather it is. This firstly mentioned in paragraph 1 of the Commentary to Art. 9 under which: 'This Article deals with adjustments to profits that may be made for tax purposes where transactions have been entered into between associated enterprises (parent and subsidiary companies and companies under common control) on other than *arm's length terms*. The Committee has spent considerable time and effort (and continues to do so) examining the conditions for the application of this Article, its consequences and the various methodologies which may be applied to adjust profits where transactions have been entered into on other than arm's length terms. Its conclusions are set out in the report entitled Transfer Pricing Guidelines for Multinational Enterprises and Tax Administrations which is periodically updated to reflect the progress of the work of the Committee in this area. *That report represents internationally agreed principles and provides guidelines for the application of the arm's length principle of which the Article is the authoritative statement.*' [emphasis added]. OECD, OECD Model Tax Convention on Income and Capital (21 November 2017), OECD, Paris 2017.
4. *See* para. 3.4 2017 OECD TPG. *See also* OECD, A Toolkit for Addressing Difficulties in Accessing Comparables Data for Transfer Pricing Analyses, Platform for Collaboration on Tax, p. 20, OECD 2017.

to the associated enterprises.[5] One way to read this paragraph (both from a literal and theoretical perspective) is by adopting a two-stage approach:

1. First, an analysis of the 'an'.[6] In particular, Article 9 of the OECD Model requires that a comparison of 'conditions' (including prices, but not only prices) made or imposed between associated enterprises with those which would be made between independent enterprises is necessary for taxpayers to determine how transfer prices should be set and for tax administrations to determine whether a transfer pricing adjustment may be performed.

In this sense, the 2017 OECD TPG emphasizes the importance of identifying the commercial or financial relations between the associated enterprises and of accurately delineating the actual transaction between the associated enterprises by analysing the economically relevant characteristics and supplementing, where necessary, the terms of any contracts with the evidence of the actual conduct of the parties.[7] In particular, 'if' this comparison leads to the conclusion that the conditions made or imposed between associated enterprises do not differ from those which would be made between independent enterprises, there is no requirement under Article 9 of the OECD Model to move on to the second step of the analysis.

2. If (on the contrary) the conditions made or imposed between the associated enterprises do differ from those agreed between independent enterprises in comparable circumstances, then Article 9 of the OECD Model allows for a recalculation of the profits which would have been accrued by the associated enterprises in the absence of such special conditions, including by adjusting them appropriately in order to make the outcome consistent with the arm's-length principle.[8] This is the second step of (our proposed reading of) Article 9, paragraph 1: verification of the '*quantum*'. How to perform this recalculation? The answer to this question is not contained in Article 9, but in the OECD TPG, this being the phase where the use of the OECD transfer pricing methods is required.

However, the choice of the appropriate transfer pricing method is only the sixth step of the OECD recommended approach as summarized in the table above. Under the current standard, there is no automatic process or pre-determined rules for the selection of a transfer pricing method in a specific case: it is the broad-based analysis, i.e., the process of accurately delineating the transaction with the identification of its economically relevant characteristics that dictates the choice of a method and not vice versa. This selection process is a sensitive and complex exercise, and, in this regard, the evolution of the OECD standard is then a key aspect.

---

5. Further information on the history of the arm's-length principle may be found in: Collier/Andrius, pp. 6–98.
6. 'An' in ancient Latin means 'if'.
7. *See* OECD, Actions 8–10: Aligning Transfer Pricing Outcomes with Value Creation: Final Report, p. 13, Paris 2015.
8. *See* Silberztein, p. 147.

III FROM THE HIERARCHY TO THE MOST APPROPRIATE METHOD STANDARD

The OECD TPG[9] identifies two categories of transfer pricing methods that can be used to establish whether the conditions in the commercial or financial relations between related parties are consistent with the arm's-length principle. Other than the traditional transaction methods, namely the comparable uncontrolled price (CUP) method, the resale price method and the cost-plus method, the OECD TPG provides for two transactional profit methods:[10] the transactional net margin method and the transactional profit split method.

Analysing the evolution of the selection process of the transfer pricing methods in the OECD TPG is helpful to clearly understand the rationale for applying the current standard.

The debate on the selection process of the transfer pricing methods is to be tracked back to 1979 when the OECD published its first principal guidance to address the allocation of income and expenses between associated enterprises.[11] The 1979 OECD Report set out[12] three specific methods (today known as the traditional transaction methods) that were to be applied according to a quite strict hierarchy: ideally, the CUP method offers the most direct way for determining an arm's-length price whereas either the cost-plus method or the resale price method may be applied. However, acknowledging the complexities that taxpayers and tax authorities may encounter in applying the traditional transaction methods, in situations where such method would not be applied in a reliable manner, the 1979 OECD Report recognized a general possibility to apply the so-called other methods.[13]

After the publication of the 1979 OECD Report, the practical application of the guidance contained therein showed inherent limitations, mainly due to the lack of information and data to apply the traditional transaction method in a reliable manner. Experience showed that apart from cases where internal comparables[14] were available, in general, it was very difficult (if not impossible) to locate external comparables showing a reliable measure of prices or gross margins earned by independent enterprises. In other cases, especially in countries where financial or other relevant information on independent enterprises were available, it was indeed possible to locate data at net margin level or other profit indicators of external comparables.

9. *See* Chapter II, para. 2.1. of the 2017 OECD TPG.
10. *See* Chapter II of the 2017 OECD TPG.
11. Further details may be found in Ahmadov, p. 184.
12. The report itself consisted of five chapters and discussed the application of the arm's-length principle and the relevant transfer pricing methods to intercompany transfer of goods and intangibles, the provision of certain intra-group services and the granting of loans under controlled transactions. In Chapter I, the Report provides a general guidance on transfer pricing methods.
13. A mixture of the traditional methods or other methods. *See* OECD, Transfer Pricing and Multinational Enterprises, Chapter I, para. 13, Paris 1979.
14. Internal comparables are comparable transactions between one party to the controlled transaction and an independent party; while external comparables are comparable transactions between two independent enterprises, neither of which is a party to the controlled transaction. *See* 2017 OECD TPG, para. 3.24.

This fact prompted the OECD to start working on fundamental revisions of the guidance by opening a discussion among more 'conservative' countries, wishing to stick to methodologies as close to prices as possible, and other countries expressing the difficulties in not considering other indicators of profitability such as net margins or similar.

Following an intense debate and analyses, in July 1995, the OECD issued a completely revised guidance: the Transfer Pricing Guidelines for Multinational Enterprises and Tax Administrations (hereinafter: '1995 OECD TPG').[15]

The 1995 OECD TPG made a clear distinction between two categories of OECD-recognized transfer pricing methods: the traditional transaction methods[16] and the transactional profit methods.[17] Consistently with the 1979 OECD Report, the traditional transaction methods were considered preferable to the other methods because they represented the most direct means of establishing whether conditions in the commercial and financial relations between associated enterprises are at arm's-length.

However, in order to take account of the instances found in the practical application of the transfer pricing methods, OECD countries agreed to broaden, albeit partially, the use of methods based on net margins or other profit indicators. In this regard, the new guidance allowed for the use of the so-called transactional profit methods, although with specific strong safeguards: (a) in exceptional cases; and (b) as a last resort. In other words, the consensus was found to permit the use of transactional profit methods, although only in the exceptional cases where no or insufficient data were available to rely solely upon or at all on the traditional transaction methods.[18] To be noted also is the use of the term 'transactional', putting a strong emphasis on the need to always stick to the 'transaction' when applying these methods.

This is probably the time when the so-called hierarchy of methods was introduced in the first place: indeed, if a category of transfer pricing method (such as the profit methods) can be used only in exceptional circumstances and as a last resort, it would be considered by implication as a less reliable method as opposed to the CUP or the other traditional methods.

However, following the publication of the 1995 OECD TPG, the actual experience in applying transactional profit methods showed that, in practice, these methods were commonly used more often than traditional methods, due to the same reasons that led OECD countries to revise the guidance contained in the 1979 OECD Report.

In particular, in those years, a dilemma became central in the debates among scholars, academics, government officials, tax advisors, corporate officials, etc.: if transactional profit methods (and particularly the transactional net margin method) are commonly used, how does this circumstance fit in with the notion contained in the 1995 OECD Report where the said methods are to be used in exceptional circumstances

15. OECD, Transfer Pricing Guidelines for Multinational Enterprises and Tax Administrations (June 1995), OECD Publishing, Paris 2015 [hereinafter: '1995 OECD TPG'].
16. Described in Chapter II, 1995 OECD TPG.
17. Described in Chapter III, 1995 OECD TPG.
18. *See* OECD, Proposed Revision of Chapters I-III of the Transfer Pricing Guidelines 9 September 2009 - 9 January 2010, Paris 2010.

only and as a last resort? In other words, the practice did not generally match with the theoretical framework contained in the OECD TPG. It is important to underline that this was not just an issue of a theoretical or philosophical nature; on the contrary, as in all cases where OECD TPG are not clear or give rise to ambiguities, the (strict) hierarchy of methods became one of the sources of controversy among countries in transfer pricing cases, ending up, ultimately, in unresolved double taxation.

In essence, the above considerations led the OECD to proceed to revise the 1995 OECD TPG, with the aim of providing a new standard and superseding the above-mentioned strict hierarchy of methods. The debate was mainly focused on the significance and importance of the comparability analysis: as said before, it is the accurate delineation of the transaction, the identification of the relevant functions performed, assets used and risks assumed, and the availability of information that should dictate the choice of a method, rather than the consequences of simplified 'labels' attributed to the parties under analysis (i.e., contract manufacturers, stripped distributors, low-risk assemblers, contract researching, etc.).

The driver for the subsequent choice of the correct transfer pricing methods being the comparability analysis, it became apparent that no method should have been considered more appropriate over another one *ex ante*.

In 2010, the OECD then issued a revised version of the Transfer Pricing Guidelines for Multinational Enterprises and Tax Administrations (hereinafter: '2010 OECD TPG') by adding new guidance on the selection of the most appropriate transfer pricing method to the circumstances of the case, on how to apply transactional profit methods (the transactional net margin method and the profit split method), how to perform a comparability analysis and how to apply the arm's-length principle in business restructurings.

More specifically, the standard adopted in the 2010 OECD TPG provided that the selected transfer pricing method should be the 'most appropriate method to the circumstances of the case',[19] replacing then the exceptional use of the transactional profit methods.

This major step forward, however, led to another question: how to determine if one method is more appropriate over another one? In order to answer this question, it was necessary to focus the analysis on identifying agreed-upon criteria to select the most appropriate method.

IV CRITERIA TO SELECT THE MOST APPROPRIATE METHOD

The 2010 OECD TPG, as previously mentioned, introduced an important revision of the guidance on the selection of the transfer pricing methods by providing that no method should be considered a priori as the most appropriate method, but its reliability and suitability are strongly linked to and dependent on the commercial or financial relations between the associated enterprises and the conditions and economically

19. In order to reflect this evolution, the OECD proposed to address all transfer pricing methods in a single chapter, Chapter II.

relevant circumstances surrounding those relations in the controlled transaction accurately delineated.[20]

This is clearly stated in paragraph 2.2. of the 2010 OECD TPG where it is recognized that the selection of a transfer pricing method always aims at finding the most appropriate method for a particular case. For this purpose, the selection process should take into account the following four criteria:

(i) the respective strengths and weaknesses of the OECD-recognized methods;
(ii) the appropriateness of the method considered in view of the nature of the controlled transaction, determined, in particular, through a functional analysis;
(iii) the availability of reliable information (particularly on uncontrolled comparables) needed to apply the selected method and/or other methods. However, 'even in cases where comparable data are scarce and imperfect, the selection of the most appropriate transfer pricing method should be consistent with the functional analysis of the parties'[21]; and
(iv) the degree of comparability between controlled and uncontrolled transactions, including the reliability of comparability adjustments that may be needed to eliminate material differences between them.

V IMPORTANCE OF THE COMPARABILITY ANALYSIS IN THE SELECTION OF THE MOST APPROPRIATE METHOD

The 2017 OECD TPG, in further emphasizing the role of the comparability analysis in order to select and apply the most appropriate transfer pricing method, has substantially confirmed the above-mentioned criteria.

When performing a comparability analysis and the economically relevant characteristics are appropriately identified (i.e., the contractual terms of the transaction, the functions performed by each of the parties to the transaction, taking into account assets used and risks assumed, the circumstances surrounding the transaction, and industry practices, the characteristics of property transferred or services provided, the economic circumstances of the parties and of the market in which the parties operate, the business strategies pursued by the parties) the accurate delineation of the transaction 'naturally' dictates the selection of the most appropriate transfer pricing method.

This explains why, according to the new guidance issued in 2010 and confirmed in 2017, there cannot be a preference for one method over any other methods based on a strict hierarchy defined *ex ante*.

The most appropriate standard, however, has not completely eliminated in substance the hierarchical approach among the recognized OECD transfer pricing methods.[22] A preference for the traditional methods, and in general of CUP, is still

20. *See* Maisto, p. 173.
21. *See* 2017 OECD TPG, Chapter III, para. 3.39.
22. *See* Maisto, p. 173.

recognized[23] when the said methods and a transactional profit method can be applied in an equally reliable manner.[24]

VI THE NEW 2018 GUIDANCE ON TRANSACTIONAL PROFIT SPLIT METHODS

With reference to the profit split method, the historical evolution of the hierarchy of methods - from its exclusion in 1979 to the new guidelines set out in 2010 where the profit split method has been deemed applicable when it is found to be the most appropriate method - reflects the increasing complexity, flexibility and integration of the multinational business model.[25] Their value creation processes often imply having functions split across several related entities, as well as the need to develop and maintain valuable intangibles in order to compete in an increasingly competitive global market.

Indeed, such an increased application of the profit split method has also been confirmed by certain documents published by several tax authorities.[26]

However, considering the above, it is important to bear in mind that in order to determine whether the transactional profit split method is likely to be the most appropriate method, it is necessary to take into account the criteria set out in paragraph 2.2. of the 2010 OECD TPG. This fundamental premise is unchanged in the 2017 OECD TPG and in the OECD Revised Guidance on Profit Splits (hereinafter: 'Revised Guidance on Profit Split').[27]

In this sense, the 2017 OECD TPG and the Revised Guidance on Profit Split recognize that there can be situations where the profit split method is found to be more appropriate than traditional transaction methods. In particular, where each of the associated enterprises 'makes unique and valuable contributions in relation to the controlled transaction, or where the parties engage in highly integrated activities, the profit split method may be considered preferable than one-sided method'.[28]

All these aspects are developed and addressed in other chapters, however, it is important to highlight here how the new guidance clarifies two fundamental aspects to be considered when evaluating the appropriateness and reliability of the profit split method.

First of all, notwithstanding that the transactional profit split method can be applied in cases where there are no comparables, a lack of comparables alone is

23. *See* 2017 OECD TPG, Chapter II, para. 2.3.
24. *See* AHMADOV, p. 184.
25. KROPPEN/DAWID/SCHMIDTKE, pp. 267 and 270.
26. *See* US Internal Revenue Service, Italian Revenue Agency, Australian Taxation Office, Canada Revenue Agency and Japan National Tax Agency.
27. OECD, Revised Guidance on the Application of the Transactional Profit Split Method: Inclusive Framework on BEPS: Action 10, OECD/G20 Base Erosion and Profit Shifting Project (June 2018), OECD Paris. www.oecd.org/tax/beps/revised-guidance-on-the-application-of-the-transactional-profitsplit-method-beps-action-10.pdf.
28. *See* 2017 OECD TPG, para. 2.4.; Revised Guidance on Profit Split, paras 2.119–2.120.

insufficient per se to lead to a conclusion that the transactional profit split is the most appropriate method.[29]

This interpretation is in line with the rationale of the most appropriate method standard under which the comparability analysis dictates the choice of the most appropriate method. At the same time, it is recognized that the 'perfect comparable', especially when the analysis is focused on external ones, might not exist or be located elsewhere. In essence, the new guidance suggests that in most circumstances it would be more appropriate to use 'imperfect' comparables under a one-sided method rather than adopting a profit split in an unreliable manner.

In other words, if reliable comparables are available, it is unlikely that the profit split method will be the most appropriate method. In this regard, the Revised Guidance on Profit Split, in cases where comparables are available, clarifies that 'depending on the facts of the case, an appropriate method using uncontrolled transactions that are sufficiently comparable, but not identical to the controlled transaction is likely to be more reliable than an inappropriate use of the transactional profit split method'.[30]

Considering the above, the OECD has not underestimated the subjectivity and extraordinary complexity inherent in the application of the profit split method, concluding that a distorted application of the profit split method may lead to a non-arm's length result that is less reliable than the application of another transfer pricing method.

The history and evolution of the profit split method in the OECD Transfer Pricing Guidelines, as summarized above, is closely linked with the development of the guidance on all the other methods and its applicability depends, ultimately, on a thorough understanding of its features, strengths and weaknesses, as addressed and discussed in other chapters of this book.

SELECTED BIBLIOGRAPHY

AHMADOV JAMIL, The 'Most Appropriate Method' as the New OECD Transfer Pricing Standard: Has the Hierarchy of Methods Been Completely Eliminated?, in: 18 International Transfer Pricing Journal 3 (16 May 2011).

AUSTRALIAN TAXATION OFFICE, Advance Pricing Arrangement Program, November 2011.

CANADA REVENUE AGENCY, Advance Pricing Arrangement Program Report, 2015.

COLLIER RICHARD & ANDRIUS JOSEPH L., Transfer Pricing and the Arm's Length Principle after BEPS, Oxford 2017.

FULLER JAMES P. & NEUMANN LARISSA, U.S. Tax Review, in: Tax Notes International, 2018/10.

ITALIAN REVENUE AGENCY, APA Bulletin, 19 March 2013.

JAPAN NATIONAL TAX AGENCY, MAP (Mutual Agreement Procedures) Report 2015.

29. *See* Revised Guidance on Profit Split, para. 2.128. *See also* FULLER/NEUMANN, pp. 903-913.
30. *See* Revised Guidance on Profit Split, para. 2.128.

KROPPEN HEINZ-KLAUS, DAWID ROMAN & SCHMIDTKE RICHARD, Profit Split, the Future of Transfer Pricing? Arm's Length Principle and Formulary Apportionment Revisited from a Theoretical and a Practical Perspective, in: SCHÖN WOLFGANG & KONRAD KAI A. (eds), Fundamentals of Transfer Pricing in Law and Economics, Verlag Berlin Heidelberg 2012.

MAISTO GUGLIELMO, OECD Revision of Chapters I-III and IX of the Transfer Pricing Guidelines: Some Comments on Hierarchy of Methods and Re-characterization of Actual Transactions Undertaken in: WEBER DENNIS & VAN WEEGHEL STEF (eds), The 2010 OECD Updates: Model Tax Convention and Transfer Pricing Guidelines – A Critical Review, Alphen aan den Rijn 2011.

SILBERZTEIN CAROLINE, The Revised Transfer Pricing Guidelines, in: WEBER DENNIS & VAN WEEGHEL STEF (eds), The 2010 OECD Updates: Model Tax Convention and Transfer Pricing Guidelines – A Critical Review, Alphen aan den Rijn 2011.

US INTERNAL REVENUE SERVICE, APMA Program Statistical Data: Announcement and Report Concerning Advance Pricing Agreements, 31 March 2016.

CHAPTER 3

The New Guidance of Chapter I of the OECD Guidelines

Xaver Ditz

I ACCURATELY DELINEATING THE TRANSACTION

Comparability is the key to applying the arm's-length principle. In line with the 2010 (Organisation for Economic Co-operation and Development) OECD Transfer Pricing Guidelines for Multinational Enterprises and Tax Administrations (hereinafter: '2010 OECD TPG'),[1] the new guidelines (hereinafter: '2017 OECD TPG')[2] emphasize from the outset the importance of the comparability between the controlled transaction and the independent transaction as being central to the application of the arm's-length principle.[3] An analysis of comparability comprises two aspects:[4] (i) an accurate delineation of the controlled transaction by identifying the commercial or financial relations between the associated enterprises, and the conditions and economically relevant circumstances involved, and (ii) a comparison between these aspects of the controlled transaction and those of comparable transactions between independent enterprises.

Chapter I of the 2017 OECD TPG addresses the first aspect, i.e., the identification of the commercial/financial relations between associated enterprises and the delineation of controlled transaction(s). Sections A to C contain general information and premises forming the basis of the arm's-length principle, which remain largely

1. OECD, Transfer Pricing Guidelines for Multinational Enterprises and Tax Administrations (18 August 2010), OECD Publishing, Paris, http://www.oecd.org/ctp/transfer-pricing/transfer-pricing-guidelines.htm.
2. OECD, OECD Transfer Pricing Guidelines for Multinational Enterprises and Tax Administrations 2017 (10 July 2017), OECD Publishing, Paris, https://doi.org/10.1787/tpg-2017-en.
3. 2017 OECD TPG, para. 1.33.
4. 2017 OECD TPG, para. 1.33.

unchanged from the 2010 version. Section D provides more tangible guidance, in particular, on how the transactions between associated enterprises can be delineated to make them operable for comparability. The accurate delineation of such transactions first requires a broad understanding of the industry and of how (i.e., by means of which assets, strategies, key functions, etc.) the multinational enterprise (MNE) group operates therein.[5] Second, the process outlined by the OECD identifies how each member of an MNE group operates therein by analysing the commercial/financial relations with its associated enterprises as expressed in transactions between them.[6]

The accurate delineation of transactions between associated enterprises is then based on an analysis of the economically relevant characteristics of the transaction. These characteristics are categorized by the 2017 OECD TPG as follows:[7]

- the contractual terms of the transaction (section D.1.1);
- the functions performed by each party to the transaction, taking into account assets used and risks assumed, including how those functions relate to the wider generation of value by the MNE group to which the parties belong, the circumstances surrounding the transaction and industry practices (section D.1.2);
- the characteristics of property transferred or services provided (section D.1.3);
- the economic circumstances of the parties and of the market in which the parties operate (section D.1.4); and
- the business strategies pursued by the parties (section D.1.5).

While the sections on the latter three characteristics (like the remaining parts of Chapter I) largely correspond to the 2010 version, the sections on the first two characteristics were revised significantly during the Base erosion and profit shifting (BEPS) project (hereinafter: 'BEPS Project').[8] In particular, the second characteristic has been extended to include the concept of risk as a decisive element in the accurate delineation of a transaction.[9]

When the OECD launched the BEPS Project in 2013, it defined transfer pricing, particularly in relation to the shifting of risks, as one of the key areas to combat in its efforts against BEPS.[10] During the revision of the 2017 OECD TPG, which was covered by Actions 8-10 of the project, the main objective was to ensure that transfer pricing outcomes were in line with 'value creation'. The OECD had identified a perceived emphasis on contractual allocations of functions, assets and risks as one of the major flaws of the previous guidelines that prevented the alignment of value creation and

5. 2017 OECD TPG, para. 1.34. Here, the new guidelines refer to the Masterfile as part of the newly established pair of transfer pricing documents in Chapter V.
6. 2017 OECD TPG, para. 1.35.
7. 2017 OECD TPG, para. 1.36.
8. OECD, Addressing Base Erosion and Profit Shifting (12 February 2013), OECD Publishing, Paris, https://doi.org/10.1787/9789264192744-en.
9. This contribution will therefore concentrate on the new element of risk and not discuss unchanged aspects further.
10. BEPS Project, p. 48.

profit allocation. This rendered the existing guidance on the application of the arm's-length principle vulnerable to manipulation.[11]

BEPS Action 9 dealt particularly with aspects of risk and capital. The final report published in October 2015 (hereinafter: 'Actions 8-10 Final Report')[12] had increased the significance of identifying and allocating risk in transfer pricing and its connection with human interactions, i.e., functions. Risk is defined as the effect of uncertainty on the objectives of a business.[13] In the OECD's reasoning, all business operations are inherently linked to risk and profit-seeking businesses take on risks in the expectation of a positive return from the commercial opportunities associated with these risks. Furthermore, as previous tax planning strategies were often based on the purely contractual reallocation of risks without any change to a business operation,[14] the Actions 8-10 Final Report proposes that the bearer of specific business risks must not be determined by contractual provisions alone but by identifying the party that can, in fact, exercise meaningful and specifically defined control over – and has the financial capacity to assume – the risk in question.

Besides defining and raising the importance of the concept of risk, the guidelines now contain a framework for identifying and allocating risk, which is based on the concepts of 'control over risk' and 'financial capacity to assume risk'.[15] Altogether, this establishes the concept of risk as the key to the allocation of profits to individual entities that are parties to a transaction.

While the new concept of risk primarily pertains to the accurate delineation of a transaction within a comparability analysis,[16] it thereby also plays an important role in the context of the new guidance on the profit split method. For example, the new guidance refers to considerations of risk for choosing a suitable transfer pricing method for a transaction. This selection must in principle aim at finding the most appropriate method for each individual case.[17] Here, the new guidance on the profit split method[18] names the sharing of economically significant risks by multiple parties to a transaction as one of the indicators for the transactional profit split being the most appropriate method.[19] Thus, in a post-BEPS world, risks can play a significant role in determining the outcome of transfer pricing analysis and the choice of the transfer pricing method.

11. OECD, Action Plan on Base Erosion and Profit Shifting (19 July 2013), OECD Publishing, Paris. http://dx.doi.org/10.1787/9789264202719-en, p. 20; Verlinden/Ledure/Dessy, p. 109.
12. OECD, Aligning Transfer Pricing Outcomes with Value Creation, Actions 8-10 - 2015 Final Reports, OECD/G20 Base Erosion and Profit Shifting Project (5 October 2015), OECD Publishing, Paris, https://doi.org/10.1787/9789264241244-en.
13. 2017 OECD TPG, para. 1.71; Actions 8-10 Final Report, para. 1.71.
14. For a critique of the interplay between transfer pricing and business models, *see* Hickman, p. 730.
15. 2017 OECD TPG, para. 1.60; Actions 8-10 Final Report, para. 1.60; Bilaney, p. 577.
16. 2017 OECD TPG, paras. 1.33 and 1.36; Actions 8-10 Final Report, paras. 1.33 and 1.36.
17. 2017 OECD TPG, para. 2.2.
18. OECD, Revised Guidance on the Application of the Transactional Profit Split Method: Inclusive Framework on BEPS: Action 10, OECD/G20 Base Erosion and Profit Shifting Project (June 2018), OECD, Paris. www.oecd.org/tax/beps/revised-guidance-on-the-application-of-the-transactional-profit-split-method-beps-action-10.pdf.
19. 2017 OECD TPG, paras 2.126 and 2.139 et seq.

Lastly, it should be noted that the concept of risk is not entirely new to transfer pricing regulations developed by the OECD.[20] The OECD's 2008 Report on the Attribution of Profits to Permanent Establishments[21] had based the definition of a permanent establishment – as a hypothetically separate and independent enterprise – on an analysis of risks attributed to the permanent establishment according to its significant people functions.[22] Furthermore, the 2010 OECD TPG had included the concept of 'control over risk', and further details were provided in the then new Chapter IX on business restructurings.[23]

The following section outlines the identification and allocation of risk in transfer pricing stated by the 2017 OECD TPG and (mostly) already in the final reports for Actions 8-10 released in October 2015.

II THE NEW FRAMEWORK ON RISKS

The process of identifying and allocating risks follows a general framework established in the revised Chapter I of the 2017 OECD TPG. This six-step approach to identifying and allocating risks[24] is intended to help taxpayers and authorities to allocate risk returns among group entities and can loosely be subdivided into an information-gathering phase (steps 1 – 3), an information-interpretation phase (steps 4 and 5) and a pricing phase (step 6).[25]

1 Identifying Economically Significant Risks with Specificity

First, an analysis is conducted of the risks borne by individual group entities involved in a transaction or – in the context of choosing a transfer pricing method – a transactional profit split. To be relevant for the transfer pricing analysis, the risk must be: (a) economically significant, i.e., the potential profits and losses arising from it must be significant in terms of likelihood and size,[26] and (b) specifiable, i.e., not only vaguely described or undifferentiated.[27] The guidance distinguishes between externally and internally driven risks and lists sources of risk that should be taken into account:

- strategic risks or marketplace risks (external);
- infrastructure or operational risks (internal);
- financial risks (external or internal);
- transactional risks (external or internal); and

20. *See* Bilaney, p. 576; Verlinden/Ledure/Dessy, p. 109.
21. OECD, Report on the Attribution of Profits to Permanent Establishments (17 July 2008), OECD, Paris.
22. *Id.*, paras 24 et seq.
23. 2010 OECD TPG, paras 1.49 and 9.10 et seq.
24. 2017 OECD TPG, para. 1.60 and secs D.1.2.1.1 to D.1.2.1.6.
25. Verlinden/Ledure/Dessy, pp. 109 et seq.
26. 2017 OECD TPG, para. 1.71; Actions 8-10 Final Report, para. 1.71.
27. 2017 OECD TPG, para. 1.72; Actions 8-10 Final Report, para. 1.72.

- hazard risks (external).

Although it is stressed that this list is non-exclusive, these risks can be considered a minimum standard requirement when performing the risk assessment.[28]

2 Contractual Assumption of Risk

The second step entails determining which group entities assume by contractual arrangement the risks identified under step 1.[29] The allocation of contractual risk was previously the starting point of a transfer pricing analysis. Under the new regulation, however, the conduct of parties can override the contractual assumption of risks whenever a misalignment is identified between conduct and contractual arrangement (*see* step 4 *infra* section 4.). From a practical standpoint, a well-drafted contractual arrangement nevertheless remains of key importance as tax authorities will have to demonstrate that conduct deviates from the risk allocation specified in contracts.[30]

3 Functional Analysis in Relation to Risk

Step 3 includes a functional analysis, which remains at the core of a transfer pricing analysis. Here, an analysis is performed to determine how the associated parties to a transaction work together in assuming and managing the identified risks. In particular, it is determined who actually performs relevant risk management functions, bears the upside or downside consequences of risk outcomes and has the financial capacity to assume the risk.[31]

Risk management functions may be either control over risk functions or risk-mitigation functions. The first functions are defined as: (i) the capability to make decisions to take on or decline a risk-bearing opportunity, together with the actual performance of the decision-making function; or (ii) the capability to make decisions on whether and how to respond to the risks associated with an opportunity, together with the actual performance of the decision-making function.[32] In essence, these functions are performed by the party who, in practice, decides which risks to accept and which opportunities to pursue. The latter functions are defined as the capability to mitigate risk, i.e., the capability to take measures that affect risk outcomes, together with the actual performance of such risk mitigation.[33]

28. Verlinden/Ledure/Dessy, pp. 109 et seq.
29. 2017 OECD TPG, s. D.1.2.1.2; Actions 8-10 Final Report, s. D.1.2.1.2.
30. Verlinden/Ledure/Dessy, pp. 109 et seq.; Petruzzi/Peng, p. 110.
31. 2017 OECD TPG, para. 1.82; Actions 8-10 Final Report, para. 1.82.
32. 2017 OECD TPG, para. 1.65; Actions 8-10 Final Report, para. 1.65.
33. 2017 OECD TPG, para. 1.61; Actions 8-10 Final Report, para. 1.61.

4 Interpreting Steps 1-3

Under step 4, the information gathered in steps 1 to 3 is evaluated in terms of whether or not the contractual assumption of risks identified is in accordance with the conduct of the parties. This requires that: (i) the associated enterprises follow the contractual terms; and (ii) that the party assuming risk (as analysed under (i)) exercises control over the risk and has the financial capacity to assume risk. If this is the case, the taxpayer may proceed directly to the final step 6.

5 The Allocation of Risk

If instead, the party assuming the risk under the contractual provision does not exercise control over the risk or does not have the financial capacity to assume the risk, the risk should be allocated to the enterprise exercising control and having the financial capacity to assume the risk.[34] If instead, the control and financial capacity are distributed among multiple associated parties, then the risk should be allocated to the associated party or group of parties exercising the most control. The other parties performing control activities should receive appropriate remuneration, taking into account the importance of the control activities performed.

6 The Pricing of a Transaction

The last step comprises the pricing of the accurately delineated transaction in accordance with the transfer pricing methods and other tools as set out in the 2017 OECD TPG, in which the assumption of risk or the mitigation of risk should be compensated with an appropriate anticipated return.[35]

III RECOGNITION OF AN ACCURATELY DELINEATED TRANSACTION PURSUANT TO ARTICLE 9 OECD MTC

The OECD contends that following the outlined approach of analysing the economically relevant characteristics of a transaction will, in general, lead to an accurate delineation of the actual transaction by taking into account both written contracts and the conduct of the parties.[36] Where the formal conditions of a transaction stipulated in contracts are inconsistent with the economically significant characteristics reflected in the conduct of the parties, the latter overrides the contractual provisions. This decision is based on a process of weighing up contractual versus actual (i.e., as shown in the conduct of the parties) risk assumption, taking into account control over risk and the financial capacity to assume risk. While this basic idea was arguably set out already in

34. 2017 OECD TPG, para. 1.98; Actions 8-10 Final Report, para. 1.98.
35. 2017 OECD TPG, para. 1.100; Actions 8-10 Final Report, para. 1.100.
36. 2017 OECD TPG, paras 1.119 et seq.

the 2010 OECD TPG (still only referring to functions, not risks),[37] it is now considerably emphasized by being put at the core (steps 4/5) of the framework.

As a non-recognition of the accurately delineated transaction through a tax administration may cause double taxation, the 2017 OECD TPG emphasizes that an accurately delineated transaction should also be recognized by tax authorities for the determination of transfer prices.[38] The 2017 OECD TPG mentions only one instance for adopting a basis different from an accurately delineated transaction under the previous guidance: where 'arrangements made in relation to a transaction … differ from those which would have been adopted by independent enterprises behaving in a commercially rational manner in comparable circumstances'.[39] In other words, the recognition of accurately delineated transactions undergoes a test of 'commercial rationality', i.e., whether or not the transaction conforms to the arrangements that would be agreed upon between unrelated parties under comparable economic circumstances.[40] As an indicator of non-conformity in the above sense, cases are mentioned in which an MNE group as a whole is worse off on a pre-tax basis.[41] In these cases, the transaction deemed to take place instead of the one actually adopted must adhere as closely as possible to the actual transaction while achieving a commercially rational result.[42]

To sum up, while the 2010 OECD TPG conceptually shifted the basis of transfer pricing analysis from a contractual provisions-based to a function-centric analysis, the OECD now recommends a risk-centric functional analysis. The function-centric approach had the advantage of being able to link returns to certain activities. While the new risk-centric approach appears to be a further refinement of the previous approach, it may fragment the analysis into ever more subtle risks, which then have to be attributed to the people controlling them. Although, in theory, it allows for a more sophisticated analysis, it also renders the transfer pricing analysis more complex and burdensome, especially for smaller businesses.[43]

At first sight, the newly added guidance for analysing risks appears conceptually sound and helpful for specifying transactions, while at the same time reducing opportunities for artificial profit shifting. However, the vagueness and high-level abstractions of the new terminology will – as with previous concepts – again require thorough analysis and plausible reasoning from both taxpayer and tax administration.

Already, the first step of identifying economically significant risks with specificity may in practice become cumbersome as very little further guidance is provided on how

37. 2010 OECD TPG, paras 1.48 and 1.64-1.69. Altogether, the 2010 OECD TPG still put the contractual arrangements at the centre of the delineation of the controlled transaction, *see also* Robillard, p. 804.
38. 2017 OECD TPG, para. 1.121.
39. 2017 OECD TPG, para. 1.122.
40. 2017 OECD TPG, para. 1.123 emphasizes that the mere non-observability of a similar transaction between independent parties is not indicative of its commercial irrationality. The evaluation of commercial rationality therefore follows theoretical considerations.
41. 2017 OECD TPG, para. 1.122. In other words, the transaction as accurately delineated is driven mainly by the tax savings effect.
42. 2017 OECD TPG, para. 1.124.
43. Verlinden/Ledure/Dessy, p. 111.

to give substance to both aspects.[44] Likewise, in theory, it seems rather simple to identify persons within the control over risk concept, but in practice, even a conclusive distinction between 'control-over-risk functions' and mere 'oversight functions' will certainly become challenging. It goes without saying that the requirements for deviating from a taxpayer's delineation of a transaction, particularly the test of 'commercial rationality', also leave considerable room for interpretation and therefore bears the risk of additional conflict.[45] Furthermore, the new guidance lacks specific provisions on the implications of the analysis, such as how to perform a reallocation of risks if - under step 5 - these are allocated to multiple associated entities of a group.[46] This may be particularly relevant in cases where a transactional profit split is being considered. All in all, the further transfer pricing moves away from clear and easily objectifiable contractual provisions, the more leeway is given to interpretation. This inevitably creates the need for more expert advice and raises the likelihood of disputes between taxpayer and tax administration. From a taxpayer's perspective, all these issues will have to be addressed by increasing the quality and quantity of documentation.[47]

SELECTED BIBLIOGRAPHY

BILANEY SUNNY KISHORE, Understanding Risk in the Era of the OECD/G20 Base Erosion and Profit Shifting Initiative, in: 70 Bulletin for International Taxation 10 (5 September 2016).

HICKMAN ANDREW, The Application of Revised Transfer Pricing Rules to Aspects of Business Models, in: 44 Intertax 10 (10 October 2016).

PETRUZZI RAFFAELE & PENG XUE, The Profit Split Method: A Holistic View of BEPS in Transfer Pricing, in: 2 Transfer Pricing International 1 (2017).

ROBILLARD ROBERT, Contractual Arrangements and the Delineation of a Transaction: A Duo in Crisis Mode, in: 45 Intertax 12 (2017).

VERLINDEN ISABEL, LEDURE DAVID & DESSY MAXIME, The Risky Side of Transfer Pricing: The OECD Base Erosion and Profit Shifting Reports Sharpen the Rules on Risk Allocation under the Arm's Length Standard, in: 23 International Transfer Pricing Journal 2 (2016).

44. *Id.*, p. 110.
45. *See also* ROBILLARD, p. 806, who criticises the new framework for being a highly subjective process empowering tax authorities to potentially disregard or reinterpret any controlled transaction as outlined by the parties involved.
46. That can also concern cases in which an MNE established committees that in fact have the control over the risk.
47. BILANEY, p. 582.

PART II Revised Guidance on the Application of the Transactional Profit Split Method

CHAPTER 4

The BEPS Action Plan and Updating the OECD Guidance on Profit Split Method

Andrew Hickman

I PROFIT SPLITS AND THE BEPS ACTION PLAN

Updating the guidance on profit splits in Chapter II of the (Organisation for Economic Co-operation and Development) OECD Transfer Pricing Guidelines (hereinafter: '2017 OECD TPG')[1] was prompted in 2013 by the OECD's Action Plan on Base Erosion and Profit Shifting (hereinafter: 'BEPS Action Plan'),[2] created in response to a request from the G20 to revise in a coordinated and comprehensive way international tax standards, taking into account the impact of globalization on countries' corporate tax regimes. In particular, the BEPS Action Plan sought to achieve better alignment of countries' taxing rights with economic activity. Out of the fifteen actions of the BEPS Action Plan, five relate to transfer pricing matters and the work has already resulted in revisions to several chapters of 2017 OECD TPG. In setting out the five actions relating to transfer pricing matters, the BEPS Action Plan includes enhanced transparency through improved documentation and refers to several types of arrangements between multinational enterprises, such as financial transactions, intangibles, over-capitalization and risks. It does not mention specific transfer pricing methods, with the exception of profit splits. This introductory section looks at some of the reasons for uniquely singling out profit splits for attention in the BEPS Action Plan and how revisions to 2017 OECD TPG have sought to address those reasons.

Before doing so, however, a generic example of a transactional profit split is offered so that readers can readily see the features that may have singled out profit

1. OECD, OECD Transfer Pricing Guidelines for Multinational Enterprises and Tax Administrations 2017, OECD Publishing, Paris, http://dx.doi.org/10.1787/tpg-2017-en.
2. OECD, Action Plan on Base Erosion and Profit Shifting, OECD Publishing. http://dx.doi.org/10.1787/9789264202719-en.

splits for special attention under the BEPS Action Plan, as well as the features that have been covered in the revised guidance (hereinafter: 'Revised Guidance on Profit Split'),[3] as outlined later in the section and in the rest of this book.

Generic example of a transactional profit split

Company A grants rights to use know-how and trademarks to Company B, an associated company, for use in Company B's business of producing and marketing certain products for sale to third-party customers. Company B possesses patented technology associated with the products. A profit split is determined to be an appropriate method and is applied by identifying the anticipated profits of Company B from the production, marketing and sale of the products using the intangibles from Company A. Those anticipated profits are created by the production and marketing activities of Company B, Company B's own intangibles, and the intangibles granted by Company A. Profits attributable to production and marketing activities are determined using benchmarks under the Transactional Net Margin Method and deducted from the profits. The residual profits are, therefore, attributable to intangibles contributed respectively by Company A and Company B. The residual profits are then split in the same proportion as the proportion of costs incurred by Company A and Company B in developing the intangibles. The outcome identifies the amount of anticipated profits attributable to the intangibles granted by Company A and determines the compensation payable by Company B to Company A.

In setting out this generic example, several features stand out. Transactions involving intangibles often give rise to consideration of applying the profit split method, and the fact that both parties to the transaction possess intangibles will tend to make methods based on comparables more difficult to apply. The process of identifying the relevant profits can be difficult since Company B may have other activities and may produce and sell other products that do not use the intangibles from Company A; in such a case, relevant revenues and costs will need to be segregated and allocations of costs may need to be estimated. The computation of anticipated profits is likely to involve a discounted cash flow valuation technique as described in Chapter VI of the 2017 OECD TPG (sections D.2.6.3 and D.2.6.4) and will give rise to practical challenges in making reliable estimations of future revenues and costs, determining the appropriate period over which to do so, and selecting an appropriate discount rate. The splitting factor used in this example is based on respective shares of development costs, but costs may not be reliable, particularly since the two sets of intangibles are

3. OECD, Revised Guidance on the Application of the Transactional Profit Split Method: Inclusive Framework on BEPS: Action 10, OECD/G20 Base Erosion and Profit Shifting Project (June 2018), OECD Paris, www.oecd.org/tax/beps/revised-guidance-on-the-application-of-the-transactional-profit-split-method-beps-action-10.pdf.

different in nature; even if reliable, costs may have been incurred over different periods and require adjustments, and relevant costs may be difficult to identify.

This illustration of a transactional profit split demonstrates that there can be considerable complexities in applying the method, at least in the form set out in this example. Therefore, further consideration would need to be given to the form of profit splits and how the method is applied if the method were to have a more extensive role in combating BEPS, as envisaged by BEPS Action 10. Nevertheless, a significant potential advantage of the profit split is that it allocates profits in accordance with respective contributions, and may seem particularly relevant in concept to achieving the BEPS objective of aligning profits with economic activity. Crucially, however, the example sheds little light on the economic activity of the parties, and in particular on the nature of Company A's intangibles, how Company A developed them, the risks it assumed and how Company B exploits them. Such absence is partly because of the inadequacies of a necessarily short example but mainly illustrates an important point. Without a thorough understanding of the actual transaction, including the risks assumed by the parties, the nature of the intangibles and how they have been developed and exploited, the application of the transactional profit split method will not by itself combat profit shifting. For example, the cost base of Company A used as the splitting factor in the profit split could include payments it made to Company B to develop the intangibles under contract on its behalf; in which case, without further analysis of the functions and risks of the parties, the profit split could risk perpetuating profit shifting rather than combating it. This point is important in understanding how the initial focus on profit splits in the BEPS Action Plan was subsumed by other changes to the OECD Transfer Pricing Guidelines, particularly covering the topics of accurately delineating the actual transaction, allocating risks, identifying intangibles and the circumstances in which the legal owner of intangibles may or may not be entitled to the returns from intangibles, as described later in this section.

Action 10 of the BEPS Action Plan invited clarification of the application of the profit split method in the context of global value chains. Action 10 is headed 'Other high-risk transactions' and focuses on the theme of transactions which would not, or which would only very rarely, occur between third parties, including circumstances in which transactions can be recharacterized. Transactions between multinational enterprises which do not occur between independent enterprises put pressure on the application of the arm's-length principle, which depends on comparison with independent parties in order to determine what would have been the conditions of the transaction had the parties been independent. The singling out of the profit split method under the BEPS Action Plan may acknowledge its uniqueness among all the transfer pricing methods in that it is less reliant on comparisons with independent parties for its application. Therefore, BEPS Action 10 implicitly poses the question of whether profit splits can play a role in a more effective application of the arm's-length principle and help to counter profit shifting.

Global value chains are mentioned in the BEPS Action Plan and one of the situations in which multinational enterprises may be perceived to operate differently to independent parties is where multinational enterprises engage in global value chains. Such global value chains can be highly integrated with considerable interdependence between the members of the multinational group with the result that it may be perceived to be difficult to separate out individual transactions with their associated separated functions, assets and risks, and to make reliable comparisons with the conditions of transactions between independent parties.[4] Indeed, critics of the arm's-length principle might say that it is futile to try do so since members of a multinational group operate as a unified business and that the concept of breaking down that unified business so that individual transactions are identified and the associated risks are determined to be located in individual enterprises is a myth perpetuated by the arm's-length principle. To those critics, the arm's-length principle is inefficient to administer and itself promotes aspects of BEPS through its apparent invitation to isolate risks, and associated profit potential, in single legal entities through contracts between them. Alternatives to the arm's-length principle tend to ignore contractual arrangements between legal entities and instead allocate shares of their consolidated profits based on shares of economic contributions. Part of the concern about the profit split method since it was first presented relates to the feature it may appear to share with non-arm's-length approaches in allocating profits in accordance with economic contributions; but at the same time, that feature could be advantageous in achieving better alignment of profits and economic activity and in responding to the issues addressed under the BEPS Action Plan.

It should be noted that Action 10 of the BEPS Action Plan did not blindly endorse the arm's-length principle. The Action Plan noted that the best course should be to address the flaws in the current system, rather than to replace it, but that nevertheless, 'special measures, either within or beyond the arm's length principle, may be required'. The possibility of 'special measures' was repeated specifically in the context of clarifying the application of the profit split method. BEPS Action 10, therefore, invites consideration of whether profit splits could play a role, either as a special measure or within the arm's-length principle, in relieving the apparent pressure on the arm's-length principle perceived to be caused by the existence of arrangements made by multinational enterprises that are unlikely to occur between independent parties, including involvement in integrated global value chains.

Another relevant feature of profit splits is that the method has tended in practice to be used in complex situations where the complexity is not only caused by the difficulty in finding meaningful comparisons with independent parties, as described above but also because the arrangement between the associated enterprises involves the transfer, use or development of unique intangibles. These two reasons are connected since it is often hard to find arrangements involving intangibles between

4. *See* OECD, BEPS Action 10: Discussion Draft on the Use of Profit Splits in the Context of Global Value Chains, 16 December 2014 - 6 February 2015.

independent parties comparable to those within a multinational group. Intangibles can be very valuable and because of the concern about shifting profits through inappropriately priced transactions involving intangibles, BEPS Action 8 is devoted to the transfer pricing of intangibles. The association in the practice of the profit split method with arrangements involving intangibles is another reason for singling out the method for reconsideration under the BEPS Action Plan.

In summary, therefore, the reasons for singling out the profit split method for specific attention under BEPS Action 10 may reflect the fact that, in practice, it often is used to price transactions involving valuable intangibles, which merit particular attention in BEPS Action 8. In addition, its application is generally less dependent on comparison with independent parties than other transfer pricing methods and may be perceived better to accommodate the unique features of the arrangements within the multinational enterprise group since it splits the profit within that group based on contributions made to earning that profit instead of, as other methods do, positing a different profit through external benchmarks based on comparison with independent parties.

As discussed in the contribution 'History and Evolution of the Profit Split Method in the OECD Guidelines', the profit split method has tended to be seen as a rather different type of transfer pricing method to other methods. For some tax administrations, taxpayers and practitioners that has been helpful since the profit split approach enables the arm's-length principle to be applied flexibly in complex situations for which comparables are unsatisfactory. For others, that has been dangerous since comparability with arrangements between independent parties is seen as the cornerstone of the arm's-length principle, and the perceived vagueness of splitting profits based on relative contributions of the parties threatens to loosen the ties with the arm's-length principle unless restrictions are placed on the application of the method. The contribution 'History and Evolution of the Profit Split Method in the OECD Guidelines'[5] discusses the ways in which OECD Transfer Pricing Guidelines have developed since 1979 the balance between flexibility and restrictions in the application of the profit split approach. BEPS Action 10 essentially posed the question of whether the balance had been struck in the right way. The first public discussion draft issued by the OECD on 16 December 2014[6] invited comments on a series of questions designed to elicit views on the scope of the use of profit splits. Generally speaking, the responses exposed polarized views on profit splits with a minority of respondents welcoming a greater role for profit splits and the majority concerned about the overuse of profit splits through lifting restrictions perceived to be essential to the appropriate application of the method. Importantly, many respondents challenged the premise of linking profit splits with global value chains and expressed concern about creating a bias towards the profit split method and against the other methods.

However, consideration of the scope of the guidance on profit splits under Action 10 was not taking place in isolation. BEPS Action 10 forms part of a grouping of related

5. See Chapter 2 in this book.
6. *See* OECD, BEPS Action 10: Discussion Draft on the Use of Profit Splits in the Context of Global Value Chains, 16 December 2014 - 6 February 2015.

transfer pricing actions that focussed on strengthening the application of the transfer pricing rules in two key areas to better provide outcomes aligned with value creation. Action 8 addressed transfers of intangibles and Action 9 addressed contractual allocations of risk and capital; both of these areas were seen as contributing to BEPS notwithstanding existing transfer pricing defences. The results of those actions were finalized in October 2015 and can now be found in 2017 OECD TPG, mainly in the updated Chapter VI and Chapter VIII and in the extensive revisions to Chapter I. Indeed, the work on intangibles was already well advanced by 2013, before the work on profit splits started, and during 2014 and 2015 work on Action 9 was prioritized since it addressed fundamental principles of any transfer pricing analysis. As explained in detail in the contribution 'The New Guidance of Chapter I of the OECD Guidelines', the revised guidance makes some important clarifications and additions that strengthen the application of the transfer pricing rules. An expected result is that the revisions would allow the arm's-length principle to deal effectively with profit-shifting situations in which significant residual profit, deriving, for example, from ill-defined intangibles, is incorrectly allocated to the legal owner or capital provider and purported residual risk-taker. In particular, the guidance clarifies that any transfer pricing analysis depends on the accurate delineation of the actual transaction, including the supplementing of contractual risk allocation by an examination of the conduct of the parties, and provides that specific risk should be allocated to the party exercising control over that risk. Contractual allocation of risk alone is not sufficient to allocate risk for transfer pricing purposes, and examples in Chapter I highlight the consequences that a risk-free return may be the limit of the profits an associated enterprise is entitled to retain in circumstances where it lacks the appropriate capability to control risk it assumes merely on paper.[7] Importantly, a party which does not control a specific risk will not be entitled to unanticipated profits or losses arising from the risk.[8] These concepts are incorporated in the revised guidance on intangibles in Chapter VI which makes it clear that the returns from the exploitation of an intangible should be allocated to a party or parties which performs and controls functions and risks related to the development, enhancement, maintenance, protection and exploitation of the intangible. That party or parties may not be the legal owner of the intangibles. Examples illustrate the application of the guidance; for instance, in Example 16, the legal owner of the intangibles performs no activities in relation to the acquisition, development or exploitation of the intangibles and does not control risks in relation to the acquisition of the intangibles or to their further development. A thorough examination of the transaction indicates that it should accurately be delineated as the provision of financing. The revisions to the guidance also strengthen the application of the arm's-length principle in two specific ways in relation to the challenges posed by the difficulties in valuing unique intangibles and the resulting risks for profit shifting. The revised guidance endorses the use of valuation techniques for intangibles, particularly those premised on the discounted value of future income streams or cash flows.[9] Such

7. 2017 OECD TPG, para. 1.103.
8. 2017 OECD TPG, para. 1.106.
9. 2017 OECD TPG, para. 6.153.

valuation techniques, like profit splits, are not reliant on comparisons with arrangements involving independent parties. The revised guidance also endorses an approach to counter information asymmetry in transactions involving hard-to-value intangibles; the approach allows consideration of *ex post* outcomes as presumptive evidence about the appropriateness of the *ex ante* pricing arrangements and can, in specified circumstances, require outcomes to be taken into account in re-evaluating the pricing.[10]

These concepts are fundamental to any transfer pricing analysis and to the application of any method. However, they have particular resonance for the profit split method since that method does allocate unanticipated profits or losses in some circumstances, and so its application is directly affected by guidance in paragraph 1.106 of the 2017 OECD TPG. Caution is expressed about assuming that a profit split would allocate residual returns to the licensor/transferor in a transaction involving intangibles,[11] and the endorsement of valuation techniques makes it clear that profit splits are not the only available method for difficult transfer pricing challenges where comparables may be lacking. The work on BEPS Actions 8 and 9 culminating in revised guidance and a strengthening of the application of the arm's-length principle, including dealing with compensation for transfers of intangibles, and with transactions that may only rarely occur between independent parties, had implications for the work on profit splits under Action 10. The approach to that work on profit splits required an assessment of whether the revisions made under BEPS Actions 8 and 9, together with greater transparency provided by Country-by-Country Reporting under Action 13, significantly curtailed opportunities for BEPS, or whether there remained weaknesses in the application of the arm's-length principle that could be remedied through changing the scope for the application of the profit split method.

II UPDATING THE OECD GUIDANCE ON PROFIT SPLITS

The second and third public discussion drafts on profits splits released in 2016[12] and 2017[13] show the emerging outcome of that assessment. Their titles are shorter than the first discussion draft and do not refer in an open-ended manner to the use of profits splits or to global value chains, but instead refer more narrowly to revised guidance. Those drafts provide updated guidance on profit splits, taking into account the revisions to the OECD Transfer Pricing Guidelines as a result of BEPS Actions 8 and 9, but do not seek to change the use of the method or to adopt special measures. The Revised Guidance on Profit Split that has now been released[14] builds on previous guidance and makes useful clarifications and the necessary connections with changes

10. 2017 OECD TPG, paras 6.186–195.
11. 2017 OECD TPG, para. 6.152.
12. OECD, BEPS Actions 8–10: Public Discussion Draft on Revised Guidance on Profit Splits, 4 July - 5 September 2016.
13. OECD, BEPS Action 10: Public Discussion Draft on Revised Guidance on Profit Splits, 22 June - 15 September 2017.
14. OECD, Revised Guidance on the Application of the Transactional Profit Split Method: Inclusive Framework on BEPS: Action 10, OECD/G20 Base Erosion and Profit Shifting Project (June 2018), OECD Paris.

made elsewhere in the OECD Transfer Pricing Guidelines, and in particular, in Chapters I and VI. By implication, the Revised Guidance on Profit Split concludes, in answer to the question posed by BEPS Action 10, that the balance struck on profit splits in previous guidance does not need to be changed, but rather reinforced, and that the profit-shifting impact of high-risk transactions has been adequately addressed by changes made in other parts of the OECD Transfer Pricing Guidelines.

The significant changes made in Chapter I that stressed the rigour of accurately delineating the actual transaction so as to identify the economically relevant characteristics of the commercial or financial relations between the parties, in conjunction with the requirement that risk allocation depends on control of that risk through capability and performance, gave confidence that the arm's-length principle could deal appropriately with the focus of BEPS Action 10 on transactions that would not occur or would only very rarely occur between independent parties. That confidence can be perceived in the revised guidance on recharacterization, as required under the first part of Action 10 since no special measure was introduced. Indeed, the discussion and examples in section D.2 of Chapter I of 2017 OECD TPG, 'Recognition of the accurately delineated transaction', suggest that the process of setting out the factual substance of the commercial or financial relations between the parties and accurately delineating the actual transaction, taking into account allocation of risks in accordance with control, deals with many of the situations that may previously have been thought to require recharacterization. The revised guidance on the recognition of the accurately delineated transaction makes it clear that if the transaction possesses the commercial rationality of an arm's-length arrangement, then every effort should be made to determine pricing under the arm's-length principle. The test is whether the actual transaction possesses the commercial rationality of arrangements that would be agreed between unrelated parties under comparable economic circumstances, not whether the same transaction can be observed between independent parties.[15] As a result of this confidence, profit splits continue to be seen in the Revised Guidance on Profit Split as part of the tools and methods to determine pricing under the arm's-length principle. Despite the requirement in BEPS Action 10 to clarify the application of the profit split method in the context of global value chains, there is no mention of global value chains in the Revised Guidance on Profit Split. One possible explanation is that revisions made under BEPS Action 9 encouraged the conclusion that global value chains no longer required specialized approaches and that the existence of global value chains did not mean that the factual substance of the commercial or financial relations between the parties in such a value chain could not be identified and the actual transaction accurately delineated. If that accurately delineated actual transaction possesses the commercial rationality of arrangements that would be agreed between unrelated parties under comparable economic circumstances, then it is capable of being priced under the tools and methods in 2017 OECD TPG (expanded to cover valuation techniques for intangibles in Chapter VI), including, but not favouring, profit splits.

15. 2017 OECD TPG, para. 1.123. *See* Ditz, The New Guidance of Chapter I of the OECD Guidelines.

The focus on accurately delineating the actual transaction in the revised Chapter I of 2017 OECD TPG is relevant to the continuing reference to profit splits in the revised guidance as the *transactional* profit split method. Indeed, the number of references (this author counted thirty-five) in the revised guidance stressing that the appropriateness of the transactional profit split method depends on the accurate delineation of the actual transaction is noteworthy. No other method discussed in Chapter II of 2017 OECD TPG is subject to such continual reminding (there is only one other reference in the entire chapter and that relates to commodity pricing). The Revised Guidance on Profit Split reinforces this aspect of how the balance has been struck on profit splits in the past and emphasizes that the revised guidance has not sought to change the scope of profit splits in response to BEPS Action 10 and affirms that the 'basic premise is unchanged'. Paragraph 1.142 of 2017 OECD TPG states that a transaction is the consequence or expression of the commercial or financial relations between the parties. The accurate delineation of the transaction requires analysis of the economically relevant characteristics of the transaction including the conditions of the transaction and the circumstances in which it takes place. It is only then that the arm's-length principle can be applied to determine the conditions that independent parties would have agreed in a comparable transaction in comparable circumstances. The reference to *transactional* profit splits firmly places profit splits within the arm's-length principle by focussing on the commercial or financial relations between the parties expressed in a transaction and by identifying the economically relevant characteristics that can then be used to determine arm's-length conditions. The transactional profit split, therefore, depends in its application on the analysis set out in Chapter I; it is part of a family of methods using the analysis in Chapter I, and is not a special measure, as potentially covered in the potential scope of Action 10, that might apportion profits without fully considering the economically relevant characteristics specific to the commercial or financial relations in a transaction between the parties.

Although the Revised Guidance on Profit Split indicates that there was, in the end, no need to change the balance previously struck on profit splits, changes have been made to the guidance to take into account certain consequences for profit splits of the updated guidance in Chapter I, depending on how a profit split is applied. The focus of the revisions, therefore, turned to make the guidance on profit splits fully aligned and consistent with the revised guidance in Chapter I. One significant aspect relates to the distinction between a transactional profit split of anticipated profits and a transactional profit split of actual profits, as discussed in the following paragraphs.

III DISTINCTION BETWEEN TRANSACTIONAL PROFIT SPLIT OF ANTICIPATED PROFITS AND TRANSACTIONAL PROFIT SPLIT OF ACTUAL PROFITS

The Revised Guidance on Profit Split explains that the profit split seeks to determine the division of profits that independent enterprises would have expected to realize and that this can be done in two ways. One way is to determine and split anticipated profits and the second approach is to determine and split actual profits. The appropriateness of the one or the other depends on the accurate delineation of the transaction because the two approaches require different characteristics to be present, particularly in terms of the parties' functions and risks. The distinction was made at the outset in the 2016 discussion draft and was relegated to a later section in the 2017 discussion draft. It now appears in paragraphs 2.136, 2.142 and 2.158-161 and in Examples 7 and 13 of the Revised Guidance on Profit Split. However, the distinction remains important for several reasons. Technically, it flows from the new guidance on risk in Chapter I of the 2017 OECD TPG, as mentioned above and, in particular, acknowledges the key point that a party that does not assume risk under the analytical framework in Chapter I will not be entitled to the returns associated with that risk, including unanticipated profits or losses.[16] A profit split of actual profits includes a sharing of the outcome of risks and is appropriate only if the parties to the profit split assume risks under the analytical framework in Chapter I. Second, the distinction is useful in showing how a profit split of anticipated profits often depends on valuation techniques described in Chapter VI (as demonstrated in Example 13, paragraph 70), and helps further to endorse such techniques by association with an appropriate method. Finally, the two ways of applying profit splits occur in practice and the guidance on each of them provides useful acknowledgement.

Example 13 in the Revised Guidance on Profit Split illustrates the difference between a profit split of anticipated profits and one of actual profits. A transactional profit split of anticipated profits is a way of setting a price at the time of the transaction for the contributions made by one of the parties. Scenario 1 of Example 13 involves the granting of rights in intangibles by Company A to an associated enterprise Company B, in circumstances where Company B uses the intangible rights in addition to its own intangibles to market and sell its products. Apart from granting rights to Company B, Company A has no further interest in the activities of Company B and does not share in the risks Company B assumes in marketing and selling its products using the intangibles granted. The circumstances described in the example are typical of licensing arrangements under which a licensee obtains rights to use an intangible to enhance its own business which it runs at its own risk. The profit split of anticipated profits applies by then determining the profits anticipated to be generated by Company B. These profits result from not only Company B's activities and its own intangible, but also from the rights in intangibles granted by Company A. The example suggests that the anticipated profits might be determined using a discounted cash flow valuation technique as described in section D.2.6.3 to D.2.6.4 of Chapter VI. Indeed, the profit split of anticipated profits not only describes a profit split approach widely used in practice but also further helps to endorse certain valuation techniques as being within the family of OECD methods. It is, therefore, likely that the example envisages the determination of Company's B's anticipated income over an appropriate time period, a determination of anticipated income attributed to production and selling and other functions, leaving the anticipated income attributable to intangibles granted by Company A and to Company B's own intangibles. The anticipated residual income

16. 2017 OECD TPG, paras 1.103 and 1.106.

attributable to the intangibles of the two companies would then be split between Company A and Company B based on a measure of the relative value of their respective contributions of intangibles. The share attributable to Company A would then be used to set a fee at the time of the arrangement for its contribution that would be payable by Company B. So, for example, if Company A was determined to have contributed 30% of the anticipated profits attributable to intangibles (and Company B the remaining 70%), then the net present value of that 30% share, discounted at an appropriate rate, could determine a lump sum payment by Company B. Alternatively, the value could be converted to a recurring royalty on sales made by Company B using the estimates of sales anticipated in the discounted cash flow calculations.

In comparing this application of the transactional profit split of anticipated profits with a transactional profit split of actual profits, it is useful to bear in mind that in this first scenario, Company A may have no further interest in Company B's commercial activities. An arm's-length fee has been determined and fully realized in the case of a lump sum, but with contingency around the amount to be realized in the case of a recurring royalty since the actual amount realized will depend on sales achieved by Company B. Notwithstanding the way in which anticipated profits were split 30:70 to set a fee for the transfer of the intangibles, Company A has no entitlement to 30% of Company B's actual profits. If Company B realized higher profits than expected, Company A would not be expected to share in these additional profits and receive a higher price for the transfer of the intangible. Conversely, if Company B failed to achieve the anticipated profits, then Company A would not be expected to lower its price or take a share in any losses reported by Company B. As paragraph 2.142 states, 'a profit split of anticipated profits will tend to concentrate the playing out of economically significant risks on one party'.

The outcome of a profit split of anticipated profits is, therefore, a price for the transaction, such as a royalty rate on sales, that is conceptually equivalent to the outcome of comparable uncontrolled price method had reliable comparables for the transaction available. In the absence of comparables, valuation techniques have been used to estimate anticipated profits attributable to the contributions of the parties; the relative contributions of intangibles made by the parties can then be used to split the anticipated profits and calculate a fee payable by one of the parties for the contribution of the other.

Scenario 2 of Example 13 varies the facts to show the application of a transactional profit split of actual profits. Whereas in Scenario 1, Company A has no further interest in the activities of Company B and does not share in the playing out of the risks Company B assumes in marketing and selling its products using the intangibles granted, in Scenario 2, Company A joins with Company B in performing marketing and distribution activities and in sharing the assumption of associated risks. Company A, therefore, directly influences the performance of Company B and the profit opportunities Company B can achieve. In this scenario, the respective contributions made by each company are determined *ex ante*, perhaps using a similar discounted cash flow technique to that described in Scenario 1, but then that ratio is used to split the actual profits of Company B in each taxable period covered by the arrangement. Thus, if the application of the transactional profit split of actual profits determined a split in the proportion 40:60, then profits in each period would be split in this proportion.

In comparison with Scenario 1, Company A has an entitlement under a profit split of actual profits to 40% of Company B's actual profits. If Company B realized higher profits than expected, Company A would automatically share in these additional profits. Conversely, if Company B failed to achieve the anticipated profits, then Company A would automatically share in the lower profits or any losses reported by Company B. Transactional profit splits of actual profits have the effect, therefore, of sharing the impact of the playing out of economically significant risks associated with the activities of the parties.

The distinction between a transactional profit split of anticipated profits, where the playing out of risks tends to be concentrated in one party, and a transactional profit split of actual profits, where risk outcomes are shared, can give rise to very different profit shares. The application of one or the other approach is not a matter of preference but instead determined by the facts of the arrangement disclosed by the accurate delineation of the actual transaction. Paragraph 2.159 makes it clear that the splitting of actual profits, that is profits which have been affected by the playing out of economically significant risks, 'would only be appropriate where the accurate delineation of the transaction shows that the parties either share the assumption of the same economically significant risks associated with the business opportunity or separately assume closely related, economically significant risks associated with the business opportunity and consequently should share in the resulting profits or losses'. Such a restriction aligns the profit split of actual profits with the revised guidance on risk in Chapter I. No such considerations apply to the profit split of anticipated profits in circumstances where the accurate delineation of the actual transaction reveals that there is no sharing in the assumption of economically significant risks which might play out for one of the parties after entering into the transaction (*see* paragraph 2.160).

IV THE STRENGTHS AND WEAKNESSES OF THE PROFIT SPLIT METHOD

In common with the guidance on other methods described in Chapter II, the strengths and weaknesses of the transactional profit split method are discussed in the Revised Guidance on Profit Split in section C.2.1. Taken together, the guidance on the strengths and weaknesses of profit splits demonstrates their usefulness in the right circumstances as determined by the analysis under section D of Chapter I but notes the practical difficulties in applying the method.

A significant strength is that a transactional profit split can take into account specific and possibly unique facts and circumstances of the associated enterprises that may not be present in independent enterprises. These unique facts and circumstances may include unique intangibles, a high degree of integration and the shared assumption of economically significant risks.

However, the Revised Guidance on Profit Split also notes significant challenges in applying a transactional profit split method. Detailed information is required to apply the method and it may be difficult to measure relevant revenue and costs for all the associated enterprises participating in the controlled transaction, and achieving the necessary segregation from the parties' other activities (*see* paragraphs 2.123, 2.155, and 2.157). In addition to challenges in identifying the profits to be combined, the way in which the profits are to be split may require detailed analysis of past, current and expected expenditure, and appropriate allocations made (*see* paragraphs 2.181-183).

V CONCLUSION ON PROFIT SPLITS AND BEPS ACTION PLAN

The singling out of profit splits under BEPS Action 10 did not, in the end, lead to any significant revision to the use of profit splits, did not pursue further the connection between profit splits and global value chains, and did not contemplate going beyond the arm's-length principle or introducing special measures. The implicit conclusion is therefore that work on other transfer pricing actions was perceived to have significantly curtailed opportunities for BEPS, and that there were no remaining matters that needed to be remedied, or could be remedied, through changing the scope for the application of the profit split method. The resulting Revised Guidance on Profit Splits is, therefore, a modest update which achieves consistency with changes elsewhere in the OECD Transfer Pricing Guidelines, reinforces the profit split method as a precision tool applied to the accurately delineated transaction in defined circumstances and resists its wider application. Whether the modest update will prove satisfactory depends partly on whether the other changes to the OECD Transfer Pricing Guidelines will prove effective in practice. Adherence to the principle of applying the profit split method to the transaction means that the new guidance on accurately delineating the substance of the transaction and on determining risk assumption needs to be effective before a transactional profit split can be reliably applied. The new guidance on identifying intangibles and determining the contribution to the value of intangibles also needs to be effective in practice before a transactional profit split can appropriately reflect the contribution of the parties.

The Revised Guidance on Profit Split does not develop the relationship between profit splits and global value chains, and the focus on transactions seeks to prevent an application of profit splits that goes beyond specific individual or aggregated transactions. The reference in paragraph 2.138 to the evaluation of highly interrelated or interdependent contributions needing to be done 'holistically' may be intended to have a narrow meaning in the context of the paragraph. However, this paragraph may over the coming years be taken to have greater resonance and the term 'holistic profit splits' may evolve to support a less transaction-based application. It is complex when examining a unified business to hypothesize transactions between independent entities, and a loosening of the transactional nature of profit splits could have offered ways to complement the other revisions to 2017 OECD TPG in order to meet BEPS objectives. As it is, the usefulness of the revised guidance on the application of the transactional profit split method in meeting BEPS objectives is dependent on the effectiveness of those other revisions.

CHAPTER 5

When Is a Transactional Profit Split Method the Most Appropriate Method?

Caroline Silberztein

I INTRODUCTION

The June 2018 Organisation for Economic Co-operation and Development (OECD) Revised Guidance on Profit Split (hereinafter: 'Revised Guidance on Profit Split')[1] is to a large extent the culmination of the OECD work on risks and intangibles in the course of the Base erosion and profit shifting (BEPS) Actions 8–10 'Aligning Transfer Pricing Outcomes with Value Creation'. According to the OECD, the 'transaction profit split can offer a useful method which has the potential, when properly applied, to align profits with value creation in accordance with the arm's length principle and the most appropriate method, particularly in situations where the features of the transaction makes the application of other transfer pricing methodologies problematic'.

One may wonder what the meaning of 'problematic' is in this context: is it where other transfer pricing methods, although appropriately selected in the application of the arm's-length principle, do not lead to an outcome that satisfies the objectives of policymakers? Or, more simply, where such other methods are not practical given the features of the transaction at hand? Of course, the former would itself be a 'problematic' answer for taxpayers, because objectives of policymakers differ from country to country and over time. For instance, tax authorities' appetite for profit split methods could differ in recession times from what it is in high growth years.

In fact, the process that led to the development of this Revised Guidance on Profit Split has fuelled controversy as to whether the arm's-length principle should remain

1. OECD, Revised Guidance on the Application of the Transactional Profit Split Method: Inclusive Framework on BEPS: Action 10, OECD/G20 Base Erosion and Profit Shifting Project, OECD Paris, June 2018. https://www.oecd.org/tax/beps/revised-guidance-on-the-application-of-the-transactional-profit-split-method-beps-action-10.pdf [hereinafter: Revised Guidance].

the overarching principle in the determination of the most appropriate method, or whether the OECD should move toward less objective determinations based on the policy objectives it defined as part of the BEPS project (hereinafter: 'BEPS Project').[2] The OECD, after considering the possible adoption of special measures in the transfer pricing area that would have diverged from the arm's-length principle, did not pursue this route and reaffirmed its support for the arm's-length principle.[3] The Revised Guidance on Profit Split should, therefore, be consistent with the rest of the OECD (2017) Transfer Pricing Guidelines for Multinational Enterprises and Tax Administrations (hereinafter: '2017 OECD TPG')[4] in which it is incorporated.

1 Is the Revised Guidance on Profit Split a Game-Changer as to the Range of Situations in Which a Profit Split Method Would Be Selected?

As acknowledged by the OECD, all transfer pricing methods (and not only the profit split method) aim at ensuring that profits of the associated enterprises are aligned with the value of their contributions and the compensation which would have been agreed in comparable circumstances at arm's length.[5] The executive summary included by the OECD in the June 2018 release states as follows:

> The OECD Transfer Pricing Guidelines have included guidance on the transactional profit split method since their first iteration in 1995. Since the revision to the Guidelines in 2010 [hereinafter: 2010 OECD TPG],[6] the transactional profit split method has been applicable where it is found to be the most appropriate method to the case at hand. This basic premise is unchanged. However, this Revised Guidance on Profit Split, while not being prescriptive, clarifies and significantly expands the guidance on when a profit split method may be the most appropriate method. It describes the presence of one or more of the following indicators as being relevant:
>
> - each party makes unique and valuable contributions;
> - the business operations are highly integrated such that the contributions of the parties cannot be reliably evaluated in isolation from each other; the parties share the assumption of economically significant risks, or separately assume closely related risks.

2. OECD, Addressing Base Erosion and Profit Shifting, OECD Publishing, Paris, https://doi.org/10.1787/9789264192744-en.
3. With the notable exception of the proposed 'Pillar 1 Approach', *see* Statement by the OECD/G20 Inclusive Framework on BEPS on the Two-Pillar Approach to Address the Tax Challenges Arising from the Digitalisation of the Economy' approved by the OECD/G20 Inclusive Framework on BEPS on 29–30 January 2020. The proposed Pillar 1 Approach contains features that, if adopted, would purposey diverge from the arm's-length principle.
4. OECD, OECD Transfer Pricing Guidelines for Multinational Enterprises and Tax Administrations 2017, OECD Publishing, Paris, https://doi.org/10.1787/tpg-2017-en.
5. Revised Guidance, para. 2.114.
6. OECD, OECD Transfer Pricing Guidelines for Multinational Enterprises and Tax Administrations 2010, OECD Publishing, Paris, http://www.oecd.org/ctp/transfer-pricing/transfer-pricing-guidelines.htm.

Thus, the basic premise (selection of the most appropriate method for the circumstances of the case following the guidance at paragraph 2.2 of the 2017 OECD TPG) remains valid.[7]

Furthermore, it is important that the standard remains the selection of the *most* appropriate method for the circumstances of the case; it is not sufficient for a profit split (or another method) to be appropriate for it to be selected, it is also necessary that no other method be more appropriate to the circumstances of the case.[8]

That being said, despite the basic framework of paragraph 2.2 being maintained, there is room for interpretation as to the extent to which the Revised Guidance on Profit Split expands the scope of situations in which a profit split method will effectively be regarded as the most appropriate. In a nutshell, while the propositions in the guidance remain relatively familiar, the examples in Annex II go much further in the direction of a broader application of profit split.

2 Some Considerations in Relation to the Examples Included in the Revised Annex II

In addition to the Revised Guidance on Profit Split, the OECD released a series of fifteen examples that will be found in Annex II to Chapter II of the 2017 OECD TPG. The reading of these examples can be somewhat disturbing in that they do not always carefully follow the Revised Guidance on Profit Split and seem to have been drafted more loosely and with less respect for the arm's-length principle. It is, therefore, important to consider the caveat that is included at the start of this new Annex: 'See Chapter II, Part III, section C of these Guidelines for general guidance on the application of the profit split method. The adjustments and assumptions about arm's length arrangements in the examples that follow are intended for illustrative purposes only and should not be taken as prescribing adjustments and arm's length arrangements in actual cases or particular industries. They are necessarily presented with limited facts … . While the examples seek to demonstrate the principles of the Sections of the Guidelines to which they refer, those principles must be applied in each case according to the specific facts and circumstances of that case. As such, the examples should not be used to interpret superficially similar cases'.

In other words, the OECD acknowledges that the examples in Annex II are imperfect; they are intended to illustrate the Revised Guidance on Profit Split in Chapter II and the latter should prevail over the former in interpretation. Accordingly,

7. As a reminder, there are four criteria set forth at para. 2.2 of the 2017 OECD TPG for the selection of the most appropriate transfer pricing method for the circumstances of the case: (i) the respective strengths and weaknesses of each OECD recognized method; (ii) the appropriateness of the method considered in view of the nature of the controlled transaction, determined in particular through a functional analysis; (iii) the availability of reliable information (in particular on uncontrolled comparables) needed to apply the selected method and/or other methods; and (iv) the degree of comparability between controlled and uncontrolled transactions, including the reliability of comparability adjustments that may be needed to eliminate material differences between them. These four criteria are all discussed to some extent in the Revised Guidance.
8. For details on the most appropriate method standard, *see* paras 2.1 to 2.12 of the 2017 OECD TPG.

we will focus on this chapter on the Revised Guidance on Profit Split more than on the examples.

II FACTORS THAT ARE DEEMED RELEVANT TO DETERMINE WHETHER A PROFIT SPLIT IS THE MOST APPROPRIATE METHOD

As part of the discussion of the four criteria identified at paragraph 2.2 of the 2017 OECD TPG for selecting the most appropriate method, the OECD identifies the following three relevant factors which may lead to the selection of a profit split:

- where each party makes unique and valuable contributions to the transaction;
- where the business operations are highly integrated so that the contributions of the parties cannot be reliably evaluated in isolation from each other; and
- where the parties share the assumption of economically significant risks, or separately assume closely related risks.

1 Accurate Delineation of the Transaction

The 2017 OECD TPG has introduced new guidance in relation to the 'accurate delineation of the transaction' which is a revised version of the old-style comparability analysis. It is of particular relevance in the process leading to the selection of the most appropriate method, especially because it will make it possible to identify the presence or absence of the three relevant factors mentioned above. The accurate delineation of the transaction relies on the identification of:[9]

- the contractual terms of the transaction;
- the functions performed by each of the parties to the transaction, taking into account assets used and risks assumed, including how those functions relate to the wider generation of value by the Multinational enterprise (MNE) group to which the parties belong, the circumstances surrounding the transaction, and industry practices;
- the characteristics of property transferred or services provided;
- the economic circumstances of the parties and of the market in which the parties operate; and
- the business strategies pursued by the parties.

The accurate delineation of the controlled transaction will thus make it possible to identify situations where each party makes unique and valuable contributions, and or where the business operations are highly integrated, and/or where the parties share the assumption of risks (or separately assume closely related risks). Furthermore, the

9. 2017 OECD TPG, para. 1.36.

accurate delineation of the transaction should make it possible to determine the extent to which:

- legal ownership of intangibles is accompanied by the performance of the important development, enhancement, maintenance, protection and exploitation functions that are identified by the OECD as necessary for the legal owner to be entitled to the corresponding share in the residual profit;[10] and/or
- contractual assumption of risk is accompanied by the performance of the important risk management and control functions that are identified by the OECD as necessary for the contractual risk-bearer to be entitled to the corresponding share in the residual profit.[11]

This is why there is a strong connection between the 2017 OECD TPG guidance on risks and intangibles and the Revised Guidance on Profit Split, which could possibly lead to a broader application of the profit split method than was the case under the 2010 OECD TPG, despite the framework of paragraph 2.2 for selecting the most appropriate method remaining unchanged.

2 Role of the 'Relevant Factors': Relevant, but Not Determinative and Not Sufficient by Themselves

The OECD notes[12] that: 'Guidance on how to determine whether the transactional profit split method is likely to be the most appropriate method is set out below, including the identification of certain features of a transaction which may be relevant. However it is important to note that there is no prescriptive rule for establishing when a particular transfer pricing method is the most appropriate method'.

It follows that while these three factors 'may be relevant', they are not determinative, i.e., a profit split method should not always be the most appropriate method just because one or more of these factors is met. This is of particular importance in cases where there is evidence that arm's length parties do not apply a profit split despite the presence of one or more of the three relevant factors in a comparable uncontrolled transaction. In effect, the arm's length principle should prevail in such cases over the presence of one or more 'relevant factor(s)'.[13]

More generally, the four criteria identified at paragraph 2.2 of the 2017 OECD TPG for selecting the most appropriate method remain applicable. While the three factors

10. 2017 OECD TPG, Chapter VI, ss B.2-B.4.
11. 2017 OECD TPG, Chapter I, s. D.1.2.1.
12. Revised Guidance, para. 2.117. Similar language is found in the Executive summary.
13. For instance, the business operations of third parties which manufacture parts for the automobile industry (hereinafter: OEM) may be highly integrated with the ones of the car manufacturer (integration in the supply chain). Nevertheless, there will be numerous cases evidencing that the car manufacturer does not necessarily share profits (or losses) with its third-party OEM. Under the 2017 OECD TPG it should be possible to exclude a profit split in comparable controlled transactions based on the fact that the OEM's business operations, despite being highly integrated, are not so highly integrated 'that the contributions of the parties cannot be reliably evaluated in isolation from each other'.

are especially relevant to assess the second criterion, i.e., appropriateness of a profit split method in view of the nature of the accurately delineated controlled transaction, the other criteria set forth at paragraph 2.2 (namely strengths and weaknesses of each method, and availability of reliable comparables data) should not be forgotten.

3 Interaction with the Arm's-Length Principle: Evidence from Third-Party Behaviours

Importantly, the OECD notes[14] that: 'It is sometimes argued that a transactional profit split method is rarely used among independent enterprises, and thus its application in controlled transactions should be similarly rare. Where such a method is determined to be the most appropriate, this should not be a factor since transfer pricing methods are not necessarily intended to replicate arm's length behaviour, but rather to serve as a means of establishing and/or verifying arm's length outcomes for controlled transactions. That said, where there is evidence that independent parties in comparable transactions apply a profit split method among themselves, such evidence should be considered in determining whether a transactional profit split method is the most appropriate method for the controlled transactions'.

Conversely, where there is evidence that independent parties in comparable transactions do not apply a profit split method, such evidence should be taken into account in determining whether a transactional profit split method is the most appropriate method for the controlled transactions and what other method, if any, may be more appropriate.[15]

III FIRST RELEVANT FACTOR: UNIQUE AND VALUABLE CONTRIBUTIONS BY EACH OF THE PARTIES TO THE TRANSACTION

The Revised Guidance on Profit Split provides that 'contributions (for instance functions performed, or assets used or contributed) will be "unique and valuable" in cases where (i) they are not comparable to contributions made by uncontrolled parties in comparable circumstances, and (ii) they represent a key source of actual or potential economic benefits in the business operations'.[16]

1 The Notion of 'Contributions'

The Revised Guidance on Profit Split does not provide a clear definition of what a 'contribution' is. Based on the 2017 OECD TPG Glossary, the notion of 'contribution' potentially includes functions performed and assets used or contributed. Further,

14. Revised Guidance, para. 2.124.
15. Revised Guidance, para. 2.129.
16. Revised Guidance, para. 2.130.

based on guidance relating to contribution analyses,[17] a contribution may include the provision of services, development expenses incurred, assets used or contributed, and/or capital invested.

It is thus very clear that the notion of 'contribution' is not restricted to intangibles. On the other hand, it is unclear whether, for the OECD, the mere assumption or bearing of risk is a 'contribution'. While this would seem logical, there is no such statement in the Revised Guidance on Profit Split, and the language at paragraph 2.127 seemingly differentiates contributions from risk assumption. Given that the OECD in the 2017 OECD TPG tends to consider that the assumption of risk cannot be separated from control and management functions, it is possible that it purposely excluded the mere assumption or bearing of risk from the list of what may constitute a unique and valuable contribution.

2 Unique Contributions

'Unique' contributions are those for which there is no comparable contribution made by uncontrolled parties in similar circumstances, i.e., contributions that cannot be 'benchmarkable'. The Revised Guidance on Profit Split further states that, 'since those contributions are "unique" and "valuable", there will be no reliable comparables information which could be used to price the entirety of a transaction in a more reliable way, through the application of another method'.[18]

Conversely, 'if information on reliable comparable uncontrolled transactions is available to price the transaction in its entirety, it is less likely that the transactional profit split method will be the most appropriate method'.[19] Therefore, the Revised Guidance on Profit Split acknowledges the use of one-sided methods in cases where reliable information on comparable uncontrolled transactions is available, resulting in transfer pricing outcomes consistent with the arm's-length principle as stated at Article 9 of the Model Tax Convention.

3 Valuable Contributions

Valuable contributions are those which 'represent a key source of actual or potential economic benefits in the business operations'.[20] While this definition is subjective, it is clear to us that 'unique and valuable contributions' should be more than 'important contributions' or 'contribution to value creation'. In effect, all the entities within a multinational group are 'important' and aim at contributing to the creation of value, otherwise they would not exist.

In our view, the characterization of a contribution as 'valuable' should not depend on its being successful – otherwise, profit split would only apply in cases of profitable activities, never in the case of loss-making activities. Doing a 'good job' is not

17. Revised Guidance, para. 2.151.
18. Revised Guidance, para. 2.119.
19. Revised Guidance, para. 2.143.
20. Revised Guidance, para. 2.130.

a unique and valuable contribution – contract R&D providers, contract manufacturers, service providers and limited risk distributors are all supposed to do a good job, as a matter of survival. There are many 'important' and 'successful' functions that are found in uncontrolled transactions, i.e., that are not unique. The arm's-length principle does not support the substitution of a profit split to a traditional method or Transactional net margin method (TNMM) in those cases.

4 'Unique and Valuable Contributions' by Each Party to the Transaction

For the OECD, 'the main strength of the transactional profit split method is that it can offer a solution for cases where both parties to a transaction make unique and valuable contributions'.[21] This is because 'in such a case, independent parties might effectively price the transaction in proportion to their respective contributions, making a two-sided method more appropriate'.

The Revised Guidance on Profit Split states that where one party to the transaction 'performs only simple functions, does not assume economically significant risks in relation to the transaction and does not otherwise make any contribution which is unique and valuable, a transactional profit split method typically would not be appropriate since a share of profits (which may be impacted by the playing out of the economically significant risks) would be unlikely to represent an arm's length outcome for such contributions or risk assumption'.[22]

In first reading, this language may seem over-cautionary: it would have been clearer to state that 'where one party to the transaction does not make any unique and valuable contribution, a profit split method is not appropriate'. However, the presence of unique and valuable contributions by each of the parties is only one – albeit the clearer[23] – of the relevant factors identified by the OECD. Based on the Revised Guidance on Profit Split, it is theoretically possible that a profit split method may apply to highly integrated transactions or transactions involving the shared assumption of risk, although one of the parties would not make any unique and valuable contribution. Of course, such an outcome would need to be carefully scrutinized for consistency with the arm's-length principle if one party makes only benchmarkable contributions.

5 Practical Examples Relevant to the 'Unique and Valuable Contributions'

Several examples in the new Annex II illustrate cases where a profit split method is likely to be applicable because of the presence of 'unique and valuable contributions' by each party to the transaction. Two of them are presented below, chosen among the most controversial ones.

21. Revised Guidance, para. 2.119.
22. Revised Guidance, para. 2.127.
23. Revised Guidance, para. 2.126.

Example 2: What makes good tea successful in the market?

'A Co, a member of T Group, is a company incorporated in Country A whose principal activity is the growing and processing of tea. A Co identifies, acquires and cultivates land with extremely good soil for growing tea. A Co has developed extensive know-how in respect of tea-growing, including maximising the desirable qualities of the tea it grows through its cultivation methods. The properties of the soil together with the cultivation methods give A Co's tea a highly sought after flavour.

A Co processes tea by undertaking the following activities: sorting leaf, grading, full or partial fermenting, blending and packaging for export as per customer order specifications. Blending entails using extensive proprietary know-how to mix the various teas in order to get blends with the unique tastes appreciated by customers of T Group. Tea produced by A Co has won international acclaim for its unique taste and aroma.

A Co sells its tea to B Co, its parent company located in Country B. B Co then repackages and brands the teas for sale in the target markets.

B Co owns and has, by its own efforts, developed the tradename and trademark which are both unique and valuable. However, the branding features the origin of the tea and the unique blend developed by A Co. B Co has carried out extensive advertising campaigns through electronic media, internet, trade fairs and publications in industry magazines resulting in the product range becoming market leader in a number of geographic markets. Tea sold by T Group commands a premium price.

The accurate delineation of the transaction in this particular case determines that both A Co and B Co are making a unique and valuable contribution and the most appropriate transfer pricing method is likely to be the transactional profit split method'.

Comments:

This example is highly debatable, and its conclusions not fully aligned with the Revised Guidance on Profit Split.

It suggests that A Co makes unique and valuable contributions consisting in the properties of the soil together with the cultivation methods (which give A Co's tea a highly sought-after flavour) and its extensive proprietary know-how to mix the various teas. On the other hand, B Co is an active brand owner and it may be assumed from the example that the leading position of the product in the market is as much due to its intrinsic qualities and to the marketing efforts undertaken by B Co.

The selection of the profit split method in this example is therefore somewhat disturbing, lacking any reference to the arm's length principle. In effect, it is unclear based on the example whether the functions, assets and risks of A Co are really unique, i.e., whether or not B Co has other options realistically available to acquire tea of comparable quality from third parties. In the latter case (where third parties exist that can produce tea of comparable quality), the example does not say whether independent growers and independent brand owners/distributors comparable to A Co and B Co would share profits at arm's length. Under the arm's length principle, a profit split method would not be the most appropriate simply because A Co produces a product of high quality.

Another question which arises is whether the qualities of the soil and the origin of the tea (which is featured in the brand) consist in unique and valuable intangibles or location-specific advantages (i.e., comparability factors according to Chapter I of the 2017 OECD TPG). In the latter case, comparability adjustments may be possible and therefore the contribution ceases to be unique and valuable.

A key question when determining the appropriateness of the profit split method for this example should be to assess what the respective roles of A Co and B Co's marketing activities are in making the taste of the tea produced and blended by A Co so appreciated by customers worldwide. The conclusion of the example may not be the same if A Co has developed a strong marketing intangible, making its tea and origin well known and appreciated, with B Co further enhancing and promoting the intangible through marketing and distribution activities; or for instance if A Co's production was unknown to the public, with B Co developing a leading trademark and offering a portfolio of branded teas to its customer base, leading and funding the marketing efforts to make this taste and origin attractive.

Example 13: Retail fashion industry penetrating a new market

'Company A, resident in Country A, is the parent company of Retail Group, an MNE group engaged in the retail fashion industry. Over the years, Company A has developed know-how and has enhanced the value of the trademark and associated goodwill of its business through intensive marketing activities. In this case, the intangibles developed and owned by Company A do not qualify as hard-to-value intangibles.

To expand the business into the Country B market, Company A enters into an agreement with Company B, a member of Retail Group resident in Country B. Under this agreement, Company A grants to Company B the rights to utilise the know-how and to use the trademarks for the purpose of fashion retailing in Country B. Company B has extensive experience in retail fashion distribution and has a strong track record in building brand recognition and loyalty in Country B through its in-house team which develops and implements innovative marketing strategies and activities.

The accurate delineation of the transaction indicates that the contributions of both companies are unique and valuable to the Retail Group's business in Country B.

The OECD then presents two scenarios in which 'the transactional profit split is determined to be the most appropriate method for determining the compensation for the rights granted by Company A to Company B on the basis that both parties to the transaction are making unique and valuable contributions'.

Comments:

The example indicates that contributions of both Company A (brand owner) and Company B (licensed distributor and marketer) are unique and valuable. This is a key assumption in the example. In our view, the thrust of this example is to illustrate a situation in which Company B is a very autonomous licensee that contributes actively to the brand building. It does not follow from this example that a profit split method would typically be the most appropriate for distribution activities, in cases where the latter are non-unique, benchmarkable activities.

IV SECOND RELEVANT FACTOR: HIGHLY INTEGRATED BUSINESS OPERATIONS

1 The Notion of 'High Integration'

According to the Revised Guidance on Profit Split, 'a high degree of integration means that the way in which one party to the transaction performs functions, uses assets and assumes risks is interlinked with, and cannot reliably be evaluated in isolation from, the way in which another party to the transaction performs functions, uses assets and assumes risks'.[24]

In the Revised Guidance on Profit Split, the following two cases of 'highly integrated activities' are identified (further discussed in sections 2. and 3. below):

- where 'the parties may perform functions jointly, own assets jointly and/or share assumption of risks to such an extent that it is impossible to evaluate their respective contributions in isolation from those of others[25]' (hereafter: joint performance); and
- where the 'integration between the parties takes the form of a high degree of inter-dependency'.[26]

24. Revised Guidance, para. 2.133.
25. Revised Guidance, para. 2.134.
26. Revised Guidance, para. 2.135.

The OECD helpfully acknowledges[27] that: 'most MNE groups are integrated to some extent .... In contrast [to cases of high integration], many instances of integration within an MNE result in situations in which the contribution of at least one party to the transaction can in fact be reliably evaluated by reference to comparable uncontrolled transactions. For example, where complementary but discrete activities are undertaken by the entities, it may be the case that it is possible to find reliable comparables since the functions, assets and risks involved in each discrete stage may be comparable to those in uncontrolled arrangements. This needs to be borne in mind in considering which transfer pricing method is the most appropriate in a particular case'.

2 'Joint Performance'

The OECD illustrates joint performance with a reference to the global trading of financial instruments by associated enterprises, which is the subject of a detailed analysis in Part III, section C of the OECD Report on the Attribution of Profits to Permanent Establishments (hereafter: 2010 AOA Report).[28] For ease of reference, the relevant fact pattern from the 2010 AOA Report is provided here:[29] 'In the integrated trading model, as in the separate enterprise model, each location has the capacity to perform the full range of trading and risk management functions necessary to conduct the business and thus performs an entrepreneurial role (assuming it also supplies its own capital). The difference is that in the integrated trading model, the trading and risk management functions with respect to a particular third party transaction may be split between locations and the gross profit arising from that transaction may be recognized in any or all of the locations. Trading or risk management in integrated form is unlikely to be found between independents and so it may not be possible to make reasonably accurate adjustments to make the data comparable. Additionally, in the integrated trading model each location cannot act independently but must co-operate with the others in order to successfully enter into a transaction and subsequently manage the resulting risk. Therefore, it may not be possible that traditional transaction methods could be applied reliably and so consideration should be given to transactional profit methods.'

In our view, it is relevant that the OECD in the 2010 AOA Report clearly acknowledges that middle office or back office functions in the setting of a global trading of financial instruments transactions are benchmarkable and would generally not be compensated through a profit split method.[30] In the 2010 AOA Report, a profit split method is appropriate for an integrated global trading activity because the activity involves several locations each of which has the capacity to perform the full range of trading and risk management functions necessary to conduct the business and thus performs an entrepreneurial role (assuming it also supplies its own capital), while each

27. Revised Guidance, para. 2.133.
28. OECD, Report on the Attribution of Profits to Permanent Establishments, OECD Paris [hereinafter: APA Report].
29. 2010 AOA Report, para. 141.
30. 2010 AOA Report, paras 143–147.

location cannot act independently but must cooperate. In such a case, a split of either the residual or the combined profits may be appropriate because the parties that are highly integrated are in essence co-entrepreneurs.

Given this background, there is a question whether 'high integration' should be an autonomous factor in the selection of a profit split method or whether its relevance should be conditioned upon the integrated activities being entrepreneurial, i.e., involving unique and valuable contributions by all the parties.

High integration of entrepreneurial functions together with support functions or benchmarkable activities should, in our view, not lead to the selection of a profit split method among them as it would not be appropriate to compensate the latter. Example 8 of Annex II is consistent with this interpretation:

Example 8: Contract manufacturing

'Company A is the parent company of M Group, an MNE group engaged in the manufacturing and distribution of electronic devices. Company A has the exclusive right to sell the devices in all territories.

Company A decides to subcontract the manufacturing of the electronic devices to Company B, another member of M Group. Under the terms of the contract, Company B will follow the directions of Company A to produce the devices. Company B will source and supply the materials necessary to produce the different parts of the final products. A key component in the manufacturing process is sourced from Company A. Company B sells the finished goods to Company A, which in turn will market and distribute the product to unrelated customers.

To perform the manufacturing activities, Company B has invested in machinery and tooling that is specifically adapted to the production of the electronic devices sold by M Group. Company B has no other customer than Company A so its entire output is acquired by Company A.

The accurately delineated transaction shows that Company B does not make any unique and valuable contributions in relation to the controlled transactions and the business of M Group. Furthermore, the risks assumed by Company B are not economically significant for the business operations of the group. While the operations of Company B are integrated to some degree with those of Company A and are dependent upon Company A, arm's length compensation for the contributions of Company B can be reliably benchmarked by reference to comparable uncontrolled transactions and the application of a one-sided transfer pricing method or methods. Under these circumstances, the transactional profit split method is unlikely to be the most appropriate method'.

Comment:

Although the example does not explicitly state so, it can be assumed that Company B is a highly integrated operation within the M group. In particular, it is indicated that Company B has no other customer than Company A. Nevertheless, the OECD acknowledges that the contributions of Company B are not unique and a profit split method is unlikely to be selected in such a case despite that level of integration.

3 High Degree of Interdependency

A 'high degree of interdependency' is another situation identified by the OECD as reflecting 'highly integrated activities'. The following example of interdependency is provided in the Revised Guidance on Profit Split:[31] 'profit split approaches may be used by independent enterprises engaged in long-term arrangements where each party has made a significant contribution (e.g., of an asset) whose value depends on the counterparty to the arrangement. In these kinds of cases, where each party makes such a contribution, and is dependent on the other party (or where the value of the contribution(s) of one party depends to a significant degree on the contribution(s) of the other party), some form of flexible pricing that takes into account, and varies with, the outcome of the risks assumed by each party arising from its dependence on the other party may be observed'.

Example 9: Combination of two intangibles

'ACo, resident in Country A, and BCo, resident in Country B, are members of AB Inc, an MNE Group. ACo owns worldwide patents on Compound A and BCo owns worldwide patents on Enzyme B. Compound A and Enzyme B are both unique. ACo and BCo have each developed their respective compound or enzyme by their own efforts, for different purposes, but each found that they were not able to be used as they had originally intended. As a result, neither Compound A nor Enzyme B has significant value at this time.

However, engineers from ACo and BCo working together subsequently determine that the combination of Compound A and Enzyme B creates a unique and valuable drug which is very effective in treating a specific disease and is likely to be highly valuable.

ACo and BCo enter into a contract according to which ACo grants BCo the right to use Compound A. BCo will combine both components to develop the new drug and will market it.

31. Revised Guidance, para. 2.135.

Under these circumstances, the high level of integration and inter-dependency between the contributions of ACo and BCo affects the value of those contributions such that each contribution is unique and valuable when considered in combination with the other. As a result, the transactional profit split method is found to be the most appropriate method for determining the compensation at which the rights to use Compound A are transferred by ACo to BCo.'

V THIRD RELEVANT FACTOR: SHARED ASSUMPTION OF ECONOMICALLY SIGNIFICANT RISKS, OR SEPARATE ASSUMPTION OF CLOSELY RELATED RISKS

The Revised Guidance on Profit Split states that a profit split method may be found to be the most appropriate method where, according to the accurately delineated transaction:[32]

- each party to the controlled transaction shares the assumption of one or more of the economically significant risks in relation to that transaction; or
- the various economically significant risks in relation to the transaction are separately assumed by the parties, but those risks are so closely inter-related and/or correlated that the playing out of the risks of each party cannot reliably be isolated.

Each of these two situations is briefly discussed below.

1 Focus on 'Economically Significant Risks'

Despite the strong emphasis of the 2017 OECD TPG on risk, it is important to recognize that every business assumes some important risk. At arm's length, an independent contract manufacturer, service provider or distributor assumes operational risks as well as the risk of losing clients and being out of business. The market and, therefore, the arm's-length principle, do not compensate the assumption of such risks through a sharing of intangible related profits with principals. A distinction is therefore needed between 'routine risks' (which may be significant to the party bearing them) and 'unique and valuable risks'.

In our view, 'economically significant risks' should be defined as unique and valuable risks, i.e., risks that are not found in the comparables and cannot be adjusted through a comparability adjustment.

Cases where an associated enterprise assumes significant risks that are not assumed by independent comparable enterprises would support the allocation of profits (or losses) to the risk-bearing associated entity that go beyond the returns earned by comparable enterprises. Depending on the nature of the risk at hand, a

32. Revised Guidance, paras 2.139 and 2.140.

comparability adjustment may be performed to adjust the comparables and take the additional risk into account; or, if the risks are of an entrepreneurial nature, their assumption may warrant a share in the residual profit from the transaction.

2 Shared Assumption by the Parties of Economically Significant Risks

Under the arm's-length principle, where each party to a controlled transaction assumes economically significant risks, each of them should be allocated the profit (or loss) associated with the specific risks it assumes, in accordance with the guidance at paragraphs 1.100–1.106 of the 2017 OECD TPG. If multiple parties share the assumption of a given risk, they should also share the profit (or loss) associated with the assumption of such risk.

That being said, the combined profit from a transaction may derive from a range of contributions, including but not limited to the shared assumption of risk. The shared assumption of risk may be associated with the contribution of unique intangibles by each party to the transaction, in which case a split of the profits derived from the transaction will be most appropriate. In other cases, contributions other that the shared assumption of risk may include unique and valuable intangibles contributed by one party only, and/or other risks that may be assumed by one party only. It can be argued that if two parties share the assumption of economically significant risks while one of them also makes other unique, valuable contributions, then the parties would logically share the profit or loss from the shared risks, not from those other contributions.

3 Separate Assumption of Closely Interrelated and/or Correlated Risks

The Revised Guidance on Profit Split indicates[33] that:

> 'A transactional profit split may also be found to be the most appropriate method where, according to the accurately delineated transaction, the various economically significant risks in relation to the transaction are separately assumed by the parties, but those risks are so closely inter-related and/or correlated that the playing out of the risks of each party cannot reliably be isolated'.
>
> 'The relevance of this factor as an indicator for the transactional profit split method will depend in large measure on the extent to which the risks concerned are economically significant such that a share of relevant profits would be warranted for each party. The economic significance of the risks should be analysed in relation to their importance to the actual or anticipated relevant profits from the controlled transactions(s), rather than in respect of their importance to any one of the associated enterprises whose business operations may extend beyond those covered by the relevant profits'.

This guidance is surprising. In effect, if the accurate delineation of the transaction shows that significant risks in relation to the transaction are separately assumed by the parties, then the profits or losses arising from the (non)materialization of those risks

33. Revised Guidance, paras 2.140–2.141.

should in theory be separately borne. Otherwise, if the profits or losses derived from the (non)materialization of the risks are jointly shared, this means that the parties jointly assume the risk, contrary to the outcome of the accurate delineation of the transaction.

Further, there are many situations at arm's length where the risks borne by one entity are influenced by other parties' risks and actions. It does not follow that the parties will share the profits or losses deriving from those risks. A good example of independent parties being impacted by separate (not shared) risks is one party's dependence on a critical component solely sourced from a second party. If the second party's business fails, the first party could be out of business. In such transactions, however, the first party would typically not agree to share profits with the second party.

This is why it is essential to highlight that the Revised Guidance on Profit Split does not address the mere separate assumption of economically significant risks, but sets as a condition for this factor to be fulfilled that 'those risks are so closely inter-related and/or correlated that the playing out of the risks of each party cannot reliably be isolated'. Some clarification to the Revised Guidance on Profit Split in this respect is provided in the following example found in Annex II:

Example 10: Separate assumption of closely interrelated and/or correlated risks

'Company A designs, develops and produces a line of high technology industrial products. A new generation of the product line incorporates a key component developed and created by Company B, an associated enterprise of Company A. This key component is highly innovative, incorporating unique and valuable intangibles. This innovation represents the key point of difference in the new generation of products. The success of the new generation of products is heavily dependent upon the performance of the key component made by Company B. The key component is specifically tailored for the new generation of products and cannot be used in any other products.

The key component was developed entirely by Company B. The accurate delineation of the transaction determines that Company B performs all the control functions and assumed all the risks in relation to the development of the component, with no involvement by Company A.

The accurate delineation of the transaction also finds that Company A performs all the control functions and assumed all the risks in relation to the overall production and sale of the new generation of products. Company A cannot control (and thus does not assume) the risks relating to the performance of the key component.

In this example, it is determined that while Company A and Company B each assumes separate economically significant risks, those risks are highly inter-dependent. As a result, it is determined that the transactional profit split method is the most appropriate method'.

Comments:

This example illustrates a case where the assumption of risk by each party to the transaction is intrinsically linked to its contributing unique and valuable intangibles and performing important control functions. It is interesting that the OECD presents it as illustrative of the separate assumption of closely related risks: it is arguably more aligned with the arm's length principle than what might be read from the Revised Guidance on Profit Split in this respect. It also echoes the above observation in relation to the definition of 'contributions' (*see* section III.1. above) that the mere assumption of risk may not be viewed by the OECD as an autonomous contribution separated from the intangibles and functions that create the risk.

4 Case Where Economically Significant Risk Assumed by One Party Is Partly Controlled by Another Party

The 2017 OECD TPG has introduced very detailed guidance on risk management and control in an effort to restrict the ability to separate the contractual assumption of risk from the performance of key functions related to that risk. It states, in particular,[34] that: 'If it is established ... that the associated enterprise assuming the risk ... does not exercise control over the risk or does not have the financial capacity to assume the risk, then the risk should be allocated to the enterprise exercising control and having the financial capacity to assume the risk. If multiple associated enterprises are identified that both exercise control and have the financial capacity to assume the risk, then the risk should be allocated to the associated enterprise or group of associated enterprises exercising the most control. The other parties performing control activities should be remunerated appropriately, taking into account the importance of the control activities performed.'

This is a part of the 2017 OECD TPG that attracted a lot of debate as it seems to open the possibility to select a profit split method to remunerate control functions in some circumstances, with no clear guidance as to what those circumstances are. The Revised Guidance on Profit Split follows the same path, addressing the situation where one party performs control functions in relation to risk that is assumed by another party:[35] 'Where a party contributes to the control of economically significant risk, but that risk is assumed by the other party to the transaction, this may, in some cases, demonstrate that it is appropriate for the first party to share in the potential upside and downside associated with that risk, commensurate with its contribution to control. *See*

34. 2017 OECD TPG, para. 1.98.
35. Revised Guidance, para. 2.137.

paragraph 1.105. However, the mere fact that an entity performs control functions in relation to a risk will not necessarily lead to the conclusion that the transactional profit split is the most appropriate method in the case.'

For ease of reference, paragraph 1.105 of the 2017 OECD TPG is reproduced here: 'A party should always be appropriately compensated for its control functions in relation to risk. Usually, the compensation will derive from the consequences of being allocated risk, and therefore that party will be entitled to receive the upside benefits and to incur the downside costs. In circumstances where a party contributes to the control of risk, but does not assume the risk, compensation which takes the form of a sharing in the potential upside and downside, commensurate with that contribution to control, may be appropriate.'

VI LACK OF COMPARABLES IS, BY ITSELF, INSUFFICIENT TO WARRANT THE USE OF A PROFIT SPLIT METHOD

The 1995 OECD Transfer Pricing Guidelines indicated[36] that 'One strength of the profit split method is that it generally does not rely directly on closely comparable transactions, and it can therefore be used in cases when no such transactions between independent enterprises can be identified.'

This has sometimes been misinterpreted as stating that a profit split method is the most appropriate in cases where reliable comparables are not found, irrespective of the reasons for such lack of comparables. In fact, one should differentiate between cases where reliable comparables are not available because the contributions made by both parties are unique and valuable, and those cases where reliable comparables are not available because of limitation in available local databases of companies operating in the local market, or of the application of a very stringent (sometimes unrealistic) comparability standard. For instance, a profit split method would not be appropriate in the case of a contract manufacturing transaction, even if there are no available data on comparable independent manufacturers operating in the same country as the controlled contract manufacturer: a lack of available information does not change the fundamental nature of the transaction and its arm's length remuneration.

The Revised Guidance on Profit Split provides[37] the following helpful clarification: 'A lack of closely comparable, uncontrolled transactions which would otherwise be used to benchmark an arm's length return for the party performing the less complex functions should not per se lead to a conclusion that the transactional profit split is the most appropriate method. Depending on the facts of the case, an appropriate method using uncontrolled transactions that are sufficiently comparable, but not identical to the controlled transaction is likely to be more reliable than an inappropriate use of the transactional profit split method. *See* paragraphs 3.38–3.39 for a discussion of limitations in available comparables.'

36. Paragraph 3.6.
37. Revised Guidance para. 2.128.

Consequently, the OECD continues to support the application of one-sided methods using reasonably comparable, although not identical, uncontrolled comparable transactions, under certain circumstances which are not explicitly defined (i.e. 'facts of the case …').

VII INDUSTRY PRACTICES

The accurate delineation of a transaction should take into consideration the main characteristics of the industry in which a company operates and the Revised Guidance on Profit Split reminds us that: 'the context of the transaction, including the industry in which it occurs and the factors affecting business performance in that sector can be particularly relevant to evaluating the contributions of the parties and whether such contributions are unique and valuable'.[38]

For the OECD, industry practices may provide relevant pointers as to whether or not to select a profit split method as the most appropriate. The Revised Guidance on Profit Split indicates[39] that: 'if information is available that independent parties do commonly use profit splitting approaches in similar situations, careful consideration should be given to whether the transactional profit split method may be the most appropriate method for the controlled transactions. Such industry practices may be a pointer to the fact that each party makes unique and valuable contributions, and/or that the parties are highly inter-dependent upon each other. Conversely, if independent parties engaged in comparable transactions are found to make use of other pricing methods, this should also be taken into account in determining the most appropriate transfer pricing method'.

VIII LOSSES

The Revised Guidance on Profit Split helpfully confirms[40] that: 'References to "profits" … should generally be taken as applying equally to losses. That is, where a transactional profit split method is determined to be the most appropriate method, it should generally also apply, and apply in the same way, regardless of whether the transaction(s) result in a relevant profit or loss.'

IX USE OF A PROFIT SPLIT METHOD AS PRIMARY METHOD OR AS A SANITY CHECK/SECONDARY METHOD

For the OECD,[41] 'The arm's length principle does not require the application of more than one method for a given transaction (or set of transactions that are appropriately aggregated …), and in fact undue reliance on such an approach could create a

38. Revised Guidance, para. 2.126.
39. Revised Guidance, para. 2.129.
40. Revised Guidance, para. 2.115.
41. 2017 OECD TPG, para. 2.12.

significant burden for taxpayers. Thus, these Guidelines do not require either the tax examiner or taxpayer to perform analyses under more than one method. While in some cases the selection of a method may not be straightforward and more than one method may be initially considered, generally it will be possible to select one method that is apt to provide the best estimation of an arm's-length price. However, for difficult cases, where no one approach is conclusive, a flexible approach would allow the evidence of various methods to be used in conjunction. In such cases, an attempt should be made to reach a conclusion consistent with the arm's-length principle that is satisfactory from a practical viewpoint to all the parties involved, taking into account the facts and circumstances of the case, the mix of evidence available, and the relative reliability of the various methods under consideration. *See* paragraphs 3.58–3.59 for a discussion of cases where a range of figures results from the use of more than one method.'

It follows that there is, in general, no requirement to use a profit split method as a sanity check or secondary method in cases where another method is selected as being most appropriate for the circumstances of the case. That being said, a profit split method can be used as a corroborative method in some complex cases, which the OECD does not define.

X HARD-TO-VALUE INTANGIBLES

At the same time as it released its Revised Guidance on Profit Split on the application of the transactional profit split method, the OECD released a document entitled 'Guidance for Tax Administrations on the Application of the Approach to Hard-to-Value Intangibles'.[42] Hard-to-value intangibles (hereinafter: HTVI) are defined in paragraphs 6.189–6.190 of the 2017 OECD TPG as follows:

> The term hard-to-value intangibles (HTVI) covers intangibles or rights in intangibles for which, at the time of their transfer between associated enterprises, (i) no reliable comparables exist, and (ii) at the time the transaction was entered into, the projections of future cash flows or income expected to be derived from the transferred intangible, or the assumptions used in valuing the intangible are highly uncertain, making it difficult to predict the level of ultimate success of the intangible at the time of the transfer.
>
> Transactions involving the transfer or the use of HTVI ... may exhibit one or more of the following features:
>
> - the intangible is only partially developed at the time of the transfer;
> - the intangible is not expected to be exploited commercially until several years following the transaction;
> - the intangible does not itself fall within the definition of HTVI ... but is integral to the development or enhancement of other intangibles which fall within that definition of HTVI;

42. OECD, Guidance for Tax Administrations on the Application of the Approach to Hard-to-Value Intangibles – BEPS Actions 8–10, OECD/G20 Base Erosion and Profit Shifting Project, OECD, Paris. www.oecd.org/tax/beps/guidance-for-tax-administrations-on-the-application-of-the-approach-tohard-to-value-intangibles-BEPS-action-8.pdf.

- the intangible is expected to be exploited in a manner that is novel at the time of the transfer and the absence of a track record of development or exploitation of similar intangibles makes projections highly uncertain;
- the intangible, meeting the definition of HTVI ..., has been transferred to an associated enterprise for a lump sum payment;
- the intangible is either used in connection with or developed under a CCA [Cost Contribution Arrangement] or similar arrangements.

The 2017 OECD TPG has introduced an administrative approach to HTVI whereby:

> Where the actual income or cash flows are significantly higher or lower than the anticipated income or cash flows on which the pricing was based, then there is presumptive evidence (from the perspective of the tax administration) that the projected income or cash flows used in the original valuation should have been higher or lower, and that the probability-weighting of such an outcome requires scrutiny, taking into account what was known and could have been anticipated at the time of entering into the transaction involving the HTVI. However, it would be incorrect to base the revised valuation on the actual income or cash flows without also taking into account the probability, at the time of the transaction, of the income or cash flows being achieved.

The administrative approach to HTVI does not prescribe a profit split method (or any other method). In fact, it is expected that it will mostly apply in practice to cases of valuations based on a discounted cashflow approach. It is, however, worth noting that, because HTVI are intangibles or rights in intangibles for which, at the time of their transfer between associated enterprises, no reliable comparables exist, cases of application of a profit split method (especially in the case of license, rather than sale, of HTVI) will be involved. Thus, cases of presumptive evidence as set forth in the 2017 OECD TPG for HTVI may also arise in cases where a profit split method has been applied, leading to an ex post revision of the underlying assumptions or the OECD:[43] 'The arm's length principle does not require the application of more than one method for a given transaction (or set of transactions that are appropriately aggregated ...), and in fact undue reliance on such an approach could create a significant burden for taxpayers. Thus, these Guidelines do not require either the tax examiner or taxpayer to perform analyses under more than one method. While in some cases the selection of a method may not be straightforward and more than one method may be initially considered, generally it will be possible to select one method that is apt to provide the best estimation of an arm's length price. However, for difficult cases, where no one approach is conclusive, a flexible approach would allow the evidence of various methods to be used in conjunction. In such cases, an attempt should be made to reach a conclusion consistent with the arm's length principle that is satisfactory from a practical viewpoint to all the parties involved, taking into account the facts and circumstances of the case, the mix of evidence available, and the relative reliability of the various methods under consideration. *See* paragraphs 3.58–3.59 for a discussion of cases where a range of figures results from the use of more than one method.'

43. 2017 OECD TPG, para. 2.12.

It follows that there is, in general, no requirement to use a profit split method as a sanity check or secondary method in cases where another method is selected as being most appropriate for the circumstances of the case. That being said, a profit split method can be used as a corroborative method in some complex cases, which the OECD does not define.

XI CONCLUDING REMARKS

The Revised Guidance on Profit Split on the application of the transactional profit split method is expected to have an immediate and significant impact on the practical approaches followed by MNEs and tax authorities on a global basis.

Interestingly, the possibility of broadening the use of profit split has attracted many comments in relation to 'fairness' and to the sustainability of the arm's-length principle. Profit split is sometimes regarded as a method that may help to counter tax avoidance through the location of residual profits in low-tax jurisdictions with little substantive activities. Further, those who advocate a broad use of profit split often do so on the grounds that subsidiaries should receive a greater share of the value created at group level, as a matter of fairness. However, the same are often reluctant to accept a broad use of the method in case of losses, arguing that subsidiaries would not be responsible for losses.

While profit split is without any doubt a valid and legitimate method in a number of circumstances, it would be naive to regard a very wide application of this method as a panacea. Its application may entail extreme complexity for taxpayers and tax authorities alike, broad uncertainties and outcomes that are potentially not aligned with the arm's-length principle.

On an administrative level, it is expected that a more extensive application of profit split will lead to more complex tax audits, resulting in an increased number of cross-border disputes and mutual agreement procedures. Disputes will likely arise about both the appropriateness of the profit split method and the determination of the profit (or loss) to be split and splitting factors. As a consequence, tax administrations that advocate a broad use of the profit split method should commit to eliminate, in a mutual agreement procedure, any double taxation that may result from the selection and application of this method or submit the case to binding arbitration. It should be recognized that the broader the use of the profit split method, the more tax administrations will need to invest resources in transfer pricing administration, both at enforcement and dispute resolution levels.

In our view, the selection of the most appropriate method (profit split or other), whether by taxpayers or tax authorities, has to be made consistently with the arm's-length principle, i.e., with what independent parties would agree (or have agreed) in comparable circumstances. That is, based on a principled, rather than an opportunistic position.

Chapter 6
Application of the Profit Split Method

Harlow Higinbotham & Vladimir Starkov

I INTRODUCTION

The key reason for applying a profit split method, as opposed to one-sided methods, to determine the arm's-length consideration in a controlled transaction is to quantify remuneration of the unique value drivers[1] present in the transaction in question. The profit split method should ordinarily be applied only in cases where the controlled parties jointly assume economically significant risks and either: (a) the remuneration of unique and valuable contributions by each of the controlled parties cannot be reliably benchmarked in other ways, e.g., by means of independent comparable transactions using one-sided methods; or (b) the controlled parties have relatively integrated operations.

In controlled transactions, contributions made by related parties may be difficult to value using uncontrolled benchmarks because of unique value chain functions in which the parties engage and due to economies of integration that may arise. Operations within a controlled group are often characterized by integrated management processes, unrestricted flows of information and cooperative behaviour of participants that result in reduced transaction costs and, often, sharing of risks and easier access to capital. Certain controlled transactions may have value drivers that are specific and unique to them, and, as such, cannot be benchmarked using unrelated comparable transactions or groups of transactions. These unique value drivers are variously referred to as 'non-routine contributions', 'intangibles' or 'entrepreneurial functions'.

The rationale for a profit split method application should be distinguished from cases where value contributions of controlled parties are potentially benchmarkable

1. The terms 'value drivers', 'contributions' and 'intangibles' are used interchangeably in this chapter.

(i.e., one or more of the parties make routine contributions), but benchmarking analysis may be difficult to perform reliably due to lack of suitable comparable benchmarks. Lack of comparable benchmarks alone should not be viewed as a sufficient reason to apply a profit split method. Functions of controlled parties for which independent benchmarks are available, either in fact or potentially, will be referred to as 'routine' functions.

The profit split method should be applied exclusively in the context of a correctly delineated controlled transaction wherein there is a fundamental sharing of economically significant risks between the parties, either on a prospective, anticipated basis or in terms of actual profit results. At arm's-length, parties entering into such arrangements can be assumed to share profits in proportion to their relative contributions to anticipated profits based on information known or reasonably foreseeable at the time that the transactions were entered into and in view of the associated risks undertaken by the parties. This core valuation principle based on arm's-length sharing of combined actual or expected profits guides the application features described below.

The correctly delineated transaction should include all of the relevant value drivers, including the economically relevant value chain, and consideration of relevant factors external to the controlled transaction, such as economic conditions, business cycles and market and competitive aspects. Often, a method referred to as the value chain analysis will be useful in providing the correct delineation of a controlled transaction.

1 Contribution Versus Residual Analyses[2]

The three distinct ways of applying the profit split method are the overall profit split method (hereinafter: 'OPSM'), the comparable profit split method (hereinafter: 'CPSM') and the residual profit split method (hereinafter: 'RPSM').

Under OPSM, the combined profits (or losses) earned by two or more parties to a controlled transaction are divided using some specified allocation key (such as costs, capital employed, assets, etc.). Under CPSM, the allocation of overall (or residual) profit (or loss) is determined based on evidence of profit allocation from an uncontrolled transaction or a group of transactions. The controlled transaction(s) selected for the CPSM should be similar to the uncontrolled transaction in the way functions, risks and assets are allocated between the uncontrolled parties in the transactions used as a benchmark and the parties to the controlled transaction. Under RPSM, the consolidated operating profit from a controlled transaction is first attributed to functions or assets used by the controlled parties, remuneration for which can be reliably established based on arm's-length evidence, while the remaining portion of the profits (the 'residual') is allocated to related parties using certain allocation keys (e.g., costs, capital employed, assets, etc.). The choice of the particular method (OPSM, CPSM or RPSM) depends on case-specific factors, for example:

2. The presentation of the methods in this section is based on HIGINBOTHAM, Chapter 10.

- CPSM – best method when arm's-length evidence of the overall profit split is available (e.g., comparable licensing transactions between unrelated parties);
- OPSM – may be the best method when non-routine intangibles and risks are owned by controlled parties in the same proportions as routine intangibles and other routine assets; and
- RPSM – best method when reliable benchmarks for routine functions are available and when non-routine intangibles and risks are owned in different proportions than routine intangibles and other routine assets.

A *contribution analysis* approach to splitting profits can be based on a variety of alternative measures of profit and related contribution factors, depending upon the availability of relevant benchmarks for the division of profits by independent enterprises engaging in comparable transactions and other internal and external data on relevant contributions, including incremental sales, employee compensation, key employee time and other factors such as assets, capital and costs. Care must be taken to achieve comparable relative contribution metrics for the parties to establish a profit-sharing paradigm that arm's-length parties would reasonably undertake in comparable circumstances.

A *residual analysis* approach to splitting profits excludes routine profits based on comparable benchmarks and focuses exclusively on the remainder residual profit and the relative contributions of the parties to the associated value drivers or entrepreneurial intangibles.

2 Distinction Between Transactional Profit Split of Anticipated Profits and Transactional Profit Split of Actual Profits

A split of the *actual* profits applies to controlled transactions that are characterized by ongoing contributions of value by related parties via the performance of non-routine activities and ongoing sharing of significant economic risks. Many ongoing transactions among related parties where more than one controlled party provides non-routine contributions and/or shares economically significant risks will be amenable to this method.

A split of *anticipated* profits may be appropriate when the related parties share ongoing unique and valuable risks but choose to establish pricing on an ex ante basis without regard to certain variances that may occur between forecasted results and actual results. The split of *anticipated* profits may also be the preferred method for such transactions as licensing of intangibles, certain financial and restructuring transactions.

Splitting anticipated profits can lead to situations when the value of intangibles at the moment of their transfer differs substantially from the value realized subsequently. This can lead to the question of whether an *ex post* adjustment to the initial valuation of the transferred intangibles may be indicated and would be expected to occur between arm's-length parties undertaking similar transactions. This issue is discussed in more detail in the section on the so-called hard-to-value intangibles included in the contribution 'When Is a Transactional Profit Split Method the Most Appropriate Method?'.

Because most 'typical' related-party transactions are characterized by an ongoing relationship by the parties and by sharing of economic risks, situations which call for sharing of anticipated profits may be somewhat less common, although in certain industries risk transfer between related parties may be customary. As an example, for groups operating in the financial industry, it is not uncommon for a controlled fund management entity to recommend particular securities or investment strategies to related investment funds. Remuneration of the management fund in such a transaction may be set according to an *ex ante* agreed formula, while the residual risk from holding the securities or executing the investment strategy will be borne by the fund.

3 Determination of the Combined Profit/Loss to Be Split

Proper application of the profit split method begins with defining the 'business' in which the unique contributions valued by this method help to determine profits and the appropriate context within which the parties at arm's-length would share in the result. As an example, a relevant transaction may be defined by the destination market of the product or products sold to unrelated parties, and would accordingly include all of the relevant related parties that contributed to the development, production, sales and post-sales activities associated with the product or products. Alternatively, the relevant 'business' may be defined as all of the applications of a given intangible property remuneration that is being rewarded under the profit split method.

As a general matter, profits or losses attributable to factors other than those accounted for in the contribution analysis should be excluded from the profit pool to be split.

The entire value chain of the controlled group relevant to the transaction or the 'business' in question must be defined. This value chain should start and end with transactions between the controlled group and unrelated parties. In practice, when an RPSM is applied, certain entities within the value chain may be entitled only to routine returns and, accordingly, such entities may be excluded from the subsequent contribution analysis or residual profit split analysis.

An important consideration for determining the appropriately delineated transaction or 'business' is the reliability of the financial data used to compute the joint profits in the transaction and the ability to determine reliably the profits to be attributed to the related parties. Segmentation of financial information generated in the ordinary course of business is a preferred method, although segmentation established for a specific controlled transaction may also be used as well as long as it reliably reflects the profits of the identified business or business segment. Keeping financial data of all related parties participating in the transaction on the same accounting standard and in the same currency is important as well, as noted in the revised guidance (hereinafter: 'Revised Guidance on Profit Split').[3]

The profit split method is applied in cases when related parties share the assumption of the same economically significant risks or separately assume closely related economically significant risks.[4] The economically significant risks, in turn, can be distinguished between the risks that a company can control and the risks that it cannot control. In those two situations, the profit split method should be applied differently. For example, a consolidated operating loss within the correctly delineated controlled transaction may be caused by conditions outside of the control of any of the related parties (e.g., external market conditions, weather conditions, exchange rates, etc.). If the loss is not attributable to the identified value drivers of the controlled transaction, then the proper method to split the loss may be to allocate the consolidated loss in proportion to all of the capital contributions in the controlled transaction, e.g., both routine and non-routine capital. This effectively amounts to the application of OPSM. If, on the other hand, a loss can be traced to the poor performance of a specific value driver controlled by only one of the related parties (e.g., failure of a product component designed or manufactured by a given affiliate of the controlled group), then the operating loss may be attributable to the accountable owner of this value driver depending upon the risk-sharing agreed between the parties.

4 Profit Split Factors

The Revised Guidance on Profit Split lists several factors that can be used to split profits, namely, costs, assets, capital, revenue, headcount, etc.[5] This list cannot be considered exhaustive, however, because the value drivers of certain controlled transactions may call for some other factors. For instance, the value of factors relevant for profit splits may sometimes be determined by other valuation methods or by reference to uncontrolled transactions (e.g., royalties for certain intangibles). Alternatively, in other situations including the digital economy, a contribution analysis based on the relative incremental value contributions of complementary value drivers, such as the technology platform versus data on individual users may be most relevant to determining the arm's-length division of the combined profits attributable to these factors. Because many of the factors listed in the Revised Guidance on Profit Split are better suited to account for relative rather than absolute values of the contributions by the related parties, we would encourage using the same factor to account for shares of all of the contributions in a given transaction.[6]

3. *See* OECD (2018), paras 2.155–2.156. As further elaborated below, it is important to ensure that both the common accounting standard and the method to account for exchange rate movements are consistent with what would be agreed by parties dealing at arm's-length.
4. OECD (2015).
5. Paragraphs 2.171–2.172.
6. While it may be possible to apply different types of split factors (e.g., headcount and capital) to a single transaction, such an application must address the question of how to divide the pool of profit from the transaction into parts that will be further split using each of the different factor

A Capital as a Profit Split Factor

Although capital is not mentioned as a profit split factor in the Revised Guidance on Profit Split, a case could be made that capital, properly defined, may have an important place among the candidate profit split factors.

In economic terms, the profits (or losses) of an enterprise provide a return on the capital invested in the enterprise (after payment of interest expenses and taxes). The capital invested in an enterprise consists of all tangible and intangible assets employed in the business, including the self-developed intangibles whose values may not be reflected on the balance sheet of an enterprise (this is the reason why the market value of a financially sound business will typically exceed the book value of the business). Since the net profit (or loss) of an enterprise provides remuneration of both tangible and intangible assets employed by the enterprise, it follows that each tangible and intangible asset employed by the enterprise has a claim on the overall net profit (loss) of the enterprise. Thus, if intangible assets employed in the business are properly identified and valued, their values, along with the values of other capital contributions that support a given transaction, can be used to allocate the total or residual profit earned in controlled transactions.

When multiple intangibles support a given controlled transaction, computing absolute values of each intangible may not be feasible (unless an uncontrolled transaction that prices some or all of those intangibles can be identified). However, it will often be possible to identify *relative* value contributions by different intangibles using the capitalized cost approach described below. Such relative values of intangibles employed by different parties to a controlled transaction may be used to allocate the total or residual profit earned in the controlled transaction.

Additionally, when tangible capital assets (e.g., cash, securities, fixed assets) are used as profit split factors, care should be taken to verify that the amounts of those capital assets are consistent with the arm's-length levels considering the functions performed and risks assumed by the party in a given transaction.

B Value Chain Analysis

Since profit split factors are ultimately used to determine the relative contributions of the two or more value drivers in a particular controlled transaction, the value chain analysis may be a useful tool to guide the selection of the factors appropriate to the transaction in hand. Since the objective of the value chain analysis is to document all value drivers of a given transaction and determine those that are most influential, this method can provide important contextual information to determine on how the profit split method may best be applied and, indeed, whether the profit split method is appropriate in the first place.

---

types. In many cases, the relative contributions of different factors may be compared in terms of their relative impact on revenues or profits using a common metric.

5 Adjustments to Profit Split Factors

Costs of intangibles development may be considered to be a reliable measure of relative contributions made by different related parties in situations where the time it takes to develop the different contributing intangibles is similar. However, it is not uncommon to encounter a timing mismatch in the development cycle of intangibles that contribute to a given controlled transaction. For instance, a development cycle for a high-technology or pharmaceutical product may span many years, while the development of marketing campaigns to promote the resulting products may require only a few months. In such cases, it is obvious that expenses recorded on an annual basis would not provide the most appropriate measure of relative contributions of value drivers by the different parties. Instead, more appropriate use of data on the intangibles development costs should take into consideration the period of development for the particular group of intangibles (as noted in paragraph 2.183 of the Revised Guidance on Profit Split), the expected useful life of the intangibles and whether different stages of development were associated with different degrees of risk (as discussed in paragraph 2.181 of the Revised Guidance on Profit Split). An effective method that allows addressing both the entrepreneurial incentive and timing mismatches in the intangibles development cycle is a capitalized cost approach. This method allows adjusting historical costs by a rate of return commensurate with the risk taken at various stages of intangibles development, account for 'gestation lags' in realizing value from the intangibles and for a gradual utilization of the intangibles over their useful life.

Costs of intangibles development incurred by related parties located in different countries may be recorded in different currencies. In some cases, relative values of currencies can change significantly over the period of time that it takes to develop and exploit the relevant intangibles. In such situations, appropriate valuations that take into account exchange rate movements and their impact on the relative valuations of capitalized costs may be necessary to achieve valuations that would be agreed by parties dealing at arm's-length.

When companies allocate resources to development activities, they forego other opportunities to invest the funds equivalent to the cost of resources spent on development. Assigning returns to the costs of developing intangibles that recognize these foregone opportunity profits that could be realized by investing the same resources into alternative financial investments with risk profiles similar to the risk of the subject intangibles development activities may be appropriate.

In certain situations, intangibles that are relevant for the profit split method application may be developed in countries with vastly different costs of living and associated wage levels. In such cases, a need for an adjustment for the differences in labour cost between affiliates (i.e., Purchasing Power Parity adjustment) may be evaluated. Differences in purchasing power between countries do not automatically imply a need for adjustment, however. Multiple factors need to be evaluated in determining whether a 'low-cost' affiliate may be entitled to an adjustment in measuring its relevant cost contributions. The conditions under which adjustment for such contributions may be appropriate include a combination of *all* of the following factors:

- 'location rents' exist in the country of the 'low-cost' affiliate;
- the controlled group is able to take advantages of the location rents;
- the 'low-cost' affiliate has secured access to the location rents; and
- price of the product (or service) is determined in the market outside of the home country of the 'low-cost' affiliate.

To illustrate how an adjustment of the intangibles development costs incurred in locations with different labour costs may work in practice, let us consider a hypothetical multinational company XYZ that develops and sells a suite of software designed to address computing needs of a specific industry (e.g., the banking sector). The suite of software sold by XYZ is regarded as one of the leading products on the market and the product is sold to customers across the world. Let us further assume that development of the software takes place only in two countries, Country A and Country B. The original version of the software was developed in Country A, and the origin of the product brand is associated with Country A, although sales affiliates of the group XYZ are responsible for developing relationships with local customers. Several years ago, the company XYZ acquired a local software development company in Country B that, prior to the acquisition, has developed and sold software with functionality that complemented the suite of products previously produced by the company XYZ. After the acquisition, the affiliate in Country B stopped selling its own software and the module being developed in Country B for the XYZ software is not sold to unrelated parties separately from the XYZ software suite. The software development teams in Countries A and B work on different software modules and develop complete modules on their own. Once the software modules are completed, they get integrated into the software suite by another development team located in Country A.

Let us also assume that examination of the facts specific to the company XYZ indicates that: (i) modules developed by Country B staff get integrated into nearly all the copies of the software suite sold by XYZ to its customers worldwide; (ii) the software development process at Country B is managed and controlled by the staff in Country B and Country A software development executives provide only general directions to the Country B development team; and (iii) for the same level of responsibilities, software developers in Country B have qualifications and skills that match those of the developers in Country A, although Country A development team has members with higher level of responsibilities than the highest-ranked team members in Country B. Let us further assume that the facts indicate that, given the same skill level, the value contributed by Country B engineers into the process of development XYZ software is on par with the value provided by Country A engineers (e.g., per hour of work), although, due to the lower cost of living in Country B, the compensation of engineers in Country B is lower than that of the engineers in Country A for the same skill level.

Given the stylized facts presented in this example, the following conclusions can be drawn. With respect to the development team in Country B, the 'location rents' are likely to exist because the price of the final product (the software suite) is set in the market outside of the 'low cost' Country B. The company XYZ is able to take advantage of the 'location rents' because it sells the software suite, including the module developed in Country B, in the world market and because its product is considered to be among the market leaders. The 'low-cost' affiliate in Country B was responsible for securing access to location rents by assembling a team of developers with capabilities to manage and control the development process of complete software modules.

Let us also assume that the accurate delineation of the controlled transaction indicates that the transactional profit split method is the most appropriate method to remunerate entrepreneurial contributions of the development teams in Countries A and B (along with entrepreneurial contributions provided by other factors, such as customer intangibles, brand, etc.) and that the most reliable method to measure entrepreneurial contributions related to the software development activities is based on the development cost. In this case, accounting for the relative contributions of the engineering staff in Countries A and B for the purposes of computing the factors for dividing the total or residual profit from the controlled transaction in question may include an adjustment of the compensation earned by the Country B engineering staff to the level of compensation earned by the Country A engineering staff of the same proficiency.

SELECTED BIBLIOGRAPHY

Higinbotham Harlow N., Chapter 10: Profit Split Methods, in: Robert T. Cole (ed.), Practical Guide to U.S. Transfer Pricing, Third Edition, 2009.

OECD (2018): OECD, Revised Guidance on the Application of the Transactional Profit Split Method: Inclusive Framework on BEPS: Action 10, OECD/G20 Base Erosion and Profit Shifting Project, OECD Paris. www.oecd.org/tax/beps/revised-guidance-on-the-application-of-the-transactional-profit-split-method-beps-action-10.pdf.

OECD (2015): OECD, BEPS Action 10: Public Discussion Draft on the Use of Profit Splits in the Context of Global Value Chains, 16 December 2014 - 6 February 2015.

CHAPTER 7

Administrative Approaches to Profit Split Method

Bruno Gibert & Celine Pasquier

I INTRODUCTION

As a result of the Organisation for Economic Co-operation and Development (OECD) Revised Guidance on the Application of the Transactional Profit Split Method published in June 2018 (hereinafter: 'Revised Guidance on Profit Split'),[1] the application of the profit split method (hereinafter: 'PSM') has been specified.[2] This shall be reflected in taxpayers' transfer pricing documentation (*see* section II.1.).

In case of a tax audit, a taxpayer will have to demonstrate to the tax administration that the method employed was appropriate, including where it has used the PSM. Where the taxpayer has not used the PSM in a situation where the Revised Guidance on Profit Split recommends using it, there is a risk that the method used by the taxpayer would be challenged by tax administrations (*see* section II.2.).

Furthermore, due to its nature and complexity, the PSM should continue to be discussed by taxpayers and tax administrations in the context of Advance Pricing Agreements (hereinafter: 'APAs') and Mutual Agreement Procedures (hereinafter: 'MAPs') (*see* section II.3.).

1. OECD, Revised Guidance on the Application of the Transactional Profit Split Method: Inclusive Framework on BEPS: Action 10, OECD/G20 Base Erosion and Profit Shifting Project (June 2018), OECD, Paris. *See* www.oecd.org/tax/beps/revised-guidance-on-the-application-of-the-transactional-profit-split-method-beps-action-10.pdf.
2. *Id.*

II ADMINISTRATIVE APPROACHES TO PSM

1 The Role of Transfer Pricing Documentation

The elaboration of a transfer pricing documentation materializes the transfer pricing policy of a taxpayer. Under the standardized approach recommended by the OECD, transfer pricing documentation is a three-tiered documentation containing a master file, a local file and a Country-By-Country Report (hereinafter: 'CbCR'). While the master file and local file existed under the previous version of the Transfer Pricing Guidelines for Multinational Enterprises and Tax Administrations (hereinafter: 'OECD TPG'), the CbCR, further to the publication of (Base erosion and profit shifting) BEPS Action 13 Report in October 2015, is a new instrument at the disposal of the tax administration to better understand at the global level the allocation of income and taxes within a multinational group while locating business activities among the various entities of such group and, hence, may push in the direction of PSM or, at least, lead to profit allocation comparisons whatever transfer pricing method has been applied.

The PSM applied between related entities is based on an agreement concluded between the parties. The application of the PSM shall be described in the local file. When presenting the application of the PSM, the local file shall justify its application and specify how the method has been applied. The documentation shall, therefore, be sufficiently detailed on the measurement and valuation of the contributions of the respective entities taken into consideration for the application of the PSM and shall specify and justify the approach retained to split the profits (contribution or residual analysis), the profits split (actual or anticipated profits and measures of profits) and profit splitting factors employed (figure or variable).

The PSM documentation shall be more extensively developed than a traditional method because it requires more data to be analysed, processed and explained. The Revised Guidance on Profit Split emphasizes that the PSM necessitates 'applying judgements in determining each of the parameters for the application of the ... method [and that] it will be particularly important to document how the method has been applied, including the determination of the relevant profits to be split, and how the profit splitting factors were arrived at'.[3] This is reflected in the 2010 OECD Transfer Pricing Guidelines for Multinational Enterprises and Tax Administrations (hereinafter: '2010 OECD TPG') provisions on the comparability analysis, which specify that 'Where the most appropriate transfer pricing method in the circumstances of the case ... is a transactional profit split, financial information on all the parties to the transaction, domestic and foreign, is needed'.[4] Given that the PSM is a two-sided method, the taxpayer's documentation shall, therefore, provide for domestic and foreign factual and financial information on the basis of which the PSM was elaborated.

3. *See* OECD, OECD Transfer Pricing Guidelines for Multinational Enterprises and Tax Administrations 2017 (10 July 2017), para. 2.123, OECD Publishing, Paris, https://doi.org/10.1787/tpg-2017-en [hereinafter: 2017 OECD TPG].
4. *See* para. 3.21. of the 2010 and 2017 OECD TPG.

2 Profit Split and Audits

A *How to Audit the PSM Applied by a Taxpayer?*

Before the launch of an audit, the CbCR prepared by the taxpayer's group and provided to the tax administration shall serve as a risk assessment tool for the tax administration. At this date, the tax administration team may only have at its disposal the CbCR to analyse the transfer pricing policy of a multinational group. The CbCR shall, in principle, be provided by the parent company of a group to its tax administration, which shall exchange it automatically with the tax administrations of the countries of the establishment of its subsidiaries and/or permanent establishments (hereinafter: 'PEs') in accordance with Directive 2016/881/EU (DAC 4) of 25 May 2016 or the Multilateral Competent Authority Agreement (hereinafter: 'MCAA') on CbCR signed in January 2016. The first exchanges of CbCR took place until 30 June 2018 on 2016 information. The tax administration of a foreign subsidiary or PE of a group shall, therefore, have access to the group's CbCR, provided that its country of establishment is within the European Union (hereinafter: 'EU') or signed the MCAA.

As such, the CbCR can neither reflect the application of a PSM nor serve the tax administration to understand how the PSM has been applied. Indeed, the CbCR does not specify intra-group transactions nor transfer pricing methods applied. In addition, figures provided in the CbCR represent aggregated amounts per tax jurisdiction.[5] But, once the tax administration has been provided with the rest of the taxpayer's documentation (master file and local file) and the tax administration is aware that the PSM has been applied, tax administrations shall cross-check high-level information obtained through the CbCR with the content of the master file and local file(s) at their disposal.

The three-tier transfer pricing documentation elaborated by a taxpayer has a compliance purpose and shall, as a whole, serve as a basis for the discussions with the tax administration in case of a tax audit. In this context, the CbCR may provide hints of profit splitting factors employed, notably based on business activities and employee information provided per entity of the group. However, the information provided by the CbCR shall not suffice as such to justify the splitting factors employed by a taxpayer given that the PSM may have been construed based on more in-depth information. The audit by the tax administration of a PSM applied by a taxpayer necessitates that the tax administration be provided in the local file with all necessary information justifying the elaboration of the PSM (*see* section II.1.).

The audit of the PSM will generally necessitate numerous exchanges between the taxpayer and the tax audit team so as to enable the tax audit to verify whether the PSM was the most appropriate transfer pricing method applicable, how the PSM was applied and how such application is justified by the taxpayer. In practice, if the PSM has been applied to cases of either unique and valuable contributions (notably with respect to

5. The accuracy of the amounts provided in the CbCR will depend on the adjustments made to align the accounting standards used to compute the amounts per tax jurisdiction.

intellectual property), highly integrated business operations or risk sharing,[6] the use of the PSM should not be challenged by the tax administration. The tax administration would then verify how the PSM was applied.

The debates which took place in the context of the revision of the OECD Guidance on the Application of the PSM demonstrated that there is no systematic route to implement the PSM and that from a taxpayer to the other, and from a business model to the other, the approach to split the profits, the profits to be split and profit splitting factors shall differ.[7] The audit of a PSM, therefore, requires a case-by-case approach from tax administrations.

B *Can a PSM Be Applied in an Audit?*

Before the launch of an audit, the information provided by the CbCR shall not suffice to justify the application of the PSM, in the same way as it cannot as such serve to justify the PSM applied by the taxpayer. The CbCR shall only serve as a risk assessment tool and could not serve as a basis for justifying the application of the PSM: 'the information in the Country-by-Country Report should not be used as a substitute for a detailed transfer pricing analysis of individual transactions and prices based on a full functional analysis and a full comparability analysis'.[8]

In addition, figures provided in the CbCR are aggregated amounts which do not enable splitting the profits generated by the group among the various entities of the group. Finally, there is a risk that using the information provided in the CbCR would lead to global formulary apportionment. Global formulary apportionment consists in allocating the aggregated profits of a multinational group among the entities of such group on the basis of a predetermined formula.[9] Global formulary apportionment differs from the PSM insofar as, unlike the PSM, it is a non-arm's length method and the remuneration allocated to a taxpayer is not tested by comparison with the profits that would be allocated between independent enterprises. As mentioned in OECD Guidance on the appropriate use of the information contained in CbCRs, '[the] appropriate use condition does not permit a tax authority to make an adjustment to the income of any taxpayer on the basis of a global formulary apportionment of income based on the data from the CbC Report'.[10] Thus, a tax administration could not deduce from a CbCR that the PSM should apply.

Instead, to determine whether the PSM should apply, the tax administration would have to analyse thoroughly the taxpayer's transfer pricing documentation, and notably the functional analysis of the taxpayer provided in the master file and local file(s). If the PSM has not been applied to cases for which the PSM is considered as the most appropriate method by OECD TPG, i.e., in cases of either unique and valuable

6. 2017 OECD TPG, paras 2.119 to 2.221.
7. *See* Finley, p. 404.
8. 2017 OECD TPG, para. 5.25.
9. 2017 OECD TPG, Definition of 'Global formulary apportionment', p. 26.
10. OECD, BEPS Action 13 on Country-by-Country Reporting, Guidance on the Appropriate Use of Information Contained in Country-by-Country Reports (September 2017), para. 17.

contributions (notably with respect to intellectual property), highly integrated business operations or risk sharing,[11] the tax administration could consider that it should apply. The tax administration could also consider that the PSM should apply to other cases, such as cases in which comparable transactions between independent parties apply a PSM. In any case, in both situations, the tax administration would have to justify the application of the PSM and the conditions of its application.[12]

With respect to the application of the PSM, the tax administration will have to assess whether the information at its disposal in the transfer pricing documentation will enable elaborating a PSM. Where the taxpayer has not applied the PSM, there is a risk that information (including financial data) provided in the taxpayer's transfer pricing documentation would not suffice. Indeed, a traditional transfer pricing documentation shall not require information as much detailed as in the PSM. The elaboration of a PSM is based on thorough value chain interviews and on the analysis of financial data from the foreign-related entity. Except if the taxpayer audited is the parent company of its related company, it may not be in possession of all necessary information to build the PSM of the tax administration. The tax administration shall have to resort to the exchange of information to obtain necessary information from the foreign entity through its country counterparty. However, even in that case, there is a risk that the information provided shall not be sufficiently exhaustive given that it will not be possible to conduct the interviews.

C Towards Simultaneous Tax Examinations?

In the circumstance of a tax administration wishing to reassess a taxpayer on the basis of the PSM, it could contemplate resorting to a simultaneous tax examination. Even though the OECD TPG does not directly recommend resorting to a simultaneous tax examination in such a situation,[13] the guidance specifies that such type of examination may be useful when information held in a foreign country is 'key to a tax investigation'.[14] A simultaneous tax examination is an 'arrangement between two or more [tax administrations] to examine simultaneously and independently, each on its own territory, the tax affairs of (a) taxpayer(s) in which they have a common or related interest with a view to exchanging any relevant information which they so obtain'.[15]

Simultaneous tax examinations shall only be carried out provided that there is a legal basis to do so, such as double tax treaties, OECD Convention on Mutual Administrative Assistance in Tax Matters or EU Directive 2011/16/EU.[16] As specified by the EU Directive, simultaneous tax examinations are investigations performed by

11. 2017 OECD TPG, paras 2.119 to 2.221.
12. *See* Bagran Ilhan, s. 1: 'The national tax authorities appear to be favouring the profit split method (PSM) as they raise more frequently the question of where the value is created in MNE's business operations. On the other hand, taxpayers have concerns that tax authorities will simply use profit splits as a backdoor to formulary apportionment'.
13. 2017 OECD TPG, paras 4.79 et seq.
14. 2017 OECD TPG, para. 4.79.
15. 2017 OECD TPG, para. 4.80.
16. Directive 2011/16/EU, Art. 12.

tax administrations on their territories which lead to the sharing of information resulting from the audit, while each tax administration remains the master of its decisions and thus of its tax reassessments. Such examinations are recommended by the OECD to address transfer pricing issues.[17] In 2018, the EU Joint Transfer Pricing Forum has pursued its works on improving its guidance on this procedure as well as the joint audit procedure[18] and issued a report entitled 'A Cooperative Approach to Transfer Pricing Controls within the EU' in October 2018.[19] On its hand, the OECD Forum on Tax Administration published another report addressing joint audits entitled 'Enhancing Tax Co-operation and Improving Tax Certainty' in March 2019.[20]

Simultaneous or joint audits could enable tax administrations to better address a taxpayer's reassessment, notably when such tax administration intends to apply the PSM.[21]

3 Approaches to the PSM in Cooperative Environments (APAs) and Dispute Resolution Procedures (MAPs)

The PSM is an appropriate transfer pricing method in the context of cooperative environments or dispute resolution procedures. APAs and MAPs are instruments which ensure respectively the prevention and the resolution of double taxation. The application of the PSM in this context is perceived as a useful tool to allocate a greater share of profit to the countries concerned while providing tax certainty to the taxpayers. This comes from the fact that the PSM, being a two-sided method,[22] finds its place naturally in these procedures that involve the two tax authorities concerned.[23]

A Approaches to the PSM in APAs

A taxpayer shall initiate an APA procedure to secure, in the future, its transfer pricing policy towards dedicated transaction(s) and prevent potential double taxation further to a tax reassessment.

17. 2017 OECD TPG, para. 4.94.
18. Joint audits are investigations performed jointly by tax administrations resulting in consistent tax reassessments.
19. *See* https://ec.europa.eu/taxation_customs/sites/taxation/files/jtpf_report_on_a_coordinated_approach_to_transfer_pricing_controls_within_the_eu_en.pdf.
20. http://www.oecd.org/fr/ctp/joint-audit-2019-enhancing-tax-co-operation-and-improving-tax-certainty-17bfa30d-en.htm.
21. *See* Kroppen/Dawid/Schmidtke, p. 22: 'If tax audits are performed simultaneously, the taxpayer could provide the same documents to both tax authorities. Both tax authorities would have the same level of information and could also align their assessment in advance'.
22. *See* Tenore, p. 3: '[The] two-sided nature [of the PSM] leads to an allocation of "the overall profit to both parties of the transaction" and therefore triggers lower risk of deviating "from a market outcome" to the extent it is "applied consistently by all jurisdictions involved (WP, §20)"'.
23. *See* Wittendorf, p. 755: 'Although the PSM is now a specified method, its application will normally be marked by significant discretionary elements. If the method is only applied on the basis of internal data, the reliability of the results will be substantially diminished. Substituting objective data with subjective judgments will naturally lead to disputes. The PSM is thus most suitable for APAs, MAPs, etc. ....'

Further to OECD BEPS works, revised OECD TPG recommends to countries, as a non-binding best practice, to conclude bilateral or multilateral APAs.[24] A taxpayer shall obtain a bilateral or multilateral APA provided that the tax administrations of the countries concerned have agreed to the remuneration allocated to them given the functions, assets and risks borne by the various entities of the group concerned. The PSM could adequately be covered by the conclusion of bilateral or multilateral APAs. It is notably referred to by OECD TPG addressing APAs when specifying that '[it] would not be appropriate to specify a profit split formula between associated enterprises if it is expected that the allocation of functions between the enterprises will be unstable. It would, however, be possible to prescribe a profit split formula if the role of each enterprise were articulated in critical assumptions....'.[25]

The conclusion of a bilateral or multilateral APA provides certainty to a taxpayer and notably with respect to the transfer pricing method employed. Considering the complexity of the PSM and the risk of challenge by a tax administration (*see* section II.2.B.), the conclusion of an APA in the context of a PSM shall be protective to taxpayers, this all the more than, the APA being bilateral or multilateral, it would bind two or more tax administrations.

In practice, the conclusion of an APA requires that the taxpayer provide an APA documentation justifying the application and conditions of application of the PSM. The documentation provided should be very similar to standard transfer pricing documentation and information to be provided to the tax administrations as extensive as under a standard transfer pricing documentation (*see* section I.1.).

B Approaches to the PSM in MAPs

A taxpayer shall initiate a MAP to resolve double taxation resulting from a tax reassessment, especially on a transfer pricing matter. Based on the position paper of the first authority of the country of reassessment, the competent authority of the other country(ies) ('second competent authority') concerned shall provide a second position paper stating whether '[it] believes that double taxation has occurred, or is likely to occur, and agrees with the remedy proposed in the position paper ...'.[26] If the competent authority believes double taxation has occurred or is likely to occur, the double taxation shall be resolved through a corresponding adjustment in the country of the second competent authority (and/or a downward adjustment in the country of the first competent authority). In accordance with Article 9(2) of the OECD Model Tax Convention, for such adjustments to be performed, competent authorities shall consult each other. No specific method is prescribed to address the double taxation issue and determine the amount of the corresponding adjustment (and/or downward adjustment). In the case of a PSM, based on the drafting of the commentaries to the OECD Model Tax Convention or OECD TPG, competent authorities should have sufficient

24. 2017 OECD TPG, para. 4.134.
25. 2017 OECD TPG, para. 4.137.
26. *See* Communication 2009/472, Annex, s. 6.4, e)(i).

leeway to readjust the characteristics of the PSM applied so as to reach an agreement.[27] Further, considering the stringent timing of a MAP, it should be very unlikely that both competent authorities would decide to resort to a PSM to address the double taxation of the case at hand (assuming the PSM was not the method applied by the taxpayer). Indeed, as well as it could lengthen a tax audit procedure, the PSM could lengthen the discussions among countries' competent authorities in a MAP context due to its complexity.

A transfer pricing reassessment may also lead to a secondary adjustment in the context of a MAP. A secondary adjustment relies on the recognition of a 'constructive transaction (a secondary transaction), whereby the excess profits resulting from a primary adjustment are treated as having been transferred in some other form and taxed accordingly. Ordinarily, the secondary transactions will take the form of constructive dividends, constructive equity contributions, or constructive loans'.[28] Such constructive transaction shall be recognized on the basis of domestic law provisions. Where secondary adjustment provisions would not exist in the country of reassessment, a secondary adjustment would not be necessary. In practice, when countries recognize secondary adjustments, they also enable the taxpayer reassessed to avoid any further taxation triggered by the secondary adjustment by providing for the repatriation of the excess profits. The recognition or the characteristics of a secondary transaction shall not be affected by the transfer pricing method applied either by the taxpayer or by the tax administration, as the secondary transaction is only triggered by the existence of a tax reassessment as such. So, the PSM should not specifically affect the conclusion of a MAP.

SELECTED BIBLIOGRAPHY

AHMADOV JAMIL, The 'Most Appropriate Method' as the New OECD Transfer Pricing Standard: Has the Hierarchy of Methods Been Completely Eliminated?, in: 18 International Transfer Pricing Journal 3 (2011).

BAGRAN ILHAN CANSU, The Use of Value Chain Analysis in a Profit Split, in: 25 International Transfer Pricing Journal 4 (2018).

FINLEY RYAN, Narrower OECD Profit-Split Guidance is a Result of U.S. Efforts, in: Tax Notes International (23 July 2018).

Communication 2009/472 on the work of the JTPF from March 2007 to March 2009 and a related proposal for a revised code of conduct for implementation of the Arbitration Convention.

KROPPEN HEINZ-KLAUS / DAWID ROMAN / SCHMIDTKE RICHARD, Profit Split, the Future of Transfer Pricing? Arm's Length Principle and Formulary Apportionment Revisited from a Theoretical and a Practical Perspective, in: Kai A. KONRAD / WOLFGANG

27. *See* AHMADOV, s. 6.: 'Transactional profit methods are no longer regarded as last resort methods, [they] are a great step forward that can help Member countries to resolve cases of double taxation under the relevant mutual agreement procedures'.
28. 2017 OECD TPG, para. 4.68.

SCHÖN (eds.), Fundamentals of International Transfer Pricing in Law and Economics, Springer 2012.

TENORE MARIO, A Two-Sided Affair: The EU Commission Favours Profit Split for the Wrong Reason, in: Kluwer International Tax Blog (30 June 2017).

WITTENDORF JENS, Transfer Pricing and the Arm's Length Principle in International Tax Law, Kluwer Law International 2010.

PART III The Profit Split Method from Other Perspectives

CHAPTER 8

Potential State Aid Exposure in Case of Tax Rulings Based on the Profit Split Method

Gabriella Cappelleri & Mario Tenore

I INTRODUCTION

The results of the most recent State aid investigations carried out by the European Commission in the area of tax rulings and transfer pricing highlight the utmost importance to be attributed to the appropriate selection and application of transfer pricing methods.

Over the past years, the European Commission's scrutiny increasingly focused on verifying whether the transfer pricing analysis performed in the context of advance pricing agreements (hereinafter: 'APAs') concluded by the Member States achieved a reliable approximation of the so-called market-based outcome.

The Commission's recent decisions have added significant uncertainties in the area of transfer pricing, which is already considered a not exact science. None of these decisions deals explicitly with the application of the profit split method. Due to this, if the Commission were to investigate the possible infringement of State aid legislation in connection with an APA endorsing the application of the profit split, the outcome of the investigation would be even more unpredictable.

Generally speaking, the Commission has made generic reference to the profit split method in some of its investigations regarding tax rulings and transfer pricing. For example, in the Belgian case dealing with the Belgian excess profit ruling system,[1] the Commission, making ample reference to paragraph 2.59 of the (Organisation for Economic Co-operation and Development) OECD Transfer Pricing Guidelines, has

1. Commission Decision of 11 January 2016 on the excess profit exemption State Aid scheme SA.37667 (2015/C) (ex 2015/NN) implemented by Belgium [hereinafter: 'Belgian Excess Profit Decision'].

affirmed that the profit split is a suitable methodology 'if each party to a transaction makes valuable, unique contributions' (paragraph 58).

In addition to the above, in its Working Paper on State Aid and Tax Rulings (hereinafter: 'DG Competition Working Paper'), the Commission has more recently recalled the profit split methodology in the context of APAs 'based on a two-sided approach, i.e. both companies to the intra-group transaction are analysed ...' (paragraph 20).

This stated, the present contribution shall provide a critical assessment of the profit split from a State aid perspective, taking into account other Commission decisions dealing with other profit methodologies, to the extent such decisions could offer useful thoughts.

II EU STATE AID AND TAX RULINGS

1 The Commission's Investigations on Tax Rulings

With the aim of guaranteeing and safeguarding the effective competitiveness in the internal market, Article 107(1) of the Treaty on the Functioning of the European Union[2] (hereinafter: 'TFEU') prevents the Member States from granting any aid 'which distorts or threatens to distort competition by favouring certain undertakings or the production of certain goods ..., in so far as it affects trade between Member States'. It follows that unlawful State aid is that which: (i) is granted by the State or through State resources, (ii) has the potential to distort competition among the Member States, (iii) favours certain undertakings,[3] and (iv) confers an economic advantage[4] on the undertaking.[5] The European Commission is in charge of ensuring that the Member States do not implement unlawful State aid.[6] Accordingly, Member States are obliged to inform the Commission of any plans to grant aid measures and to wait for the Commission's approval before enforcing the same.[7] Moreover, the Commission may open formal

2. Consolidated Version of the Treaty on the Functioning of the European Union, Official Journal C 326/91, 26 October 2012 [hereinafter: 'TFEU'].
3. The Court of Justice of the European Union [hereinafter: 'CJEU'] has consistently defined 'undertakings' as entities engaged in an economic activity, regardless of their legal status under national law and of whether the entity is set up to generate profits (*see* Judgment of the CJEU of 12 September 2000, *Pavlov and Others*, Joined Cases C-180/98 to C-184/98, ECLI:EU:C:2000:428, para. 74; Judgment of the CJEU of 10 January 2006, *Cassa di Risparmio di Firenze SpA and Others*, Case C-222/04, ECLI:EU:C:2006:8, para. 107).
4. An 'economic advantage' within the meaning of Art. 107(1) TFEU is 'any economic benefit which an undertaking could not have obtained under normal market conditions, that is to say in the absence of State intervention' (*see* the notice issued by the Commission on 19 July 2016, Commission Notice on the notion of State aid as referred to in Art. 107(1) of the Treaty on the Functioning of the European Union, 2016/C 262/01 [hereinafter: '2016 Notice'], para. 66). Furthermore, *see* Judgment of the CJEU of 11 July 1996, *SFEI and Others*, Case C-39/94, ECLI:EU:C:1996:285, para. 60; Judgment of the CJEU of 29 April 1999, *Spain v. Commission*, Case C-342/96, ECLI:EU:C:1999:210, para. 41.
5. For a comprehensive overview of the notion of State aid as referred to in Art. 107(1), *see* the 2016 Notice.
6. Article 108 TFEU.
7. Article 108(3) TFEU.

investigations if it discovers that a measure that could be considered State aid has been adopted without its prior consent.[8]

The above rules cover a large number of measures, including those pertaining to the area of direct business taxation.[9] Indeed, while on the one hand Member States are completely free to design their own direct taxation systems,[10] on the other hand, they must remit their fiscal measures to the State aid control.[11]

Since 2013, the European Commission has strengthened its scrutiny into Member States' fiscal schemes with the aim of verifying whether they comply with State aid rules. In particular, the Commission focused its attention on a number of APAs.[12,13] During its assessments, the Commission did not call into question the granting of APAs by itself (which are recognized as important tools for providing legal certainty)[14] but rather scrutinized if the transfer prices agreed therein conferred a selective advantage

8. Commission investigations usually consists of two stages: a first preliminary examination (which can result in the Commission concluding that the aid is compatible) and a subsequent formal (in-depth) investigation, which may be initiated by the Commission where it has serious doubts about the aid's compatibility with the State aid rules, or where it faces procedural difficulties in obtaining the necessary information from the Member State concerned (for further reference, *see* Council Regulation (EU) No. 734/2013 of 22 July 2013, amending Regulation (EC) No. 659/1999).The Commission's decision can be appealed by Member States and by interested parties to the General Court. Decisions from the General Court can subsequently be appealed to the CJEU under Art. 263 TFEU.
9. This had already been clarified by the CJEU in 1974 (*see* Judgment of the CJEU of 2 July 1974, *Italy v. Commission*, 173/73, EU:C:1974:71).
10. Since taxation is not mentioned among the competences that the Member States conferred on the European Union (*see* Arts 3-5 TFEU), it remains within the competences of the Member States.
11. Under this perspective, Art. 107(1) TFEU should be interpreted as prohibiting unequal treatment in taxation of undertakings in a similar factual and legal situation. In particular, fiscal measures selectively advantaging certain taxpayers over others - albeit in a similar factual and legal situation - may constitute State aid. On the contrary, fiscal measures of a general nature, applicable with no distinctions to all undertakings, cannot in principle constitute State aid. *See* Commission's Directorate-General for Competition, DG Competition Working Paper on State Aid and Tax Rulings, Background to the High Level Forum on State Aid of 3 June 2016, para. 2.
12. In June 2013, the Commission began State aid investigations into tax rulings granted by Cyprus, Ireland, Luxembourg, Malta, the Netherlands and the United Kingdom. By the end of 2014, all Member States had been asked by the Commission to provide information about their tax ruling practice. The inquiry led, in mid-2014, to the opening of three formal State aid investigations by the Commission on tax rulings granted by Ireland (to Apple), Luxembourg (to Fiat) and the Netherlands (to Starbucks). Further investigations were opened by the Commission later the same year and in 2015 on tax rulings granted by Luxembourg (to Amazon and to McDonald's) and by Belgium (the Excess Profit scheme). With specific reference to the APAs investigated, the Commission adopted four negative decisions with recovery with respect to the tax rulings granted by the Netherlands to Starbucks, by Luxembourg to Fiat and Amazon, and by Ireland to Apple. All these decisions were appealed and Court cases are currently pending before the General Court of the European Union.
13. The Glossary of the 2017 OECD Transfer Pricing Guidelines for Multinational Enterprises and Tax Administrations defines the term 'APA' as '[a]n arrangement that determines, in advance of controlled transactions, an appropriate set of criteria (e.g. method, comparables and appropriate adjustments thereto, critical assumptions as to future events) for the determination of the transfer pricing for those transactions over a fixed period of time'.
14. This was explicitly confirmed by the Commission in para. 169 of the 2016 Notice.

upon the addressees, i.e., lowered their tax liability in the relevant Member State as compared to companies in a similar factual and legal situation.[15]

According to the Commission, a tax ruling confers State aid insofar as the ruling leads to a lowering of the tax burden by deviating from the tax that the beneficiary would otherwise be obliged to pay under the general corporate tax system (i.e., the market-based outcome).[16]

The reference to 'market-based' outcome clearly evokes the 'arm's-length principle' set forth by both the OECD Model Tax Convention (hereinafter: 'OECD Model')[17] and the OECD Guidelines.[18] However, these two concepts, although similar, originate from different sources. Indeed, the Commission clarified that the arm's-length principle applied in its State aid assessments 'is not that derived from Article 9 of the OECD Model Tax Convention and the OECD TP Guidelines, which are nonbinding instruments, but a general principle of equal treatment in taxation falling within the application of Article 107(1) of the Treaty, which binds the Member States and from whose scope the national tax rules are not excluded'.[19]

As a consequence, the arm's-length principle adopted by the Commission must be considered a direct application of Article 107(1) TFEU, which prohibits unequal treatment in the taxation of undertakings in a similar factual and legal situation.[20,21]

---

15. The 2016 Notice, paras 128 and 129, clarifies that 'the selectivity of the measures should normally be assessed by means of a three-step analysis. First, the system of reference must be identified. Second, it should be determined whether a given measure constitutes a derogation from that system insofar as it differentiates between economic operators who, in light of the objectives intrinsic to the system, are in a comparable factual and legal situation. Assessing whether a derogation exists is the key element of this part of the test and allows a conclusion to be drawn as to whether the measure is prima facie selective. If the measure in question does not constitute a derogation from the reference system, it is not selective. However, if it does (and therefore is prima facie selective), it needs to be established, in the third step of the test, whether the derogation is justified by the nature or the general scheme of the (reference) system. If a prima facie selective measure is justified by the nature or the general scheme of the system, it will not be considered selective and will thus fall outside the scope of Article 107(1) of the Treaty.... However, the three-step analysis cannot be applied in certain cases, taking into account the practical effects of the measures concerned. It must be emphasised that Article 107(1) of the Treaty does not distinguish between measures of State intervention in terms of their causes or aims, but defines them in relation to their effects, independently of the techniques used. This means that in certain exceptional cases it is not sufficient to examine whether a given measure derogates from the rules of the reference system as defined by the Member State concerned. It is also necessary to evaluate whether the boundaries of the system of reference have been designed in a consistent manner or, conversely, in a clearly arbitrary or biased way, so as to favour certain undertakings which are in a comparable situation with regard to the underlying logic of the system in question'.
16. 2016 Notice, para. 171.
17. OECD, Model Tax Convention on Income and on Capital, Condensed Version 2017 (OECD 2017).
18. OECD, Transfer Pricing Guidelines for Multinational Enterprises and Tax Administrations (OECD 2017), as amended by the recently published Revised Guidance on the Application of the Transactional Profit Split Method: Inclusive Framework on BEPS: Action 10, OECD/G20 Base Erosion and Profit Shifting Project, OECD Paris [hereinafter: 'OECD Guidelines'].
19. *See* Belgian Excess Profit Decision, para. 150.
20. 2016 Notice, para. 172.
21. In 2006, the CJEU explicitly endorsed the arm's-length principle for determining whether a fiscal measure prescribing a method for an integrated group company to determine its taxable profit

Such a principle is applied by the Commission regardless of whether a Member State has incorporated it into its national legal system and in what form.[22] Nonetheless, the Commission specified that when examining if an APA complies with State aid rules, it 'may have regard' to the OECD Guidelines since the latter represent an internationally agreed standard on transfer pricing and provide useful guidance on how to ensure that a transfer pricing methodology produces an outcome in line with market conditions.[23]

The Commission regards the OECD Guidelines as 'an existing manual in the area of transfer pricing that is the result of expert discussions in the context of the OECD and elaborate on techniques aimed to address common challenges of the application of the arm's length principle to concrete situations' (Starbucks, paragraph 66).

Consistency with the OECD Guidelines is viewed as a sort of 'protection' from illegal State aid. Compliance with the OECD Guidelines is an indication that the APA beneficiary is not treated more favourably compared to a stand-alone entity whose taxable profit is determined by the market.

The approach followed by the Commission in its assessments of tax rulings has been heavily debated in the literature,[24] with the Commission often being blamed of overriding the OECD Guidelines by transposing its own independent arm's-length principle, as described in the following paragraph.

Although the Commission's primary focus is whether the methodology endorsed in the APA approximates a 'market-based outcome', there are indications that the Commission seems 'biased against' or 'worried about' possible Base erosion and profit shifting (BEPS) effects. The following illustrates this.

In the Fiat Finance and Trade decision, the EU Commission seems to reject so-called spontaneous compensating adjustments, being worried of the possible misalignments between taxable profits and commercial profits which could be a source of double non-taxation. In the Commission's view, downward compensating adjustments should be undertaken only if they match with an actual upward adjustment in the other jurisdiction.[25]

In the Starbucks Decision, the concern focuses on stateless income which would arise due to the deduction of royalties in one jurisdiction not being matched by a corresponding taxation in another jurisdiction.[26]

---

gives rise to a selective advantage for the purposes of Art. 107(1) TFEU. For further reference, *see* Joined Cases C-182/03 and C-217/03 *Belgium and Forum 187 ASBL v. Commission* EU:C:2006:416.

22. 2016 Notice, para. 172.
23. *See, inter alia,* ROBINS; WATTEL, pp. 791 and ff.; TAFERNER/WOUDA KUIPERS, pp. 134 and ff; GUNN/LUTS, pp. 119 and ff.; and DE BROE, pp. 290 and ff.
24. ROSSI-MACCANICO, *"Fiscal State Aids, Tax Base Erosion and Profit Shifting"*, 2015 EC Tax Review 2, p. 63.
25. Paragraph 310 of the Fiat decision illustrates this principle: '[A]n arm's length remuneration must not be lower than the difference between the income and the charges of the company ... the entire recorded profit must be taxed, because a third party would not accept to reduce its remuneration if none of its counterparties would make justified claims to receive a higher remuneration ... .'
26. Paragraph 340, 'In other words, the un-taxed profits paid as a royalty by SMBV to Alki LP for the roasting IP should have been fully taxable in the Netherlands.'

Should one follow this line of reasoning, in the absence of no base erosion it is uncertain whether the existence of a selective tax advantage could be found even in cases in which a tax ruling relies on a manifestly wrong application of the OECD Guidelines (e.g., with regard to the chosen transfer pricing methodology). Where the chosen transfer pricing methodology is applied in a symmetrical manner (i.e., if it does not lead to double non-taxation), the existence of the selective tax advantage could be seen as justified or not going 'beyond what is necessary and proportionate to avoid cases of unresolved double taxation' (*see* Belgium Excess Profit System decision, paragraph 89).

The symmetrical effect of transfer pricing methodologies has also been spotted by one prominent scholar, according to whom '[t]he Commission should realize that a State aid investigation in the area of transfer pricing may be a zero sum game. If it is established that company A in Member State A has understated its profits on transactions with group company B in Member State B because company A benefited from an APA that derogated from the arm's-length principle, Member State A will be required to recover the aid from company A equal to the tax that it has forfeited on the understated profits. However, such profits may very well also have been included in the tax base of company B which has paid tax thereon in Member State B'.[27]

III THE TRANSFER PRICING ANALYSES UNDER THE COMMISSION'S VIEW: FOCUS ON THE APPLICATION OF THE PROFIT SPLIT METHODOLOGY

1 General Remarks on the Commission's Assessment

When performing its State aid assessments, the Commission first examines the intra-group transactions covered by the APA and the relevant functional analysis. In a second step, the Commission focuses on the transfer pricing method endorsed by the APA, with the aim of verifying if the same leads to a reliable approximation of a market-based outcome according to the circumstances of the case.[28] Under the Commission's view, 'any deviation from the best estimate of a market-based outcome must be limited and proportionate to the uncertainty inherent in the transfer pricing method chosen or the statistical tolls employed for that approximation exercise'.[29]

The Commission recognizes the use of each of the five methods described in the OECD Guidelines[30,31] and may, in principle, also accept methods not recommended by

27. De Broe, p. 292.
28. *See* para. 519 of the Commission Decision of 4 October 2017 on State aid SA.38944 (2014/C) (ex 2014/NN) implemented by Luxembourg to Amazon [hereinafter: 'Amazon Decision'].
29. 2016 Notice, para. 171.
30. Namely, the comparable uncontrolled price method [hereinafter: 'CUP'], the cost plus method [hereinafter: 'CPM'], the resale price method [hereinafter: 'RPM'], the transactional net margin method [hereinafter: 'TNMM'] and the profit split method [hereinafter: 'PSM'].
31. *See* Amazon Decision, para. 250; Commission decision of 30 August 2016 on State aid SA.38373 (2014/C) (ex 2014/NN) (ex 2014/CP) implemented by Ireland to Apple [hereinafter: 'Apple Decision'], para. 92; Belgian Excess Profit Decision, para. 55; Commission decision of 21 October

the OECD, provided that the resulting transfer prices comply with the arm's-length principle inherent in Article 107(1) TFEU.[32] According to the Commission, if a transfer pricing arrangement follows the guidelines provided by the OECD, including those concerning the choice of the most appropriate method,[33] an APA endorsing that arrangement is unlikely to give rise to State aid.[34] In the DG Competition Working Paper, the Commission, although it confirms the natural hierarchy of the methods, seems to express a general preference under specific circumstances for the so-called two-sided methods.[35]

2 The Position of the EU Vis-à-Vis the Profit Split Method

With specific regard to the use of profit split, as above anticipated, it is also recommended in the DG Competition Working Paper in light of its two-sided nature, which leads to an allocation of 'the overall profit to both parties of the transaction' and, therefore, triggers the lower risk of deviating 'from a market outcome' to the extent it is 'applied consistently by all jurisdictions involved' (WP, paragraph 20).

Implicitly, it seems that the State aid risk exposure, in case of adoption of the profit split methodology, is reduced as a consequence of the fact that the methodology as such is subject to scrutiny in two jurisdictions.

In the DG Competition Working Paper, the Commission seems to lose sight on its priority, i.e., whether the methodology (the profit split methodology) applied by the taxpayer leads to a reliable approximation of the market-based outcome. The Commission's main concern is achieving the allocation of the 'full amount of profits'. This seems to be their reassurance against possible BEPS cases (once again it confirms that the Commission's analysis is biased by BEPS cases in its State aid analysis). The problem is that ensuring that everything gets taxed, does not mean you are making sure that everything gets taxed at arm's-length or that everything is taxed in line with 'market-based outcomes'. It could, therefore, be said that – from the point of view of State aid – the use of such methodology could be criticized to the extent it is not viewed

2015 on State aid SA.38375 (2014/C ex 2014/NN) which Luxembourg granted to Fiat [hereinafter: 'Fiat Decision'], para. 88; Commission decision of 21 October 2015 on state aid SA.38374 (2014/C ex 2014/NN) implemented by the Netherlands to Starbucks [hereinafter: 'Starbucks Decision'], para. 67.

32. The Commission maintains that multinational corporate groups retain the freedom to apply methods not described in the OECD Guidelines to establish transfer prices, provided that those prices satisfy the arm's-length principle. In this regard, the Commission recalls para. 2.9 of the 2010 and 2017 OECD Guidelines, according to which '[s]uch other methods should however not be used in substitution for OECD-recognised methods where the latter are more appropriate to the facts and circumstances of the case' (*see*, for example, para. 250 of the Amazon Decision).
33. *See* para. 2.2 of the OECD Guidelines.
34. 2016 Notice, para. 173.
35. *See* para. 20 of the DG Competition Working Paper, according to which 'Some rulings are based on a two-sided approach, i.e. both companies to the intra-group transaction are analysed, where there is less room to deviate from a market outcome. This is, in particular, the case for the profit split method, where both sides of the transaction are allocated a share of the overall profit. The profit split method does not rely on a reference to comparable transactions in the market but will, if applied consistently by all jurisdictions involved, divide the full amount of profits between the two companies to the intra-group transaction.'

as the most appropriate method and/or its application does not rely on correct parameters. The references to the most appropriate method and correct parameters could be a point of clash within the EU itself. Indeed, it should be noted that the technical body of the EU (i.e., the EU Joint Transfer Pricing Forum) has conducted activities aimed at simplifying these aspects.[36]

3 Envisaged Risks Connected to the Application of the Profit Split Method

As indicated in the previous section, the selection of the most appropriate transfer pricing method – and, possibly, of a two-sided method – is, however, not sufficient per se to preclude an APA from being characterized by the Commission as conferring a selective advantage upon its addressee.

Indeed, the Commission's scrutiny also regularly focuses on the practical application of the selected method, with the aim of ensuring that the latter actually produced a market-based outcome. In a number of cases, the Commission raised specific methodological issues associated with the application of the transfer pricing method selected within an APA. Such issues concerned, for example, the choice of the tested party, the identification of the profit-level indicator and the criteria used for comparability analysis purposes.[37] In this respect, the Commission clarified that 'even if the most appropriate method is chosen, when it is used in combination with overly favourable parameters the remuneration arrived at using that method might nevertheless underestimate the tax liability of the taxpayer and thus give rise to an advantage for the purposes of Article 107(1) of the TFEU'.[38]

It follows that the taxpayer may, in response to the Commission's statement, adopt two different approaches. In a first scenario, the economic and financial analysis at the basis of the application of the selected transfer pricing method could be robust and articulated to try to prove that a market-based outcome has been reached.[39] However, in this respect, care should be taken that a robust and articulated application of the profit split would not be seen as artificial by Commission. Indeed, it should be recalled that the latter stated in the press release on the Fiat State aid case that: 'the two

36. It is believed that such an approach may entail a risk of departure from the arm's-length principle. One wonders, however, whether or not the deviations from the standard application criteria defined in the new OECD Guidelines and proposed by the EU Joint Transfer Pricing Forum in order to simplify the practical application of the method can, on the other hand, constitute a risk in terms of State aid.
37. *See*, for example, the Fiat Decision, where the Commission, with reference to the selected profit level indicator (i.e., the return on equity), challenged the amount of capital to be remunerated, the use of the hypothetical regulatory capital as profit level indicator, the inconsistent application of the Basel II framework to calculate that capital, the inappropriate deductions from the capital to be remunerated and the level of required return applied to the capital to be remunerated.
38. *See* para. 244 of the Fiat Decision.
39. Indeed, the application of such methodology is a complex exercise and, to a certain extent, a subjective one since it involves discretion in identifying (i) the combined profits to be split, (ii) the operating expenses associated with the transactions and (iii) the appropriate allocation keys, etc.

tax rulings under investigation endorsed artificial and complex methods to establish taxable profits for the companies'.

On the contrary, a second approach to be followed by the taxpayer could be that proposed by the Commission Service to the Joint Transfer Pricing Forum. According to the Commission Service, 'It would therefore be worth investigating whether a list of pre-determined splitting factors per industry or business structure could be developed by analysing which are the splitting factors with the highest recurrence per each industry or sector.' By contrast, limiting the analysis to State aid purposes,[40] this approach, although it may compromise the application of the arm's-length principle, could, however, limit the risk of State aid. Indeed, in the opinion of the Commission, if the selection of parameters related to the transfer pricing method were to be left to the sole discretion of the taxpayer, integrated cross-border groups would be selectively advantaged over non-integrated companies (which necessarily fix their prices at arm's length without having the chance to adjust their tax base).[41]

SELECTED BIBLIOGRAPHY

De Broe Luc, The State Aid Review against Aggressive Tax Planning: 'Always Look a Gift Horse in the Mouth', 24 EC Tax Review 6 (2015).

Gunn Anna & Luts Joris, Tax Rulings, APAs and State Aid: Legal Issues, 24 EC Tax Review 2 (2015).

Robins Nicole, The Tax State Aid Investigations, and the Role of Economic and Financial Analysis, 19 Derivates & Financial Instruments 5 (2017).

Rossi-Maccanico Pierpaolo, Fiscal State Aids, Tax Base Erosion and Profit Shifting, 24 EC Tax Review 2 (2015).

Taferner Anja & Wouda Kuipers Jurjan, Tax Rulings: In Line with OECD Transfer Pricing Guidelines, but Contrary to EU State Aid Rules?, 56 European Taxation 4 (2016).

Wattel Peter J., Stateless Income, State Aid and the (Which?) Arm's Length Principle, 44 Intertax 11 (2016).

40. Indeed, from a transfer pricing prospective, this could lead to a departure from the arm's-length principle.

41. *See* para. 242 of the Fiat Decision.

CHAPTER 9

The Work of the Joint Transfer Pricing Forum on the Profit Split Method

Mauro Faggion & Simone Di Vaia

I BACKGROUND

The work programme of the Joint Transfer Pricing Forum (hereinafter 'JTPF') for the 2015–2019 mandate refers to the profit split method as one of the topics on which the JTPF will provide output and foresees that work will focus on the practical application of the profit split method in the European Union (EU).

At the JTPF meeting of 8 March 2018, it was decided to circulate a questionnaire in order to gather information on practical issues. In particular, the questionnaire wanted to collect information about the types of cases and facts that the profit split method has been used, identifying which industries the profit split method could be applied to and exploring the reasons that make the profit split method an appropriate method in this context.

The results[1] of the survey were presented at the JTPF meeting of 26 June 2018 and the main points are summarized below.

II SECTORS AND INDUSTRIES WHERE THE PROFIT SPLIT METHOD IS APPLIED AND COMMON FEATURES OF THE SUPPLY CHAIN

The first research area of the questionnaire aimed to analyse if it was possible to establish a link between the profit split method and some particular industry.

1. The summary of the survey is available here: https://ec.europa.eu/taxation_customs/business/company-tax/transfer-pricing-eu-context/joint-transfer-pricing-forum/eu-joint-transfer-pricing-forum-meeting-26-june-2018_en.

The twenty-eight replies received by the JTPF Secretariat (seventeen from the Member States and eleven from non-governmental members) did not show any direct correlation between the profit split method and one specific industry. On the contrary, both the Members states and the non-governmental members mentioned a broad array of sectors and industries where the profit split method has been applied.

From the more specific sectors where the profit split method has been applied, the most prevalent ones were, by order of frequency, the financial sector, industrial equipment, the automotive industry, the IT sector, the trade in consumer goods, the pharmaceutical industry, the food industry and the oil and gas industry.

III REASONS TO CONSIDER THE PROFIT SPLIT METHOD THE MOST APPROPRIATE METHOD

The survey investigated the reasons why the profit split method has been considered as the most appropriate method. The answers showed that the situations where the profit split method was applied closely followed the situations described in the Organisation for Economic Co-operation and Development (OECD) Transfer Pricing Guidelines. In particular, the following cases have been mentioned:

- both parties have unique and valuable contributions to the core value drivers of the business, especially in terms of existing IP or DEMPE[2] functions on developed IP;
- highly integrated business models;
- common sharing of risks; and
- unique business models with no suitable comparable uncontrolled prices (CUPs), one-sided methods not applicable, neither party being suitable to be considered as a tested party (e.g., strong senior management on both sides).

Several replies mentioned the use of the profit split method as a ‘sanity check’ to support a benchmarking study, to avoid extreme results from the application of other methods and in the context of reaching an agreement with the tax authorities.

IV MAIN CHALLENGES IN APPLYING THE PROFIT SPLIT METHOD

The third main area of the survey focused on the main challenges arising in the application of the profit split method.

Among the main practical issues, the determination of the appropriate splitting factors, the valuation of the contributions and the identification of the profits to be split were mentioned.

In particular, the choice of the appropriate splitting factors, their relative weights and the valuation of the contributions seems to have been mentioned in practically all of the replies as one of the main challenges in applying the profit split method.

2. Development, enhancement, maintenance, protection and exploitation.

The majority of Member States reported problems with the availability, comparability and general quality of data from all parties that should participate to the profit split, also mentioning related issues with the subjectivity of the analysis and reliability of forecasts. In addition, the Member States noted difficulties in having to conduct a separate value-chain analysis and identifying the key value drivers from outside the company. The non-governmental members pointed out the concern related to the defence of the profit split method in a context of potential audit and the challenges in implementing, maintaining and monitoring the profit split method once it is set up.

1 Choosing the Measure of Profit

The survey also investigated which measure of profit to be split is more often considered in practice. The majority of the replies seem to have mentioned the Earnings before interest and taxes (EBIT)/operating profit as the measure of profit to be split, arguing that it most accurately reflected the level at which the related risks were taken and at which the unique and valuable contributions were made.

That measure would sometimes be adjusted to include interest expenses or exchange rate gains/losses to the extent that they were directly related to the main activities. A couple of replies also mentioned the use of Earnings Before Interest, Taxes, Depreciation, and Amortization (EBITDA), gross profit or incremental profit (with/without the use of IP).

2 Choosing Profit Splitting Factors

The survey also tried to investigate the most recurrent splitting factors. As we have already said, the choice of the splitting factors was indicated as one of the main challenges arising from the application of the method. As to the reasons why those profit splitting factors were chosen, most of the replies indicated a link between those profit splitting factors and the contribution towards the key value drivers of the business (e.g., intangibles or significant people functions). The survey reports a wide array of splitting factors. Among them, we can mention the significant people functions, the salaries, including bonus payments (also capitalized over a number of years) and headcount (weighted by salary), cost-base related to DEMPE functions, operating costs and working capital.

The survey is completed with some examples.

V JTPF AREA OF WORK

In order to address the difficulties arisen from the survey, the Commission Service at the meeting of 24 October 2018 put forward a discussion paper[3] that scoped four main potential areas of work:

3. The document is available here: https://ec.europa.eu/taxation_customs/eu-joint-transfer-pricing-forum-meeting-24-october-2018_en.

(1) When to use the profit split method (PSM)? As the first area of work, the Secretariat proposed to better clarify and describe the situation in which the PSM should be considered the most appropriate method.
(2) How to split the profit? As the second area of work, the Secretariat proposed to analyse and better describe the most recurrent splitting factors.
(3) Is there a need for simplification? The third potential area of work meant to investigate the need for simplification. The Secretariat proposed to streamline the application of the PSM in order to achieve more certainty, efficiency and fairness.
(4) How to simplify the application of the PSM? As a possible way of simplification, the paper suggests following the two-stage approach based on the residual analysis of the OECD Guidance which is better described in the following paragraph.

VI A PROPOSAL FOR SIMPLIFICATION

With particular reference to the high degree of subjectivity linked to the choice of the splitting factors, the Commission Service put forward a proposal to simplify the application of the profit split method.[4]

According to the proposal, the residual analysis should be preferred. As it is well known, under the residual analysis the combined profits from controlled transactions are allocated between the associated enterprises based on a two-step approach:

First step: arm's-length remuneration of the so-called routine functions (i.e., activities making non-unique contributions). The remuneration of the routine functions transaction is determined by applying one of the traditional transactional transfer pricing methods or the transactional net margin method (TNMM).

Second step: the residual profit (or loss) that remains after having remunerated the routine activities is allocated among the parties based upon a reasonable approximation that would result in a division of profits that independent parties would expect to realize.

According to the Commission Service, the first step of the analysis does not present particular challenges as the routine activities are easy to benchmark and their remuneration is determined by applying the other transfer pricing methods (in practice, more often the TNMM). The real challenge arises when it comes to the question of how to split the residual profit which is undermined from the high level of

4. The idea of using the profit split method in a simplified manner in order to bridge the gap between the arm's-length principle and a formulaic approach is not new in the academic arena. *See* for example Avi-Yonah, Reuven S. 'Allocating Business Profits for Tax Purposes: A Proposal to Adopt a Formulary Profit Split.' K.A.Clausing & M.C.Durst, co-authors. Fla. Tax Rev. 9, no. 5 (2009): 497–553. More recently Michael P. Devereux, Alan Auerbach, Michael Keen, Paul Oosterhuis, Wolfgang Schön & John Vella, 'Residual Profit Allocation by Income', working paper 2019.

subjectivity and the lack of prescriptive guidelines. To face these issues, the Commission Service proposed to investigate whether the use of a formula or a list of predetermined splitting factors per industry or business structure could be developed.[5]

For the Commission Service, simplifying the profit split method does not mean rejecting the arm's-length principle but rather implies addressing the limits of its application, as those may arise in certain specific situations. In fact, the survey showed that splitting the residual profit is a subjective exercise and even the most accurate functional/value-chain analysis would be unlikely to rectify this inherent subjectivity. The argument of the Commission Service is based on the consideration that the profit split method usually features as the most appropriate method for profit allocation if there are unique and valuable contributions by more than one party to the transaction. In this context, comparables may be almost impossible to identify. In addition, one would need to rely heavily on the contribution of intangibles, which may also involve some extra subjectivity.

Furthermore, in the absence of objective evidence that the arm's-length principle is always reflected in the outcome of applying the profit split method, there is no reason why the attribution of the residual profit through predetermined splitting factors or the use of a formula would turn out to conflict with the established principles for a fair allocation of profit.

It is specified in the proposal of the Commission Service that the proposed simplification of the mechanism should not be taken as a rejection of the arm's-length principle but rather as a way to address the limits of its application, as these may arise in certain specific situations. Indeed, the arm's-length umbrella is still to be used to determine: (i) when the profit split method should be applied; and (ii) the remuneration of routine activities (first step).

As it results from the summary record,[6] during the meeting of October, the members reached consensus on a two-stage process whereby at the first stage, the focus should be on clarifying certain concepts related to the PSM and eventually at the second later stage on exploring the way of simplification.

In particular, the work should focus on: (i) clarifying in which circumstances the Profit split method may be considered the most appropriate transfer pricing method; and (ii) how to split the profit based on the concepts described in the revised OECD Guidance as well as by providing an inventory of the recurrent splitting factors.

It should be noted that the Commission Service's proposal of simplification comes some months before of the OECD document on addressing the tax challenges of

5. This approach can be assimilated to the contribution method developed for the arm's-length tests of global trading by fully integrated financial institutions. *See*, Hay/Horner/Owens, Past and Present Work in the OECD on Transfer Pricing and Selected Issues, p. 423. The OECD reports on global trading also recognize the use of a multifactorial formula. *See*, for example, OECD, The Taxation of Global Trading Financial Institutions (17 March 1998).
6. Available here https://ec.europa.eu/taxation_customs/sites/taxation/files/jtpf-24-10-2018-summary-record_en.pdf.

the digitalization of the economy which that was published some months later in March 2019.[7]

Indeed, two out of the three proposals contained in the OECD document suggest that a modified residual profit split method be used to reallocate a share of the residual profit of Multinational Enterprises (MNE) groups to market jurisdictions.

The 'user participation proposal' suggests allocating a share of residual profits to user jurisdictions to recognise the value created through user participation. Similarly, the 'marketing intangibles' proposal states the allocation could be done under a revised residual profit split analysis.

Both proposals advocate for a simplified mechanics to split the profit that could be based on a metric to be politically agreed and go beyond the arm's-length principle.

VII THE REPORT ON 'THE APPLICATION OF THE PROFIT SPLIT METHOD WITHIN THE EU'

On March 2019, the JTPF published the final report on '*The application of the profit split method within the EU*'.

The Report is intended to summarize the work done under the first part of a two-stage process, beginning with the clarification of certain concepts, while the second stage will explore simplification.

Under this first stage, the EU Report aims to complement the OECD Transfer Pricing Guidelines by clarifying situations when to use profit split as the most appropriate transfer pricing method and how to split the profit, based on the revised OECD Transfer Pricing Guidelines, as well as providing an inventory of potential splitting factors.

1 The Use of the Profit Split Method

The Report discusses both when the profit split method should be applied and when should be not applied.

In line with the OECD Transfer Pricing Guidelines, the Report endorses the use of the profit split method in cases of:

- a unique and valuable contribution by each party to the controlled transaction;
- a high level of integration regarding business transactions to which the transaction relates; and/or
- the shared assumptions of economically significant risks or separate assumption of economically closely related risks by the parties to the transaction.

By contrast, the Report specifies that the PSM should not be applied when:

7. OECD Public Consultation document on Addressing the tax challenges of the digitalisation of the economy available here: http://www.oecd.org/tax/beps/public-consultation-document-addressing-the-tax-challenges-of-the-digitalisation-of-the-economy.pdf.

- one of the parties to the transactions performs only simple functions and does not make a unique and valuable contribution; and/or
- the transaction can be appropriately benchmarked, comparable transactions and functions can be identified.

The lack of comparable alone is not considered sufficient for determining that the profit split method should be selected as the most appropriate method

In this case, the Report suggests taking a pragmatic approach broadening, if needed, the search criteria by looking at independent enterprises with slightly different business models situated in other geographical markets but being active in the same industry or engaged in different industries but situated in the same geographical market.

Through a section of questions and answers, the Report emphasizes that each of the three conditions (unique and valuable contribution, high level of integration, shared assumption of risks) may by itself be sufficient to justify the application of the profit split.

Further, it is clarified that a unique and valuable contribution should represent a key source of actual or potential economic benefit in business operations and the profit split be applied even if the potential benefit is not realized. Within this concept, the important factor is not whether a (potential) economic benefit is realized or not, but whether the success of the contribution is the key to the success of the business operations.

The Report also emphasizes that the presence of a cross-entity and cross-border business unit structure should not per se be an indication of a highly integrated business operation and warrant the use of a profit split. The functions of a cross-border business units structure vary from one business to another and therefore and assessment needs to be performed on a case-by-case basis.

The first part of the Report is completed with examples both positive (when to use the profit split method) and negative (when not to use the profit split method).

2 How to Split the Profit

The Report recalls that the profit split method should seek to split the relevant profit on an economically valid basis in order to approximate the results that would have been achieved between independent enterprises in comparable circumstances.

The Report does not say anything on how to determine the profit to be split but provides instead a nonexclusive list and brief overview of the most common splitting factors, which are grouped in five broad categories.

A People-Based Factors

The first category of splitting factors is people-based, which may be taken into consideration when the value creation is driven by the workforce and personnel knowledge and skills.

In this case, either the factor of employee compensation and/or headcount may be used. In general, the splitting factor based on remuneration seems to be preferable compared to the headcount since it takes into account how much the MNE values the contribution of various employees. Headcount may be preferable where differences in the cost of living and other factors make it difficult to use remuneration.

In order to apply the people-based factors, it is important: to map the employees, to describe the functions carried out by the employees and to identify those related to DEMPE functions.

Among the cons of using these splitting factors, the Report mentions the subjectivity of the selection of the key employees.

B Cost-Based Factors

The cost-based splitting factors are often used in the joint performance of the value-creating activities. The contribution in the form of a value-creating activity is then reflected on the costs borne in the performance of that activity.

The Report mentions five key allocation factors under the cost-based factors: operating expenses, cost of goods sold, marketing costs, brand development expenses and R&D costs.

The operating expenses: Operating expenses (OPEX) are expenses that a business incurs in carrying out an organization's day to day activities but these are directly associated with the production. Although OPEX may be related to routine functions at times, they may be used as a splitting factor when the value creation is driven by the intensity of the activities performed by the entities.

The cost of goods sold: Cost of goods sold (COGS) is the accumulated total of all costs used to create a product or service, which has been sold. COGS generally includes the cost of the materials used in creating the good, along with the direct labour costs used to produce the good or service. Although COGS may also be related to routine functions at times, it may be used as a splitting factor when value creation is driven by the production activity.

The marketing costs are associated with the delivering of goods or services to customers and they may be used as a splitting factor when the value creation is driven by the marketing activity.

The Report differentiates the brand development expenses, i.e., the cost specifically linked to the brand. They may be used as a splitting factor when the value creation is driven by the brand.

Finally, the R&D expenses are costs a company incurs in the process of developing new goods and services to best suit the company's and consumer's need. They may be used as splitting factors, especially where two or more entities concur to development of an intangible.

In relation to the cost-based factors, the Report notes that it could be difficult to decide the amount of cumulative values. For example, the R&D costs to develop an intangible may be incurred over a number of the years.

C Sales/Volume-Based Factors

Under this category, the Report groups the turnover and volume of trade as possible splitting factors.

However, it is recognized that these factors are most often used in combination with other splitting factors that reflect efforts in sales and distribution activities but also efforts in R&D depending on the industry and group strategy.

The Report mentions that these factors are objective if determined on the basis of uncontrolled transactions. On the other hand, these factors may not be a good indicator of value creation, as turnover and volume of trades are not necessarily aligned with DEMPE functions.

D Asset-Based Factors

Under this category, the Forum lays down four allocation keys: the value of key business assets, assets under management, royalty rates, and franchise agreement. All key allocations can be a solution to complicated cases involving intangibles, however, it may be difficult to find comparables. The asset value that is used as a splitting factor would have to be measured in accordance with the arm's-length principle rather than accounting value where there is likely to be a material difference between the two.

VIII CONCLUDING REMARKS

The JTPF Report is an attempt to clarify certain concepts related to the application of the profit split method under the current OECD Transfer Pricing Guidelines.

According to the survey run by the JTPF, such a method is not used very often at present within the EU. This appears to be related to the high degree of subjectivity of the method that may expose to risk of litigation.

The JTPF recognizes that the profit split method could be applied more often in the near future due to the emergence of new business models and therefore it is essential monitoring the practical application of the method in order to evaluate whether to further clarify the mechanism and eventually explore ways of simplification.

It remains to be seen whether an agreement would be reached at the OECD on the use of a modified profit split method in the context of the work on the tax challenges arising from digitalization and eventually what would be the relation of the new profit attribution rule with the traditional profit split method.

SELECTED BIBLIOGRAPHY

AVI-YONAH, REUVEN S., '*Allocating Business Profits for Tax Purposes: A Proposal to Adopt a Formulary Profit Split*.' Fla. Tax Rev. 9, no. 5 (2009).

MICHAEL P. DEVEREUX, ALAN AUERBACH, MICHAEL KEEN, PAUL OOSTERHUIS, WOLFGANG SCHÖN AND JOHN VELLA, '*Residual Profit Allocation by Income*', working paper 2019.

HAY DIANE / HORNER FRANCES / OWENS JEFFREY, Past and Present Work in the OECD on Transfer Pricing and Selected Issues, in: Intertax, 22, no. 10 (1994).

CHAPTER 10

The Impact of Profit Split to Indirect Taxes, with Emphasis on European VAT

Andrea Parolini

I INTRODUCTION

The debate on ramifications of transfer pricing policies on indirect taxes echoed the increasing attention that transfer pricing gained in the past years due to changes in business models and the relevance of multinational groups in modern interconnected economies.

The question looks prima facie rather simple: When a transfer pricing adjustment is executed is there any need to also rectify the consideration of the underlying supplies of goods or services for the purposes of consumption taxes?

At first glance, one should conclude that such adjustments, aimed to realign the price of the goods transferred or the services provided at the conditions ordinarily determined by market forces, should have an impact also on consumption taxes.[1] However, an in-depth analysis shows that such a conclusion would be inaccurate since transfer pricing methods, including the profit split method, are grounded on concepts that have little to share with the principles on which consumption taxes are based.

This chapter tries to outline the principles governing the computation of the taxable basis for consumption taxes on the basis of the provisions laid down in Council Directive 2006/112/EC of 28 November 2006 on the common system of value added tax (hereinafter: 'VAT Directive') and to compare such principle with the arm's-length principle laid down in Article 9 of the OECD Model Convention in order to understand the interaction between the two with the scope to understanding if transfer pricing

1. *See* OECD, OECD Transfer Pricing Guidelines for Multinational Enterprises and Tax Administrations 2017 (10 July 2017), Chapter 1, para. 1.2, OECD Publishing, Paris, https://doi.org/10.1787/tpg-2017-en [hereinafter: '2017 OECD TPG'].

adjustments based on the transactional profit split method may have an impact on VAT. A final remark on the ramifications of transfer pricing Adjustments on custom obligations in the context of the Regulation (EU) No 952/2013 of the European Parliament and of the Council of 9 October 2013 laying down the Union Customs Code (hereinafter: 'UCC') will be performed.

II THE NOTION OF 'TAXABLE AMOUNT' IN THE VAT DIRECTIVE

Article 73 VAT Directive stipulates that the taxable amount (i.e., the taxable base) for VAT purposes of a supply of goods or services shall include everything which constitutes 'consideration' obtained or to be obtained by the supplier, in return for the supply, from the customer or a third party, including subsidies directly linked to the price of the supply.

The Court of Justice of the European Union (hereinafter: 'CJEU') clarified that the concept of consideration for VAT purposes has a subjective nature so that it is not influenced by the objective value that a good or service may have on a given market. In particular, according to the CJEU:

> [T]he consideration must be capable of being expressed in monetary terms and ... it is a subjective value, since the basis of assessment is the consideration actually received and not a value estimated according to objective criteria.[2]

The CJEU has been requested to deal with cases in which the consideration of a given supply was lower than the cost price of the goods or services supplied. In this respect, the CJEU opined that:

> [T]he fact that the price paid for an economic transaction is higher or lower than the cost price is irrelevant to the question whether a transaction is to be regarded as a transaction affected for consideration. The latter concepts require only that there be a direct link between the supply of goods or the provision of services and the consideration actually received by the taxable person.[3]

It follows from the above jurisprudence that for a supply of goods or services to be regarded as effected for consideration, the existence of a direct link between the supply made and the consideration received must be satisfied.[4] Hence, a supply of goods or services is taxable for VAT purposes if there is a legal relationship between the supplier of goods or services and the customer pursuant to which there is reciprocal

2. CJEU, 23 November 1988, Case C-230/87, *NaturallyYours Cosmetics Ltd*, para. 16. The same principle has been expressed in a following decision dated 2 June 1994, Case C-33/93, *Empire Stores*, para. 18 and in 20 January 2005, Case C-412/03, *Hotel Scandic Gåsabäck AB*, para. 21.
3. CJEU, 20 January 2005, Case C-412/03, *Scandic*, paras 22 and 36.
4. The CJEU stated that the direct link condition is not met when the consideration is a 'mandatory charge' which is imposed by virtue not of a contractual but a statutory obligation (*see* CJEU, 8 August 1988, Case C-102/86, *Apple and Pear Development Council*; 1 July 1982, Case C-222/81, *BAZ Bausystem*). According to certain doctrine, this is the case of the so-called primary adjustment in the field of transfer pricing rules. Primary adjustments are the adjustments made for income tax purposes by the tax authorities in the jurisdiction of one related party. The amount of the adjustment is set by the tax authorities with the aim of adjusting the price to an arm's-length price (*see* SANTORO).

performance and the remuneration received by the supplier constitutes the value actually given in return for the supply to the recipient.[5]

On the contrary, the arm's-length principle for income tax purposes is a general principle to allocate taxable base among different States preventing that transactions between related parties are priced according to subjective values with the aim to avoid shifting profits from one jurisdiction to another.

The rationale behind the rules governing the computation of VAT taxable base and transfer pricing is therefore substantially different.[6] That different structure, purpose and principles of income taxes and VAT justify the different valuation rules, namely the arm's-length principle for corporate income taxes and the subjective value for VAT purposes.

III INTERACTION BETWEEN ARM'S-LENGTH PRINCIPLE AND THE 'TAXABLE AMOUNT' RELEVANT FOR VAT PURPOSES

An interaction between the two principles may be found in Article 80 VAT Directive where the Member States are granted the possibility to opt for introducing a provision in order to disregard the consideration actually received by a supplier in favour of the 'open market value' of a transaction.

Such a rule is aimed to prevent VAT evasion and it can be invoked only for those cases where supplies of goods or services are carried out between related parties and provided that the supplier or the recipient does not have a full right of deduction. The VAT Directive acknowledges the possibility that the arm's-length price may be used under certain conditions as the taxable base of a transaction while as a general rule it provides for the taxable base to be everything which constitutes consideration as the subjective value actually received (*see* section II).

However, this optional rule represents a derogation from the standard provision (i.e., subjective value) laid down by Article 73 VAT Directive which should be strictly limited to tackle evasion and avoidance schemes.

Although Article 80 VAT Directive could indeed be seen as reflecting the arm's-length principle for VAT purposes, there is one fundamental difference between the scope of applications of those provisions: while the arm's-length principle applies generally in all intra-group transactions under the transfer pricing rules used for the purposes of direct taxation, the scope of the arm's-length principle set out under the VAT Directive is much narrower.

There are just three situations where the VAT taxable base must reflect the open market value:

5. *See* CJEU, 3 Mar. 1994, Case C-16/93, *R.J. Tolsma*. For the sake of completeness, it should be borne in mind that the VAT Directive provides for specific derogations to the general principle that a supply of goods or services should be effected for consideration to fall within the scope of VAT. Reference is made to Art. 16 and Art. 26 of the VAT Directive that are mainly connected with the private use or other application for non-business purposes of business goods or services.
6. Corporate income tax is levied by each jurisdiction according to its own set of rules. VAT is a general indirect tax on consumption and it is not imposed at a profit level. It applies to each single transaction without taking into account the total profit of loss of a taxable person.

- when the consideration is lower than the open market value and the customer does not have full right of deduction of the input VAT;
- when the consideration is lower than the open market value and the supplier does not have full right of deduction of the input VAT; and
- when the consideration is higher than the open market value and the supplier does not have a full right of deduction of the input VAT.

Indeed, in any of the above three events, artificially altering the price of the transaction would frustrate the proper collection of VAT. Nevertheless, it stems from the jurisprudence of the CJEU that the three events listed in Article 80 VAT Directive represent a closed list:

> [W]here goods or services are supplied at an artificially low or high price between parties who both enjoy a full right of deduction of VAT, there cannot be any evasion or avoidance of tax at that stage. It is only at the stage of the final consumer, or of a mixed taxable person enjoying only a proportional right of deduction, that an artificially low or high price can lead to a loss of tax revenue.
>
> Consequently, it is only where the person concerned by the transaction does not enjoy a full right of deduction that there is a risk of tax evasion or avoidance which Article 80(1) of the directive allows the Member States to prevent.[7]

According to the CJEU, national VAT law cannot impose the open market value to be relevant for determining the VAT taxable base of a transaction between parties that have full right of deduction.[8]

Article 72 VAT Directive lays down what is meant by open market value for VAT purposes:

> '[O]pen market value' shall mean the full amount that, in order to obtain the goods or services in question at that time, a customer at the same marketing stage at which the supply goods or services takes place, would have to pay, under conditions of fair competition, to a supplier at arm's-length within the territory of the Member State in which the supply is subject to tax.

Article 72 VAT Directive makes explicit reference to the arm's-length principle. In this respect, it has been observed that the definition of 'open market value' has certain similarities with that which may be developed applying the arm's-length principle in the field of income taxes.[9] However, it should be borne in mind that those two concepts are aimed for achieving different results. While the arm's-length principle consists in the general criterion for the allocating profits between multinational groups, the open market value is a derogation to the general rule governing the application of VAT and its application is subject to strict conditions. Moreover, the rationale behind every consumption tax - that is to ensure collection of tax where goods or services are effectively exploited - requires a further consideration on the territorial scope of the concept of arm's-length value. Indeed, Article 72 VAT Directive seems to narrow the

7. CJEU, 26 Apr. 2012, Joined Cases C-624/10 and C-129/11, *Balkan and Sea Properties ADSITs*, paras 44 and 45.
8. *See also* Matesanz.
9. *See* Parolini, p. 123.

border of the arm's-length value in order to reflect the value of goods and services in the same country where those goods and services are subject to VAT. Such a territorial requirement seems to be broader if one looks to the practical application of arm's-length value for income tax purposes where reference to markets of different countries is often a starting point for benchmarking comparable transactions.

IV RELEVANCE OF TP ADJUSTMENTS BASED ON THE PROFIT SPLIT METHOD FOR VAT PURPOSES

It follows from the above-mentioned analyses that the possibility to characterize a transfer pricing adjustment, whether based on the profit split method or not, as a consideration in respect of a previous supply of goods depends on the following conditions:

(i) the existence of a direct link between the consideration and the original supply of goods or services; and
(ii) the possibility to apply the derogation laid down by Article 80 of the VAT Directive.

1 The Existence of a 'Direct Link'

As outlined above, in order for a transfer pricing adjustment to impact on the taxable amount for VAT purposes, it is necessary to identify the existence of a direct link between the consideration and the original supply of goods or services performed. Such a direct link can be established if there is a contractual relationship between the supplier and the customer according to which it can be inferred that the additional (or lower) remuneration received by the supplier constitutes the consideration actually received in return of the supply of the specific goods.

In this respect, the analysis performed above shows that the mere circumstance that a transfer pricing adjustment is executed following the action of any tax authority or it is performed by the parties intervening in the supply is not sufficient by itself to exclude or conclude that such transfer pricing adjustment could also have an impact for the purposes of VAT.[10] Part of the doctrine argues that any adjustment assessed by any tax authorities cannot be ascribed to a change of the initial taxable base of a given transaction as it does not alter the consideration agreed between the parties. However, as observed by the VAT Committee, the conclusion can be, to a certain extent, not correct where the additional price of a transaction requested by any tax authority actually results from the agreement between the parties where it is stated that transfer pricing adjustments have to be included in the sale price of a certain good or service.[11] In this respect, transfer pricing clauses (if any) laid down in the intra-company

10. *See* Santoro and Matesanz.
11. VAT Committee, Working Paper 923 dated 28 February 2017, *Possible VAT implications of Transfer Pricing*.

arrangements can be used as an evidence of the connection between the transfer pricing adjustment and the sale price where they provide for adjustment clauses subject to periodical assessment.[12]

It is also evident that the identification of a direct link is influenced by the transfer pricing methodology adopted by taxpayers. Namely, transaction-based methods, such as the comparable uncontrolled price method, would determine the prices on a transaction-by-transaction basis so that the price paid would show clearly the link with the executed transactions and consequently its relevance for VAT purposes. Instead, should profit-based methods be applied, the above-mentioned link could be less evident, or absent, and therefore, the VAT impact could be different.[13] In this respect, in principle, adjustments executed applying the transactional profit split method are not apt to impact on VAT. Such method, according to the clarifications provided by the OECD 'identifies the relevant profits to be split for the associated enterprises from a controlled transaction and then splits those profits between the associated enterprises on an economically valid basis that approximates the division of profits that would have been agreed at arm's length'.[14] Being based on the splitting of profits, the profit split method is not apt to alter the underlying consideration and, therefore, should not impact on VAT since there is no direct link between the supplies of goods or services and the adjustment performed.

This conclusion is, in principle, not affected by the fact that the transfer pricing adjustments are performed on a voluntary basis, based on a transfer pricing agreement, or executed following an audit of any tax authority. That said, one cannot neglect that a certain degree of uncertainty can materialize in situations in which transfer pricing agreements shaped on the profit split method provide for contradictory clauses leading to imply that the adjustment constitutes an alteration of the originally agreed consideration for supplies of goods and services. Also, in this case, however, any uncertainty should be overtaken on the basis that adjustments based on the transactional profit split method, if properly executed, do not refer to a specific transaction so that they are not directly linked with a supply of goods or services.

2 Application of Article 80 of the VAT Directive

It has been acknowledged by the VAT Committee that 'if all transfer pricing adjustments led to a modification of the VAT taxable amount, the general principle of Article 73 of the VAT Directive could be undermined and the open market value would "de facto" end up becoming the norm'.[15]

12. *See* Lucas Mas, para. 3.2.
13. *See* Rouberol; Bakker/Obuoforibo, p. 208.
14. *See* OECD, Revised Guidance on the Application of the Transactional Profit Split Method: Inclusive Framework on BEPS: Action 10, OECD/G20 Base Erosion and Profit Shifting Project (June 2018), p. 11 OECD, Paris. www.oecd.org/tax/beps/revised-guidance-on-the-application-of-the-transactional-profit-split-method-beps-action-10.pdf.
15. VAT Committee, Working Paper 923 dated 28 February 2017, *Possible VAT implications of Transfer Pricing*.

In the context of VAT, the use of the 'open market value' to identify the taxable amount, therefore, constitutes an exception and the use of such exception is limited to the case envisaged in Article 80 VAT Directive.[16]

This, of course, creates a tension between transfer pricing policies and VAT, the tension that in the past has been highlighted by the Commission with reference also to other articles of the VAT Directive.[17]

It is worth noting that Article 80 VAT Directive has its own objective scope and applies independently from the arm's-length principle for income tax purposes. The case is less theoretical than one could expect since legislation implementing Article 80 VAT Directive could apply in a purely domestic setting – to the extent, the Member State concerned opted for its implementation – even if it decided not to apply the arm's-length principle for domestic transactions for income tax purposes.

Moreover, the scope of Article 80 VAT Directive departs from the provision on associated enterprise laid down in tax treaties in a number of aspects, one of them being the personal scope of application of the provision. In fact, the scope of Article 80 VAT Directive is broader compared to the one laid down in Article 9 OECD Model since it covers situations in which no entrepreneurial activities are carried on by one of the persons involved in the supply, such as in the case of employment or family links. Notwithstanding the above, the analysis of the wording of Article 80 VAT Directive shows that a group of companies *lato sensu* may be caught by the implementing measures of Article 80 VAT Directive.

Another difference between Article 80 VAT Directive derives from the situations in which it may be invoked. Article 9 OECD Model has a very broad application, whereas Article 80 VAT Directive is confined to cases in which one (or both) parties have a limited right to deduct input VAT and the taxable amount of the supply is higher or lower compared to the open market value. In this sense, the application of Article 80 VAT Directive is clearly a provision aimed at tackling abusive transactions, while the OECD recognizes that 'transfer pricing should not be confused with the consideration of problems of tax fraud or tax avoidance, even though transfer pricing may be used for such purposes'.[18]

---

16. It is worth noting that the VAT Expert Group, in its document VEG n. 071 REV2 issued on 18 April 2018 argued, on the basis of Art. 80 VAT Directive, that transfer pricing adjustments should be considered irrelevant for VAT purposes every time both parties have a full right to deduct.
17. *See* Commission staff working document – Accompanying document to the Proposal for a Council Directive amending Directive 2006/112/EC on the common system of value added tax, as regards the treatment of insurance and financial services (COM(2007) 747) – Impact Assessment (SEC/2007/1554 final). Reference is made to Art. 132(1)(f) VAT Directive that provides for an exemption in the public interest for an independent group of persons. Such an exemption, however, applies to the extent the group claims from their members 'the exact reimbursement of their share of the joint expenses' with no markup. As pointed out by this author that under Art. 132(1)(f) VAT Directive the 'the circumstance that the supplier does not generate any profit from its activity represents a relevant divergence with the arm's length principle and thereby may generate conflicts with domestic income tax legislation and tax treaty. The application of a margin of profit on the service, by contrast, may satisfy the arm's length principle but would jeopardize the application of the exemption'. (*see* Parolini, p. 121).
18. *See* OECD, OECD Transfer Pricing Guidelines for Multinational Enterprises and Tax Administrations 2017 (10 July 2017), Chapter I, para. 1.2, OECD Publishing, Paris, https://doi.org/10.1787/tpg-2017-en.

As a final issue, one could also question whether the 'open market value' of supply could be determined following the OECD Transfer Pricing Guidelines (TPG). From a preliminary analysis, this question should be replied in the negative if one considers that the CJEU clearly affirmed that the OECD Convention is irrelevant for the purposes of resolving VAT cases.[19] Notwithstanding the above, the application of the OECD TPG in the field of VAT should not be excluded a priori (*see* section III). However, such application should be strictly confined to methods based on comparable transactions, not being applicable in the field of VAT profit-based methods, such as the transactional profit split.[20]

In conclusion, one could expect that in situations in which Article 80 VAT Directive may apply (i.e., situations in which the parties involved suffer limitations of their right to deduct), a transfer pricing adjustment based on the application of the transactional profit split may stimulate a VAT assessment. However, such an assessment could not be based on the outcome of the analysis performed for transfer pricing purposes since the transactional profit split method would depart from the definition of 'open market value' laid down in Article 72 VAT Directive.

V TRANSFER PRICING AND CUSTOMS VALUATION WITHIN THE EU

The debate on the impact of transfer pricing adjustments and customs evaluation is not new.[21] However, the issue, in the context of the UCC, has finally been resolved by the CJEU in Case C-529/16, *Hamamatsu Photonics Deutschland GmbH,* issued on 21 December 2017,[22] in which the Court dealt with the relationship between transfer pricing adjustments a posteriori and valuation method for customs purposes laid down by Regulation 2913/1992 (now replaced by the UCC).[23] In its judgment, the CJEU first

19. CJEU, 23 Mar. 2006, Case C-210/04, *FCE Bank*, para. 39.
20. This shareable conclusion was first reached by SANTORO, p. 156.
21. *See* MAISTO, p. 111, where the author highlights that the profit split method and the transactional net margin method are compatible with the methods laid down for custom evaluation in the context of the General Agreement on Tariffs and Trade. *See also* VAT Committee, Working Paper 923 dated 28 February 2017, *Possible VAT implications of Transfer Pricing*, para. 3.3. *See also* World Custom Organization, *Guide to Customs Valuation and Transfer Pricing*, Brussel, 2018. With reference to the application of the PSM in the context of the GATT/WTO Valuation Cod, *see also* JOVANOVICH, s. *2.(e), which* states: 'The profit split method is a difficult case because nothing in the GVC appears to refer to this method. However, nothing in the GVC prevents the use of this method either. This absence of clear support in the language of the GVC makes us think that the use of the profit split – in the context of Art. 1.2(a) – must be as restrictive as possible.'
22. The case has been commented by J. TUOMINEN and also by DE ANGELIS/ELSHOF.
23. Hamamatsu Photonics Deutschland GmbH (Hamamatsu) was a German subsidiary of the Japanese company Hamamatsu and it acted as distributor of optical devices purchased from the parent company. The transfer pricing policy of the group, agreed upon with the German tax authorities under an APA, provided that the consideration paid by Hamamatsu to purchase the devices distributed was to be adjusted in order to allow the latter to realize a target operating margin. The case referred to the CJEU concerns the relevance of such adjustments deriving from the importation of optical devices from Japan during 2009 and 2010. In those years, Hamamatsu accounted an operating margin below the threshold agreed in the APA. As a consequence, the Japanese parent company carried out a downward adjustment in order for Hamamatsu to

recalled that Article 29 of Regulation 2913/1992 provided that the customs value for imported goods is the transaction value, i.e., the price paid or payable for the goods when they are sold for being imported into the EU. It follows from the jurisprudence of the CJEU that the transaction method is the primary criterion for customs valuation which should be derogated only if the price actually paid or payable for the goods cannot be determined.[24] According to the CJEU, in particular, the transaction method reflects the real economic value of the imported goods and, in general, the price paid or payable could be adjusted where necessary in order to avoid the setting of arbitrary or fictitious customs value.[25] The CJEU further emphasized that - according to its jurisprudence - a subsequent adjustment of transaction value is limited to specific cases such as, for instance, the presence of defected or damaged goods. On the basis of the above, the CJEU concluded that Regulation 2913/1992 does not impose any obligation on importers to apply for adjustment of the transaction value on the basis of a transfer pricing adjustment. That conclusion should also be applicable under the new UCC even though the CJEU did not comment expressly on that point.

VI CONCLUSIONS

The analysis performed in this chapter shows, on the one hand, that ramifications of transfer pricing adjustments in the field of consumption taxes are not automatic and that profit-based methods, such as the transactional profit split method, are not apt to be applied in the specific field.

In the context of European VAT, however, an adjustment based on the profit split method could stimulate any tax authority to perform an adjustment also for VAT purposes to the extent companies involved do not enjoy a full right of deduction.

However, such an assessment could not be based on the outcome of the analysis performed for transfer pricing purposes since the transactional profit split method would depart from the definition of 'open market value' laid down in Article 72 VAT Directive.

SELECTED BIBLIOGRAPHY

BAKKER ANUSCHKA / OBUOFORIBO BELEMA, Transfer Pricing and Customs Valuation, IBFD Publications BV (2009).

achieve its target profitability. Hamamatsu considered that transfer pricing adjustment as relevant for the purpose of determining the customs taxable base of the goods and filed a refund claim for the higher customs duties paid on the price that was declared to the customs authorities at the time of importation. The German customs authorities refused the refund claim arguing that the transfer pricing adjustment was not relevant for customs purposes as no allocation of the adjustment amount to the individual imported goods was made. The case was brought before the Munich Federal Court that referred the question to the CJEU seeking confirmation about the interpretation of the provisions governing the valuation of goods for customs purposes.

24. CJEU 12 Dec. 2013, Case C-116/12, *Christodoulou and Others*.
25. CJEU 19 Mar. 2009, Case C-256/07, *Mitsui & Co.*

De Angelis Enrico / Elshof Theo, The Interplay Between Transfer Pricing and Customs Valuation in Case of Retroactive Profit Adjustments: The Position of the ECJ in the Case Hamamatsu Photonics Deutschland GmbH (C-529/16), 25 ITPJ 4 (2018).

Jovanovich Juan Martin, Chapter 6 – Comparison Between Customs Valuation and OECD Transfer Pricing Guidelines, in: Bakker/Obuoforibo (eds.), Transfer Pricing and Customs Valuation, IBFD Publications BV (2009).

Lucas Mas Mayra O., Chapter 7 – Value Added Tax, in: Bakker/Obuoforibo (eds.), Transfer Pricing and Customs Valuation, IBFD Publications BV (2009).

Maisto Guglielmo, Cross-Border Valuation on Income Tax, Customs Duties and VAT, 55 Bull. Intl. Fiscal Docn. 3 (2001).

Matesanz Fernando, Transfer Pricing Adjustments and VAT, 29 IVM 1 (2015).

Parolini Andrea, European VAT and Groups of Companies, in: Guglielmo Maisto (ed.), International and EC Tax Aspects of Group of Companies, IBFD (2008).

Rouberol Isabelle, Interaction Between Transfer Pricing and VAT Adjustments in the European Union, 27 IVM 5 (2016).

Santoro Emanuela, Transfer Pricing and Value Added Tax in the European Community: Is There Room for Interaction and, If So, Where?, 14 ITPJ 3 (2007).

Tuominen Juha, The Link Between Transfer Pricing and EU Customs Valuation Law: Is There Any and How Could It Be Strengthened?, 25 ITPJ 6 (2018).

VAT Committee, Working Paper 923 dated 28 February 2017, Possible VAT implications of Transfer Pricing.

Part IV Comparative Analysis

CHAPTER 11

A Comparative Analysis of the UN and OECD Approaches on the Transactional Profit Split Method and Formulary Apportionment

Michael Kobetsky

I INTRODUCTION[1]

The challenge of allocating profits to members of a multinational enterprise (MNE) group is to achieve equity between the jurisdictions by allocating profits on the basis of sound economic principles that are consistently applied to avoid double taxation and prevent tax avoidance. The Organisation for Economic Co-operation and Development (OECD) Transfer Pricing Guidelines for Multinational Enterprises and Tax Administrations (hereinafter: '2017 OECD TPG')[2] are premised on the arm's-length principle for allocating profits to members of a MNE group. The 2017 OECD TPG, incorporating Base

1. Author's note: In April 2019, the UN Committee of Experts issued draft revised text on the transactional profit split method for inclusion in the UN Manual: Committee of Experts on International Cooperation in Tax Matters, 'Co-coordinator's Report of the Work of the Sub-Committee on Transfer Pricing', 8 April 2019. The draft revised text was prepared for consideration by the UN Committee of Experts for its April 2019 meeting. A draft was issued again on 29 September 2019 for consideration at the UN Tax Committee of Experts' October 2019 meeting. The guidance in the UN Manual on the transactional profit split method will be updated in the next version of the UN Manual in 2021. The main focus of the draft revised text is to achieve consistency between the guidance in the UN Manual and the Revised Guidance in the OECD TPG. The draft revised text issued in April and September 2019 were issued after this chapter was drafted. This chapter does not consider the draft revised text. The chapter is based on the current version of the UN Manual.
2. OECD, OECD Transfer Pricing Guidelines for Multinational Enterprises and Tax Administrations 2017, OECD Publishing, Paris, https://doi.org/10.1787/tpg-2017-en [hereinafter: '2017 OECD TPG'].

Erosion and Profit Shifting (BEPS) Actions 8–10, seek to allocate profits to jurisdictions on the basis of value creation.[3] The United Nations Practical Manual on Transfer Pricing for Developing Countries (2017) (hereinafter: 'UN Manual')[4] is also based on the arm's-length principle.

There has been considerable debate about the relative merits of the arm's-length system and formulary apportionment approaches for allocating profits to members of a MNE group. Formulary apportionment is unequivocally rejected in the 2017 OECD TPG as being an arbitrary and inappropriate method for the allocation of profits between associated enterprises. Nevertheless, the OECD is proposing to use formulary apportionment measures, *inter alia*, for BEPS Action 1 on addressing the Tax Challenges Arising from the Digitalisation of the Economy.[5] In 2020, the OECD/G20 Inclusive Framework endorsed 'Pillar One' of the 'Unified Approach' that uses formulary measures, to allocate certain profits of MNEs, using digital business models, to market jurisdictions (BEPS Action1).[6] While the arm's-length principle and formulary apportionment are viewed as alternatives, the transactional profit split method in the OECD's Revised Guidance on the Application of the Transactional Profit Split Method[7] (hereinafter: 'OECD Transactional Profit Split Method report') and UN Manual provides the opportunity for the use of formulary apportionment factors in certain situations.

This chapter compares and contrasts the transactional profit split method in the UN Manual to the OECD Transactional Profit Split Method report. The OECD Transactional Profit Split Method report was approved by the Inclusive Framework on BEPS[8] and was incorporated into the OECD TPG in June 2018.[9] The chapter considers the difference between the status of the 2017 OECD TPG and the UN Manual. Finally, the chapter considers formulary apportionment in the context of the transactional profit split method. The analysis focuses on the advantages and disadvantages of formulary apportionment and the relative merits of using apportionment factors in the transactional profit split method.

A key difference between the UN Manual and the OECD Transactional Profit Split Method report on the transactional profit split method is that the OECD guidance is substantially more detailed; the OECD guidance is 17 pages with an accompanying annex of examples of 15.5 pages, whereas the UN guidance on the transactional profit

3. OECD/G20, Aligning Transfer Pricing Outcomes with Value Creation, Actions 8-10 - 2015 Final Reports, OECD Publishing, Paris, https://doi.org/10.1787/9789264241244-en.
4. (United Nations, New York, 2017) [hereinafter: 'UN Manual'].
5. P. Saint-Amans, Director of the OECD Centre for Tax Policy and Administration, at the International Fiscal Association Congress in 2018, announced that the OECD was agnostic on the arm's-length principle: *see* JOHNSTON, p. 1165.
6. *See Supra* n. 131.
7. OECD, Revised Guidance on the Application of the Transactional Profit Split Method: Inclusive Framework on BEPS: Action 10 (June 2018),
8. 'The OECD/G20 Inclusive Framework on BEPS (IF) was established to ensure interested countries and jurisdictions, including developing economies, can participate on an equal footing in the development of standards on BEPS related issues, while reviewing and monitoring the implementation of the OECD/G20 BEPS Project.': https://www.oecd.org/tax/flyer-inclusive-framework-on-beps.pdf.
9. OECD Transactional Profit Split Method report, p. 11.

split method and examples is around 8.5 pages in total. The OECD's transactional profit split method was substantially revised in the OECD Transactional Profit Split report as a BEPS Action 10 measure. The UN Manual[10] 2017 update was completed more than twelve months before the OECD/G20 published its revised transactional profit split method guidance.[11] The UN's guidance on the transactional profit split method in the UN Manual will be amended at the proposed update in 2021. A significant difference between the OECD and UN approaches to the transactional profit split method is that the UN allows the transactional profit split method to be used if there are no comparables, whereas the OECD approach does not treat the transactional profit split method as being the most appropriate method solely because reliable comparables are unavailable. Nevertheless, the three situations in which the OECD Transactional Profit Split Method is considered to be the most appropriate method (those involving high degrees of integration, unique and valuable contributions by the associated enterprises and when the associated enterprises share the same or closely related economically significant risks) are situations in which comparables are usually unavailable. Another difference between the two approaches is that the OECD provides detailed guidance that the transactional profit split method may be the most appropriate method if, according to the accurately delineated transaction, the associated enterprises share the same economically significant risks or closely related risks.[12] In contrast, the UN Manual does not provide detailed guidance on this issue other than to state that the transactional profit split method is based on the relative value of each associated enterprise's contribution which includes, *inter alia*, risks incurred.[13]

1 The Status of the 2017 OECD TPG and the UN Manual

There is a difference in the status of the UN Manual and the 2017 OECD TPG. OECD member countries and certain non-member countries are expected to follow the 2017 OECD TPG.[14] In contrast, the United Nations Committee of Experts on International Cooperation in Tax Matters (hereinafter: 'UN Tax Committee') is a subsidiary body of the United Nations Economic and Social Council.[15] The UN Tax Committee members are appointed by the UN Secretary General for a term of four years. The Tax Committee members are nominated by governments and they participate in their capacity as experts, but the Tax Committee is not an intergovernmental committee.[16] The UN Tax

10. The UN Manual was launched on 7 April 2017 in New York: http://www.un.org/esa/ffd/publications/united-nations-practical-manual-on-transfer-pricing-for-developing-countries-2017.html.
11. The OECD Transactional Profit Split Method report was published on 21 June 2018.
12. OECD TPG, paras 2.139–2.142.
13. UN Manual, para. B.3.3.13.3.
14. 'Recommendation of the Council on the Determination of Transfer Pricing between Associated Enterprises': Recommendation (95)126. The recommendation on the 'Determination of Transfer Pricing between Associated Enterprises' was adopted by the OECD Council on 13 July 1995 after being proposed by the Committee on Fiscal Affairs. The recommendation has since been amended several times and was last amended on 3 April 2017.
15. http://www.un.org/esa/ffd/ffd-follow-up/tax-committee.html.
16. http://www.un.org/esa/ffd/tax-committee/about-committee-tax-experts.html.

Committee has subcommittees that assist the UN Tax Committee in its work, such as the Subcommittee on Article 9 (Associated Enterprises): Transfer Pricing,[17] which assists the UN Tax Committee in updating the UN Manual. The UN Manual does not reflect country positions because the UN Tax Committee is not an intergovernmental committee, though it is an expert committee.

II UN PROFIT SPLIT METHOD

1 Background

The transactional profit split method in the UN Manual allocates profits from controlled transactions between associated enterprises on the basis of the profits that would have been derived by the enterprises if they were independent enterprises dealing with each other on arm's-length terms.[18] The transactional profit split method seeks to remove the effect on profits arising from the special conditions in controlled transactions between associated enterprises.[19] The UN Manual's guidance on the transactional profit split method refers to identifying the profits to be allocated between the associated enterprises.[20] The UN Manual considers the issue of anticipated and actual profits, *inter alia*, for timing issues for comparability purposes[21] and for the use of the transactional profit split method for intangibles.[22]

The transactional profit split method in the UN Manual begins by identifying the profits derived between associated enterprises from controlled transactions. These profits are then allocated to the associated enterprises on the basis of each enterprise's relative contribution to the profits reflecting the functions each enterprise has performed, the risks that each enterprise has borne, and the assets used by each enterprise.[23] If available, the profit allocation should be based on external market data disclosing the profit split that would be used by independent parties in the same or similar circumstances. Such external market data would only be available in exceptional circumstances. According to the UN Manual, the transactional profit split method is applicable to the allocation of profits from controlled transactions 'involving tangible property, intangible property, trading activities or financial services'.[24]

2 Methods to Allocate Profits

The UN Manual uses two methods to allocate profits: the contribution analysis and the residual analysis.[25] The contribution analysis allocates the total profits from controlled

17. UN Manual, p. iii.
18. UN Manual, para. B.3.3.13.2.
19. *Id.*
20. UN Manual, para. B.3.3.13.3.
21. UN Manual, paras B.2.4.2.3-7.
22. UN Manual, paras B.5.3.30-33.
23. UN Manual, para. B.3.3.13.3.
24. *Id.*
25. UN Manual, para. B.3.3.14.1.

transactions according to paragraph B.3.3.14.2. of the UN Manual 'on the basis of the relative value of functions performed by those associated enterprises engaged in the controlled transactions'.[26] The UN Manual notes that to the extent possible, external market data should be used which indicates the manner in which independent enterprises would allocate profits in similar circumstances.[27]

In some cases, it may be possible to calculate the relative value of each enterprise's contribution directly 'then determining the actual value of the contribution of each enterprise may not be required'.[28] As stated above, the UN Manual notes that the profit being allocated under the contribution analysis would normally be net profits.[29] Nevertheless, in certain situations, it may be appropriate to commence with gross profits and to deduct the expenses attributable to each associated enterprise.[30]

The residual analysis of the combined profits from controlled transactions under the transactional profit split method allocates profits under a two-step approach. Under the first step, profits are allocated to each enterprise for their routine contributions to the combined profits.[31] The profit allocation is based on the allocation of profits that independent enterprises would have used in the same or similar circumstances. The UN Manual states that the transactional net margin method is used to determine each associated enterprise's return under the first step.[32]

The second step involves the allocation of residual profits remaining after the first step, based on the facts and circumstances of the associated enterprises.[33] If the residual profit arises from 'intangible property', then the allocation should be based on the relative value of each enterprise's contributions of intangible property.[34] The residual analysis is usually applied to situations in which both associated enterprises contribute valuable intangible property.[35] In addition, the UN Manual states that the second step is usually not based on comparables.[36]

The UN Manual notes that the following approaches are acknowledged as being used in some unnamed jurisdictions to determine the respective value of each enterprise's contribution to intangible property:

- external market benchmarks that reflect the fair market value of intangible property;
- the capitalized cost of developing intangible property and the associated improvements, less an appropriate amount of amortization premised on the useful life of the intangibles; and

26. UN Manual, para. B.3.3.14.2.
27. *Id.*
28. UN Manual, para. B.3.3.14.3.
29. *Id.*
30. *Id.*
31. UN Manual, para. B.3.3.14.4.
32. *Id.*
33. *Id.*
34. *Id.*
35. UN Manual, para. B.3.3.14.5.
36. *Id.*

- the sums incurred in developing the intangibles in recent years if the expenditures of each associated enterprise have been constant and the useful life of the intangible property of the associated enterprises is similar.[37]

The UN Manual claims that the residual transactional profit split method is commonly used in practice in preference to the contribution approach.[38] The UN Manual also states that the residual transactional profit split method 'breaks up a complicated transfer pricing problem into two manageable steps'.[39] The UN Manual also states that the residual transactional profit split method reduces the potential for disputes between MNEs and tax authorities because the residual transactional profit split method reduces the profit to be split under the 'potentially more controversial second step'.[40]

3 Comparable Profit Split Method

In addition, the UN Manual outlines a different version of the transactional profit split method called the 'comparable profit split method', which it claims is used in certain countries, but the country names are not provided.[41] Under the comparable profit split method, the net profit from controlled transactions is compared to profit allocations between independent enterprises operating 'in similar activities and under similar circumstances'.[42] The comparable profit split method is dependent on external market data to determine the relative contributions of associated enterprises.[43] The UN Manual points out that the difference between the residual transactional profit split method and comparable profit split method is that the former can be used in the absence of external market data, but the latter relies on external market data.[44] Nevertheless, the UN Model states that the contribution analysis and comparable profit split methods are not often used because of the lack of reliable market data.[45]

4 Strengths and Weaknesses of the Transactional Profit Split Method

The UN Manual claims that the transactional profit split method has the following strengths:

- it may be used for highly integrated associated enterprises in which a one-sided analysis is inappropriate;

37. UN Manual, para. B.3.3.14.6.
38. UN Manual, para. B.3.3.14.7.
39. *Id.*
40. *Id.*
41. UN Manual, para. B3.3.15.1.
42. *Id.*
43. *Id.*
44. *Id.*
45. UN Manual, para. B.3.3.15.2.

- it may be used in situations in which the traditional transfer pricing methods are inapplicable because reliable comparable transactions are unavailable;
- it avoids extreme results for one associated enterprise because it is a two-sided analysis; and
- it is able to allocate the profits attributable to synergies between intangible property and profits arising from economies of scales.[46]

The weaknesses of the transactional profit split method include:

- the 'theoretical weakness'[47] of the second step, such as assuming that the value derived from the synergy between intangible property is based on the relative inputs of the associated enterprises;
- the reliance on access to data from foreign-associated enterprises which may create difficulties for both associated enterprises and their respective tax authorities; and
- the UN Manual acknowledges that measurement problems arise from using the transactional profit split method. It is claimed that it may be difficult to determine the combined revenue and costs of associated enterprises arising from controlled transactions. In addition, it may be challenging to allocate the costs between controlled and uncontrolled transactions of the associated enterprises.[48]

5 When to Use the Transactional Profit Split Method

The UN Manual provides that the transactional profit split method may be used for associated enterprises that have highly interrelated transactions that cannot be examined on a separate basis using the other transfer pricing methods.[49] This arises if the 'transactions that are so interdependent that they cannot be evaluated on a separate basis using a traditional transaction method'.[50] The example provided in the UN Manual of where the transactional profit split method could be used is a global financial services business.[51] The UN Manual notes that if both parties to the controlled transaction 'own valuable intangible property'[52] for which comparable transactions are unavailable, the transactional profit split method may be the most appropriate method.[53]

The transactional profit split method involves the selection of factors that resulted in the combined profit of the associated enterprises, determining the weighting

46. UN Manual, para. B.3.3.16.1.
47. UN Manual, para. B.3.3.16.2.
48. *Id.*
49. UN Manual, para. B.3.3.17.1.
50. *Id.*
51. *Id.*
52. UN Manual, para. B.3.3.17.2.
53. *Id.*

for each factor and then allocating the profits between the enterprises.[54] The UN Manual points out that the contribution analysis is difficult to apply because comparable data on the manner in which independent parties would have split such profits is usually unavailable.[55]

The UN Manual provides guidance on the use of the transactional profit split method in the chapter for intangibles.[56] The UN Manual directs that in deciding whether the transactional profit split method is the most appropriate method for a transaction, the availability of adequate data on the combined profits and the factors to be used to allocate the profits 'should be taken into account as this can affect the reliability of the method'.[57] In relation to transactions involving the transfer of intangibles or the rights in intangibles, the UN Manual notes that three main questions need to be considered.[58] First, what are the combined profits arising from the transactions that will be split? Second, will the split be based on *ex ante* or *ex post* profits? The UN Manual states that the profit split approach selected must consider which parties assume the risks because '*ex post* results may differ from *ex ante* profits'.[59] Finally, what are the appropriate profit splitting factors? Selection of the profit splitting factors is described in the UN Manual as depending on 'expected contributions by each party to the transaction'.[60]

III THE OECD TRANSACTIONAL PROFIT SPLIT METHOD

The OECD Transactional Profit Split Method report provides detailed threshold tests for determining if the transactional profit split method is the most appropriate method. The OECD Transactional Profit Split Method states that: 'The transactional profit split method seeks to establish arm's length outcomes or test reported outcomes for controlled transactions in order to approximate the results that would have been achieved between independent enterprises engaging in a comparable transaction or transactions.'[61] The OECD Transactional Profit Split Method report provides that the transactional profit split method may also be used to allocate losses between associated enterprises if the transactional profit split method is the most appropriate method.[62] Although the UN Manual makes no reference to the use of the transactional profit split method for allocating losses, it would be expected that the UN Manual would be consistent with OECD Transactional Profit Split Method report.

54. UN Manual, para. B.3.3.17.4.
55. *Id.*
56. UN Manual, paras B.5.6.30–33.
57. UN Manual, para. B.5.6.30.
58. UN Manual, para. B.5.6.31.
59. *Id.*
60. *Id.*
61. OECD TPG, para. 2.114.
62. OECD TPG, para. 2.115.

1 When the Transactional Profit Split Method Is Applicable

As with the other methods, the OECD Transactional Profit Split Method report prescribes the accurate delineation of the controlled transaction to determine if the transactional profit split method is applicable.[63] This is to determine the commercial and financial relations between the associated enterprises and to examine the activities of each associated enterprise. A key problem in transfer pricing is finding reliable comparables, which is a significant challenge when the associated enterprises have contributed valuable intangibles. The OECD Transactional Profit Split Method report notes that a 'lack of closely comparable, uncontrolled transactions'[64] should not, by itself, be used as the basis for the use of the transactional profit split method.[65]

The UN Manual takes the contrary approach and supports the use of the transactional profit split method if 'the traditional methods [sic][66] prove [to be] inappropriate due to a lack of comparable transactions'.[67] Consequently, the UN Manual supports the use of the transactional profit split method if comparables are unavailable. In practice, it may be argued that there is no difference between the UN and OECD Approaches as the situations in which the transactional profit split method is the most appropriate method are likely to be when reliable comparable transactions are unlikely to be available.

The OECD Transactional Profit Split Method report provides that the transactional profit split method may be the most appropriate transfer pricing method in the following three situations.

A Unique and Valuable Contributions by the Parties

If both parties to a controlled transaction contribute unique and valuable contributions, the OECD Transactional Profit Split Method report indicates that the transactional profit split method may be the most appropriate method.[68] The determination of the existence of unique and valuable contributions may depend on the industry sector and the factors that affect business performance in the sector.[69] The OECD Transactional Profit Split Method report states that if each party to a controlled transaction contribute unique and valuable intangibles, it will also be necessary to determine if the parties assume economically significant risks in connection with the intangibles.[70]

The UN approach is consistent with the OECD approach on the requirement that both parties contribute valuable intangibles. The UN Manual states that if one party

63. OECD TPG, para. 2.125.
64. OECD TPG, para. 2.128.
65. OECD TPG, para. 2.128.
66. The reference in the quote to 'traditional methods' would include the transactional net margin method which is not a traditional transfer pricing method.
67. UN Manual, para. B.3.3.16.1.
68. OECD TPG, para. 2.126.
69. *Id.*
70. 2017 OECD TPG, para. 131.

'owns valuable intangible property',[71] the other party will be the tested party using the cost-plus method, resale price method or transactional net margin method.[72] The UN Manual provides that if both associated enterprises own valuable intangible property 'for which it is impossible to find comparables',[73] the transactional profit split method might be the most reliable method.[74]

A difference between the OECD and UN approaches is that the UN refers to the narrower ownership of 'intangible property', whereas the OECD refers to associated enterprises contributing unique and valuable intangibles.[75] The Glossary to the UN Manual contains the following definition of 'intangibles': 'Intangibles are property that has no physical existence but whose value depends on the legal rights of the owner. Examples of intangibles are intellectual property such as patents, copyright and trademarks.'[76] Intangible property refers to intangibles that are protected by law and may be transferred between parties. In contrast, knowledge or commercial information, such as know-how, acquired by a party is not intangible property and is not protected by law. Know-how[77] is an intangible asset and may be licensed by contract. The term 'intangibles' or 'intangible asset' is much broader than intangible property. The references to 'intangible property' in the UN Manual appear to be a drafting oversight as Chapter B.5. on 'Transfer Pricing Considerations for Intangible Property' is consistent with the OECD approach in only referring to the term 'intangibles'. The 2017 OECD TPG has the following definition of intangibles:

> In these Guidelines, therefore, the word 'intangible' is intended to address something which is not a physical asset or a financial asset, which is capable of being owned or controlled for use in commercial activities, and whose use or transfer would be compensated had it occurred in a transaction between independent parties in comparable circumstances. Rather than focusing on accounting or legal definitions, the thrust of a transfer pricing analysis in a case involving intangibles should be the determination of the conditions that would be agreed upon between independent parties for a comparable transaction.[78]

The UN Manual's definition of intangibles in Chapter B5 reflects the definition of intangibles in the 2017 OECD TPG:

> For the purposes of this chapter [B.5. Transfer Pricing Considerations for Intangible Property[79]] the term 'intangible' encompasses something which is neither a physical nor a financial asset, which is capable of being owned or controlled for commercial purposes, whose use or transfer would be compensated had it occurred between independent enterprises in comparable circumstances. Whether something is recognized as an intangible for legal or accounting purposes is an

71. UN Manual, para. B.3.3.17.2.
72. *Id.*
73. *Id.*
74. *Id.*
75. OECD TPG, para. 2.131.
76. UN Manual, Glossary, p. 639.
77. 'Know-how' is defined in the *Oxford English Dictionary* (3rd Edition, 2010) as: 'Knowledge of how to do some particular thing; skill, expertise, esp. in regard to a practical or technical matter.'
78. 2017 OECD TPG, para. 6.6.
79. B.5. should be titled 'Transfer Pricing Considerations for Intangibles'.

informative starting point but not determinative. It is not the case that all valuable intangibles are legally protected, registered or recognized for accounting purposes.[80]

As discussed above, the UN Manual provides guidance in the chapter on intangibles on the use of the transactional profit split method for intangibles.[81]

B Highly Integrated Business Operations

One of the factors required to justify the use of the transactional profit split method is a high degree of integration within a MNE group. This is defined as meaning that one associated enterprise's contributions through its functions, assets and risks are interlinked with its associate enterprises to such an extent that they cannot be evaluated separately.[82] The OECD Transactional Profit Split Method report claim that in many situations of integration within a MNE group, the contributions of at least one party to the transaction can be 'reliably evaluated by reference to comparable uncontrolled transactions'.[83] The example provided in the OECD Transactional Profit Split Method report to support the contention that reliable comparables may be available is where an associated enterprise performs complementary and discrete activities. The functions, assets and risks at each discrete point may be comparable to uncontrolled transactions.[84]

C Shared Assumption of Economically Significant Risks and Separate Accounting of Closely Related Risks

The OECD Transactional Profit Split Method report states that the transactional profit split method may be the most appropriate method if the accurately delineated transaction indicates that the associated enterprises share the assumption of economically significant risks.[85] The transactional profit split method may also be the most appropriate method if associated enterprises separately assume the economically significant risks and these risks are closely interrelated or correlated to the extent that the risks assumed by each party cannot be separated.[86] The use of the transactional profit split method in these circumstances depends on the extent to which the allocation of profits to the parties is necessary because they are assuming economically

80. UN Manual, para. B.5.2.3.
81. UN Manual, paras B.5.6.30-33.
82. OECD TPG, para. 2.133.
83. *Id.*
84. *Id.*
85. OECD TPG, para. 2.139.
86. OECD TPG, para. 2.140.

significant risks.[87] The economically significant risks should be considered by reference to their connection with the actual or anticipated profits from the controlled transactions.[88]

The OECD Transactional Profit Split Method report notes that if the transactional profit split method is the most appropriate method on the basis of economically significant risks, as considered in the above paragraph, it is likely that a split of actual profits should occur rather than a split of anticipated profits.[89] '[T]he actual relevant profits to be split, will reflect the playing out of the risks of each party.'[90] On the other hand, a split of anticipated profits is claimed by the OECD to focus on the 'playing out of economically significant risks on one party'.[91] The OECD Transactional Profit Split Method report requires that the sharing of actual or anticipated profits should depend on the accurate delineation of the transaction.[92]

This OECD consideration of the transactional profit split method, in the context of economically significant risks, is not replicated in the UN Manual's guidance on the transactional profit split method. The UN Manual's guidance on the transactional profit split method refers to risk as one factor contributing to controlled transactions for which a profit allocation may be required.[93]

2 Transactional Profit Split of Anticipated Profits and Actual Profits

The OECD Transactional Profit Split Method report states that the determination of the profits to be split may be actual profits or anticipated profits, or a combination of both, and that they should be aligned with the accurately delineated transaction.[94] If the transactional profit split method is the most appropriate method, the splitting of profits is conditional upon when the accurate delineation of the transaction establishes that the parties share the assumption of the same economically significant risks for a business activity or separately assume closely related risks for the transaction; in these situations, the parties should share the resulting profits or losses.[95]

The OECD Transactional Profit Split Method report directs that the transactional profit split method should be applied without hindsight.[96] Regardless of whether the profits being split are the anticipated profits or the actual profits derived by the associated enterprises, the basis on which the profits are split, the selection of profit splitting factors and method for calculating the profits, any contingencies and any adjustments must be determined on the basis of information known by the associated enterprises or reasonably foreseeable by them at the time the controlled transactions

87. OECD TPG, para. 2.141.
88. *Id.*
89. OECD TPG, para. 2.142.
90. *Id.*
91. *Id.*
92. *Id.*
93. UN Manual, para. B.3.3.13.3.
94. OECD TPG, para. 2.158.
95. OECD TPG, para. 2.159.
96. OECD TPG, para. 2.161.

were entered into.[97] An exception to this approach would be if there were unforeseen events that would have resulted in the renegotiation of the agreement if it had been between independent parties.[98] On the use of the transactional profit split method for intangibles, the UN Manual raises the issue of whether *ex post* or *ex ante* profits should be split.[99] Apart from this comment, the UN Manual's guidance on the transactional profit split method does not reflect the OECD directions on the use of *ex ante* or *ex post* profits for the transactional profit split method.

3 Strengths and Weaknesses of the Transactional Profit Split Method: UN and OECD Approaches

The OECD Transactional Profit Split Method report provides a detailed explanation of the advantages and disadvantages of using the transactional profit split method. On the other hand, the UN Manual outlines in point form the advantages and disadvantages.[100] The OECD Transactional Profit Split Method report states that the main advantage of the transactional profit split method is that it provides a pricing solution when both associated enterprises to a transaction make unique and valuable contributions.[101] In such situations, independent parties might price the transaction on the basis of their respective contributions justifying the use of a two-sided method.[102] Moreover, it would be expected that there would be a lack of reliable comparables with which to price the unique and valuable contributions made by associated enterprises.[103] In these situations, it is appropriate to allocate combined profits on the basis of the respective values of the contributions to the controlled transaction actually made by the associated enterprises. The respective contributions would be determined on the basis of the relative value of each associated enterprise's functions, assets and risks.[104] Again, in this situation, the other transfer pricing methods will be ineffective because reliable comparables will be unavailable. The transactional profit split method is also appropriate for associated enterprises that are highly integrated, in which a one-sided analysis would be not appropriate.[105]

In contrast, the OECD Transactional Profit Split Method report provides that if the accurate delineation of actual controlled transactions establishes that an associated enterprise only performs simple functions, does not share the economically significant risks associated with the transaction, or does not make a contribution which is unique and valuable, the use of the transactional profit split method would be inappropriate because it is unlikely to reflect an arm's-length situation.[106] In comparison, the UN

97. *Id.*
98. *Id.*
99. UN Manual, para. B.5.6.31.
100. UN Manual, paras B.3.3.16.1-2.
101. OECD TPG, para. 2.119.
102. *Id.*
103. *Id.*
104. *Id.*
105. OECD TPG, para. 2.120.
106. OECD TPG, para. 2.127.

Manual notes that the transactional profit split method is able to allocate between associated enterprises the profits arising from synergies between 'intangibles assets' contributed by them and profits arising from economies of scale.[107]

The OECD Transactional Profit Split Method report notes that a strength of the transactional profit split method is the flexibility it provides in the allocation of profits by considering the specific and perhaps unique facts and circumstances of the associated enterprises that might not be reflected in transactions between independent enterprises.[108] If there 'is a high degree of uncertainty for each of the parties in relation to a transaction',[109] the transactional profit split method provides flexibility to allocate profits to each associated enterprise.[110] In a transaction between associated enterprises that involves the shared assumption of closely related economically significant risks, the transactional profit split method allows a profit allocation that reflects 'the actual outcome of the risks associated with the transaction'.[111] On the other hand, the UN Manual states that the transactional profit split method may be suitable for integrated operations for which a one-sided analysis is inappropriate.[112]

The OECD Transactional Profit Split Method report claims that another strength of the transactional profit split method is that each of the parties to a transaction is separately evaluated in the pricing of the transaction; this is explained as involving a determination of the contributions of each associated enterprise and valuing their respective contributions to determine the arm's-length allocation of profits to each associated enterprise.[113]

The OECD and UN approaches differ on whether the transactional profit split method avoids extreme results for one of the associated enterprises because it is a two-sided approach.[114] The UN Manual claims that one of the associated enterprises will not be left with an extreme result.[115] In contrast, the OECD Transactional Profit Split Method report on transactional profit split method does not mention whether the transactional profit split method avoids extreme and improbable results that may occur under a one-sided transfer pricing method.

Both the OECD and UN approaches claim that a weakness of the transactional profit split method is the difficulty of obtaining the necessary information about the operations of associated enterprises. The OECD Transactional Profit Split Method report also claims that it may be difficult for both taxpayers and tax authorities to determine the combined income and costs for the associated enterprises participating in controlled transactions.[116] This exercise would involve analysing the financial records of the parties to controlled transactions to determine income, costs and net profits arising from these transactions and segregating the items from the parties'

107. UN Manual, para. B.3.3.16.1.
108. 2017 OECD TPG, para. 1.121.
109. *Id.*
110. *Id.*
111. *Id.*
112. UN Manual, para. B.3.3.16.1.
113. OECD TPG, para. 2.122.
114. UN Manual, para. B.3.3.16.1.
115. *Id.*
116. OECD TPG, para. 2. 123.

uncontrolled transactions. In addition, this requires recording the accounts of associated enterprises on a common basis and making the necessary accounting and currency adjustments.[117] Identifying the appropriate profit split factors is a difficult process that involves judgement.[118] It is important for taxpayers to document the application of the transactional profit split method including the determination of the profits that were split and the reasoning for the selection of the profit splitting factors.[119] On the other hand, the UN Manual only refers to the difficulty of obtaining information from foreign-associated enterprises.[120]

The OECD Transactional Profit Split Method report claims that as the transactional profit split method is rarely used by independent enterprises, this cannot be used to argue that any use of the transactional profit split method should be limited.[121] If the transactional profit split method is the most appropriate method, the corresponding limited use of the transactional profit split method by independent enterprises is not a relevant factor 'since transfer pricing methods are not necessarily intended to replicate arm's length behaviour, but rather to serve as a means of establishing and/or verifying arm's length outcomes for controlled transactions'.[122]

IV FORMULARY APPORTIONMENT

The UN Manual claims that an alternative to the arm's-length principle is global formulary apportionment.[123] Although formulary apportionment is only used at the subnational level in countries, such as the US and Canada, the European Union (EU) is considering implementing a Common Consolidated Corporate Tax Base (CCCTB) for EU countries.[124] The CCCTB proposal uses formulary apportionment to allocate profits of a MNE group operating within the EU and accordingly the transfer pricing rules would not apply.[125] Despite the assertion that formulary apportionment and the arm's-length principle are alternative allocation mechanisms, the OECD's revision of the transactional profit split method provides the opportunity for the use of formulary apportionment factors to split profits under the transactional profit split method.

Formulary apportionment is a profit-allocation method in which profits are allocated to jurisdictions on the basis of certain factors. Under formulary apportionment, a MNE group is treated as a single or unitary entity and the income of the group is calculated on an aggregate basis. The advantages of formulary apportionment are simplicity and countering tax avoidance.[126] But formulary apportionment is not a panacea; there are practical problems with using formulary apportionment, such as the

117. *Id.*
118. *Id.*
119. *Id.*
120. UN Manual, para. B.3.3.16.2.
121. OECD TPG, para. 2.124.
122. *Id.*
123. UN Manual, para. B.1.4.14.
124. European Commission, Proposal for a Council Directive on a Common Consolidated Corporate Tax Base, (COM(2016) 683, 2016/0336 (CNS)), pp. 2-3.
125. *Id.*
126. Clausing, The U.S. State Experience, p. 354; *see also* Durst, p. 6.

measurement of the components and the tax base.[127] Commentators have advocated for some time that formulary apportionment is a superior profit-allocation method.[128] Nevertheless, there is considerable scope for the transactional profit split method to use formulas specifically selected for a MNE group to split profits from intangibles.[129]

In October 2019, the OECD Secretariat issued a public consultation document[130] on the 'Unified Approach' under Pillar One[131] (hereinafter: the 'Unified Approach'), which includes formulary measures to allocate certain profits to market jurisdictions for MNEs using highly digitalized business models. The 'Unified Approach' creates a nexus measure that is based on sales and does not require the physical presence of a MNE in the market jurisdiction. The OECD Secretariat claimed that this 'approach largely retains the current transfer pricing rules based on the arm's-length principle but complements them with formula-based solutions in areas where tensions in the current system are the highest'.[132]

In January 2020, the Inclusive Framework endorsed the Unified Approach as the foundation for the consensus-based solution to be finalized in 2020.[133] The Inclusive Framework noted that: 'The proposed reallocation of taxing rights under Pillar One would require improved tax certainty, including effective and binding dispute prevention and resolution mechanisms. In the design and implementation of the solution, the IF [Inclusive Framework] also acknowledges the need to minimise complexity.'[134] The Unified Approach consists of a three-tiered mechanism to allocate profits:

- Amount A – a share of the residual profit allocated to market jurisdictions using a formulaic approach that is based on either the MNE group level or the business line level. This is a new taxing right for the market jurisdictions and does not require the MNE to have a physical presence in the jurisdiction. The basis for Amount A is the active and continuous participation of a MNE in the economy of a market jurisdiction.
- Amount B – a fixed remuneration for baseline marketing and distribution functions that take place in the market jurisdiction. This amount is based on the arm's-length principle.

127. Clausing, *id.*
128. Musgrave/Musgrave, p. 85; Bird/Brean, p. 1392.
129. *See* Fleming/Peroni/Shea, pp. 54–55.
130. OECD, Public discussion document, 'Secretariat Proposals for a "Unified Approach" Under Pillar One'. [hereinafter: the 'Unified Approach']
131. In January 2019, the Inclusive Framework issued a short Policy Note (Addressing the Tax Challenges of the Digitalisation of the Economy – Policy Note, as approved by the Inclusive Framework on BEPS on 23 January 2019, OECD 2019), which allocated the proposed measures for dealing with the tax challenges arising from the digitalization of the economy into two broad measures, Pillar One and Pillar Two. Pillar One deals with allocation of taxing rights. Pillar One has three proposals, the 'user participation' proposal, the 'marketing intangibles' proposal and the 'significant economic presence' proposal. Pillar Two is designed to ensure that multinational enterprises pay a minimal level of tax on profits. Pillar Two is intended to address the remaining BEPS issues.
132. *Id.*
133. OECD/G20, *id*, p. 4, para. 2.
134. OECD/G20, *id.*

- Amount C – is any additional profit if the activities of an MNE in a jurisdiction exceed the baseline activity dealt with by Amount B. Amount C also involves the need for improved dispute resolution mechanisms.[135]

1 Advantages of Formulary Apportionment

A *Simplicity*

The key advantage that formulary apportionment offers is simplicity.[136] The net income of a MNE group is allocated to jurisdictions using a formula with specified apportionment factors. The main factors for allocating income under formulary apportionment are sales, labour and capital. Under formulary apportionment, the legal distinction between associated enterprises is disregarded and the MNE group is treated as a unitary business. In comparison, the arm's-length principle is considered by some commentators to be complex.[137] The length of the 2017 OECD TPG,[138] *inter alia*, is cited as evidence of the complexity of the transfer pricing system.[139] It is asserted that the arm's-length principle is relatively simple, but challenges arise in finding reliable comparables. In most cases involving the use of the transactional net margin method, there is a need for a detailed and extensive examination of a transfer pricing database to find comparables, which is costly and complex.

Commentators have noted that formulary apportionment involves complex factual issues, such as determining the tax base to be apportioned if it is based on a unitary business.[140] In addition, selecting the apportionment factors and defining the apportionment factors and the weight to be given to them for the purposes of the transactional profit split method involves judgment.[141] Formulary apportionment is usually proposed as a single formula for all taxpayers, but it has the capacity to have different formulas for different business sectors. If formulary apportionment is used in the transactional profit split method, it has the advantage that the formula can be tailored for a particular MNE group.

B *Compliance and Administration Costs*

It is very costly for taxpayers to comply with transfer pricing rules as the core of transfer pricing is comparability. The key shortcoming of transfer pricing is the availability and reliability of comparables. The taxpayer is required to first analyse the accurately

135. OECD/G20, Statement by the OECD/G20 Inclusive Framework on BEPS on the Two-Pillar Approach to Address the Tax Challenges Arising from the Digitalisation of the Economy, (January 2020), p. 8, para. 10.
136. Avi-Yonah/Clausing/Durst, p. 512; Bruner/Rassier/Ruhl, p. 14.
137. Hellerstein, p. 108; Avi-Yonah/Clausing/Durst, pp. 502, 512–513.
138. The 2017 TPG is 603 pages.
139. Hellerstein, p. 108.
140. Hellerstein, *id.*; Avi-Yonah/Clausing/Durst, pp. 522–523.
141. Hellerstein, *id.*

delineated transaction between the associated enterprises and to then find appropriate and reliable uncontrolled transactions. Finally, the taxpayer is required to select the most appropriate transfer pricing method. It has been asserted that the costs of administering and complying with formulary apportionment would be lower than those under transfer pricing.[142] The compelling point Hellerstein makes is that one factor at the subnational level in the United States in rejecting the arm's-length system was the cost of complying with and administering the arm's-length system.[143]

C *Reflects Economic Reality*

It has been argued that the arm's-length principle does not reflect economic reality.[144] MNE groups operate as integrated unitary businesses through the use of high-speed and high-quality communications and business systems.[145] Associated enterprises in a MNE group do not treat each other as separate entities. Uncontrolled transactions are claimed to be so different from controlled transactions that it has been argued that the arm's-length principle provides limited guidance in setting transfer prices.[146] It is claimed that formulary apportionment factors are not financial determinations but reflect actual economic activity.[147] Moreover, economists researching the effect of profit shifting by US MNEs on the US national accounts used formulary apportionment to measure offshore profit shifting as the difference between profits earned under formulary apportionment and profits earned under the arm's-length principle.[148] But these economists are not advocating a shift to formulary apportionment despite the benefits of formulary apportionment as a measurement mechanism.[149]

2 Disadvantages of Using Formulary Apportionment

A *Arbitrary Allocation*

One of the main criticisms of formulary apportionment is that it is arbitrary.[150] The OECD asserts that formulary apportionment does not consider market conditions, the facts and circumstances of the associated enterprises and the management's allocation of resources resulting in an arbitrary allocation of profits.[151] In addition, a formula based on costs, assets, payroll and sales provides a fixed rate of profit per currency unit of each component to the associated enterprises irrespective of the functions, assets,

142. Hellerstein, p. 109; Avi-Yonah/Clausing/Durst, p. 511.
143. Hellerstein, *id.*, citing Hellerstein/Hellerstein, para. 8.03; Avi-Yonah/Clausing/Durst, p. 498.
144. US General Accounting Office, pp. 61–62.
145. Kobetsky, p. 79.
146. US General Accounting Office, p. 61.
147. Clausing, The Effect of Profit Shifting, p. 929.
148. Bruner/Rassier/Ruhl, pp. 2–3.
149. *Id.*, p. 15.
150. 2017 OECD TPG, para. 1.25.
151. *Id.*

risks and efficiencies of each associated enterprise.[152] This criticism infers that the arm's-length principle provides an accurate allocation of profits. Nevertheless, as stated above, the OECD is now claiming to be agnostic on the arm's-length principle.[153] In contrast, it has been contended that formulary apportionment is not as arbitrary as the current international tax system which was (prior to the OECD/G20 BEPS Project) subject to corporate tax planning behaviours, such as certain group members establishing residency in low-tax jurisdictions, their transfer pricing planning and their organizational structure.[154] Transfer pricing rules were effectively manipulated by certain MNEs to allocate profits to low-tax jurisdictions resulting in an allocation of profits which did not reflect economic activity under the 2017 OECD TPG prior to the OECD/G20 BEPS Project.[155] This manipulation, *inter alia*, resulted in the OECD/G20 BEPS Project. In response to the assertion that formulary apportionment is arbitrary, it may be contended that any allocation method is arbitrary.[156]

B Double Taxation

The OECD claims that the most significant concern of global formulary apportionment is preventing double taxation and ensuring single taxation.[157] It is argued in the 2017 OECD TPG that the most significant challenge for formulary apportionment is obtaining agreement on a formula and defining a group for the purposes of unitary taxation.[158] To avoid double taxation, consensus would be required on a broad range of issues, including measuring the tax base of the group, the apportionment factors, the weight that is to be allocated to each factor and a common accounting system.[159] In particular, the OECD contends that jurisdictions are unlikely to agree on a universal allocation formula.[160] It has been asserted that formulary apportionment would reduce double taxation even if countries used different formulas.[161] Under formulary apportionment, a taxpayer would be able to predict the tax consequences of its investments in given jurisdictions.[162] Under the arm's-length system, it is uncertain how a jurisdiction would apply its transfer pricing rules in the absence of an advance pricing agreement. Consequently, it is claimed that the risk of unpredictable double taxation is higher under the arm's-length principle.[163]

152. *Id.*
153. *Supra* n. 5.
154. Clausing, The Effect of Profit Shifting, p. 929; Avi-Yonah/Clausing/Durst, pp. 516–517; Brauner, p. 615.
155. OECD/G20, Aligning Transfer Pricing Outcomes with Value Creation, Action 8–10: Final Reports, p. 9; OECD, Addressing Base Erosion and Profit Shifting (2013), pp. 10, 52–53.
156. Li, pp. 855–856; Avi-Yonah/Clausing/Durst, pp. 516–517.
157. 2017 OECD TPG, para. 1.22.
158. *Id.*
159. *Id.*
160. *Id.*
161. Durst, p. 11; Avi-Yonah/Clausing/Durst, p. 520.
162. Durst, p. 11.
163. *Id.*

C Potential for Profit Shifting

The 2017 OECD TPG asserts that taxpayers may be able to manipulate the factors in the formula to shift income to low-tax jurisdictions.[164] The examples cited of techniques for manipulating formulary apportionment are: entering unnecessary financial transactions; moving mobile assets to favourable tax locations; and requiring an associated enterprise to hold inventory levels above levels that would normally be held.[165] This assertion has been questioned as it ignores the cost of moving assets and employees to low-tax jurisdictions to exploit formulary apportionment.[166] Moreover, it has been claimed that the formulary factors of payroll, assets and sales used in US subnational taxation are not tax-sensitive in the manner predicted by the OECD.[167] Nevertheless, under a multiple factor formula, there is an incentive to locate factors in low-tax jurisdictions.[168]

3 The Apportionment Factors

A Sales

The inclusion of the sales factor in formulary apportionment recognizes the business reality that demands that an enterprise's products and services are a key part of any enterprise's business operations.[169] Economists consider that demand creates income and is, therefore, an appropriate factor to be included in a formula as it reflects the contribution of a jurisdiction to an enterprise's profits.[170] Sales may be allocated on the basis of destination or on the basis of origin – involving the entity that sells the products or provides the services. The allocation of income in relation to sales, on a destination basis, would allocate profits to the jurisdiction in which the products are predominantly sold or services are provided.[171] The main reason for using a destination-based sales factor rather than an origin-based factor is that entities that buy the products or receive the services are not susceptible to manipulation.[172] It is claimed that a distortion from a destination-based tax is lower than an origin-based tax and, therefore, meets the neutrality criterion.[173] The distortion arising from an origin-based system

164. 2017 OECD TPG., para. 1.23.
165. *Id.*
166. Blay, p. 47.
167. Clausing, The Effect of Profit Shifting, p. 929. The article refers to the following publication for a more detailed consideration of this issue: Clausing, The U.S. State Experience under Formulary Apportionment; Blay, *id.*
168. Clausing, *id.*
169. European Commission, Taxation Papers, The Delineation and Apportionment of an EU Consolidated Tax Base for Multi-jurisdictional Corporate Income Taxation: a Review of Issues and Options, Working Paper No. 9/2006, p. 52.
170. *Id.*
171. *Id.*
172. *Id.*
173. *Id.*

was examined in BEPS Action 7[174] in which MNEs providing digital advertising services to customers in host countries claimed that the sales were formally made by enterprises in low-tax jurisdictions, such as Ireland or Singapore, to avoid taxation in the host countries. The enterprises claimed that under the business profits article of a tax treaty, the enterprise resident in a low-tax country was not taxable in the host country as the enterprise avoided creating a permanent establishment in the host country.

Some commentators reject the notion that demand is an income-producing factor and claim that profits should not be attributed to sales.[175] These commentators argue that a better approach is to use supply apportionment factors.[176] A further argument against using sales as an apportionment factor is that it conflicts with the arm's-length system which does not assign taxing rights over company income on the basis of demand and that such a reform is not justified.[177] In the context of the EU proposals for a CCCTB, it may be asserted that the sales factor would result in profits of EU enterprises being allocated to the jurisdictions in which the consumers or service recipients are located rather than the jurisdictions in which production occurs or where services are provided from. Consequently, the basis for rejecting a sales factor is that it is an extreme change from the current system of allocating company profits.[178]

The most compelling argument in favour of using a sales factor is simplicity. It would be relatively simple to measure the sales factor for the purposes of apportionment.[179] In defining the sales factor, a range of issues requires consideration. First, the sales factor may be defined as the gross sales resulting from the ordinary business operations of an enterprise, such as income from the sale of tangible and intangible assets and income from rendering services.[180] Second, should the factor include profits derived from transactions outside the ordinary operation of a business, such as the sale of capital assets?[181] Third, should intra-group sales be excluded?[182] It is argued that intra-group transactions should be excluded from the sales factor to prevent the risk of profit shifting to low-tax jurisdictions.[183] Thus, the sales factor should be restricted to sales to independent buyers.

B *Payroll*

The payroll factor for apportioning profits reflects the labour cost of producing assets or providing services. Payroll is measured by determining the total costs of labour, such as salary, bonuses and commissions. The payroll factor allocates profits to the jurisdiction in which the labour force is located. Labour is the least mobile factor. It has

174. OECD/G20, Preventing the Artificial Avoidance of Permanent Establishment Status, Action 7, 2015 Final Report, (Paris, 2015, OECD), p. 10.
175. European Commission, Taxation Papers, *supra* n. 169, at pp. 52–53, citing SCHÄFER/SPENGEL.
176. *Id.*, p. 53.
177. *Id.*
178. *Id.*
179. *Id.*
180. *Id.*
181. *Id.*
182. *Id.*
183. *Id.*

been asserted that the cash-flow definition of payroll is relatively simple; it is easy to measure and to use to allocate profits to jurisdictions in which the workforce is located.[184] Problems may arise in measuring certain types of remuneration, such as non-cash benefits and pensions.[185] The definition of the payroll factor may need to distinguish between employees and independent contractors as the payroll factor will usually be restricted to employees. In many jurisdictions, the distinction between employees and independent contractors has proven to be very difficult and contentious.

One clear concern with the payroll factor is that it assumes that productivity is equal in all jurisdictions.[186] Salaries are likely to be significantly different between jurisdictions and such salary differences between jurisdictions result in a higher attribution to high-cost labour countries. This may be inappropriate if productivity is not also higher in those jurisdictions.

C Assets

Assets may be an appropriate apportionment factor because assets are a major income-producing factor.[187] Nevertheless, there are several practical problems in using assets. It is difficult to measure the value of assets.[188] Valuations may be market values, but it would be costly and imprecise to attempt to determine such values for assets. If identical or similar assets are not traded by independent parties, the value of assets suffers from the problem of lack of comparables. One approach is to use the International Financial Reporting Standards to determine market values and an alternative approach is to use historical costs. Regardless of the method, the cost of valuing assets is a significant challenge in formulary apportionment.

The key asset of many large MNEs is high-value and unique intangibles.[189] Intangibles are problematic. It is difficult to allocate certain intangibles to one jurisdiction and valuing them is even more difficult as they are rarely traded between independent parties.[190] One approach is to base the value of intangibles on the cost of creating and maintaining an intangible.[191] The obvious limitation of this approach is that the market value of an intangible will be significantly greater than the cost of creating and maintaining the intangible.[192]

184. European Commission, Taxation Papers, *supra* n. 169, at p. 47.
185. *Id.*
186. *Id.*
187. European Commission, Taxation Papers, *supra* n. 169, at, p. 49.
188. *Id.*
189. European Commission, Taxation Papers, *supra* n. 169, at p. 51.
190. *Id.* pp. 50–51.
191. *Id.* p. 50.
192. *Id.*

V CONCLUSION

The OECD Transactional Profit Split Method report on the transactional profit split method is detailed and sets out the circumstances in which the transactional profit split method may be the most appropriate method. In comparison, the UN Manual provides more limited guidance on the transactional profit split method. One difference between the two methods is the extensive threshold requirements set out in the OECD Transactional Profit Split Method report requiring the associated enterprises to be highly integrated, to both make unique and valuable contributions and to share the same or closely related economically significant risks.

There is some overlap between the transactional profit split method and formulary apportionment. The transactional profit split method under the UN and OECD approaches enables departure from the need to seek comparable transactions, which are very unlikely to be available. The Achilles heel of the arm's-length principle is the costly and challenging search for comparable transactions for benchmarking purposes in some situations. The transactional profit split method under both the UN and OECD approaches provides the scope for the use of a flexible formula to allocate profits on a case-by-case basis between associated enterprises once the appropriate factors have been identified and the relative weighting determined. Nevertheless, the transactional profit split method is rarely likely to be the most appropriate method under the OECD Transactional Profit Split Method report because of the threshold requirements.

The OECD/G20 Inclusive Framework's 'Unified Approach' proposal to allocate certain profits of MNEs using highly digitalized business models to market jurisdictions using formulaic methods is a significant development as it reflects a departure from strict adherence to the arm's-length principle. This is a significant development for allocating profits of MNEs using highly digitalized business models to market jurisdictions in the twenty-first century. Nevertheless, challenges remain for the Inclusive Framework to establish a consensus that is also acceptable to the US which is not an Inclusive Framework member.

SELECTED BIBLIOGRAPHY

AVI-YONAH REUVEN S. / CLAUSING KIMBERLY A. / DURST MICHAEL C., Allocating Business Profits for Tax Purposes: A Proposal to Adapt a Formulary Profit Split, in: Florida Tax Review 2009/497.

BLAY PAUL A., Reviving Transfer Pricing Enforcement Through Formulary Apportionment, in: Tax Development Journal 2017/28.

BREAN DONALD J.S. / BIRD RICHARD M., The Interjurisdictional Allocation of Income and the Unitary Taxation Debate, in: Canadian Tax Journal 1986/34.

BRUNER JENNIFER / RASSIER DYLAN G. / RUHL KIM J., Multinational Profit Shifting and Measures Throughout Economic Accounts, in: National Bureau of Economic Research 2018, Working Paper No. 24915.

BRAUNER YARIV, Formula Based Transfer Pricing, in: Intertax 2014/10.

CLAUSING KIMBERLY A., The U.S. State Experience under Formulary Apportionment: Are There Any Lessons for International Reform?, in: National Tax Journal, June 2016/69.

CLAUSING KIMBERLY A., The Effect of Profit Shifting on the Corporate Tax Base in the United States and Beyond, in National Tax Journal, December 2016/69.

DURST MICHAEL C., The Tax Policy Outlook for Developing Countries: Reflections on International Formulary Apportionment, in: ICTD Working Paper 2015/32.

FLEMING J. CLIFTON / PERONI ROBERT J. / SHEA STEPHEN E., Formulary Apportionment in the U.S. International Income Tax System: Putting Lipstick on a Pig?, in: Michigan Journal of International Law 2014/1.

HELLERSTEIN JEROME R. / HELLERSTEIN WALTER, State Taxation, 3rd edition, Valhalla 1998.

HELLERSTEIN WALTER, The Case for Formulary Apportionment, in: International Transfer Pricing Journal May 2005/12.

JOHNSTON STEPHANIE SOONG, OECD Makes Headway on Long-Term Answers to Tax Digital Economy, in Tax Notes International, September 2018/91.

KOBETSKY MICHAEL, International Taxation of Permanent Establishments: Principles and Policy, 2011.

LI JINYAN, Global Profit Split: An Evolutionary Approach to International Income Allocation, in: Canadian Tax Journal 2002/823.

MUSGRAVE R.A. / MUSGRAVE P.B., Inter-Nation Equity, in BIRD M. RICHARD / HEAD G. JOHN (eds.), Modern Fiscal Issues: Essays in Honor of Carl S. Shoup, Toronto 1972.

SCHÄFER ANNE / SPENGEL CHRISTOPH, The Impact of ICT on Profit Allocation Within Multinational Groups: Arm's Length Pricing or Formula Apportionment?, Zentrum für Europäische Wirtschaftsforschung Discussion Papers No. 03-53, 2003.

US General Accounting Office, International Taxation, Problems Persist in Determining Tax Effects of Intercompany Prices (1992).

PART V Countries Experience

CHAPTER 12

Countries Experience: Status Quo and Likely Evolutions – France

Bruno Gibert

I INTRODUCTION

1 Legal Framework

In France, there is no specific legislative provision detailing the transfer pricing methodology. Transfer pricing methodology is derived from the general legal provision set forth in Article 57 of the French Tax Code on transfer pricing, as interpreted by case law and commented in the French tax administration (FTA) guidelines (BOI-BIC-BASE-80-10-10-20140218, n° 130 to 200). In substance, the FTA guidelines on transfer pricing methodology are aligned with (Organisation for Economic Co-operation and Development) OECD principles. However, Article 57 explicitly allows the use of profit-based transfer pricing methods (§4).

2 Transfer Pricing Method Selection

The profit split method (hereinafter: 'PSM') is referred to by the FTA guidelines as being the most reliable method where projects or activities within a group are highly integrated and it is not possible to determine or justify a valuation for each operation.

The guidelines also indicate that such method can also be used where traditional methods cannot be used because of a lack of reliable independent comparables, or where both parties to a transaction make unique and valuable contributions. They specify that 'the method shall only be used as a last recourse, which requires to have first demonstrated that the other methods are not relevant. It is very intuitive, but it is useful for validating the consistency of the results obtained using the main method employed to set transfer prices'.[1]

II PRACTICAL APPLICATION OF THE PSM IN FRANCE

At the local level, the tendency to resort to the PSM by the FTA is developing in the context of tax audits. As a comparison, among taxpayers, the use of the method seems to remain stable and limited.

1 Application of the PSM in Designing the Group Transfer Pricing Policy

Given that it is a two-sided method, resorting to the PSM requires more time and resources than applying a one-sided method. It is, therefore, more expensive for the taxpayers and also for the FTA. In terms of efficiency, the PSM appears to be the method favoured by taxpayers only if the specificities of the transaction demonstrate that the PSM is the most appropriate method in accordance with the OECD Transfer Pricing Guidelines (hereinafter: 'OECD TPG'). This refers to cases of unique and valuable contributions (notably with respect to intellectual property), highly integrated business operations or risk-sharing.

According to our information, the PSM is used in France, but not on a large scale to date. The evolution of the OECD Guidance applicable to the PSM may lead taxpayers to review the basis of their transfer pricing method to ensure that it is still in line with the OECD TPG. In particular, the value chain analysis could lead taxpayers to investigate this option; we have had some signs in this direction but which are to be confirmed.

2 The Operators' Experience When Liaising with the FTA: Audits

To date, to our knowledge, there have been only a few reassessments of taxpayers applying the PSM by the FTA. Further, we are not aware of FTA reassessments based upfront on the PSM. As mentioned above, the application of the PSM is expensive for the FTA. It also requires that the FTA has at its disposal all necessary factual and financial information to elaborate the PSM. The lack of reliable information in that respect may finally deter the FTA from resorting to this method. We have recently been confronted by such a situation where the FTA indicated that according to them, the PSM would be the best method, but they finally renounced given the workload involved and the difficulty to obtain the necessary information.

1. BOI-BIC-BASE-80-10-10-20140218, n° 190, last sentence: '*Cette méthode ne doit être utilisée qu'en dernier recours, ce qui suppose d'avoir démontré que les autres méthodes ne sont pas pertinentes. Très intuitive, elle est toutefois utile pour valider a posteriori la cohérence des résultats obtenus à l'aide de la méthode principale utilisée pour fixer les prix de transfert.*'

From our experience, when a PSM was audited by the FTA, the method itself was not challenged but the conditions under which the method was applied (how the profits were split, as well as splitting factors) were challenged on the basis of the functional analysis performed by the taxpayer and the economic studies carried out. The audit of a PSM leads to an in-depth review of the taxpayer's transfer pricing documentation and prolonged exchanges between the FTA and the taxpayer. The FTA may also request the taxpayer to provide it with a study by an independent expert justifying the PSM applied, notably through a value chain analysis.

A recent information report filed on 12 September 2018 by the French Finance Commission before the National Assembly concluding on an information mission relating to the international tax evasion of enterprises[2] analysed the opportunity for the FTA to use the PSM more frequently. The report emphasized that, in line with a former report from the General Inspectorate for Finance dated March 2013,[3] the FTA should apply the PSM more frequently when it appears to be appropriate regarding the organization and business model of the group audited. It specified that the aim is not to systematize the use of the PSM but to encourage its use when it is justified, in place of methods which would be less appropriate with regards to the facts of the case. The report added that there is indeed much interest in such approach for enterprises and tax revenues, given that: (i) for enterprises, the use of the PSM would provide tax certainty and reduce the risk of double taxation; (ii) for the FTA, the use of a more appropriate method would strengthen the reassessments performed and limit the risk of contentious cancellation; and (iii) for tax revenues, the PSM would appear to be more interesting from a budgetary point of view.

In future, the FTA may therefore tend to apply the PSM more frequently. However, even if the access to information by the FTA has significantly improved, it may still have to face the barrier of necessary factual and financial information to build the method in the specific case of a taxpayer (e.g., the country-by-country report and transfer pricing documentation would not provide sufficient information in that respect).

3 The Operators' Experience When Liaising with the FTA: APA Procedures and MAPs

In France, the PSM is mainly used by taxpayers intending to conclude an advance pricing agreement (hereinafter: 'APA'). The reason why there have been few tax reassessments of a PSM to date in France is thus most probably also linked to the number of APAs (bilateral or multilateral) concluded to secure the PSM applied by a taxpayer.

2. *Rapport d'information déposé par la Commission des finances, de l'économie générale et du contrôle budgétaire en conclusion des travaux d'une mission d'information relative à l'évasion fiscale internationale des entreprises, présenté par Madame Bénédicte Peyrol et Monsieur Jean-François Parigi et enregistré à la Présidence de l'Assemblée nationale le 12 septembre 2018*, pp. 98-99.
3. IGF, *Mission de comparaison internationale sur la lutte contre l'évasion fiscale via les échanges économiques et financiers intra-groupe, mars 2013*, p. 16.

In case of a PSM tax audit leading to a tax reassessment, the taxpayer will generally initiate a mutual agreement procedure (hereinafter: 'MAP') to resolve the double taxation. In such a situation, the MAP can serve as a basis for the conclusion of an APA (bilateral or multilateral) under the same transfer pricing conditions as the MAP. The APA shall only be applicable for the future, as France does not provide for retroactive APAs.

Given its nature and complexity, the application of the PSM in future in France will probably rely on the same existing trend: it shall mainly be addressed by both taxpayers and the FTA in the context of APAs.

ANNEX 1 LEGAL FRAMEWORK

French Legal Provisions

Article 57 of the French Tax Code

ANNEX 2 RELEVANT REGULATIONS AND CASE LAW

FTA Guidelines

BOI-BIC-BASE-80-10-10-20140218, n°190

French Transfer Pricing Case Law Referring to Methodology

Administrative Court of Appeal of Versailles, 5 May 2009, N° 08VE02411, 3th and 5th chambres, *Man Camions et Bus*
Administrative Court of Appeal of Versailles, 5 December 2011, N° 10VE02491, 6th chambre, *Unilever France holdings*
Conseil d'Etat, 8th-3rd chambres réunies, 6 June 2018, N° 409645 and N° 409647, *SCS General Electric Medical Systems*

CHAPTER 13

Countries Experience: Status Quo and Likely Evolutions – Germany

Xaver Ditz

I INTRODUCTION

1 Legal Framework

German tax law lists suitable transfer pricing methods in section 1(3) of the Foreign Tax Act (hereinafter: 'FTA'; '*Außensteuergesetz*'). Additional guidance on the applicability of transfer pricing methods is provided by administrative guidelines. The most important regulations regarding transfer pricing methods are the Administrative Guidelines for the Examination of Income Allocation in the Case of Internationally Related Enterprises (hereinafter: 'Transfer Pricing Principles') of 23 February 1983 (*Grundsätze für die Prüfung der Einkunftsabgrenzung bei international verbundenen Unternehmen*) and the Administrative Guidelines for the Examination of Income Allocation between Associated Parties with Cross-Border Business Relations with Respect to Determination and Cooperation Duties, Adjustments and Mutual Agreement and EU Arbitration Procedures (hereinafter: 'Procedural Principles') of 12 April 2005 (*Grundsätze für die Prüfung der Einkunftsabgrenzung zwischen nahestehenden Personen mit grenzüberschreitenden Geschäftsbeziehungen in Bezug auf Ermittlungs- und Mitwirkungspflichten, Berichtigungen sowie auf Verständigungs- und EU-Schiedsverfahren*). While tax laws are binding for taxpayers *and* tax authorities, administrative guidelines are, in principle, only binding for tax authorities. In practice, however, administrative guidelines are more or less treated as binding for both parties, as taxpayers must explain whenever they intend to differ from the administrative interpretation of the rules. Also, administrative guidelines, in fact, govern transfer pricing issues due to their extensive guidance in comparison to other sources.

In line with the (Organisation for Economic Co-operation and Development) OECD Transfer Pricing Guidelines (hereinafter: 'OECD TPG'), the arm's-length principle forms the basis for transfer pricing regulations in German tax law.[1] The arm's-length principle was introduced into German tax law with section 1 FTA in 1972, which partly corresponds to Article 9 of the OECD Model Tax Convention. However, despite the similarity between the FTA and the Model Tax Convention, Germany has not formally implemented the OECD TPG into national law, which is why - technically - these cannot be used directly as an argument in transfer pricing disputes. Germany nevertheless accepts the OECD TPG as an interpretation as long as they are not contradictory to domestic tax law.[2]

II TRANSFER PRICING METHOD SELECTION

Section 1(3), first sentence, FTA mentions only the traditional transfer pricing methods, i.e., the comparable uncontrolled price method (CUP), the resale price method (RPM) and the cost-plus method (CPM). German tax law prefers the CUP method for intercompany supplies, the RPM method for distribution entities[3] and the CPM method for the provision of intercompany services.[4] The CUP method is often applied using hypothetical calculations based on the specific differences between an intercompany transfer and a (partly) comparable third-party transfer. Although traditional methods are regarded as preferable (hierarchy of methods), section 1(3), second sentence, FTA also allows for 'other methods' in cases where the traditional methods cannot be applied.

The German administrative guidelines, which follow the OECD TPG quite closely, do allow for the application of the transactional net margin method (TNMM) and the profit split method, considering them 'other methods'. Section 3.4.10.3(c) of the Procedural Principles mentions the profit split method as an acceptable procedure where the traditional methods cannot be (reliably) applied, and explicitly refers to the relevant section on the profit split method in the OECD TPG 1995.[5]-[6] The Procedural Principles illustrate the application of the profit split method with the example of allocating profits between two or more entities acting as entrepreneurs within the same MNE group (e.g., 'global trading'). Unlike the profit split method (and the TNMM), however, section 3.4.10.3(d) of the Procedural Principles explicitly excludes the application of the comparable profit method for German tax purposes.

Besides administrative guidelines, standard German transfer pricing commentaries accept profit-oriented methods, such as the profit split method, and the TNMM. In

1. Section 1(1) FTA; Federal Ministry of Finance, Transfer Pricing Principles, s. 2.1.
2. OECD, OECD Transfer Pricing Guidelines for Multinational Enterprises and Tax Administrations 2017 (10 July 2017), OECD Publishing, Paris, https://doi.org/10.1787/tpg-2017-en [hereinafter: 2017 OECD TPG].
3. Federal Ministry of Finance, Transfer Pricing Principles, s. 3.1.3. Example 1.
4. Federal Ministry of Finance, Transfer Pricing Principles, s. 6.4.1.
5. Then, paras 3.5 et seq. OECD TPG 1995; now, paras 2.114 et seq. OECD TPG 2017.
6. OECD, Transfer Pricing Guidelines for Multinational Enterprises and Tax Administrations (June 1995), OECD Publishing, Paris 2015.

general, the profit split may be used where participants of one or multiple transactions share economically significant risks, e.g., in the case of closely integrated business structures, where both parties make unique and valuable contributions.[7] Although methods other than the CUP, RPM or CPM method may be rejected by the tax authorities for the determination of transfer prices in standard situations, profit-oriented methods may nevertheless be used and accepted to recalculate and support/supplement transfer prices that have been determined by applying traditional transactional methods. For example, profit-based methods may be applied to determining appropriate licence fees. Furthermore, when an activity or a function or elements thereof are transferred, discounted cash flow methods based on transferred profit potentials become applicable.

III PRACTICAL APPLICATION OF THE PROFIT SPLIT METHOD IN GERMANY

1 Significant Profit Measures

As neither German tax law nor administrative guidelines include more specific provisions on the application of the profit split method, commentaries and other literature sources[8] mainly refer to the guidance provided in the OECD TPG. Consequently, up to now, these sources refer mainly to the previous 2010 guidance. Experience shows that, in practice, the OECD guidance can be cited and is accepted for justifying the application of the profit split method. However, because profit splits are rarely conducted in German tax practice, as of yet it remains to be seen how the new guidance will be implemented in Germany.

The profit to be distributed between the associated enterprises is understood to be an operating profit.[9] In general, therefore, the EBIT (earnings before interest and taxes) is, therefore, used and adjusted where necessary. However, in individual cases where it is justifiable, it is also possible to jointly determine the gross profit and apportion it to the related parties involved.[10] This is the case, in particular, when it is difficult to allocate the operating costs incurred by associated enterprises to the transaction under scrutiny. In this case, each company must then cover its own operating costs using the gross profit allocated this way.

When applying the profit split method, it is furthermore necessary to clarify whether the split is based on planned profits (an *ex ante* approach) or on actual profits which have been realized (an *ex post* approach). According to the OECD TPG 2010, depending on the circumstances of each individual case, both the use of planned or

7. Baumhoff/Liebchen, in: Mössner et al., para. 4.292; Greinert, in: Flick/Wassermeyer/Baumhoff et al., § 1 AStG, para. 842; Greinert, in: Wassermeyer/Baumhoff, para. 5.124.
8. *See* e.g., Baumhoff/Liebchen, in: Mössner et al., para. 4.291 et seq.; Greinert, in: Flick/Wassermeyer/Baumhoff et al., § 1 AStG; paras 841 et seq.; Greinert, in: Wassermeyer/Baumhoff, paras 5.123 et seq.; Jacobs/Endres/Spengel, in: Jacobs, pp. 582 et seq.
9. OECD, TPG 2010, para. 2.131; now in OECD, TPG 2017, para. 2.162.
10. *Id.*

actual profits can be justified.[11] Experience up until now shows that in the German transfer pricing practice the splitting of anticipated profits can be considered the standard case, while a split of actual profits is not often observed. As the new guidance on splitting actual versus anticipated profits is more differentiated and seemingly links this decision to the question of which indicator for the application of the profit split method is present,[12] it remains to be seen whether and how this more differentiated approach will be adopted by German practice.

2 Methods

The allocation of profits is based on an analysis of the functions performed, risks taken and assets used by the associated enterprises, which can be taken from the functional analysis performed for transfer pricing purposes.

Still following the OECD TPG 2010, different approaches to profit splitting are mentioned in German literature,[13] in particular, not only the contribution analysis and the residual analysis[14] but also the method of capital employed.[15] However, because of their importance, only the contribution analysis and the residual analysis are discussed in more detail. These are also for the main part observable in taxation practice. For a contribution analysis, the profit from a transaction is determined and apportioned between related parties depending on their respective contribution or value added to the transaction in question. The contribution or value added is determined by means of a functional analysis, whereby the contribution should be determined, if possible, based on the value of a service or on the basis of actual market values.[16] During a residual analysis, the total profit is divided into two steps:[17] (1) In the first stage, each company participating in the transaction is granted a 'routine return' for its non-unique contributions. The recommendation is to derive the routine returns using the known traditional methods or the TNMM, i.e., by employing transfer prices derived from an arm's-length comparison. (2) The profit or loss remaining after subtracting the routine return ('residual profit') is then distributed in the second stage, taking into account the individual contributions of the associated enterprises, e.g., the use of significant patents, know-how or brands.

3 Valuation Rules in Practice

The practical application of the profit split method requires the selection of an allocation key. The recommendation in the OECD TPG is to select an allocation key

11. OECD, TPG 2010, paras 2.127 et seq.
12. OECD, TPG 2017, paras 2.158 et seq.
13. Baumhoff/Liebchen, in: Mössner et al., para. 4.293; Greinert, in: Flick/Wassermeyer/Baumhoff et al., § 1 AStG; Rn. 847 et seq.; Greinert, in: Wassermeyer/Baumhoff, paras 5.129 et seq.; Jacobs/Endres/Spengel, in: Jacobs, p. 583.
14. OECD, TPG 2010, paras 2.119 et seq.; now in OECD, TPG 2017, paras 2.149 et seq.
15. OECD, TPG 2010, para. 2.145.
16. OECD, TPG 2010, para. 2.119; now in OECD, TPG 2017, para. 2.150.
17. OECD, TPG 2010, para. 2.121; now in OECD, TPG 2017, para. 2.152.

which strongly correlates with the generation of profits.[18] Practical experience shows that a wide variety of allocation keys are used, including asset- or capital-oriented keys (e.g., invested assets, net working capital or intangible assets used); cost-oriented keys (e.g., research and development expenditure or advertising costs incurred); and employee-oriented keys (e.g., number of employees or working hours). Also, in practice, these keys are typically applied using the associated enterprises' internal data.

In addition, a number of 'rules of thumb' have been established in German transfer pricing practice. For example, the Knoppe formula, which attributes 25%–33.3% of the *ex ante* profits to the licensor, is commonly used to determine or validate transfer prices for licensing intangible assets.

Again, it is difficult to assess whether the refinements in the outline of the respective sections in the OECD TPG 2017 will have an effect on actual practice. It can be expected that at least in those sections where the updates include more specific provisions, e.g., by referring to concrete examples applicable in certain cases,[19] these updates will likely also be adopted by German transfer pricing practice.

SELECTED BIBLIOGRAPHY

Wassermeyer Franz / Baumhoff Hubertus, Verrechnungspreise international verbundener Unternehmen, 2014.

Schönfeld Jens / Ditz Xaver, Doppelbesteuerungsabkommen, 2nd Edition 2019.

Flick Hans / Wassermeyer Franz / Baumhoff Hubertus / Schönfeld Jens et al., Außensteuerrecht, Loose-Leaf, 87th Supplement, 10.2018.

Jacobs Otto H., Internationale Unternehmensbesteuerung, 8th Edition, 2016.

Vögele Alexander / Borstell Thomas / Engler Gerhard, Verrechnungspreise, 4th Edition, 2015.

Mössner Jörg-Manfred et al., Steuerrecht international tätiger Unternehmen, 5th Edition, 2018.

18. OECD, TPG 2010, para. 2.136/2.138; now in OECD, TPG 2017, para. 2.179/2.181.
19. *See* the significantly extended Annex II of the OECD, TPG 2017.

ANNEX 1 LEGAL FRAMEWORK

Section 1 Foreign Tax Act: Adjustments of income

(1) If a taxpayer's income from business dealings with foreign countries with a related person is reduced because the taxpayer's foundation for the determination of his income is based on other conditions, particularly prices (transfer prices), than those that would have been agreed upon between unrelated parties under the same or similar circumstances (arm's-length principle), then, notwithstanding other provisions, his income shall be determined as if it would have accrued under conditions made between unrelated parties. A taxpayer in terms of this provision is also a partnership or a co-entrepreneurship; a partnership or a co-entrepreneurship itself is a related person, if it meets the requirements of Subsection 2. For the application of the arm's-length principle, it is assumed that unrelated parties are aware of all essential circumstances of the business dealing and act on principles of a prudent business manager. If the application of the arm's-length principle causes any further adjustments than the other provisions, the further adjustments will have to be made in addition to the other provisions.

(2) A person is a person related to the taxpayer:
   1. if such person holds, directly or indirectly, a participation equal to or in excess of one-fourth of the taxpayer's capital (substantial participation), or if such person is able to exercise a controlling influence, directly or indirectly, on the taxpayer, or, vice versa, if the taxpayer holds a substantial participation in such person's capital or is able to exercise a controlling influence, directly or indirectly, on such person; or
   2. if a third person holds a substantial participation both in such person's and the taxpayer's capital or is able to exercise a controlling influence, directly or indirectly, on both of them; or
   3. if such person or the taxpayer, in reaching agreement on the conditions of a business transaction, is able to exercise influence through channels outside such transaction, or if one of them has an interest of his own that the income accrue to the other party.

(3) For a business dealing within the meaning of paragraph 1, 1st sentence the transfer price has to be determined primarily by the comparable uncontrolled price method, the resale price method or the cost-plus method, if arm's-length prices can be determined, which are fully comparable for these methods after appropriate adjustments regarding the performed functions, the employed assets and the assumed chances and risks (functional analysis) are made; different values form an arm's-length range. If fully comparable arm's-length values cannot be determined, limited comparable values shall be used after having made appropriate adjustments under the application of an appropriate transfer price method. If in cases of the 2nd sentence several limited comparable arm's-length values are determined, the range shall be narrowed. If the price which is used by the taxpayer, in cases of the 1st sentence is outside the

range or in cases of the 2nd sentence outside the narrowed range, the median is applicable. If limited comparable arm's-length values cannot be determined, the taxpayer has to perform a hypothetical arm's-length test in compliance with paragraph 1, 3rd sentence. The taxpayer has to determine the minimum price of the supplier and the maximum price of the recipient in consideration of functional and risk adequate discount rate (range of potential agreement) as a result of a functional analysis and internal financial planning; the range of potential agreement will be determined by the profit expectations (profit potentials). The price, which complies with the arm's-length principle with the utmost probability shall be used; if no other price is substantiated; the median shall be used as a basis. If the taxpayer's range of potential agreement is unfounded and because of this another range of potential agreement is the basis, it is possible to waive the income adjustment, if the taxpayer's underlying price is within the other range of potential agreement. If in cases of the 5th sentence a function including the corresponding chances and risks and the transferred or disposed assets and other benefits is relocated (relocation of functions), the taxpayer has to determine the range of potential agreement based on a relocation of the function as a whole (transfer package). In cases of the 9th sentence the determination of the transfer prices has to be accepted for all affecting assets and services and after all appropriate adjustments, if the taxpayer substantiates that no essential intangible assets and advantages are exchanged or transferred for use with the function, or that the overall result of the individual price determination, measured on the price determination for the transfer package as a whole, complies with the arm's-length principle. If in cases of 5th and 9th sentences essential intangible assets and advantages are object of the business dealing and the actual profit development differs substantially from the profit development that was the basis for the estimation of the transfer prices, it has to be assumed disputable that at the time when the deal was concluded uncertainties concerning the price agreements existed and unrelated parties would have agreed on an appropriate adjustment provision. If the parties have not concluded an adjustment provision and a substantial difference in terms of the 11th sentence occurs within the first 10 years after the transaction, for the adjustment according to paragraph 1, 1st sentence an appropriate one-time adjustment amount that amends the original transfer price has to be calculated in the year subsequent to the year in which the difference took place.

(4) Business dealings in terms of this provision are:

1. single or multiple related economic incidents (transactions) between a taxpayer and a person related to him,
   a) which are part of the taxpayer's or the related person's activity that Sections 13, 15, 18 or 21 of the Income Tax Act are applicable on or, in case of a foreign-related person, would be applicable on, if the transaction would be domestic as well as under participation of a fully liable taxpayer and a domestic-related person; and

b) which are not based on an underlying company agreement (a company agreement is an agreement which directly leads to a change of the shareholder's position);
2. transactions between a taxpayer's company and his permanent establishment located in another State (assumable contractual relationships).

If a transaction is not based on a contractual agreement, it is to assume that independent prudent business managers would have concluded contractual agreements or would assert claims on legal positions, which are taxation objects, unless the taxpayer shows a credible alternative individually.

(5) The provisions of Subsections 1, 3 and 4 are applicable analogously, if the conditions, especially the transfer prices, of a business dealing in terms of Subsection 4 Sent. 1 No. 2, on which the allocation of income between a domestic enterprise and its foreign permanent establishment or the determination of income of a domestic permanent establishment of a foreign enterprise based for tax purposes, do not meet the arm's-length principle and, therefore, reduce the domestic income of a limited taxpayer or increase the foreign income of a resident taxpayer. With respect to the application of the arm's-length principle, a permanent establishment has to be treated as an independent enterprise, unless the permanent establishment's affiliation to its enterprise requires a different treatment. In order to treat the permanent establishment as a separate and independent enterprise, the following allocations have to be performed in a first step:
1. an allocation of the enterprise's functions, which is exerted by the permanent establishment's personal (personal functions),
2. an allocation of the enterprise's assets, which the permanent establishment needs in order to perform its assigned functions,
3. an allocation of the enterprise's business chances and risks, which the permanent establishment takes over because of the functions performed by it and the assets allocated to it, and
4. an adequate equity (additional surplus).

Based on this allocation, the nature of the business dealings between the enterprise and its permanent establishment as well as the transfer pricing for these business dealings have to be determined in a second step. Sent. 1 to 4 are applicable analogously to permanent representatives. The possibility to create a balancing item according to Section 4g of the Income Tax Act is not limited. Sent. 1 to 4 are not applicable to business dealings between a shareholder and his partnership or between a co-entrepreneur and his co-entrepreneurship, regardless of the involvement being of direct or indirect nature according to Section 15 Subsection 1 Sent. 1 No. 2 Sent. 2 of the Income Tax Act; Subsection 1 applies for these business dealings. If a double taxation treaty is applicable and if the taxpayer claims that its provisions contradict Sent. 1 to 7, the treaty has only priority, as far as the taxpayer proves that the other state exercises its right to tax in accordance with this treaty and, therefore, the application of Sent. 1 to 7 would lead to double taxation.

(6) The Federal Ministry of Finance is authorized to regulate details of the arm's-length principle in terms of Subsections 1, 3 and 5 as well as details with respect to its uniform application, and to stipulate principles for the determination of an additional surplus in terms of Subsection 5 Sent. 3 No. 4 by decree-law, with consent of the Federal Council (*Bundesrat*).

ANNEX 2 RELEVANT REGULATIONS AND CASE LAW

Federal Ministry of Finance, Administrative Principles for the Examination of Income Allocation in the Case of Internationally Related Enterprises [Transfer Pricing Principles] (Verwaltungsgrundsätze für die Prüfung der Einkunftsabgrenzung bei international verbundenen Unternehmen), 23 February 1983, Federal Tax Gazette Part I 1983, p. 218.

Federal Ministry of Finance, Administrative Principles for the Examination of Income Allocation between Associated Parties with Cross-border Business Relations with Respect to Determination and Cooperation Duties, Adjustments and Mutual Agreement and EU Arbitration Procedures [Procedural Principles] (Grundsätze für die Prüfung der Einkunftsabgrenzung zwischen nahestehenden Personen mit grenzüberschreitenden Geschäftsbeziehungen in Bezug auf Ermittlungs- und Mitwirkungspflichten, Berichtigungen sowie auf Verständigungs- und EU-Schiedsverfahren), 12 April 2005, Federal Tax Gazette Part I 2005, p. 570.

Federal Ministry of Finance, Intra-group use of the company name (Namnesnutzung im Konzern), 7 April 2017, Federal Tax Gazette Part I 2017, p. 701.

CHAPTER 14

Countries Experience: Status Quo and Likely Evolutions – Italy

Aurelio Massimiano & Marco Valdonio

I INTRODUCTION

1 Legal Framework

Italian transfer pricing rules are dealt with by Article 110(7) of the Italian Income Tax Code,[1] which, as recently amended by Law Decree 24 April 2017, No. 50[2] (hereinafter: 'Law Decree'), explicitly incorporates in the law the arm's-length principle in line with the definition set forth by both the (Organisation for Economic Co-operation and

1. Presidential Decree 22 December 1986, No. 917. For a general overview on the Italian transfer pricing domestic legislation, *see* VALDONIO/MASSIMIANO/SEVERI, Italy, in Guide to International Transfer Pricing Law: Tax Planning and Compliance Strategies – 7th Edition.
2. Law Decree 24 April 2017, No. 50 (converted, with amendments, by Law 21 June 2017, No. 96) introduced important amendments to Italian domestic transfer pricing rules. Further to revising Art. 110(7), it modified the domestic rules concerning corresponding adjustments, which were previously only allowed by domestic legislation following the conclusion of a mutual agreement procedure (hereinafter: 'MAP'). The Law Decree introduced a new rule aimed at broadening the conditions under which corresponding adjustments can be recognized also on a unilateral basis (Art. 31-*quater*(1)(c) of Presidential Decree 29 September 1973, No. 600). More in detail, apart from the case of conclusion of a MAP, the new rule contemplates two further cases where a corresponding adjustment is allowed: (i) as a result of transfer pricing adjustments deriving from activities of international cooperation among tax authorities whose results have been shared between the participant states; and (ii) upon formal application by the taxpayer to the Italian tax authorities [hereinafter: 'ITA'] following a transfer pricing primary adjustment done in compliance with the arm's-length principle done by a foreign state (provided that such state has stipulated a treaty with Italy that provides for an adequate exchange of information). For further details on the issue, *see* MASSIMIANO/SEVERI, The New Italian Transfer Pricing Provision Concerning Unilateral Corresponding Adjustments.

Development) OECD Model Tax Convention[3] and the OECD Guidelines (hereinafter: 'OECD TPG').[4] In particular, the current wording of the domestic primary rule now establishes that the prices for intercompany cross-border[5] transactions should be determined on the basis of the 'conditions and prices that would have been agreed between independent parties acting on an arm's length basis and in comparable circumstances'.[6]

This reference to the arm's-length principle thus allows domestic transfer pricing legislation to be fully aligned with the OECD principles set forth by the OECD TPG. Following the formal introduction of the arm's-length principle into domestic legislation, the Ministry of Economy and Finance issued, on 14 May 2018, a decree setting out clarifications for the purposes of the application of the arm's-length principle within the context of domestic transfer pricing provisions (hereinafter: 'the Decree').[7]

3. OECD, *Model Tax Convention on Income and on Capital, Condensed Version 2017* (OECD Publishing, 2017) [hereinafter: OECD Model Tax Convention].
4. OECD, OECD Transfer Pricing Guidelines for Multinational Enterprises and Tax Administrations (OECD Publishing, 2017).
5. Article 5(2) of Law Decree 14 September 2015, No. 147, clarified that the provisions of Art. 110(7) of the Italian Income Tax Code do not apply to transactions occurring among Italian enterprises.
6. Literally, Art. 110(7) of the Italian Income Tax Code, as amended by Law Decree of 24 April 2017, No. 50, provides that: 'Items of income arising from transactions with non-resident companies that, directly or indirectly, control the enterprise, are controlled by it or are controlled by the same company controlling the enterprise are determined based on the conditions and prices that would have been agreed between independent parties acting on an arm's-length basis and in comparable circumstances, if such determination results in an increase of income. The same applies if the determination results in a decrease of income, according to the procedures and conditions set forth by Article 31-*quater* of Presidential Decree of 29 September 1973, No. 600'. By contrast, the previous wording of Art. 110(7) of the Italian Income Tax Code (in force until April 2017) referred to the so-called 'normal value', without any reference to the 'conditions'. The 'normal value' is a domestic law concept that is substantially similar to, but not entirely in line with, OECD standards. The 'normal value' is defined by Art. 9(2) of the Italian Income Tax Code as follows: 'Normal value ... means the price or consideration applied on average for goods or services of the same kind or similar, in arm's-length conditions and at the same market level, at the time and place where goods and services are purchased or rendered or, in the lack of it, at the nearest time and place. For the determination of normal value, reference is made as far as possible to price lists or tariffs of the person rendering the goods or services or, in the lack of it, to official lists, considering usual discounts.' The concept of 'normal value' remains within Italian tax domestic legislation but applies with reference to other matters, such as for the purposes of the determination of the value of in-kind transactions when they do not take place in a cross-border intercompany context (the concept of 'normal value' utilized for the purposes of exit taxation has also been replaced by the above concept of arm's-length value through the legislative decree No. 142 of 29 November 2018 implementing EU Directive 2016/1164/EU, as amended by Directive 2017/952/EU - the so-called ATAD1 and ATAD2 Directives).
7. In that regard, the Decree confirmed the willingness of the Italian tax legislator to be fully compliant with international best practices. The Decree further expressly mentions the references to the OECD Model Tax Convention, the OECD TPG and the Final Report on Actions 8–10 of the OECD/G20 Base Erosion and Profit Shifting Project, thus implying that such documents constitute relevant sources for the purposes of the application of the arm's-length principle, in line with international best practices. The Decree does not expressly mention the work within the European Union (and particularly the outcome of the EU JTPF work programme which also had a significant focus on the use of the transactional PSM in the EU) but, in all events, such work should also be considered as 'international best practices'. For further details on the Decree, *see* the article: Cappelleri/Cataldi, Guidance from the Italian Legislator on the Correct Application of the Arm's Length Principle: Alignment to the OECD Standards.

It should be noted that although this formal alignment of the formulation of the domestic transfer pricing provision with the OECD definition is of recent introduction, the position of the Italian tax authorities (hereinafter: 'ITA') (*see*, for example, the guidance provided for transfer pricing documentation requirements[8] or on the patent box regime[9]), and case law (namely Italian Supreme Tax Court[10]) is that it also fully refers to the OECD TPG as the driving guidance for the purposes of the application of the arm's-length principle in the past.[11]

2 Transfer Pricing Method Selection

The primary Italian transfer pricing rule does not expressly indicate the possible methods to be adopted for the purpose of setting arm's-length prices or for verifying compliance with the arm's-length principle of the conditions applied in an intercompany cross-border transaction.

Prior to the introduction of the Decree (*see* section 1 above), however, this topic was covered by the administrative practice of the ITA. A first reference can be found in Circular Letter no. 32/9/2267 of 22 September 1980 (hereinafter: 'the 1980 Circular') providing for guidelines on transfer pricing issued in 1980.[12] Such circular was mainly based on the 1979 OECD TPG and, with respect to the identification of the applicable transfer pricing methods, it followed a strict hierarchy of methods and, therefore, classified the profit split method (hereinafter: 'PSM') as a 'last resort' methodology.[13]

8. Circular Letter No. 58/E of 15 December 2010 on transfer pricing documentation requirements.
9. Circular Letter No. 11/E of 4 April 2016 on patent box regime.
10. *See* Decisions No. 22023 of 13 October 2006, No. 11226 of 16 May 2007 and No. 8130 of 22 April 2016.
11. In this respect, it must be noted that some of the guidance provided by the ITA in Circular Letter No. 32/9/2267 of 22 September 1980 (e.g., the reference to lender's market when performing a comparability analysis of intra-group financing or to the 'safe harbour' royalty rates provided for pricing at arm's-length the licensing of intangibles) were not consistent with the provisions of the OECD TPG. Such inconsistency created a number of difficult interpretative issues that, in part, are still valid considering that the 1980 Circular has not been repealed. In addition, it should be noted that over the past years, Italian jurisprudence expressed its preference for the CUP method in some decisions issued by the Supreme Tax Court (*see*, *inter alia*, Decisions No. 17953 of 19 October 2012, No. 22010 of 25 September 2013 and No. 24005 of 23 October 2013), also partially justified by the internal reference to the 'normal value' concept.
12. For further details on the issue, *see* Maisto, Tax Treatment in Italy of International Transactions between Affiliated Companies.
13. In particular, the 1980 Circular was the first comprehensive guidance on transfer pricing issued by ITA (formerly Ministry of Finance). As mentioned in the text, such circular was essentially based on the OECD report Transfer Pricing and Multinationals of 1979 (even if with some differences) and has nearly been the exclusive source for interpreting Italian transfer pricing rules over the past years. More in detail, the 1980 Circular listed the methods that could be applied for the purposes of determining transfer pricing rules by distinguishing among two categories: (i) 'traditional' methods (i.e., the traditional transaction-based methods), namely the comparable uncontrolled price method (CUP), the resale price method (RPM) and the cost plus method (CPM); and (ii) alternative' methods, i.e., the profit split method (PSM) and comparable profit method (substantially similar to the transactional net margin method). In the 1980 Circular, and with a following circular letter issued in 1981 (Circular Letter No. 42 of 12 December 1981, hereinafter: 1981 Circular), it was clearly stated that the traditional methods are the methods of preference where suitable pricing or gross profit data is available for comparison.

Nonetheless, as already indicated in section 1, the OECD TPG, as updated over the years,[14] continued to represent the main source of interpretation, in both in the ITAs' auditing practice and case law, and such reference was confirmed by the ITA both when issuing the relevant provisions for the purposes of transfer pricing documentation (where the 'most appropriate method rule' was first formally mentioned, *see supra* n. 13) and in the advance pricing agreement (APA) statistical report, last issued in 2013. In such latter document, it was indicated that the profit split was applied in 23% of the agreements concluded, implicitly confirming that the transaction profit methods have lost their 'last resort' status (as indicated also in the 1980 Circular) and may be used more frequently if they prove to be the most appropriate methods.

After the change of the primary rule with Law Decree 24 April 2017, No. 50, the Decree restated the entire topic and provided for a detailed summary of the criteria (fully in line with the OECD TPG[15]) for selecting the most appropriate transfer pricing method with respect to the circumstances of the case.

More in detail, Article 4 of the Decree, after detailing the mentioned criteria, lists the transfer pricing methods recognized by Italian tax law, which basically refer to those provided by the OECD TPG. In this respect, it is worth noting that even though traditional methods are still preferred over profit-based methods, the legislator (in accordance with paragraph 2.3 of the OECD TPG) 'softened' the hierarchy since the CUP, where the relevant conditions for its application are met, is deemed to be the most

Hence, a strict hierarchy of methods could be identified. The alternative methods were left to residual cases where reliable comparability information is not available or where the transactions are very complex, interrelated or involve the use of non-routine valuable intangibles or other value drivers. According to the 1980 Circular, the alternative transactional profit methods could be considered as checking methods of any of the three 'traditional' methods or when there is no possibility to apply them. For completeness sake, it should be noted that the 1981 Circular seems to open a bit more the possibility to use the PSM where it is possible to identify in the free market arrangements that are based on an allocation of the profits arising from a business activity. The 1981 Circular also makes a basic example where it is indicated that the enterprise that takes care of the entire manufacturing process should be attributed two thirds of the global profit, whereas the distribution entity should be entitled to the remaining one third. It must be observed, however, that in the practice of tax authorities and tax practitioners such position was quickly considered as obsolete and no longer represents a material point of reference for the purposes of the application of the arm's-length principle.

14. For further details on the issue, *see* Maisto, OECD Revision of Chapters I-III and IX of the Transfer Pricing Guidelines: Some Comments on Hierarchy of Methods and Re-characterization of Actual Transactions Undertaken.
15. As per Art. 4(1) of the Decree, the most appropriate transfer pricing method has to be selected by taking into account the following criteria: (a) strengths and weaknesses of each method considering the circumstances of the case; (b) the adequacy of the method taking into account the relevant economic conditions of the controlled transaction; (c) the availability of reliable information, in particular, related to third-party comparable transactions; and (d) the degree of comparability between controlled and uncontrolled transactions, including the reliability of comparability adjustments that may be needed to eliminate differences between them.

appropriate method provided that all methods can be applied with the same level of reliability.[16]-[17]

Should a profit method be selected when a traditional transactional method could have in principle been applied in an equally reliable manner,[18] the taxpayer has to explain the reasons why the latter had been excluded. In this respect, explanations about the reasons for which a certain method has been selected are always required for attesting the consistency of the results derived with the arm's-length standards.

As a last remark, it should be noted that Article 4 of the Decree specifies that in the case of an audit, the ITA must verify compliance of a controlled transaction with the arm's-length principle based on the method adopted by the taxpayer, provided that such method has been selected following the most appropriate method rule and the above-mentioned provisions concerning the use of alternative methods.[19] The Decree thus implicitly confirms that if the taxpayer has applied a method, the burden of proof is shifted to the ITA, which, in order to use a method different from the one applied by the taxpayer, must first demonstrate that the latter has been selected without complying with the guidelines provided by Article 4.[20]

16. The expression 'same level of reliability' basically recalls the 'equally reliable manner' concept provided by para. 2.3 of the OECD TPG.
17. As indicated above, over the past years, Italian jurisprudence expressed its preference for the CUP method in certain decisions issued by the Supreme Tax Court (*see supra* n. 11).
18. Some commentators have pointed out that the Decree does not include the wording of para. 2.4 of the OECD TPG stating that there are situations in which a transactional profit split is more appropriate than a one-sided method. The commentators who highlighted this believe that the absence of such specification can be interpreted as a resistance of the tax authorities against the application of the PSM. However, it is believed that this latter interpretation does not take into account the fact that the Decree does not constitute a complete transposition of the OECD TPG. As a consequence, the absence in the Decree of the examples provided by the OECD TPG in the mentioned para. 2.4 - demonstrating that under certain circumstances, transactional profit methods are deemed to be more appropriate than traditional transaction methods - does not mean that the Italian tax legislator is reluctant to the application of the PSM. Moreover, para. 2.4 is included in the translation of the guidelines made by the ITA, even if it has never been formalized.
19. *See also*, Provincial Tax Court of Milan, Section No. 3, 15 October 2018, No. 4604, Regional Tax Court of Milan, Section No. 3, 19 November 2018, No. 5005, Regional Tax Court of Milan, Section No. 3, 28 January 2019, No. 714 and Regional Tax Court of Milan, Section No. 2, 7 November 2019, No. 4698.
20. The wavering position of Italian case law has created uncertainties regarding which party must bear the burden of proof in transfer pricing cases. According to the Supreme Court jurisprudence, the burden of proof in transfer pricing cases primarily lies on the ITA (*see, inter alia*, Decisions of the Supreme Court No. 22023 of 13 October 2006 and No. 11226 of 16 May 2007). However, the are some recent cases where the Supreme Court concluded that the burden of proving that the transfer prices are appropriate lies with the taxpayer (*see, inter alia*, Supreme Court Decisions No. 15298 and No. 15282 of 21 July 2015, No. 6331 of 1 April 2016, No. 7493 of 15 April 2016, No. 13387 of 30 June 2016, No. 20805 of 6 September 2017, No. 214010 of 15 September 2017, No. 9673 of 19 April 2018, No. 28335, No. 28337 and No. 28338 of 7 November 2018, No. 898 of 16 January 2019, No. 9615 of 29 January 2019; No. 9615 of 4 April 2019; No. 2757 of 26 June 2019, No. 17511 and No. 17512 of 28 June 2019, No. 5645 and No. 5646 of 2 March 2020).

II PRACTICAL APPLICATION OF THE PROFIT SPLIT METHOD IN ITALY

1 Application of the Profit Split Method in Designing the Group Transfer Pricing Policy

As mentioned above, neither Italian tax law nor administrative guidelines include detailed provisions on how to apply the PSM; thus, the most comprehensive tool is represented by the guidance provided in the OECD TPG.

The absence of detailed guidance has increased the difficulties encountered by taxpayers and tax practitioners in the application of the PSM. The main difficulties experienced concern both the identification of the information necessary for the implementation of the method[21] and the concrete application of the method.[22]

Having said that, recent business practice experience shows that the PSM is typically used in Italy in certain specific business sectors, such as the financial services industry.[23] However, it is possible to see the selection of the PSM also in specific situations across several other segments, such as in the automotive industry, the construction industry (for complex construction projects) and the pharmaceutical sector or even in other industrial companies.

In addition, the PSM might be considered as the most appropriate method in case of profits to be split, on the basis of the key entrepreneurial risk-taking (hereinafter: 'KERT') functions, in a permanent establishment/branch structure (this frequently happens for banks and insurance companies and, more in general, in the financial

21. One of the most significant obstacles in applying the PSM is indeed the difficulty encountered in defining the degree of detail of the information needed to compute the appropriate profit split and in accessing financial information related to foreign affiliates (especially when the local entity is a subsidiary of a foreign group). In such cases, there might be constraints (legal restrictions or internal policies) that might limit the possibility for the parent company to share financial information of other group companies with the subsidiary, even if the subsidiary contributes to the value creation of the group; for these reasons a one-sided method is often preferred in consideration of its simplicity of application. With respect to the determination of the profits to be split, a second issue relates to the fact that in certain cases, segmented profit and loss accounts need to be established, typically involving information system constraints and subjective decisions as to the allocation of indirect expenses. This is why, to overcome such difficulties, it becomes advisable to discuss and agree on each and every case with the ITA in advance (e.g., by applying for an APA procedure).
22. If a residual profit split is being applied, certain challenges may derive from the distinction between routine and non-routine contributions, as well as local and global costs, and from the difficulty in ensuring that the same accounting criteria are used in the various jurisdictions. The 'right' answers will depend on the particular facts and circumstances of each business. Moreover, whatever industry is involved, the application of a profit split approach can entail significant data and definitional issues, with particular respect to the allocation factors. In this regard, the determination of the most reliable allocation keys often becomes a subjective exercise and, obviously, introducing subjectivity to the allocation of profits can foreseeably lead to diverging views by the interested parties, i.e., in confrontation with the tax authorities.
23. In particular, asset management transactions, where multiple individuals based in different jurisdictions share the responsibility for a particular trading book, are especially suitable for the application of the PSM. Profits in these cases may be split by relying upon certain business variables that are internally tracked for management reporting purposes, thereby mitigating significantly the uncertainty around potential challenges of the allocation keys.

services industry), where all the different offices make unique and valuable contributions to the related transactions and information on comparable entities might not be enough for applying any other method.

Regarding the method for application of the PSM, the residual and contribution methods are both used in practice. However, it should be highlighted that the contribution analysis is not easily applied in most of the industries since no sufficient information on profit splits between unrelated comparable enterprises is actually available. With particular respect to the financial services sector, the contribution analysis is commonly done on the basis of the criteria used, for management accounting purposes, to identify the value contributed by each phase of the activity (e.g., origination, back office, etc.).

In some other cases, the contribution analysis is conducted more on a cost-based approach basis[24] or with respect to the average salary per key person or on the basis of the bonus of key employees.

As a final remark, it must be taken into account that in order to apply the PSM and demonstrate to the tax authorities that the application of that profit split results in an arm's-length outcome from an Italian perspective, taxpayers need to undertake a detailed assessment of the contributions made by each party to the transaction with reference to the functions performed, assets contributed and risks assumed. That analysis needs to involve objective assessments, making reference, as much as possible, to evidence and not to rely on subjective assessments or assumptions (unless they are based on facts).[25] Particular care is required for tracing and justifying all the relevant factors that led to the application of the profit split.[26] This may prevent

24. For example, a multinational group, having an Italian exclusive franchisee for the group brand, applied a PSM using the marketing expenses incurred as splitting factor due to the unique and valuable marketing intangibles generated by advertising activities performed by the Italian entity. This approach is coherent with para. 2.181 of the 2018 Guidance on the Application of the Transactional PSM. By contrast, experience showed that the R&D expenses are not a proper driver for splitting the profits due to the uncertainty of the related results (it may happen that a relevant amount of R&D expenses incurred does not actually lead to a corresponding increase of the value of the intangible and vice versa) and the different timing gap existing between discovery/research phase, development and exploitation.
25. In this regard, the decision of the Regional Tax Court of Milan, Section No. 22, 15 November 2017, No. 4680 pointed out that in cases where the profit is split on the basis of an evaluation of the relative relevance of the functions, assets and risks to the value added to the controlled transaction, such evaluation should be supported by reliable objective data in order to limit arbitrariness. However, the decision was favourable to the taxpayer which applied the PSM in an unreliable manner.
26. Under Italian tax law, multinational enterprises are not subject to special documentation requirements with regard to transfer pricing and there are no penalties specific to transfer pricing violations. However, in case of adjustment of a taxpayer's taxable profit by the ITA, administrative tax penalties applicable to general violations do apply to transfer pricing (in most cases between 90% and 180% of the higher tax assessed as a consequence of the adjustment). Such administrative penalties are not applicable when the following two requirements are met: (i) the taxpayer has filed a communication with the ITA in which it has declared that it can provide appropriate transfer pricing documentation in line with the guidelines issued by the ITA; and (ii) during tax investigations by the ITA, the taxpayer provides it with such appropriate transfer pricing documentation.

potential audit that could otherwise challenge that the method has been applied in an arbitrary manner and not supported by proper evidence.

2 The Operators' Experience When Liaising with ITA: Audits

In the past, considering the quite limited experience of auditors on the determination of the value of unique and valuable contributions or highly integrated transactions, the application of a one-sided method was much more common (the selected method was generally the transactional net margin method, in the absence of reliable CUP information).

The trend has recently evolved; indeed, Italian tax auditors, during their audit activities on Italian companies (especially those having transactions with principals located in low-tax jurisdictions), tend to assess or estimate the overall profitability raised on the value chain by all parties involved and to apply, if possible, a profit split approach, often justifying the application of such method with the high degree of integration.[27] This approach follows specific guidance of the central authorities and, of course, echoes the outcome of the (Base erosion and profit shifting) BEPS Project.[28] In light of the above, nowadays, tax auditors that address transfers pricing cases regularly request the audited taxpayer to provide financial data (generally the accounts) of all of the parties involved in the value chain (or at least the more significant ones, such as the principal company)[29] and tend to use such information to: (a) test the appropriateness of the profit declared by the audited company in terms of a slice of the overall profit; and (b) in many cases to apply PSM in place of one-sided methods. The PSM, based on presumptive data, in some cases has also been used in the lack of information provided by the audited company (e.g., in cases where the audited company did not have access to the accounting information of the foreign company the tax auditors used information retrieved in their systems, such as value-added tax (VAT) returns).

27. In that respect, it is worth noting that the common parent organizations of multinational groups with line of reporting going beyond the legal entities is sometimes scrutinized by tax authorities for challenging the existence of a high degree of integration that requires the application of the profit split.
28. Circular No. 1/2018 of the Tax Police is of particular interest because it affirms that 'this method is likely to be used in cases in which the parent company is tax resident in Italy and can, therefore, provide evidence on the internal procedures adopted for the allocation of the group profit among the subsidiaries according to their participation in the value chain'.
29. Depending on the case, such type of request may actually exceed the powers of tax auditors since such information refers to a company that is not the audited company (in certain cases this may also raise legal problems or policy constraints where there are restrictions to deliver financial information outside the group in the absence of an obligation to do so). For this reason, in many cases, auditors request the information by referring to a general 'collaboration' approach, rather than as a real mandatory request, leaving the possibility for the audited company not to meet such request. That said, it is not uncommon – in a subsequent settlement scenario – that the failure to provide financial information on the other group companies might become counterproductive due to the fact that the ITA might take a very rigid approach or even withdraw from settlement discussions for the lack of information provided.

The increased use by the ITA of the PSM is also reflected by recent Italian case law.[30] Indeed, certain judgments show that the ITA tends to also apply the PSM in cases where there is a lack of information on the value chain or the taxpayer has not demonstrated the applicability of other methods.[31]

The experience derived from the audits on Italian companies showed that the ITA dealt both with cases having transactions involving unique and valuable intangibles and cases where they identified highly integrated business operations.[32] With regard to transactions involving unique and valuable intangibles, an important issue arises when valuation techniques are used in intercompany transactions involving intangibles. Indeed, the application of the valuation techniques by the ITA has often been inconsistent, varying from case to case.[33]

Referring to highly integrated businesses, it is worth mentioning that in certain cases, the ITA have first recharacterized the functional profile of the subsidiaries operating in Italy as having a more substantial/value-added role and, on the basis of such recharacterization, have then applied the profit split.[34]

The splitting factors, as already mentioned, depend on the type of business of the audited company. In some cases, the tax authorities have applied a weighting of multiple factors,[35] consistently with the new provisions of the Final

30. For the most recent PSM-related Italian case law, refer to: Regional Tax Court of Milan, Section No. 11, 22 May 2017, No. 2255, Regional Tax Court of Milan, Section No. 22, 15 November 2017, No. 4680, Regional Tax Court of Milan, Section No. 22, 17 January 2018, No. 1891, Provincial Tax Court of Varese, Section No. 2, 27 March 2018, No. 228, Regional Tax Court of Milan, Section No. 3, 12 November 2018, No. 5431, Regional Tax Court of Milan, Section No. 19, 19 November 2018, No. 5005, Regional Tax Court of Milan, Section No. 15, 14 January 2019, No. 1295.
31. *See* Regional Tax Court of Milan, Section No. 11, 22 May 2017, No. 2255, and, on the same case, Provincial Tax Court of Milan, Section No. 36, 5 May 2015, No. 3960.
32. The decision of the Provincial Tax Court of Milan, Section No. 17, 15 December 2015, No. 265 is of particular interest as it concerned an assessment issued by the ITA, which considered that the permanent establishment of a foreign bank was engaged in the sale of banking products. According to the ITA, this activity could be defined as a KERT function highly integrated in the business operations. The Provincial Tax Court upheld the appeal of the taxpayer, ruling that the activities performed by the permanent establishment could not qualify as a KERT function and therefore the profit split should not be applied by the tax authorities. *See also* the Regional Tax Court of Milan, Section No. 22, 17 January 2018, No. 1891 and Regional Tax Court, Section No. 3, 18 November 2018, No. 5431. As for the applicability of the PSM to transactions involving unique and valuable intangibles, *see* Provincial Tax Court of Varese, Section No. 2, 27 March 2018, No. 228 which considered that the PSM was not applicable as one of the parties carried out the full R&S function and coordination activities while the other party performed routine activities.
33. In particular, the approach used to determine the assumptions about growth rates, discount rates, terminal value, etc., may vary significantly depending on the office carrying out the assessment.
34. In those cases, the theory that the PSM would be applicable was based on the argument that the functional analysis performed by the ITA showed that the principal foreign company fragmented highly integrated functions across several group companies. Thus, the ITA claimed that the activities performed by each single Italian subsidiary of the group must be assessed in the light of other activities that constitute highly integrated functions of a cohesive business and which the other subsidiaries carried on in Italy. In such circumstances, the ITA disregarded the application of one-sided methods and selected the PSM as the most appropriate method.
35. In particular, in a case involving an asset management company, the tax authorities have weighted assets under management and employee compensation.

Report.[36] However, it should be noted that, in several cases, the ITA followed a mere presumptive approach for determining the drivers for splitting the profits due to the information asymmetries between tax auditors and taxpayers or simply conducted a quite subjective contribution analysis and weighing.

Another recent tax audits' trend showed more frequent use of the PSM during the tax assessment phase and, in particular, with reference to tax assessments that originally claim the tax residence of a foreign entity by alleging that the same is, instead, tax resident in Italy.

More in detail, during the settlement discussion, it has often been demonstrated that the elements on which the tax assessments were grounded could at most lead to a transfer pricing adjustment (being some functions of Italian related entity not properly remunerated) but they were not indicative of a deemed residence in Italy of the foreign entity.

Such a typical structure challenged by the ITA provides for a non-Italian resident asset management company that outsources various services (e.g., distribution, investment advisory, custody) to the foreign-related entities formally acting as service providers. The transfer pricing policy commonly structured by multinational groups operating in the asset management industry for remunerating those outsourced services provides for a markup (usually amounting to 5%) on the costs incurred by the local entity. However, during the assessment phase, the ITA often pointed out that, on the basis of the actual conduct of the parties, the Italian service company was not acting as a mere service provider but was actually performing investment management and product development activities. Indeed, the functional analysis of the transactions in place among the group entities has often shown that the local 'service' companies also supplied skills and know-how aimed at customizing and developing the products to be offered on the market. Based on the above, a large part of the profit generated at the level of the non-resident management company was due to the contribution of the local entity. Given, then, the supply of a valuable intangible asset by the Italian entity and the high degree of functional integration between the parties, the ITA deemed it more appropriate to adopt a PSM attributing the residual profit on the basis of proper allocation keys, i.e., the volume of assets under management managed by the parties involved in the transaction and the personnel costs incurred by the same parties.

36. Paragraph 2.170 states that 'Depending on the facts and circumstances of the case, the factor can be a figure ..., or a variable ... which could be calculated on the basis of a single profit splitting factor or a weighting of multiple factors.'

3 The Operators' Experience When Liaising with Italian Tax Authorities: APA Procedures

Italian domestic legislation provides for an 'APA' procedure[37] addressed to 'enterprises with international activity'[38] which intend to agree in advance with the ITA the most appropriate transfer pricing criteria and methodologies applicable to transactions carried out with related parties. Aside to that, within the context of the applicable international treaties, similar APAs can also be reached on a bilateral or multilateral basis.

In this context, the ITA released specific statistics in 2013[39] that show an increase in the use of the PSM in APAs executed in 2012 (i.e., 23% of total cases compared to 26% for previous years).[40] Although no statistics have been published for subsequent years, informal communications seem to indicate that the implementation by the APA Office of the PSM has increased in subsequent years.

This is also due to the introduction of the patent box regime in Italy, which in most cases (i.e., in all cases where a CUP cannot be identified) was resolved by recourse to a residual PSM approach.[41]

Based on available information, it may be considered that in recent APA experience, the conclusion as to the applicability of the PSM in an APA context is based on a process that is consistent with the OECD TPG.[42] This is also confirmed by the

37. Article 31*ter* of Presidential Decree No. 600 of 29 September 1973. Such an agreement is binding for the tax period in which the agreement has been made and for the four subsequent periods, unless changes occur in the relevant factual or legal circumstances, it may be renewed. After the expiration of the above-mentioned period, recourse to such a procedure allows the prevention of possible future conflicts between the tax authorities and the enterprise with regard to the computation of transfer prices or any other issues falling within the scope of the procedure.
38. As defined by Art. 1 of the implementing decree issued by the ITA on 21 March 2016.
39. Second official bulletin on APA of 19 March 2013.
40. The relatively frequent application of the PSM in APAs may be justified by the following arguments: (i) an APA procedure is characterized by a greater transparency between taxpayer and the APA Office compared to tax audits. Such difference, justified by the cooperative approach within the APA procedure, leads to a significant reduction of information asymmetries existing between taxpayers and tax authorities that accordingly facilitates the identification of proper splitting factors and therefore the correct application of the PSM; (ii) given that an APA is a complex and in-depth procedure, it is likely that taxpayers put forward to the APA Office the most complex cases where the applicability of the PSM may be more frequent than standard cases.
41. On the application of the method in the patent box procedures, *see* GUATRI/VILLANI, Le valutazioni per il transfer pricing degli intangibili.
42. In particular, the PSM was considered the most appropriate method in cases when there is a high degree of integration between associated enterprises that make unique and valuable contributions, as for example in the automotive or chemical industries, or in case of attribution of profits to a permanent establishment. An example of executed APAs providing for the application of the PSM relates to a case in which both the manufacturer and the distributor belonging to the same multinational group contributed to increase the value of the group brand, due to the high integration between the principal and the local entities which gave a substantial contribution to the definition of the strategic manufacturing policies and the strategies for acquiring new market shares. A contribution PSM was adopted through which the relevant profits accrued from controlled transactions were divided between the associated enterprises on the basis of the value of the contributions made by each of the associated enterprises participating in those transactions. The evaluation of such contributions has been determined as the ratio between potential

outcome of the procedures relating to the patent box regime. Indeed, in that regard, the ITA[43] confirmed that in most circumstances the most appropriate method for determining the pricing related to the transfer or use of intangibles is the CUP method and, if the use of such method is not reliable, the PSM.

SELECTED BIBLIOGRAPHY

CAPPELLERI/CATALDI, Guidance from the Italian Legislator on the Correct Application of the Arm's Length Principle: Alignment to the OECD Standards, in: International Transfer Pricing Journal, 5/2018.

GUATRI/VILLANI, Le valutazioni per il transfer pricing degli intangibili, 2018.

MAISTO, Tax Treatment in Italy of International Transactions Between Affiliated Companies, in: International Bureau of Fiscal Documentation, 1983.

MAISTO, OECD Revision of Chapters I-III and IX of the Transfer Pricing Guidelines: Some Comments on Hierarchy of Methods and Re-characterization of Actual Transactions Undertaken, in: The 2010 OECD Updates, 2011.

MASSIMIANO/SEVERI, The New Italian Transfer Pricing Provision Concerning Unilateral Corresponding Adjustments, in: International Transfer Pricing Journal, 1/2019.

VALDONIO/MASSIMIANO/SEVERI, Italy, in: Guide to International Transfer Pricing Law: Tax Planning and Compliance Strategies - 7th Edition, 2017.

operating profit of each single entity over the integrated potential operating profit of all the companies involved in the transaction, like the typical contributions determined within a joint venture agreement.

43. *See* Circular Letter No. 11/E of 7 April 2016.

ANNEX 1 LEGAL FRAMEWORK

Legislative references

- Article 110(7) of Presidential Decree No. 917 of 22 December 1986: 'Items of income arising from transactions with non-resident companies that, directly or indirectly, control the enterprise, are controlled by it or are controlled by the same company controlling the enterprise are determined based on the conditions and prices that would have been agreed between independent parties acting on an arm's length basis and in comparable circumstances, if such determination results in an increase of income. The same applies if the determination results in a decrease of income, according to the procedures and conditions set forth by Article 31-*quater* Presidential Decree No. 600/1973'.
- Article 31-*quater*(1)(c) of Presidential Decree No. 600 of 29 September 1973
- Article 59 of Law Decree No. 50 of 24 April 2017 (converted, with amendments, by Law No. 96 of 21 June 2017)
- Decree of the Ministry of Economy and Finance of 14 May 2018.

ANNEX 2 RELEVANT REGULATIONS AND CASE LAW

Circular Letters

- Circular Letter no. 32/9/2267 of 22 September 1980
- Circular Letter no. 42 of 12 December 1981
- Circular Letter no. 58/E of 15 December 2010
- Circular Letter no. 11/E of 4 April 2016
- Circular No. 1/2018 of the Tax Police

Case Law

- Decision of the Supreme Court no. 22023 of 13 October 2006
- Decision of the Supreme Court no. 11226 of 16 May 2007
- Decision of the Supreme Court no. 17953 of 19 October 2012
- Decision of the Supreme Court no. 22010 of 25 September 2013
- Decision of the Supreme Court no. 24005 of 23 October 2013
- Decision of the Supreme Court no. 15282 of 21 July 2015
- Decision of the Supreme Court no. 6331 of 1 April 2016
- Decision of the Supreme Court no. 7493 of 15 April 2016
- Decision of the Supreme Court no. 8130 off 22 April 2016
- Decision of the Supreme Court no. 13387 of 30 June 2016
- Decision of the Supreme Court no. 20805 of 6 September 2017
- Decision of the Supreme Court no. 214010 of 15 September 2017
- Decision of the Supreme Court no. 9673 of 19 April 2018
- Decision of the Supreme Court no. 28335 of 7 November 2018
- Decision of the Supreme Court no. 28337 of 7 November 2018
- Decision of the Supreme Court no. 28338 of 7 November 2018
- Decision of the Supreme Court no. 898 of 16 January 2019
- Decision of the Supreme Court no. 9615 of 29 January 2019
- Decision of the Supreme Court no. 9615 of 4 April 2019
- Decision of the Supreme Court no. 2757 of 26 June 2019
- Decision of the Supreme Court no. 17511 of 28 June 2019
- Decision of the Supreme Court no. 17512 of 28 June 2019
- Decision of the Supreme Court no. 5645 of 2 March 2020
- Decision of the Supreme Court no. 5646 of 2 March 2020
- Decision of the Provincial Tax Court of Milan, Section No. 36, no. 3960 of 5 May 2015
- Decision of the Provincial Tax Court of Milan, Section No. 17, no. 265 of 15 December 2015
- Decision of the Regional Tax Court of Milan, Section No. 11, no. 2255 of 22 May 2017
- Decision of the Regional Tax Court of Milan, Section No. 22, no. 4680 of 15 November 2017

- Decision of the Regional Tax Court of Milan, Section No. 22, no. 1891 of 17 January 2018
- Decision of the Provincial Tax Court of Varese, Section No. 2, no. 228 of 27 March 2018
- Decision of the Provincial Tax Court of Milan, Section No. 3, no. 4604 of 15 October 2018
- Decision of the Regional Tax Court of Milan, Section No. 3, no. 5431 of 12 November 2018
- Decision of the Regional Tax Court of Milan, Section No. 19, no. 5005 of 19 November 2018
- Decision of the Regional Tax Court of Milan, Section No. 15, no. 1295 of 14 January 2019
- Decision of the Regional Tax Court of Milan, Section No. 3, no. 714 of 28 January 2019
- Decision of the Provincial Tax Court of Milan, Section No. 2, no. 4698 of 7 November 2019

Chapter 15

Countries Experience: Status Quo and Likely Evolutions – Spain

Joan Hortalà i Vallvé

I INTRODUCTION

1 Legal Framework

The Spanish tax legislator has since the earliest stages of the Corporate Income Tax devoted a section of the code to address related-party transactions and their potential adjustments. The first Corporate Income Tax Law enacted in 1978 (*Ley del Impuesto sobre Sociedades*)[1] included in Article 16 the arm's-length principle,[2] the definition of related parties and the right of tax authorities to adjust related-party transactions which are not arm's-length, provided the adjustment does not result in an increase of revenues or a reduction of expenses.[3] The regulations (*Reglamento del Impuesto sobre Sociedades*)[4] also refer to the arm's-length principle, but there is no method defined or suggested, leaving to the taxpayers and tax auditors the effective application of the arm's-length principle to related transactions. Besides a reform in 1991, the Corporate Income Tax was completely redrafted in 1995.

1. Ley 61/1978 del Impuesto sobre Sociedades (27 December) ('BOE' num. 312, 30 December 1978, pp. 29429–29437).
2. '[C]*uando se trate de operaciones entre Sociedades vinculadas, su valoración a efectos de este Impuesto se realizará de conformidad con los precios que serían acordados en condiciones normales de mercado entre sociedades independientes.*' '[R]elated party transactions should be valued for Corporate Income Tax according to prices that would have been agreed in ordinary market conditions between independent companies.' A translation of current Art. 18 is included at the end of the chapter.
3. Note that the Spanish law adjustment of non-arm's length related-party transactions is an autonomous remedy that does not require recurring to anti-abuse rules.
4. Real Decreto 2631/1982, de 15 de octubre, por el que se aprueba el Reglamento del Impuesto sobre Sociedades ('BOE' nom. 252, of 21 October 1982, pp. 29017–29019).

On 1 January 1996, an entirely new Corporate Income Tax was enacted.[5] The new Law aligns Spanish transfer pricing with (Organisation for Economic Co-operation and Development) OECD Transfer Pricing Guidelines (hereinafter: 'OECD TPG') issued in 1995 and introduces the transactional profit split method (PSM) for the first time. However, the new Law still deviates in several aspects and areas from the OECD recommendations. First, and probably one of the most controversial differences, Spanish law did not include the transactional net margin method (hereinafter: 'TNMM'), leaving the 'PSM' as the last resort method when none of the traditional methods is suitable to check the appropriateness of a related transaction with the arm's-length principle. The transactional PSM could hardly play the last resort role attributed due to the specific transactional PSM information needs, leading tax practitioners, and even auditors, to rely on traditional methods using net margins (the sole reliable method when non-internal comparable exist and databases are required, a kind of disguised TNMM). Moreover, the wording of the Law suggested that only the tax auditors were authorized to readjust a related transaction, whereas a taxpayer was obliged to apply the agreed related-party transaction price regardless of its alignment with the arm's-length principle.[6] In addition, the tax authorities were only authorized to readjust a transfer price if the final outcome resulted in lower or deferred taxation in Spain but required the tax authorities to make bilateral adjustments to avoid double taxation.

The Law was developed by Regulations,[7] which make no reference to methods or other practical guidelines on the application of the transfer pricing, merely including two chapters, the first one (Chapter IV, Article 15) regulates the procedural aspects of the reassessment of a transfer pricing audit, and the second one develops the advance price arrangements (hereinafter: 'APA') programme for the first time in Spain (Chapter V, Articles 16–28). It is worth highlighting that Article 19.2 when listing the indents to be included in the documentation filed by the taxpayer(s) with the APA request expressly asks for a reasoned selection of the transfer pricing method (letter c), but also the distribution among the parties involved of the profits derived from the transaction to which the APA transfer pricing method suggested applies. We will come back to this concept later on, as it is a key element to understand the role of the transactional PSM in the audits in Spain.

A substantial reform of the Corporate Income Tax was subsequently introduced in 2006,[8] redrafting Article 16 of Ley 43/1995 to better align it with the OECD TPG. The new Spanish transfer pricing legal framework introduces TNMM (Article 16.4); taxpayers are also compelled to adjust non-arm's length related transactions (Article

5. Ley 43/1995, de 27 de diciembre, del Impuesto sobre Sociedades ('BOE' nom. 310 of 28 December 1995, pp. 37072–37128).
6. The Law stated that the tax authorities might value, within the statute of limitation period, at market price transactions between related parties: '*La Administración tributaria podrá valorar, dentro del período de prescripción, por su valor normal de mercado, las operaciones efectuadas entre personas o entidades vinculadas ....*'
7. Real Decreto 537/1997, de 14 de abril, por el que se aprueba el Reglamento del Impuesto sobre Sociedades ('BOE' nom. 98, of 24 April 1997, pp. 13084–13132).
8. Ley 36/2006, de 29 de noviembre, de medidas para la prevención del fraude fiscal, ('BOE' nom. 286, of 30 November 2006, pp. 42087–42118).

16.1.1°);[9] tax authorities should correct non-arm's length related transactions irrespective of the impact on the taxpayer's taxable base (Article 16.1.2°); introduces transfer pricing documentation pending of a further regulation development (Article 16.3), secondary adjustments (Article 16.8), and specific transfer pricing penalties, closely related to the documentation (Article 16.10). With regards to transfer pricing method selection (Article 16.4): traditional methods are preferred to transactional (but not within them: comparable uncontrolled price, cost-plus and resale minus are equally eligible); if none of the traditional transfer pricing methods is suitable, any of the transactional, i.e., transactional PSM or TNMM, are eligible.

Current Corporate Income Tax is ruled by Ley 27/2014,[10] which dedicated Article 18 to transfer pricing. It has not introduced substantial changes other than some technical improvements, such as no hierarchy of transfer pricing methods for application purposes (Article 18.4).

II PRACTICAL APPLICATION OF THE TRANSACTIONAL PSM IN SPAIN

1 Court Cases Addressing Transactional PSM

The number of court cases addressing the transactional PSM is very limited, which is consistent with the almost negligible application of this method in practice.

One might believe that when the Spanish legislator in the 1995 reform characterized the transactional PSM as a last resort method, it would have become popular and widely used. However, practitioners faced significant difficulties to apply it and relied on TNMM even if not included in the tax code, sometimes by forcing traditional methods to use net margins instead of gross ones or just directly invoking the OECD TPG as an ancillary source of law, arguing that the ultimate rationale of the Spanish legislation was the OECD TPG.

The Spanish Supreme Court ruled on 21 February 2017 (rec. 2970/2015) on this matter. The taxpayer, a Spanish subsidiary of a multinational group, was reassessed by the Spanish tax audit team (STAT) in 2009 for fiscal years 2003 to 2005 for its transactions with a Dutch-related party. The tax auditors understood that the transfer pricing policy was unappropriated and applied the TNMM to realign audited related transactions. The Court ruled that TNMM was introduced in 2006 and could be retroactively applied by the tax auditors to readjust related parties' transactions. It is interesting to highlight that one of the judges disagreed with the Supreme Court decision and expressed his personal view: he understood that the application of transfer pricing methods is a procedural rule and should not be governed, like substantial tax measures, by the retroactivity principle. More interesting from a

9. '*Las operaciones efectuadas entre personas o entidades vinculadas se valorarán por su valor normal de mercado. Se entenderá por valor normal de mercado aquel que se habría acordado por personas o entidades independientes en condiciones de libre competencia.*'
10. Ley 27/2014, de 27 de noviembre, del Impuesto sobre Sociedades ('BOE' nom. 288, of 28 November 2014).

transfer pricing perspective is that he qualified the taxpayer behaviour as non-cooperative, not attending information requests made by the tax auditors, crucial in applying the transactional PSM. The judge pointed out that the transactional PSM could not act as a last resort method because its application requires information from all parties involved and tax auditors might not always access a relevant portion of it.

Another case was ruled by the Central Tax Court[11] on 10 July 2008. In this case, the taxpayer group filed income taxes where the companies were all making profits whereas the common shareholder, an individual entrepreneur, was declaring losses for that activity. The tax auditor understood that none of the traditional transfer pricing methods was eligible and the Court confirmed that the lack of available external comparable data and the integrated activities performed by the entities audited justified the transactional PSM application, which placed all the taxpayers involved, including the shareholder, in a profit-making position.

2 Tax Audit Practice Concerning Transactional PSM

The transactional PSM has rarely been used by taxpayers and exceptionally applied by tax auditors. The difficulties inherent to this method are widely described in the literature and has been recognized by the OECD.

However, it is a common practice of tax auditors to rely on a simplified transactional PSM as a test to check the appropriateness of the results derived from the application of other transfer pricing methods, mainly TNMM. Most transfer pricing audits conclude in practice with an overall analysis of the taxpayer value chain, identifying the split of the group final net margin among the entities involved, to verify whether the Spanish members of the group obtain a reasonable tranche of that net profit considering their overall value creation.[12]

As already mentioned, this practice is even embedded within the Spanish legislation when requesting this analysis in the elements to confirm the documentation to apply for an APA.

3 Most Likely Development of the Transactional PSM in Spain

There is a common understanding that transfer pricing evolution following the (Base erosion and profit shifting) BEPS Project (hereinafter: 'BEPS Project') and, in particular, Actions 1 and 8 to 10 will derive in an increased application of the transactional PSM. The 2017 update of the OECD TPG already envisages transactional PSM emerging

11. The Central Tax Court is not properly a Court belonging to the Spanish judicial system, but a Court made of tax inspectors and depending from the Ministry of Finance, acting as the last revision body within the Ministry for a tax auditor decision before appealing to the ordinary courts of justice.
12. When applying such a 'simplified' PSM, tax authorities analyse the overall net return on sales generated by the group as a whole, then consider which are the activities performed in Spain to allocate a reasonable percentage considering the facts around the case (splitting factors would vary according to the taxpayer industry and the functions, assets and risks in Spain). The goal is not to fix an appropriate remuneration but rather to avoid an incongruent result.

as a preferred method. The digital economy players have difficulties to find among traditional transfer pricing methods an appropriate solution for allocation of profits aligned with the arm's-length. Neither does TNMM properly assist practitioners when facing a transfer pricing application to taxpayers with highly integrated value chains. One can argue that the updated 2017 OECD TPG is somehow less favourable to transactional PSM than the BEPS Project, most probably to avoid this method to gateway a formulary apportionment system.

The transactional PSM will continue playing a fundamental role as a second test used to check the validity of a primary test, as explained in the section related to tax audit practice with regards to the transactional PSM. The transactional PSM is the most intuitive and straightforward test to ensure that profits attributed to a certain jurisdiction are not negligible or excessive when framed within the value creation of a group.

Undoubtedly the information required to properly apply the transactional PSM is still a major objection to expand it, although the major hardness falls on the relative weight attributed to the two key-value boosters: either capital or human abilities, which is tainted of political connotations.

SELECTED BIBLIOGRAPHY

Calderón Carrero José Manuel, Precios de transferencia e impuesto sobre sociedades: (un análisis de la normativa española desde una perspectiva internacional, comunitaria y constitucional), Valencia 2005.

Cordón Ezquerro Teodoro, Fiscalidad de los precios de trasferencia (operaciones vinculadas), Madrid 2010.

del Campo Azpiazu Carolina, Acciones 8, 9 y 10: Alineando resultados de precios de transferencia y generación de valor, in: Various authors, El Plan de Acción BEPS. Una reflexión obligada, Madrid 2017, p. 219° ss.

Jiménez-Valladolid de L'Hotellerie-Fallois Domingo Jesùs, El método de la distribución de beneficios (profit-split) como mecanismo para atribuir beneficios en cadenas de valor integradas y su aplicación a la economía digital, in: Saturnina Moreno Gonzàles, Tendencias y desafíos fiscales de la economía digital. 1st edn, Pamplona 2017, p. 423° ss.

ANNEX 1 LEGAL FRAMEWORK

Corporate Income Tax Law

Article 18. Controlled transactions.

1. Transactions carried out between related persons or entities should be assessed at their market value. The market value is understood as the price which would have been agreed between unrelated persons or entities in free market conditions.

2. Parties are considered related in the following situations:

a) Party with at least a 25% participation in its partners or participants.
b) An entity and its administrators, unless the administrators' remuneration is for exercising functions.
c) An entity and the spouses or persons joined by relations of kinship, on a direct line or collateral, for consanguinity or affinity up to the third degree of the partners or participants, counsellors or administrators.
d) Two entities in the same group (according to the criterion established in article 42 Commercial Code).
e) An entity and the administrators of another entity, when both entities are in the same group.
f) An entity and another entity owning indirectly at least 25% of the share capital or own funds.
g) Two entities in which the same partners, participants or their spouses, or persons joined by relations of kinship, in direct or collateral line, for consanguinity or affinity up to the third degree, take part directly or indirectly in at least 25% of the share capital or own funds.
h) A resident entity in Spain and its permanent establishments abroad.

In the cases that the association is defined taking into account the association of the partners or parties with the entity, the participation must be equal to or greater than 25 percent. In relation to the mention of the administrators, will include the administrators de jure or de facto.

There is a group when an entity can be used to control another party in accordance with the principles established in article 42 of the Commercial Code, regardless of their residence and the obligation to present consolidated annual accounts.

3. The persons or related entities, in order to justify the transactions performed have been valued at their market value, must keep the specific documentation established by regulation at the disposal of the tax authorities, in accordance with principles of proportionality and sufficiency, such documentation shall have a simplified content in relation to related persons or entities whose net amount of the turnover, defined in the terms established in article 101 of this Law, is less than EUR 45 million.

In any case, the simplified content of the documentation will be applicable to the following transactions:

1. Transactions performed by taxpayers of the Personal Income Tax, carrying out an economic activity, to which the objective estimation method with entities in which those or their spouses, ascendants or descendants, applies Individually or jointly among all of them, have a percentage equal to or greater than 25 percent of the share capital or equity.
2. Transactions of businesses transmissions.
3. Transactions regarding operations of securities or shares representing the participation in the equity of any type of entities not admitted to trading in any of the regulated securities markets, or that are admitted to trading on regulated markets located in countries or territories qualified as tax heavens.
4. Transactions on real estate.
5. Transactions on intangible assets.

The specific documentation will not be required:

a) To the transactions carried out between entities that are integrated in the same tax consolidation group, without prejudice to the provisions of article 65.2 of this Law.
b) Transactions carried out with its members or with other entities that are members of the same consolidated tax group by the economic interest groupings, in accordance with the provisions of Law 12/1991, of April 29, on Economic Interest Groupings, and the temporary unions of companies, regulated by Law 18/1982, of May 26, on the tax regime of groupings and temporary unions of companies and companies of regional industrial development, and registered in the special register of the Ministry of Finance and Public Administration. However, the specific documentation will be required in the case of temporary unions of companies or comparable to temporary unions, which are subject to the regime established in article 22 of this Law.
c) Transactions carried out in the area of public offerings of sales or of public offers for the acquisition of securities.
d) In relation to the operations carried out with the same person or related entity, provided that the amount of the set of transactions does not exceed EUR 250,000, in accordance with the market value.

4. For the assessment of the market value, any of the following methods will be applied:

a) Comparable uncontrolled price method, comparing the price of the asset or service in a transaction between related persons or entities with the price of an identical asset or service or one with similar characteristics in a transaction between unrelated persons or entities in comparable circumstances, performing where needed the corrections necessary to obtain equivalence and consider the specifics of the transaction.
b) Cost-plus method, adding to the purchase value or production cost of the asset or service the typical margin in identical or similar transactions with unrelated

persons or entities or, failing this, the margin unrelated persons or entities apply to comparable transactions, performing where needed the corrections necessary to obtain equivalence and consider the specifics of the transaction.

c) Resale price method, subtracting from the resale price of an asset or service the margin applied by the actual retailer in identical or similar transactions with unrelated persons or entities or, failing this, the margin unrelated persons or entities apply to comparable transactions, performing where needed the corrections necessary to obtain equivalence and consider the specifics of the transaction.

d) Profit split method, assigning to each related person or entity jointly performing one or more transactions the part of the joint profit arising from such transaction or transactions, depending on a criterion suitably reflecting the conditions subscribed by unrelated persons or entities in similar circumstances.

e) Transactional net margin method, attributing to the transactions carried out with a related person or entity the net profit, calculated on costs, sales or the most suitable scale depending on the characteristics of the transactions, which the taxpayer or, where applicable, third parties might have obtained in identical or similar transactions carried out between unrelated parties, performing where needed the corrections necessary to obtain equivalence and consider the specifics of the transaction.

The choice of the method will take into account, among other circumstances, the nature of the controlled transactions, the availability of reliable information and the degree of comparability between controlled and uncontrolled transactions.

When it is not possible to apply the above-mentioned methods, other methods and valuation techniques that are in accordance with the principle of free market can be applied.

5. In the case of provision of services between persons or related entities, valued in accordance with the provisions of section 4, it shall be required that the services provided produce or may produce an advantage or utility to the recipient.

In the case of services provided jointly in favour of several persons or related entities, and provided that the individualization of the service received or the quantification of the determining elements of their remuneration is not possible, it will be possible to distribute the total consideration among the beneficiary persons or entities, according to some distribution rules that are considered to be rational. This criterion will be considered fulfilled when the applied method takes into account, in addition to the nature of the service and the circumstances in which it is provided, the benefits obtained or likely to be obtained by the persons or entities targeted.

6. For the purposes of the provisions of section 4 above, the taxpayer may consider that the agreed value coincides with the market value in the case of provision of services by a partner, natural person, a related entity and meets the following requirements:

a) More than 75 percent of the income of the entity comes from the exercise of professional activities and has the appropriate material and human resources for the development of the activity.
b) The amount of the compensation corresponding to all the partners for the rendering of services to the entity is not less than 75 percent of the result prior to the deduction of the compensation corresponding to all the members for the provision of their services.
c) The amount of the corresponding compensations for each of the partners meets the following requirements:
   1.º It is determined based on the contribution made by these to the good functioning of the entity, being necessary to state in writing the qualitative and /or quantitative applicable criteria.
   2nd. It shall not be less than 1.5 times the average salary of the employees of the entity that perform functions analogous to those of the partners of the entity. In the absence of the latter, the amount of the aforementioned remunerations may not be less than 5 times the Public Indicator of Multiple Effects Income.

Failure to comply with the requirement established in this number 2 in relation to any of the partners will not prevent the application of the provisions of this section to the other partners.

7. In the case of agreements for the distribution of costs of goods or services signed between related persons or entities, the following requirements must be met:

a) Related persons or entities that sign the agreement will have access to the property or other rights that have similar economic consequences on the assets or rights that are subject to acquisition, production or development as a result of the agreement.
b) The contribution of each person or related entity must take into account the forecast of profits or advantages that each one of them expects to obtain from the agreement in response to a criterion of rationality.
c) The agreement must contemplate the variation of its circumstances or persons or related entities, establishing the compensatory payments and adjustments deemed necessary.

The agreement signed between related persons or entities must comply with the requirements established by the regulation.

8. In the case of taxpayers who have a permanent establishment abroad, in those cases in which this is established in an agreement to avoid international double taxation, these apply, and will be included in the taxable base of those estimated incomes for internal transactions carried out with the permanent establishment, valued at market price.

9. Taxpayers may request the Tax Authorities to determine the value of the transactions carried out between related persons or entities prior to their performance. This request will be accompanied by a proposal that will be based on the principle of free market.

The Tax Authorities may formalize agreements with other Administrations in order to jointly determine the market value of the transactions.

The valuation agreement will take effect with respect to the transactions carried out after the date on which it is approved, and will be valid for the tax periods specified in the agreement itself, without exceeding the four tax periods following that of the date in which it is approved. Likewise, its effects could reach the transactions of previous tax periods provided that the right of the Administration to determine the tax debt by means of the timely liquidation or the final settlement of the transaction subject to the request has not been elapsed.

In the event of significant variation in the economic circumstances existing at the time of the approval of the Tax Authority agreement, this may be modified to adapt it to the new economic circumstances.

The proposals referred to in this section may be dismissed after the resolution period has elapsed.

The procedure for the resolution of the valuation agreements of related transactions, as well as that of their possible extensions, will be established by regulations.

10. The Tax Authorities may verify the transactions between related persons or entities and, when appropriate, make the corrections that may be appropriate in the terms agreed between unrelated parties in accordance with the principle of free market, in respect of the subject transactions to this Tax, to the Personal Income Tax or to the Non-Resident Income Tax, with the documentation provided by the taxpayer and the data and information available to him. The Tax Authorities will be bound by the said correction in relation to the rest of the related persons or entities. The correction made will not determine the taxation for this Tax or, as the case may be, for the Personal Income Tax or for the Non-Resident Income Tax of an income higher than that actually derived from the transaction for all the people or entities that have made it. In order to carry out the comparison, that part of the income that is not included in the tax base will be taken into account, since an objective estimation method may be applied.

11. In those transactions in which it is determined that the agreed value is different from the market price, the difference between both values will have, for the related persons or entities, the tax treatment that corresponds to the nature of the rents shown as consequence of the existence of the said difference. In particular, in the cases in which the association is defined in terms of the connection between partners or entities, the difference will have, in general, the following treatment:

a) When the difference is in favour of the partner or parties, the part that corresponds to the percentage of participation in the entity will be considered as remuneration of its own funds for the entity and as participation in benefits for the member. The part of the difference that does not correspond to that percentage, will have for the entity the consideration of remuneration of own funds and for the partner or participant of perceived utility of an entity for the condition of partner, shareholder, associate or parties in accordance with the provisions of article 25.1.d) of Law 35/2006, of November 28, on the Personal Income Tax and partial modification of the laws on Corporate Taxes, on the Non-Resident Income Tax and about the Net Wealth Tax.

b) When the difference is in favour of the entity, the part of the difference that corresponds to the percentage of participation in the same will be considered as a contribution of the partner or participant to the entity's own funds, and will increase the value of acquisition of the participation of the partner or parties. The part of the difference that does not correspond to the percentage of participation in the entity, will be considered as income for the entity, and of liberality for the partner or participant. In the case of taxpayers of the Non-Resident Income Tax without a permanent establishment, the income will be considered as a capital gain in accordance with the provisions of article 13.1.i).4.° of the rewritten text of the Tax Law on the Income of Non-residents, approved by Royal Legislative Decree 5/2004, of 5 March.

The provisions of this section shall not be applied when restitution of assets between the related persons or entities in the terms established by the regulations. This restitution will not determine the existence of income in the affected parties.

12. The verification of related-party transactions will be regulated by regulations, in accordance with the following rules:

1. The verification of the related operations will be carried out within the procedure initiated with respect to the taxpayer whose tax situation is subject to verification. Without prejudice to the provisions of the following paragraph, these actions shall be considered exclusively with the said tax obligor.
2. If against the provisional liquidation practised to such taxpayer as a result of the verification, the latter interposed the corresponding appeal or claim, this circumstance will be notified to the other persons or related entities affected, in order that they may appear in the corresponding procedure and present the appropriate allegations.

   Once the appropriate terms have elapsed without the taxpayer having lodged an appeal or claim, the liquidation practiced to the other affected persons or related entities will be notified, so that those who wish may opt jointly for filing the appropriate appeal or claim. The filing of the appeal or claim will interrupt the statute of limitations of the right of the Tax Authority to make the appropriate settlements to the taxpayer and to the other persons or entities affected, to whom such interruption will be communicated, beginning again the computation of such deadline when the liquidation practiced by the Administration has become final.
3. The finality of the settlement will determine its effectiveness and firmness in relation to other persons or related entities. The Tax Authorities will carry out

the corresponding regularizations, unless said regularizations have been made by the concerned person or entity, in the terms established by regulation.

4. The provisions of this section shall apply with respect to the persons or related entities affected by the correction that are taxpayers of Corporate Tax, Personal Income Tax or Non-Resident Income Tax.
5. The provisions of this section shall be considered without prejudice to the provisions of international treaties and conventions that have become part of the domestic legal system.
6. When the verification of the value of the transaction is carried out within the verification referred to in this section, the provisions of section 2 of article 57 and article 135 of Law 58/2003 will not apply, of December 17, General Tax Law.

13. 1. Tax infringement constitutes the lack of contribution or incomplete contribution, or with false data, of the documentation that, in accordance with the provisions of section 3 of this article and its implementing regulations, the related person or entity must be in possession of such in case the Tax Authorities requested, when the Tax Authorities does not make corrections in application of the provisions of this article.

This infraction will be considered a serious infraction and will be sanctioned in accordance with the following rules:

a) The fine will consist of a fixed pecuniary fine of EUR 1,000 for each piece of information and EUR 10,000 for each set of data, omitted, or false, referring to each of the documentation obligations established by regulation for the group or for each person or entity as a taxpayer.
b) The fine foreseen in the previous letter will have as a maximum limit the lower of the two following amounts:
   - 10 percent of the total amount of the operations subject to this Tax, to the Personal Income Tax or to the Non-Resident Income Tax generated in the tax period.
   - 1 percent of the net amount of the turnover.

2. The following cases constitute a tax offence, provided that corrections are made by the Tax Authorities, in application of the provisions of this article with respect to the operations subject to this Tax, to the Personal Income Tax and Non-Resident Income Tax:
   (i) The lack of provision or the incomplete provision of documentation, or providing false data in such documentation, in accordance with the provisions of section 3 of this article and its implementing regulations, must be kept by the related people or entities in case the Tax Authority requires it.
   (ii) That the market value derived from the documentation provided for in this article and in its implementing regulations is not that declared in the Corporate Tax, Personal Income Tax or Non-Resident Income Tax.

These infractions will be considered a serious infraction and will be fined with a proportional pecuniary fine of 15 percent on the amount of the amounts resulting from the corrections that correspond to each transaction. This fine will be incompatible with the one applicable by the application of articles 191, 192, 193 or 195 of the General Tax Law, on the basis of tax bases that would have led to the imposition of the infraction provided in this number 2.

3. The corrections made by the Tax Authority in application of the provisions of this article with respect to transaction subject to this Tax, to the Personal Income Tax or Non-Resident Income Tax, which determine lack of income, improper obtaining of tax refunds or improper determination or accreditation of items to be offset in future declarations or net income is incorrectly declared without producing a lack of income or obtaining returns due to compensation in a verification or investigation procedure pending amounts of compensation, having complied with the specific documentation obligation referred to in section 3 of this article, it will not constitute the commission of the infractions of articles 191, 192, 193 or 195 of Law 58/2003, of December 17, General Tax Law, on the part of tax bases that would have given rise to the aforementioned corrections.
4. The fines provided in this section will be compatible with that established for resistance, obstruction, excuse or refusal to the actions of the tax administration in Article 203 of the General Tax Law, for the neglect of the requirements made.

With respect to the fines imposed in accordance with the provisions of this article, the provisions of paragraphs 1.b) and 3 of article 188 of the General Tax Law shall apply.

14. The market value for the purposes of this Tax, the Personal Income Tax or the Non-Resident Income Tax, will not produce effects with respect to other taxes, unless expressly provided otherwise. Likewise, the value for the purposes of other taxes will not affect the market value of the transactions between related persons or entities to this tax, the Personal Income Tax or the Non-Resident Income Tax, unless otherwise provided express to the contrary.

ANNEX 2 CASE LAW

Resolución del Tribunal Económico Administrativo Central (Spanish Central Tax Court Resolution) 1995/2006 de 10 de julio de 2008.

Sentencia de la Audiencia Nacional, sala de lo Contencioso-Administrativo, Sección 2ª (National Audience Court) Sentencia num. 59/2016 de 28 enero (rec. 78/2013).

Tribunal Supremo, Sala de lo Contencioso-Administrativo, Sección 2ª (Supreme Court) Sentencia num. 293/2017 de 21 febrero (rec. 2970/2015).

Audiencia Nacional, Sala de lo Contencioso-administrativo, Sección 2ª, (National Audience Court) Sentencia 102/2016 de 11 Feb. 2016, (rec. 89/2013).

Audiencia Nacional, Sala de lo Contencioso-administrativo, Sección 2ª, (National Audience Court) Sentencia 66/2016 de 28 Ene. 2016, (rec. 79/2013).

CHAPTER 16

Countries Experience: Status Quo and Likely Evolutions - Switzerland

Raoul Stocker & Patrick Schmid

I INTRODUCTION

1 Legal Bases for Corporate Taxation

A The Swiss Tax System

Legal entities in Switzerland are subject to taxation as independent entities. Independent means that they are taxed independently of the person who controls the entity. In Switzerland, multiple kinds of taxes are levied from entities, such as Corporate Income Tax (CIT), Capital Tax, Withholding Tax (WHT), Real Estate Gains Tax and Value Added Tax (VAT). In order to apply the principles of transfer pricing to an intra-group transaction, the following taxes are mainly to consider: CIT, VAT, WHT and Stamp Duties.

The Swiss federalism leads to the fact that entities are taxed on three different levels: federal, cantonal and communal. Depending on the respective tax, all or only some of the levels have tax sovereignty.[1] While only the federal tax authorities can levy WHT, Stamp Duties and VAT, the tax sovereignty for CIT and Capital Tax is split between federal, cantonal and communal tax authorities.

1. *See* STOCKER/RAAB, ch. T mn. 2.

B Adjustment of the Taxable Profit

a Hidden Profit Distribution

Switzerland has not implemented any specific transfer pricing rules as such.[2] Intercompany transactions between companies and shareholders or affiliated parties, however, must be determined according to the arm's-length principle that is embedded in the Federal Direct Tax Act (*Bundesgesetz über die direkte Bundessteuer*, FDTA) and the Federal Tax Harmonization Act (*Bundesgesetz über die Harmonisierung der direkten Steuern der Kantone und Gemeinden*, FTHA). As stated in Article 58(1) FDTA and Article 24(1) FTHA, the taxable net profit of a corporate entity consists of the balance of its income statement adjusted by commercially non-justified expenses and by revenues not credited to the income statement. Hence, the named articles constitute the legal bases for the tax authorities to correct a corporate entity's net profit as stated in its income statement for tax purposes, while they limit, at the same time, the correction to the commercially non-justified expenses and the revenues not credited to the income statement.

According to established and long-standing jurisprudence of the Swiss Federal Supreme Court (*Bundesgericht*, BGer) in connection with hidden profit distributions, tax authorities are allowed to adjust transfer prices if the following three requirements are cumulatively met:[3]

- a service is rendered without receiving adequate remuneration in return, such as the service is considered to be a withdrawal of the entity's funds as it reduces the entity's profit;
- the transaction benefits a shareholder or a related party of the shareholder and its legal grounds lie in the shareholding relationship, i.e., the benefit is directly or indirectly received, whereby it is assumed that the benefit is unusual and does not follow appropriate business conduct; and
- the disproportion between service and remuneration must have been recognizable to the acting bodies, such as it can be assumed that the preferential treatment was intentional.

Additionally, it is required that the disproportion between service and remuneration is obvious, which is why only large differences qualify for fiscal adjustments (i.e., 25% or more of the market value).[4] This requirement is not met, i.e., a disproportion between service and remuneration is not recognizable to the acting bodies if there is a

2. However, particular provisions exist for public-private enterprises acting in the public interest, which render services mainly to affiliated parties (Art. 58(3) FDTA). *See also* s. II.
3. DFT 82 I 291; DFT 105 Ib 84; DFT 113 Ia 25; DFT 140 II 88 (92), cons. 4.1 (recently with four, but substantively identical requirements); decision 2C_11/2018 of the Federal Supreme Court, 10.12.2018, cons. 7.2; decision A-103/2011 of the Federal Administrative Court, 21.9.2011, cons. 4.4; *see also* STOCKER, Potential Effects; BRÜLISAUER/MÜHLEMANN, Art. 58 mn. 222.
4. Decision A-103/2011 of the Federal Administrative Court, 21.9.2011, cons. 4.4; decision A-4091/2016 of the Federal Administrative Court, 24.1.2018, cons. 2.4.2; STOCKER/RAAB, ch. T mn. 21.

comprehensive, well-documented and plausibly justified independent transfer pricing study that results in a comparable remuneration in a comparable market.[5]

In order to assess whether or not a disproportion between service and remuneration of intercompany transfer prices exists, Swiss practice established the application of objective criteria (i.e., arm's-length principle), that are based on the OECD Transfer Pricing Guidelines for Multinational Enterprises and Tax Administrations (hereinafter: 'OECD TPG') due to a lack of specific regulations in the Swiss tax legislation.[6]

Mainly, shareholders qualify as recipients of hidden profit distributions. Swiss doctrine requires the respective shareholder to hold a controlling position, as he would not otherwise be able to cause a hidden profit distribution.[7] However, the Federal Supreme Court clarified that such controlling position does not require a majority stake.[8] Under certain circumstances, even a minority shareholder can hold a controlling position.[9] In addition to the shareholder himself, namely affiliated parties to the shareholder can qualify as recipients of hidden profit distributions. To qualify as such, they must especially relate to the shareholder (e.g., family connection, affiliated companies).[10]

b *Cross-Border Transactions of MNEs*

In the case of multinational entities (MNEs) that perform cross-border transactions, Swiss practice applies also the OECD TPG for assessing their intercompany transfer prices.[11] The OECD TPG nonetheless does not constitute treaty law or legislative decrees but are rather seen as guidelines for the interpretation of Article 9 of the OECD Model Convention (hereinafter: 'OECD Model').[12] Because no restrictions on the scope of application can be detected, Swiss practice applies the OECD TPG to all cross-border transactions, including those with entities in non-treaty states.[13] Analogously, the above principles also apply to transactions between the head office and its permanent establishments.[14]

Even though the Swiss legislator withheld in general from implementing specific transfer pricing regulations into the national tax legislation, there exist a number of administrative directives, so-called Circular Letters, that refer implicitly or explicitly to

5. Decision 2005-114 of the Federal Tax Appeals Committee, 8.6.2006, cons. 3 b) cc).
6. Decision 2C_11/2018 of the Federal Supreme Court, 10.12.2018, cons. 7.3 et seq.; *see* Circular Letter No. 4 of the FTA, 19.3.2004, regarding the taxation of service companies.
7. STOCKER/STUDER, p. 387.
8. DFT 115 Ib 238 (246), cons. 6 c).
9. DFT 115 Ib 238 (246), cons. 6 c): Namely, in cases where several minority shareholders act together in order to reach a common goal.
10. STOCKER/STUDER, p. 387.
11. Decision DB.2011.50 of the Zurich Tax Appeal Court, 29.6.2015, cons. 3 c) aa). As the OECD Guidelines are not geographically restricted, Swiss tax administrations apply them also to cross-border transactions with non-treaty states.
12. DFT 143 II 136 (149), cons. 5.2.3; Decision A-2122/2016 of the Federal Administrative Court, 31.1.2017, cons. 5.4.2.1; Decision DB.2011.50 of the Zurich Tax Appeal Court, 29.6.2015, cons. 3 c) aa).
13. STOCKER/STUDER, p. 387; STOCKER, Potential Effects, p. 210.
14. For the application of the AOA in Swiss practice, *see* BRÜLISAUER, Art. 7, mn. 462 et seq.

the determination of intercompany transfer prices.[15] In this respect, Circular Letter No. 4 of the Federal Tax Administration (hereinafter: 'FTA') of 12 March 2014 (Taxation of Service Companies) reminds the cantonal tax administrations to take into account the OECD TPG when taxing MNEs.

Among the administrative directives, some of them refer to safe harbour regulations. This means that the tax authorities accept a determination of transfer prices within a predefined range without any additional specific documentation or justification.[16] Taxpayers, however, are free to prove that their remuneration holds the arm's-length principle, even if it lies outside the safe harbour range.[17]

According to the OECD, no adjustment should be made if the remuneration of the controlled transaction (e.g., price or margin) lies within a certain arm's length range.[18] Swiss jurisdiction and doctrine have confirmed in the most recent cases that this concept also applies in Switzerland.[19] The Federal Supreme Court stated in its leading case that the arm's-length remuneration is not determined by one single value rather by a value between a maximum and a minimum.[20] In cases where the remuneration lies outside the arm's-length range, the adjustment, therefore, has to be made to the most advantageous value from the taxpayer's point of view.[21]

2 Retroactivity of OECD TPG

With the publication of the 2017 OECD Transfer Pricing Guidelines (hereinafter: 2017 OECD TPG)[22] and the Revised Guidance on Profit Split,[23] the question arises whether newer versions of the OECD TPG can apply with retroactive effect. It is the opinion of the OECD that changes and additions to the commentaries - and presumably the OECD TPG - are generally applicable to the interpretation and application of conventions concluded before their adoption, as they reflect 'the consensus of the OECD member countries as to the proper interpretation of existing provisions and their application to specific situations'.[24] Swiss doctrine and its jurisdiction, however, are inconsistent on

15. For example, Circular Letter No. 6 of the FTA of 6.6.1997 regarding hidden equity; Circular Letters of the FTA of 19-20.2.2018 regarding interest payments in Swiss Francs or in foreign currency between affiliated entities (updated annually); *see* Stocker/Raab, ch. T mn. 23 et seq.
16. For example, Circular Letter No. 6 of the FTA of 6.6.1997, *id.*; Circular Letters of the FTA of 19 and 20.2.2018 regarding interest payments in Swiss Francs or in foreign currency between affiliated entities (updated annually); Circular Letter No. 8 of the FTA of 18.12.2001 regarding international profit allocation.
17. Circular Letters of the FTA of 19 and 20.2.2018, *id.*, p. 2.
18. 2017 OECD TPG, para. 3.60.
19. Decision A-4091/2016 of the Federal Administrative Court, 24.1.2018, cons. 2.4.2.
20. DFT 107 Ib 325 (332), cons. 4.
21. Meuter/Studer/Stocker, s. 38; Brülisauer/Krummenacher, Art. 24 mn. 246.
22. OECD, OECD Transfer Pricing Guidelines for Multinational Enterprises and Tax Administrations 2017 (10 July 2017), OECD Publishing, Paris, https://doi.org/10.1787/tpg-2017-en.
23. OECD, Revised Guidance on the Application of the Transactional Profit Split Method: Inclusive Framework on BEPS: Action 10, OECD/G20 Base Erosion and Profit Shifting Project (June 2018), OECD Paris. www.oecd.org/tax/beps/revised-guidance-on-the-application-of-the-transactional-profitsplit-method-beps-action-10.pdf.
24. OECD, Model Tax Convention on Income and on Capital: Condensed Version 2017, Paris 2017, Introduction, mn. 36; Amendments to the articles of the OECD Model and changes to the

this topic and the Federal Supreme Court has not yet had the chance to eliminate this uncertainty.[25] According to a lower instance court's decision, however, the version of the OECD TPG has to be consulted that was in place at the time of the disputed facts.[26] In any case, the Federal Supreme Court stated that under certain circumstances, judges are allowed to consult a newer version of the commentaries, and presumably also of the OECD TPG. This is the case, for example, when the commentaries or OECD TPG contain no change to the existing regime but only precise or explain its meaning.[27] It remains to be clarified, however, whether a newer version contains a change to the existing regime or only a precision or explanation.[28]

II TRANSFER PRICING METHOD SELECTION

The comparable uncontrolled pricing method (hereinafter: 'CUPM') presents the most preferred transfer pricing method in Switzerland.[29] Besides the CUPM, the resale pricing method (hereinafter: 'RPM') and the cost-plus method (hereinafter: 'CPM') are also widely used. For service companies, however, one should know that the CPM does not necessarily present the most suitable transfer pricing method. In its Circular Letter No. 4, the FTA stated that the CPM is 'not an appropriate method (or only in very exceptional cases)' for financial services or management functions.[30] This restriction implies that the choice of the adequate transfer pricing method should be based on an analysis of the risks assumed and the functions performed.[31] In this regard, the FTA follows the OECD concept known as functional analysis.[32] According to such, a first step identifies the significant people functions relevant to the assumption of risk and those relevant to the ownership of assets.

Limitations apply to public-private entities acting in the public interest that render services mainly to affiliated parties (e.g., joint ventures in the electricity sector). Article 58(3) FDTA restricts the authorized transfer pricing methods for valuing their services: only traditional transaction methods, such as CUPM (*Marktpreis*), CPM (*Gestehungskosten zuzüglich eines angemessenen Aufschlages*) and RPM (*Endverkaufspreis abzüglich einer angemessenen Gewinnmarge*) are allowed.

In Switzerland, the profit split method (hereinafter: 'PSM') applies only in rare cases. Occasionally, the cantonal tax authorities tend to apply PSM in the finance and

Commentaries that are a direct result of these amendments, however, are not relevant to the interpretation and application of previously concluded conventions.

25. Decision A-2122/2016 of the Federal Administrative Court, 31.1.2017, cons. 5.4.2.1; MEUTER/STUDER/STOCKER, ss 41 et seq.
26. Decision DB.2011.50 of the Zurich Tax Appeal Court, 29.6.2015, cons. 3 c) bb).
27. Decision 2A.239/2005 of the Federal Supreme Court, 28.11.2005, cons. 3.4.5; Decision A-2122/2016 of the Federal Administrative Court, 31.1.2017, cons. 5.4.2.1; Decision A-4693/2013 of the Federal Administrative Court, 25.6.2014, cons. 4.2.
28. More detailed in STOCKER/SCHMID, Entschädigung immaterieller, pp. 94 et seq.
29. Decision 2C_11/2018 of the Federal Supreme Court, 10.12.2018, cons. 7.4; STOCKER/STUDER, p. 388.
30. Circular Letter No. 4 of the FTA of 19.3.2004 regarding the taxation of service companies.
31. STOCKER/STUDER, p. 388.
32. *See* Decision 2C_11/2018 of the Federal Supreme Court, 10.12.2018, cons. 7.6.

banking sector (e.g., *the* field of investments and asset management).[33] However, the tax authorities' opinion that one particular transfer pricing method must apply, may be problematic in light of the OECD TPG. In cases where the taxable person is able to demonstrate that other methods can apply, the tax authorities' approach contradicts the goal to always find the most appropriate method for a particular case.[34]

In 2015, the Zurich Tax Appeal Court dealt with transfer prices in connection with portfolio management services.[35] While selecting the applicable transfer pricing method, the CUPM took precedence over the PSM, which was preferred by the cantonal tax authorities.[36] According to the commissioned expert opinion, no unique and valuable contributions could be attributed to the participants, which would have been necessary for applying the PSM.[37] Therefore, also due to the available data, the CUPM was considered the more appropriate method. The PSM applied only to check the outcome of the CUPM and confirm its results.[38]

III PRACTICAL APPLICATION OF PSM

1 General Remarks

As mentioned above, the CUPM is widely considered the most appropriate transfer pricing method due to its direct comparability to the terms between independent enterprises.[39] However, CUPM requires sufficient data in order to achieve reliable results.[40] Such data is sometimes not available, which is why other transfer pricing methods have to be considered.

In most cases, it is not possible to apply one single transfer pricing method to all identified functions in order to establish whether the conditions are consistent with the arm's-length principle.[41] Instead, it appears to be useful to divide the identified functions into: (i) non-unique contributions; and (ii) unique and valuable contributions.[42] In a first step, the respective turnover is deducted by the remuneration for the non-unique contributions. In a second step, the remaining amount is then allocated to the unique and valuable contributions.

---

33. Stocker/Studer, p. 390; *see also* s. III.
34. 2017 OECD TPG, para. 2.2.
35. Decision DB.2011.50 of the Zurich Tax Appeal Court, 29.6.2015, cons. 4 c.
36. *Id.*, cons. 4 c) bb); however, it has to be noted that underlying facts of the case took place in 2006/2007, which is why the Zurich Tax Appeal Court referred to the OECD TPG 2010 (cons. 3 c) bb)).
37. *Id.*, cons. 4 c) bb).
38. *Id.*, cons. 4 c) cc).
39. Zuckschwerdt/Meuter, p. 29.
40. Decision DB.2011.50 of the Zurich Tax Appeal Court, 29.6.2015, cons. 3 a) aa).
41. Tschirner/Stocker, p. 56; Stocker/Raab, ch. T mn. 65.
42. Stocker, Internationale Erfolgsabgrenzung, s. 375.

2 Investment Funds

In order to determine the arm's-length remuneration for the unique and valuable contributions in the investment funds business, Switzerland's practice follows the recommendation of the OECD and applies the residual profit split method (hereinafter: 'RPSM').[43] As mentioned above, in a first step, non-unique contributions (e.g., administration services) are compensated according to traditional transaction methods if possible.[44] In a second step, the remaining (residual) profit is allocated to the enterprises contributing unique and valuable services. The allocation is generally achieved by using one or more allocation keys.[45] The salary of the involved asset managers is considered to be one of these.[46]

The typical business model of investment funds includes both non-unique as well as unique and valuable contributions.[47] However, it is not always possible to clearly classify all functions as either non-unique or unique and valuable contributions. It is, therefore, necessary to analyse each case individually. The usual business model of investment funds includes the following groups of functions:[48]

- marketing and distribution;
- customer service;
- administration;
- portfolio management;
- advisory; and
- risk management.

It appears indisputable that portfolio management and risk management functions classify as unique and valuable contributions.[49] Here, CUPM can apply only in rare cases due to the fact that portfolio management functions are particularly closely related to the person of the fund manager and are a matter of trust.[50] This is the reason why portfolio management functions are rarely outsourced by private equity funds and single hedge funds and, thus, comparable prices at arm's-length are hardly existent. Although outsourcing of portfolio management functions can be found in cases of open investment funds (e.g., funds of hedge funds), the outsourced functions are not comparable to those of private equity and single hedge funds.[51] If CUPM cannot apply and the functional analysis rules out other traditional transaction methods, the only remaining transfer pricing method is the PSM.

43. 2017 OECD TPG, para. 2.115; Zuckschwerdt/Meuter, p. 32; Tschirner/Stocker, p. 57; Stocker/Raab, ch. T mn. 71.
44. Tschirner/Stocker, *id.*; Stocker, Internationale Erfolgsabgrenzung, s. 378.
45. Tschirner/Stocker, *id.*; OECD Guidelines 2017, para. 2.140.
46. Tschirner/Stocker, *id.*; Stocker, Internationale Erfolgsabgrenzung, ss 447 et seq.
47. Stocker/Raab, ch. T mn. 56.
48. Stocker/Raab, *id.*
49. Tschirner/Stocker, p. 56.
50. Zuckschwerdt/Meuter, p. 5.
51. Zuckschwerdt/Meuter, p. 29.

As for marketing functions, it depends on the extent of the activities whether they classify as non-unique or as unique and valuable contributions. In constellations where extensive marketing functions are exercised, they might create marketing intangibles (e.g., well-known trademark).[52] Such marketing functions no longer qualify as non-unique functions and must be remunerated accordingly.[53]

The classification of customer services and distribution functions depends on the complexity of the performed functions and associated risks.[54] In some cases, it might help to analyse the target group of the particular investment fund.[55] Price comparisons between independent parties show that customer services and distribution functions generally are the highest remunerated functions of the supply chain.[56] Often, up to 50 % of the management fees are allocated to these functions.

Advisory functions are generally considered as valuable and unique functions.[57] However, it might be difficult to separate advisory functions from portfolio and risk management functions; in particular, if competences of a portfolio manager are sub-delegated to an investment advisor.[58] In this case, the advisory functions are rather valuable and unique contributions. If the advisory function, however, contains only the monitoring of relevant media and no analyses are carried out that result in specific advises, the advisory functions classify as non-valuable (routine) contributions.[59]

3 Remuneration for Intangibles

Intangibles play an important role in today's business of MNEs. There are basically two kinds of intangibles imaginable. First, there can be marketing intangibles (e.g., trademark, customer list or particular distribution channel) and second, there can be know-how intangibles (e.g., patent, software, trade secrets).[60] If determining the arm's-length remuneration is not possible by applying the CUPM, Swiss practice demands the application of an RPSM to define the remuneration of the involved functions, risks and assets to develop, enhance, maintain, protect and exploit intangibles.[61]

4 Global Trading and Commodities Trading

According to the OECD, the term global trading refers to the capacity of financial institutions to execute customer's orders in financial products in markets around the

52. Tschirner/Stocker, p. 56.
53. More detailed in Stocker/Schmid, Markenrechte, pp 216 et seq.
54. Tschirner/Stocker, p. 56; Stocker/Raab, ch. T mn. 67.
55. Stocker/Raab, *id.*
56. Tschirner/Stocker, p. 56; Stocker/Raab, *id.*
57. Stocker/Raab, ch. T mn. 68.
58. *Id.*
59. *Id.*
60. Tschirner/Stocker, p. 58.
61. Tschirner/Stocker, *id.*; Miyatake, p. 29.

world and/or around the clock.[62] This activity includes underwriting and distributing products on a worldwide basis, acting as a market-maker in physical securities and in derivative instruments, acting as a broker for client transactions on stock and commodities exchanges around the world, and developing new products to meet the needs of the financial institution's clients.[63]

Like investment funds, global trading is also one of the businesses for which data on comparable prices between independent parties exist only in rare cases.[64] The main reason for this lack of comparable data is the high level of integration and the strong cooperation of global trading activities executed in more than one location.[65] These circumstances do not allow a valuation of individual transactions.[66] Therefore, CUPM rarely applies, which is why Swiss practice follows the OECD recommendation and pleads for the application of the PSM.[67] In cases where the functions are performed in more than one location, it will be necessary to determine the relative contribution of each location to the performance of the function;[68] in other words, the allocation keys must be determined. Similar to investment funds, the compensation of the involved traders in each location is considered to be one of the main allocation keys because there appears to be a good correlation between the earning of the profit for the firm and the earning of compensation for the individuals.[69]

In order to determine the arm's-length compensation for activities in connection with commodities trading that takes place in more than one location, the Swiss practice established the application of the RPSM by analogy with the method used for investment funds. In a first step, a management fee equal to 1%–2%, recalculated in a sort of cost-plus remuneration to cover local costs, of the assets under management is allocated to the trader's functions (i.e., CPM).[70] They compensate for non-unique contributions of the respective location. In a second step, a performance fee equal to 20%–30% of the profit realized or generated is allocated to the trader's contributing

62. OECD, Report on the Attribution of Profits to Permanent Establishments, 2008, part III, para. 8.
63. *Id.*
64. Stocker, Internationale Erfolgsabgrenzung, s. 367; OECD, Report on the Attribution of Profits, *id.* part III, para. 119.
65. Report on the Attribution of Profits, *id.*, part III, paras 28 and 119 et seq. Traders in each trading centre (generally London, New York and Tokyo or Hong Kong) set prices and trade off a portfolio of positions called a 'book' while the market is open in that location. When the markets close in one location, responsibility for trading the 'book' is passed to the next trading location, where the open positions form the starting point for trading. Traders in the new location may close position passed to them and open new ones. In addition to the 'book passing' method, there also exists a more seamless manner, with traders in one location trading at the same time and from the same book as traders in another location.
66. Stocker, Internationale Erfolgsabgrenzung, s. 367.
67. Stocker, *id.* s. 375; Brülisauer, Art. 7, mn. 527.
68. OECD, Report on the Attribution of Profits to Permanent Establishments, 2008, part III, para. 187.
69. *Id.*; Stocker, Internationale Erfolgsabgrenzung, ss 442 et seq., highlights the weaknesses of compensation-based allocation keys and advocates a risk-based alternative (i.e., value at risk [VaR]).
70. Tschirner/Stocker, p. 55.

unique and valuable services.[71] The remaining profits belong to the investors (i.e., capital providers).

5 Allocation to Intercantonal Permanent Establishments

An intercantonal enterprise is an enterprise which maintains one or more permanent establishments in Switzerland but outside the canton of its head office.[72] In these cases, due to Swiss federalism, more than one canton claims tax sovereignty. Thus, taxable profit and equity have to be allocated between the head office and the permanent establishment(s). The profit (and equity) allocation within Switzerland takes place on a pro rata basis, i.e., profit and equity are allocated proportionally.[73] In order to determine the respective proportion, there are mainly two methods: either the proportion bases on the accounting results of the intercantonal enterprise and its permanent establishment(s) (i.e., direct method) or the proportion bases on specific allocation keys (i.e., indirect method).[74] The Federal Supreme Court stated repeatedly that the direct method takes preference over the indirect method and it should always apply, provided it shows the degree of each permanent establishment's contribution to the overall profit or loss.[75] In cases where there are no separate profit and loss statements or if they are unsuitable for determining the allocation to the permanent establishment(s), the indirect method should apply.[76]

For the indirect method, different allocation keys are taken into account depending on the enterprise's business. For trading and service enterprises, the allocation keys are derived from the turnover of the head office and its permanent establishment(s).[77] For manufacturing enterprises, the allocation keys equal the production factors (i.e., capital and labour).[78] The capital factor itself consists of the attributed assets at book value plus possible rent expenses, which are capitalized at 6%.[79] The labour factor consists of the employees' salaries attributed to the place of labour exploitation and not that of the paying agent.[80] The employees' salaries are capitalized at 10%.[81]

An additional share of the profit (i.e., a fixed percentage between 10% to 30% depending on the importance of the management functions of the head office) is allocated to the head office, depending on the impact of the central management on the overall result or the independence of the permanent establishment(s), respectively.[82]

71. *Id.*
72. LOCHER, p. 97; TEUSCHER/LOBSINGER, § 30 mn. 4 et seq.
73. LOCHER, *id.*
74. LOCHER, p. 98.
75. DFT 93 I 415 (422), cons. 3.
76. *Id.*
77. LOCHER, p. 103.
78. LOCHER, p. 104; TEUSCHER/LOBSINGER, § 31 mn. 24.
79. TEUSCHER/LOBSINGER, *id.*
80. *Id.*
81. *Id.*
82. TEUSCHER/LOBSINGER, § 31 mn. 25 (manufacturing enterprises) and mn. 36 (trading and service enterprises).

In its leading case in 1910, the Federal Supreme Court stated that the principle of a pro rata allocation also applies in cases where one or more permanent establishments generate a loss.[83] Because the indirect method allocates profit and loss according to allocation keys, the loss-generating permanent establishments participate in the profit of successful permanent establishments and vice versa. Such loss assumption is final and there is no possibility for chargeback in case the loss-generating permanent establishment generates profits in future business periods.[84] In cases where an intercantonal enterprise generates an overall loss, Swiss jurisdiction and doctrine are inconsistent on how the loss carryforwards should be allocated.[85]

In summary, the indirect method for allocation of the profit and loss of intercantonal enterprises corresponds to the PSM. In case there is a fixed percentage allocated to the head office, the method is close to the RPSM.

6 Checking the Results in Complex Cases

In complex cases, the PSM applies to check the previously determined results deriving from other transfer pricing methods. If the remuneration according to the PSM lies within a certain range of the previously determined results (i.e., 15%), they are considered to be at arm's-length.

SELECTED BIBLIOGRAPHY

BRÜLISAUER PETER, in: ZWEIFEL/BEUSCH/MATTEOTTI (eds.), Commentary, International Taxation, Basel 2015.

BRÜLISAUER PETER / KRUMMENACHER OLIVER, in: ZWEIFEL/BEUSCH (eds.), Commentary, FTHA, 3rd edn, 2017.

BRÜLISAUER PETER / MÜHLEMANN MARCO, in: ZWEIFEL/BEUSCH (eds.), Commentary, FDTA, 3rd edn, 2017.

LOCHER PETER, Einführung in das interkantonale Steuerrecht, 2015, 4th edn.

MIYATAKE TOSHIO, Transfer Pricing and Intangibles, in: Cahiers de droit fiscal international, 2007, vol. 92a.

MEUTER HANS ULRICH / STUDER CHRISTOPH / STOCKER RAOUL, Praxisfälle zum Transfer Pricing, at: IFF-Seminar zum internationalen Steuerrecht, 21-22.11.2017.

STOCKER RAOUL, Internationale Erfolgsabgrenzung beim Global Trading mit Finanzinstrumenten, Diss., Bamberg 2006.

STOCKER RAOUL, Potential Effects of the OECD Base Erosion and Profit Shifting Initiative on Swiss Transfer Pricing Rules and Swiss Companies, in: 69 Bull. Intl. Taxn. 4/5, 2015.

STOCKER RAOUL / RAAB JÜRGEN, in: VÖGELE/BORSTELL/ENGLER (eds.), Verrechnungspreise, 4th edn, 2015.

83. DFT 36 I 576 (581), cons. 3.
84. TEUSCHER/LOBSINGER, § 31 mn. 10.
85. For a detailed discussion on the topic, *see* TEUSCHER/LOBSINGER, § 34, mn. 40 et seq.

STOCKER RAOUL / SCHMID PATRICK, Entschädigung immaterieller Vermögenswerte: Auswirkungen des Updates 2017 der OECD-Verrechnungspreisleitlinie, in: TPI 2/2018.

STOCKER RAOUL / SCHMID PATRICK, Markenrechte: Entschädigung des rechtlichen Eigentümers vs Ausübung von DEMPE-Funktionen, in: TPI 4/2018.

STOCKER RAOUL / STUDER CHRISTOPH, Bestimmung von Verrechnungspreisen, in: ST 5/2009.

TEUSCHER HANNES / LOBSINGER FRANK, in: ZWEIFEL/BEUSCH/MÄUSLI-ALLENSPACH (eds.), Commentary, Intercantonal Taxation, 2011.

TSCHIRNER MARC A. / STOCKER RAOUL, Verrechnungspreise im grenzüberschreitenden Anlagefondsgeschäft, in: FStR 2010.

ZUCKSCHWERDT CHRISTOPH / MEUTER HANS ULRICH, Verrechnungspreisproblematik beim grenzüberschreitenden Management von Private-Equity und Hedge-Funds, in: ZStP 1/2009.

ANNEX 1 LEGAL FRAMEWORK

Federal Direct Tax Act (*Bundesgesetz über die direkte Bundessteuer*), Art. 58(1).
Federal Tax Harmonization Act (*Bundesgesetz über die Harmonisierung der direkten Steuern der Kantone und Gemeinden*), Art. 24(1).

ANNEX 2 RELEVANT REGULATIONS AND CASE LAW

Circular Letter No. 4 of the FTA, 19.3.2004 (taxation of service companies).
Circular Letter No. 6 of the FTA, 6.6.1997 (hidden equity).
Circular Letter No. 8 of the FTA, 18.12.2001 (international profit allocation).
Circular Letters of the FTA, 19 and 20.2.2018 (interest payments in Swiss Francs or in foreign currency between affiliated entities [updated annually]).
DFT 143 II 136.
DFT 140 II 88.
DFT 115 Ib 238.
DFT 113 Ia 25.
DFT 107 Ib 325.
DFT 105 Ib 84.
DFT 82 I 291.
Decision 2C_11/2018 of the Federal Supreme Court, 10.12.2018.
Decision 2A.239/2005 of the Federal Supreme Court, 28.11.2005.
Decision A-4091/2016 of the Federal Administrative Court, 24.1.2018.
Decision A-2122/2016 of the Federal Administrative Court, 31.1.2017.
Decision A-4693/2013 of the Federal Administrative Court, 25.6.2014.
Decision A-103/2011 of the Federal Administrative Court, 21.9.2011.
Decision 2005-114 of the Federal Tax Appeals Committee, 8.6.2006.
Decision DB.2011.50 of the Zurich Tax Appeal Court, 29.6.2015.

CHAPTER 17

Countries Experience: Status Quo and Likely Evolutions – United Kingdom (England and Wales)

Steve Edge & Alicia Tan

I INTRODUCTION

The United Kingdom (UK) transfer pricing rules are contained in Part 4 of the Taxation (International and Other Provisions) Act 2010 (hereinafter: 'TIOPA 2010'). Specific mention is made in that Act of the arm's-length principle – which forms the basis of UK transfer pricing law.[1]

UK legislation does not provide detailed rules on how that arm's-length position is to be determined or what methodology should be used in what situations. However, pursuant to section 164 of TIOPA 2010, UK transfer pricing law is to be construed in a manner that best secures consistency with the most up-to-date (Organisation for Economic Co-operation and Development) OECD Model Tax Convention[2] and the OECD Transfer Pricing Guidelines (hereinafter: 'OECD TPG').[3] The transactional profit split method can, therefore, be used in the UK in appropriate transfer pricing cases.

Additional guidance as to how the UK transfer pricing rules operate and how the transactional profit split method would be applied is contained in the UK tax authority's operating manuals.[4] These manuals are not binding law, but provide a useful steer as to how the law will be applied in practice. Although these manuals are, strictly

1. TIOPA 2010, s. 147.
2. OECD, Model Tax Convention on Income and on Capital, Condensed Version 2017 (OECD Publishing, 2017).
3. OECD (2017), OECD Transfer Pricing Guidelines for Multinational Enterprises and Tax Administrations 2017, OECD Publishing, Paris, https://doi.org/10.1787/tpg-2017-en.
4. Her Majesty's Revenue & Customs' Manuals, particularly the International Manual (INTM).

speaking, internal guidance for UK tax officials, they are also made available to the public, and therefore, the UK tax authority does not tend to depart from the guidelines contained in the manuals without good justification. There is also much importance placed on treating taxpayers fairly and consistently – and these manuals play a part in that effort.

II TRANSFER PRICING METHOD SELECTION

The OECD TPG do not prescribe any hierarchy between the various transfer pricing methods. In most cases, the UK tax authority takes the view that the application of any methodology should result in the same outcome since the underlying purpose of all of the methods is to determine the arm's-length position.

However, there is a broad preference in the OECD TPG for traditional transactional methods over profit allocation or split methods. Similarly, the UK tax authority has stated that the comparable uncontrolled price (hereinafter: 'CUP') or comparable uncontrolled transaction (hereinafter: 'CUT') methods are generally accepted as the most effective ways of assessing what the parties would have done in an arm's-length situation.

That being said, the emphasis in the OECD TPG is on using the most appropriate method for any particular case. This is also the approach that the UK tax authority takes to method selection.[5]

In particular, the UK tax authority has noted that the transactional profit split method can offer a viable solution for 'very complex trading relationships involving highly integrated operations'.[6] In other words, it becomes a more attractive option in situations where it is difficult to evaluate transactions on a separate and distinct basis.

For transactional profit split to be considered the most appropriate option, the UK tax authority would have to establish that, in an arm's-length context, the parties would be unable to value in any accurate way their respective contributions to the joint venture, which would leave them to propose a profit share in whatever proportion seemed appropriate. This is most often the case in situations involving hard-to-value intangible assets.[7]

III PRACTICAL APPLICATION OF THE PROFIT SPLIT METHOD

The OECD TPG specify that the transactional profit split methodology should divide the profits on an 'economically valid basis'[8] and that this should approximate the transactional profit split that would have been agreed at the time of the transaction between parties operating at arm's-length. What constitutes an 'economically valid

5. HM Revenue & Customs Manuals, INTM421010.
6. HM Revenue & Customs Manuals, INTM421070.
7. *See*, for example, *Ultraframe (UK) Ltd v. Eurocell Building Plastics Ltd* [2006] EWHC 1344 (Pat), which was a commercial case that discussed transactional profit split in the context of royalty payments that would have been made between a licensor and licensee.
8. 2017 OECD TPG, para. 2.114.

basis' typically depends on the allocation of economic functions and risks – this goes back to the functional analysis that is fundamental to transfer pricing in general.

Whatever outcome the transactional profit split methodology produces should also be a credible one. A theoretically valid transactional profit split model – or, indeed, any other transfer pricing model – that produces an outcome that is not economically sound is unlikely to stand up to scrutiny.[9]

The OECD TPG specify two approaches to operating the transactional profit split method in practice: (i) the contribution analysis; or (ii) the residual analysis.[10]

The contribution analysis method involves dividing the total combined profits from the controlled transactions in line with the relative value of the functions carried out by the various parties. This requires the UK tax authority to develop a close understanding of how the trade works and what adds value to it. For example, if it was the intrinsic nature of the product being sold that generated the profits, then more profit should be allocated to the R&D and product development functions. Conversely, if it was the success of the marketing activity and customer contacts that generated the profits, then more profit should be allocated to the sales and distribution function. Of course, the UK tax authority points out that if determining what adds value to the trade was that simple, then it is likely that the CUP method would be used instead and there would be no need to rely on a transactional profit split.

Under the residual analysis method, the parties are first allocated with a share of the total combined profits that ensures that they are adequately remunerated with a basic return proportionate to the functions carried out. This basic return would not take into account any return that might be due to the parties on the basis of valuable contributions (such as intangible assets) made by the participants. The residual profit is then split between the parties based on an analysis of how parties operating at arm's-length would have allocated this remainder. At this stage, the respective contributions and relative bargaining positions of the parties should be taken into account.

Where the transactional profit split method is used, the UK tax authority is, in effect, recognizing that neither party can proceed in the business that is to be carried on by the joint venture without the other – in other words, that it cannot carry on the business of the joint venture by recruiting staff or contracting for services or developing IP or technology in an efficient or economic way. In commercial practice, of course, many joint ventures end up being terminated after a relatively short period because, as the parties work together, one of them concludes that it can replace the contribution made by the other or that the relative value of the two parties' contributions has changed significantly.

When advance price arrangements (hereinafter: 'APAs') were first used in the UK (before we had formal legislation and had to rely on an agreement reached with another tax authority (typically the US) under a mutual agreement procedure), most

9. *See*, for example, *Arbuthnott v. Bonnyman* [2014] EWHC 1410 (Ch), where the court rejected methodologies that led to an unreasonable and incredible result, despite the fact that the manner in which those methods had been applied was technically sound.
10. 2017 OECD TPG, paras 2.124–2.129.

were done in the banking sector where it was relatively easy to attribute a return to capital from a typical banking or financial services business.[11] After rewarding administrative or routine charge allocations, the residual return could then be split among front office teams in the bank's offices, based on their relative amounts of incentive compensation. In effect, this lets the sales staff and traders' remuneration indicate where profits were really being generated. This has worked fairly satisfactorily over the years in the financial services sector.

However, transactional profit split methodology has been less successful in non-financial services situations and particularly in the IT or consumer brands sectors, where profit would typically be allocated first to administrative, routine or other activities that can be priced on a cost-plus, transactional net margin or CUP basis. Using transactional profit split in such cases often leaves too much going to the IP or IT residual. This is particularly an issue where this results also in income being attributed to operations where there is relatively little substance to support the return - perhaps because of an R&D cost share or a tax-structured supply chain.

To the extent there is remaining doubt, the answer can be validated or adjusted by a simple check which attributes distribution returns to each operation around the world consistently with the UK agreed commission or margin, and then seeks to establish what the implied return on IP investment is and how reasonable that is. If the outcome from that exercise looks completely unrealistic, the UK tax authority may conclude that the distribution return in the UK has not been set at the right level, or otherwise that the assessment of the impact of collective activities has been wrongly determined (the so-called fragmentation effect).

Using the transactional profit split method in this way, however, is simply a cross-check and not a primary method. Other cross-checks can be used in conjunction, to check the global allocation of profits or appropriateness of the return to the UK, in order to ensure that the outcome is an appropriate and plausible arm's-length solution.

While transactional profit split is commonly used in this way as a cross-check now that greater global information is available to the tax authorities in the UK following the introduction of the diverted profits tax, transactional profit split per se remains very limited as a primary method.

SELECTED BIBLIOGRAPHY

Alison Lovejoy, Transfer Pricing Litigation: In-House Tax - Transfer Pricing, in: Tax Journal, Issue 998, 33 (2009).

Pim Fris and Graham Poole, Analysis - Transfer Pricing More Demanding, in: Tax Journal, Issue 1019, 13 (2010).

John Henshall, Global Transfer Pricing: Principles and Practice (2016).

11. *See*, for example, *DSG Retail Limited v. HMRC* [2009] STC (SCD) 397, where a transactional profit split methodology was considered the most appropriate and the allocation of profits was determined by reference to the typical return that an insurance company might expect on its capital. The majority of the residual was allocated to the retailer, to take into account the value of the intangibles it held.

ANNEX 1 LEGAL FRAMEWORK

Part 4 of the Taxation (International and Other Provisions) Act 2010.
Section 147 **Tax calculations to be based on arm's length, not actual, provision**

(1) For the purposes of this section 'the basic pre-condition' is that—
  (a) provision ('the actual provision') has been made or imposed as between any two persons ('the affected persons') by means of a transaction or series of transactions,
  (b) the participation condition is met (see section 148),
  (c) the actual provision is not within subsection (7) (oil transactions), and.
  (d) the actual provision differs from the provision ('the arm's length provision') which would have been made as between independent enterprises.
(2) Subsection (3) applies if—
  (a) the basic pre-condition is met, and
  (b) the actual provision confers a potential advantage in relation to United Kingdom taxation on one of the affected persons.
(3) The profits and losses of the potentially advantaged person are to be calculated for tax purposes as if the arm's length provision had been made or imposed instead of the actual provision.
(4) Subsection (5) applies if—
  (a) the basic pre-condition is met, and
  (b) the actual provision confers a potential advantage in relation to United Kingdom taxation (whether or not the same advantage) on each of the affected persons.
(5) The profits and losses of each of the affected persons are to be calculated for tax purposes as if the arm's length provision had been made or imposed instead of the actual provision.
(6) Subsections (3) and (5) have effect subject to—
  (a) section 165 (exemption for dormant companies),
  (b) section 166 (exemption for small and medium-sized enterprises),
    (ba) section 206A (modification of basic rule where allowances restricted for certain oil-related expenditure),
  (c) section 213 (this Part generally does not affect calculation of capital allowances),
  (d) section 214 (this Part generally does not affect calculation of chargeable gains),
  (e) section 447(5) and (6) of CTA 2009 (this Part generally does not affect how exchange gains or losses from loan relationships are accounted for),
  (f) section 694(8) and (9) of CTA 2009 (this Part generally does not affect how exchange gains or losses from derivative contracts are accounted for) [F3, and
  (g) section 938N of CTA 2010 (this Part treated as of no effect for the purposes of Part 21B of CTA 2010 (group mismatch schemes)).

(7) The actual provision is within this subsection if it is made or imposed by means of any transaction or deemed transaction in the case of which the price or consideration is determined in accordance with any of sections 225F to 225J of ITTOIA 2005 or any of sections 281 to 285 of CTA 2010 (transactions and deemed transactions involving oil treated as made at market value).

Section 151 **'Arm's length provision'**

(1) In this Part 'the arm's length provision' has the meaning given by section 147(1).
(2) For the purposes of this Part, the cases in which provision made or imposed as between any two persons is to be taken to differ from the provision that would have been made as between independent enterprises include the case in which provision is made or imposed as between two persons but no provision would have been made as between independent enterprises; and references in this Part to the arm's length provision are to be read accordingly.

Section 164 **Part to be interpreted in accordance with OECD principles**

(1) This Part is to be read in such manner as best secures consistency between—
 (a) the effect given to sections 147(1)(a), (b) and (d) and (2) to (6), 148 and 151(2), and
 (b) the effect which, in accordance with the transfer pricing guidelines, is to be given, in cases where double taxation arrangements incorporate the whole or any part of the OECD model, to so much of the arrangements as does so.
(2) Subsection (1) has effect subject to—
 section 147(1)(c) and (7) (oil-related provision to which Part does not apply),
 sections 205 and 206 (rules for oil-related ring-fence trades),
 section 217(3) to (7) (provision for sales of oil),
 section 447(5) and (6) of CTA 2009 (this Part generally does not affect how exchange gains or losses from loan relationships are accounted for), and
 section 694(8) and (9) of CTA 2009 (this Part generally does not affect how exchange gains or losses from derivative contracts are accounted for).
(3) In this section 'the OECD model' means—
 (a) the rules which, at the passing of ICTA (which occurred on 9 February 1988), were contained in Article 9 of the Model Tax Convention on Income and on Capital published by the Organisation for Economic Co-operation and Development, or
 (b) any rules in the same or equivalent terms.
(4) In this section 'the transfer pricing guidelines' means—
 (a) the version of the Transfer Pricing Guidelines for Multinational Enterprises and Tax Administrations approved by the Organisation for Economic Co-operation and Development (OECD) on 22 July 2010 as revised

by the report, Aligning Transfer Pricing Outcomes with Value Creation, Actions 8-10 - 2015 Final Reports, published by the OECD on 5 October 2015, or

(b) such other document approved and published by the OECD in place of that (or a later) version or in place of those Guidelines as is designated for the time being by order made by the Treasury,

including, in either case, material which is published by the OECD as part of (or by way of update or supplement to) the version or other document concerned and which is designated for the time being by order made by the Treasury.

(5) In this section 'double taxation arrangements' means arrangements that have effect under section 2(1) (double taxation relief by agreement with territories outside the United Kingdom).

ANNEX 2 RELEVANT REGULATIONS AND CASE LAW

HM Revenue & Customs Manuals, INTM421010, INTM421070.
Ultraframe (UK) Ltd v. Eurocell Building Plastics Ltd [2006] EWHC 1344 (Pat).
DSG Retail Limited v. HMRC [2009] STC (SCD) 397.
Arbuthnott v. Bonnyman [2014] EWHC 1410 (Ch).

CHAPTER 18

Countries Experience: Status Quo and Likely Evolutions – United States

Yariv Brauner

I INTRODUCTION

The practice of profit splits in the United States is fraught with ambiguity. On the one hand, it is common, especially in complex cases, and always considered in analysis involving important intangibles (although dominated by its companion methodology, the comparable profit method or CPM[1]). On the other hand, profit split is mostly considered a residual, almost forced methodology, more appropriate to cases where the all-important search for comparables lead to very little.

This perception of profit split is interesting if one considers its origins, in intuitive court analyses (described below) at times when such courts determined that they had been ill-equipped by the then available legal framework to tackle difficult transfer pricing cases and, therefore, issued their best-judgment rulings that included effectively profit split analysis. Lately, the Internal Revenue Service (IRS), recovering from its original literal arm's-length rhetoric, continuously attempted to use profit split in complex cases that eventually resulted in litigation, only to be rebuffed by the same courts that have generally used the IRS' own literal arm's-length rhetoric against it, siding, time after time with the taxpayers. The recent favour that profit split enjoys goes, of course, beyond the IRS as the Organisation for Economic Co-operation and Development (OECD) retreats from its own narrow arm's-length rhetoric to promote the expansion of the role of profit splits in transfer pricing.[2] This trend has not yet affected the rules and application of profit split in the United States, yet one may see the

1. Both introduced by the 1994 regulations to resolve the inefficacy of the traditional transfer pricing methods that had been more reliant on comparability.
2. Note, however, that the IRS version of profit split, as described below, is different from the current OECD version. Its use is more limited in scope, and risk is a key valuation factor.

impact on the recent tax reform (the 2017 Tax Cuts and Jobs Act) that increases support for apportionment in the domestic setting.

II TRANSFER PRICING METHOD SELECTION

The US transfer pricing regime dates back almost to the enactment of the federal income tax at the beginning of the twentieth century, yet it is common to view the finalization of the 1968 regulations, promulgated pursuant to Internal Revenue Code section 482,[3] as the starting point of the modern American transfer pricing regime. These Regulations are essentially the same as those in place today. They highlighted the arm's-length standard as the basis for transfer pricing adjustments and provided, for the first time, rules for specific types of transactions, including intercompany services, licensing or sale of intangibles and the sale of tangible property. Nonetheless, taxpayers were able to engage in advantageous tax planning with intangible transfers, especially taking advantage of the tax benefits that the operation in Puerto Rico had presented them, leading to serious concerns within the government about the efficacy of the rules. A series of cases involving such tax planning were taken to court, generally granting wins to taxpayers and typically rendering a decision based on rough splits of profits – eventually to become the profit split method – based on best judgements rather than on the newly finalized rules.[4] Reform of the Puerto Rico tax benefits was tried, showing little improvement, leading to more general reform discussions and the eventual sole amendment of section 482, adding a 'commensurate with income' requirement for payments for the use of intangibles, and the publication of a policy paper, known as the 'White Paper' of 1988. Both focused on the difficulty of applying the literal arm's-length standard to transfers of intangibles and the inherent lack of good comparables to such transfers.

This work eventually led to a new regulations project, with final regulations published in 1994. These regulations, most importantly: (i) formalized the best method rule, clarifying that there is no predetermined hierarchy among the prescribed transfer pricing methods; (ii) accepted the concept of arm's-length range, which, in effect, acknowledged the impossibility of applying the literal arm's-length based on exact comparables in all cases – the paradigm that caused many of the government's losses prior to that; and (iii) added the comparable profits and profit split methods, non-straightforward arm's-length methods, to the arsenal of permissible transfer pricing methods. These latter methods came to dominate the practice of transfer pricing in the United States despite resistance, initially mainly from the OECD, related to whether they truly reflect arm's-length resistance that disappeared as the OECD itself accepted a variation of these methods in its transfer pricing guidelines.

The core of the US transfer pricing regime has not changed much since. Most of the activity has focused on procedural matters, penalties and the institutionalization of advanced pricing agreements (APA) and controversies tended to be resolved away

3. All references are to the Internal Revenue Code (26 U.S.C.) and the Treasury Regulations unless otherwise specified.
4. For a review of these cases, *see*, e.g., BRAUNER, p. 79.

from the courts until recently, when the almost standard use by US multinationals (MNEs) of the cost-sharing safe harbour was exposed to result in large revenue loss to the US Treasury.

1 Profit Split Method

A Origins

The origins of profit split analysis in the United States is, as already mentioned, in a line of transfer pricing cases involving difficulties of valuating transferred intangibles.[5] The transfer pricing methods prescribed by the 1968 regulations were ineffective in these cases where data regarding comparables were either insufficient, unavailable or both. Most of these cases involved transfers of intangibles to Puerto Rican arms of US MNEs to enjoy certain tax incentives in Puerto Rico. All these cases were decided in a rough justice fashion, seemingly while the courts assume that no precedence could be drawn from them. The analysis was sometimes very brief and in other cases more elaborate, yet the final decision had always been equity rather than accuracy-based, simply an application of the court's best judgment.

The 1988 White Paper mentioned the tendency of the courts to decide on splits in the range of 40:60, mentioning also the 50:50 split in a specific tax section applicable to US territories (Puerto Rico), and asserting the incompatibility of these solutions with the existing legal regime.

B The Regulations

The 1994 regulations finally prescribed profit split as a transfer pricing methodology, equal to others under the best method rule.[6] The final regulations removed certain procedural restrictions imposed in prior (1993) Temporary Regulations based on that profit split relied, at least mostly, on internal rather than third-party data, eliminating the residual nature of the method.[7] They provide that the relative value of each controlled taxpayer's contribution to the relevant business activity must be determined based on the functions performed, risks assumed and resources employed by each participant in the relevant business activity. This allocation corresponds to the division of profit or loss that would result from an arrangement between uncontrolled taxpayers, each performing functions similar to those of the various controlled taxpayers engaged in the relevant business activity. The profit allocated to any member of a group is not limited to the total operating profit of the group from the relevant business activity. The combined operating profit or loss from the business activity should not necessarily be shared equally or in any other arbitrary proportion. The regulations prescribe two specific methods: (i) comparable profit split and (ii) residual profit split.

5. *See supra* n. 3.
6. 59 Fed. Reg. 34971 (8 July 1994).
7. The final regulations also eliminated an important substantive requirement: that each controlled taxpayer must own valuable non-routine intangibles.

Since then profit split became an important method in the US practice of transfer pricing. It is used in various circumstances, but primarily in complex APA or MAP cases, PE allocations and in financial transactions.

Comparable profit split derives from the combined operating profit of uncontrolled taxpayers whose transactions are comparable to those of the controlled taxpayers in the relevant business activity. Each uncontrolled taxpayer's percentage of the combined operating profit or loss is used to allocate the combined operating profit or loss of the relevant business activity. This method cannot be used if the uncontrolled parties' combined operating profit (a percentage of the combined assets) significantly varies from that earned by the controlled taxpayers. Comparability depends on all the factors of the best method rule,[8] but particularly on the comparison of the operating profit of the controlled and uncontrolled taxpayers. In addition, the similarity of the contractual terms between the parties is particularly important in profit split application. All material differences require adjustments.

For a method to be considered best, its reliability must be tested. The reliability of the comparable profit split analysis depended particularly on the reliability of the allocation of costs, income and assets between the relevant business activity and the similarity in accounting practices. A reasonable allocation formula may be used if it is not possible to make the allocation based on factual relationships. This would hurt the reliability, however, in the same way that allocations relate to non-compared activities. Finally, if data related to one side in the transaction is better than for both sides, other (one-sided) methods are viewed as more reliable, meaning that, to a certain extent, comparable profit split remained a residual method in many cases.

The residual profit split method takes the combined operating profit or loss from the relevant business activity and allocates it between the controlled taxpayers, first, by allocating market profits (determined by other transfer pricing methods) to each party for its routine contributions and second, by allocating the residual profit between the parties based on the relative investment in the relevant (non-formerly allocated to) intangibles.

Routine contributions are contributions similar to those made by third parties involved in similar business activities for which it is possible to ascertain market returns, not including the group's 'crown jewels' (valuable intellectual property). Functional analysis identifies these contributions in an otherwise normal transfer pricing analysis. Comparability and reliability are then determined based on the methods used for the first step. The reliability of the second step heavily depends on the quality of the data available and the extent of (generally more reliable) external market benchmarks used.

In practice, the use of profit split is often supported by the use of one of the traditional (1968 regulation) methods to test one or both sides separately and then examine the results in comparison with the outcome under profit split. This is particularly true in bilateral cases (APA or MAP). Finally, the regulations anticipate

8. Treas. Reg. § 1.482-6(c)(2)(ii)(A).

that profit split may also be used to allocate losses, using the same principles, yet with no guidance on how to conduct such an analysis.

III PRACTICAL APPLICATION OF THE PROFIT SPLIT METHOD

1 Application of the Profit Split Method in Designing the Group Transfer Pricing Policy

Generally, profit split comes into consideration in the United States when both related parties make non-routine contributions. Multiple authorities stress that when only one party makes such contributions, other transfer pricing methods are likely to be considered more reliable and hence 'better'.

The ties between profit split and unique intangibles are, therefore, strong. Note that the value of intangibles contributed is also required to be determined, and the regulations propose ways to make such valuations: external market benchmarks that reflect the intangible's fair market value, capitalization of development costs, etc., yet very little concrete guidance exists.

Other IRS guidance, such as the practice unit titled: 'Residual Profit Split Method - Outbound',[9] includes examples for transactions where profit split may be used: (i) sales of tangible goods if the seller uses non-routine manufacturing intangibles to make the goods, and another controlled party purchases and resells the goods using its non-routine marketing intangibles; (ii) controlled party licenses non-routine manufacturing intangibles to a second controlled party who then manufactures goods using those manufacturing intangibles and sells the goods using its own non-routine marketing intangibles; and (iii) commercial sales of a software if two controlled parties each contribute non-routine software intangibles to the product and the controlled parties share the revenue from the sales. The practice unit repeats the mantra that ideally market data should be used to determine the relative value of the parties' respective non-routine contributions, yet it acknowledges that the method tends to be used when these are not available, as is typically the case with transactions such as those mentioned, and, therefore, the unit proceeds to permit an estimation of such value based on the capitalized cost of developing the (non-routine) intangibles by the parties (reduced by appropriate amortization). The unit acknowledges the unreliable relationship between cost and value, especially when only internal data is used in the valuation process, and attempts to caution the IRS agents, for example, in cases where one party makes an initial very risky investment followed by the other party's much less follow-up investment. Although not dramatic, this guidance to IRS agents demonstrates the unease that the use of profit splits generates in the common practice of US transfer pricing.

9. *See* https://www.irs.gov/pub/int_practice_units/ISOPUOP_1_7_04.pdf.

2 The Taxpayers' Experience When Liaising with US Tax Authorities and Tax Courts

As already mentioned, recent transfer pricing litigation involved cost-sharing arrangements, yet the core issue in all complex cases is the allocation of value among a parent, usually in the United States, where R&D originates, and a subsidiary, usually in a low-tax jurisdiction, where other activities and 'risk-taking' takes place. The IRS regularly argued for an approach that assesses the business in aggregate, followed by an apportionment of value among the parts of the business, very much in line with the profit split methodology. The Tax Court has repeatedly rejected this approach, electing to side with taxpayers that insisted on assessing each tested transaction in isolation, promoting a CUP/CUT analysis, opting the liberal use of adjustments rather than admitting the lack of appropriate comparables.[10]

In some cases, however, taxpayers benefit from more flexible positions, especially in the context of APA proceedings. Naturally, taxpayers applying for APAs are in positions more amenable to compromise and the opacity of these proceedings prevent the in-depth study of these proceedings, yet anecdotal evidence does not point to the increasing insistence of the government on the use of the profit split in the context of APA proceedings (at least not in successful cases).

SELECTED BIBLIOGRAPHY

Brauner Yariv, Value in the Eye of the Beholder: The Valuation of Intangibles for Transfer Pricing Purposes, in: 28 Virginia Tax Review 79 (2008).

10. A good example for this approach is the recent decision in *Amazon.com, Inc. & Subsidiaries v. Comm'r* 148 T.C. No. 8 (23 March 2017). Note that rarely the courts do accept the aggregate approach. *See*, e.g., *Guidant LLC et al. v. Commissioner*, Nos 5989-11, 5990-11, 10985-11, 26876-11, 5501-12, 5502-12, United States Tax Court (19 July 2016).

ANNEX 1 LEGAL FRAMEWORK

Section 482 of the Internal Revenue Code (26 U.S.C. § 482) and the U.S. Treasury Regulations promulgated thereunder (26 C.F.R. § 1.482-6).

§ 1.482-6 Profit split method.

(a) *In general.* The profit split method evaluates whether the allocation of the combined operating profit or loss attributable to one or more controlled transactions is arm's length by reference to the relative value of each controlled taxpayer's contribution to that combined operating profit or loss. The combined operating profit or loss must be derived from the most narrowly identifiable business activity of the controlled taxpayers for which data is available that includes the controlled transactions (relevant business activity).**(b)** *Appropriate share of profits and losses.* The relative value of each controlled taxpayer's contribution to the success of the relevant business activity must be determined in a manner that reflects the functions performed, risks assumed, and resources employed by each participant in the relevant business activity, consistent with the comparability provisions of § 1.482-1(d)(3). Such an allocation is intended to correspond to the division of profit or loss that would result from an arrangement between uncontrolled taxpayers, each performing functions similar to those of the various controlled taxpayers engaged in the relevant business activity. The profit allocated to any particular member of a controlled group is not necessarily limited to the total operating profit of the group from the relevant business activity. For example, in a given year, one member of the group may earn a profit while another member incurs a loss. In addition, it may not be assumed that the combined operating profit or loss from the relevant business activity should be shared equally, or in any other arbitrary proportion. The specific method of allocation must be determined under paragraph (c) of this section.
(c) *Application -*

(1) *In general.* The allocation of profit or loss under the profit split method must be made in accordance with one of the following allocation methods – (i) The comparable profit split, described in paragraph (c)(2) of this section; or
  (ii) The residual profit split, described in paragraph (c)(3) of this section.
(2) *Comparable profit split -*
  (i) *In general.* A comparable profit split is derived from the combined operating profit of un controlled taxpayers whose transactions and activities are similar to those of the controlled taxpayers in the relevant business activity. Under this method, each uncontrolled taxpayer's percentage of the combined operating profit or loss is used to allocate the combined operating profit or loss of the relevant business activity.
  (ii) *Comparability and reliability considerations – (A) In general.* Whether results derived from application of this method are the most reliable measure of the arm's length result is determined using the factors described under the best method rule in § 1.482-1(c).

(*B*) *Comparability* -

(*1*) *In general.* The degree of comparability between the controlled and uncontrolled taxpayers is determined by applying the comparability provisions of § 1.482-1(d). The comparable profit split compares the division of operating profits among the controlled taxpayers to the division of operating profits among uncontrolled taxpayers engaged in similar activities under similar circumstances. Although all of the factors described in § 1.482-1(d)(3) must be considered, comparability under this method is particularly dependent on the considerations described under the comparable profits method in § 1.482-5(c)(2) or § 1.482-9(f)(2)(iii) because this method is based on a comparison of the operating profit of the controlled and uncontrolled taxpayers. In addition, because the contractual terms of the relationship among the participants in the relevant business activity will be a principal determinant of the allocation of functions and risks among them, comparability under this method also depends particularly on the degree of similarity of the contractual terms of the controlled and uncontrolled taxpayers. Finally, the comparable profit split may not be used if the combined operating profit (as a percentage of the combined assets) of the uncontrolled comparables varies significantly from that earned by the controlled taxpayers.

(*2*) *Adjustments for differences between the controlled and uncontrolled taxpayers.* If there are differences between the controlled and uncontrolled taxpayers that would materially affect the division of operating profit, adjustments must be made according to the provisions of § 1.482-1(d)(2).

(C) *Data and assumptions.* The reliability of the results derived from the comparable profit split is affected by the quality of the data and assumptions used to apply this method. In particular, the following factors must be considered -

(*1*) The reliability of the allocation of costs, income, and assets between the relevant business activity and the participants' other activities will affect the accuracy of the determination of combined operating profit and its allocation among the participants. If it is not possible to allocate costs, income, and assets directly based on factual relationships, a reasonable allocation formula may be used. To the extent direct allocations are not made, the reliability of the results derived from the application of this method is reduced relative to the results of a method that requires fewer allocations of costs, income, and assets. Similarly, the reliability of the results derived from the application of this method is affected by the extent to which it is possible to apply the method to the parties' financial data that is related solely to the controlled transactions. For example, if the relevant business activity is the assembly of components purchased from both controlled and uncontrolled suppliers, it may not be possible to apply the method solely to financial data related to the controlled transactions. In such a case, the reliability of the results derived from the application of this method will be reduced.

(2) The degree of consistency between the controlled and uncontrolled taxpayers in accounting practices that materially affect the items that determine the amount and allocation of operating profit affects the reliability of the result. Thus, for example, if differences in inventory and other cost accounting practices would materially affect operating profit, the ability to make reliable adjustments for such differences would affect the reliability of the results. Further, accounting consistency among the participants in the controlled transaction is required to ensure that the items determining the amount and allocation of operating profit are measured on a consistent basis.

(D) *Other factors affecting reliability.* Like the methods described in §§ 1.482-3, 1.482-4, 1.482-5, and 1.482-9, the comparable profit split relies exclusively on external market benchmarks. As indicated in § 1.482-1(c)(2)(i), as the degree of comparability between the controlled and uncontrolled transactions increases, the relative weight accorded the analysis under this method will increase. In addition, the reliability of the analysis under this method may be enhanced by the fact that all parties to the controlled transaction are evaluated under the comparable profit split. However, the reliability of the results of an analysis based on information from all parties to a transaction is affected by the reliability of the data and the assumptions pertaining to each party to the controlled transaction. Thus, if the data and assumptions are significantly more reliable with respect to one of the parties than with respect to the others, a different method, focusing solely on the results of that party, may yield more reliable results.

(3) *Residual profit split* -

(i) *In general.* Under this method, the combined operating profit or loss from the relevant business activity is allocated between the controlled taxpayers following the two-step process set forth in paragraphs (c)(3)(i)(A) and (B) of this section.

(A) *Allocate income to routine contributions.* The first step allocates operating income to each party to the controlled transactions to provide a market return for its routine contributions to the relevant business activity. Routine contributions are contributions of the same or a similar kind to those made by uncontrolled taxpayers involved in similar business activities for which it is possible to identify market returns. Routine contributions ordinarily include contributions of tangible property, services and intangible property that are generally owned by uncontrolled taxpayers engaged in similar activities. A functional analysis is required to identify these contributions according to the functions performed, risks assumed, and resources employed by each of the controlled taxpayers. Market returns for the routine contributions should be determined by reference to the returns achieved by uncontrolled taxpayers engaged in similar activities, consistent with the methods described in §§ 1.482-3, 1.482-4, 1.482-5 and 1.482-9.

(B) *Allocate residual profit -*

(1) Non-routine contributions generally. The allocation of income to the controlled taxpayer's routine contributions will not reflect profits attributable to each controlled taxpayer's contributions to the relevant business activity that are not routine (non-routine contributions). A non-routine contribution is a contribution that is not accounted for as a routine contribution. Thus, in cases where such non-routine contributions are present, there normally will be an unallocated residual profit after the allocation of income described in paragraph (c)(3)(i)(A) of this section. Under this second step, the residual profit generally should be divided among the controlled taxpayers based upon the relative value of their non-routine contributions to the relevant business activity. The relative value of the non-routine contributions of each taxpayer should be measured in a manner that most reliably reflects each non-routine contribution made to the controlled transaction and each controlled taxpayer's role in the non-routine contributions. If the non-routine contribution by one of the controlled taxpayers is also used in other business activities (such as transactions with other controlled taxpayers), an appropriate allocation of the value of the non-routine contribution must be made among all the business activities in which it is used.

(2) *Non-routine contributions of intangible property.* In many cases, non-routine contributions of a taxpayer to the relevant business activity may be contributions of intangible property. For purposes of paragraph (c)(3)(i)(B)(1) of this section, the relative value of nonroutine intangible property contributed by taxpayers may be measured by external market benchmarks that reflect the fair market value of such intangible property. Alternatively, the relative value of non-routine intangible property contributions may be estimated by the

capitalized cost of developing the intangible property and all related improvements and updates, less an appropriate amount of amortization based on the useful life of each intangible property. Finally, if the intangible property development expenditures of the parties are relatively constant over time and the useful life of the intangible property contributed by all parties is approximately the same, the amount of actual expenditures in recent years may be used to estimate the relative value of non-routine intangible property contributions.

(ii) *Comparability and reliability considerations* -

(A) *In general.* Whether results derived from this method are the most reliable measure of the arm's length result is determined using the factors described under the best method rule in § 1.482-1(c). Thus, comparability and the quality of data and assumptions must be considered in determining whether this method provides the most reliable measure of an arm's length result. The application of these factors to the residual profit split is discussed in paragraph (c)(3)(ii)(B), (C), and (D) of this section.

(B) *Comparability.* The first step of the residual profit split relies on market benchmarks of profitability. Thus, the comparability considerations that are relevant for the first step of the residual profit split are those that are relevant for the methods that are used to determine market returns for the routine contributions. The second step of the residual profit split, however, may not rely so directly on market benchmarks. Thus, the reliability of the results under this method is reduced to the extent that the allocation of profits in the second step does not rely on market benchmarks.

(C) *Data and assumptions.* The reliability of the results derived from the residual profit split is affected by the quality of the data and assumptions used to apply this method. In particular, the following factors must be considered -

(1) The reliability of the allocation of costs, income, and assets as described in paragraph (c)(2)(ii)(C)(1) of this section;

(2) Accounting consistency as described in paragraph (c)(2)(ii)(C)(2) of this section;

(3) The reliability of the data used and the assumptions made in valuing the intangible property contributed by the participants. In particular, if capitalized costs of development are used to estimate the value of intangible property, the reliability of the results is reduced relative to the reliability of other methods that do not require such an estimate, for the following reasons. First, in any given case, the costs of developing the intangible may not be related to its market value. Second,

the calculation of the capitalized costs of development may require the allocation of indirect costs between the relevant business activity and the controlled taxpayer's other activities, which may affect the reliability of the analysis. Finally, the calculation of costs may require assumptions regarding the useful life of the intangible property.

(D) *Other factors affecting reliability.* Like the methods described in §§ 1.482-3, 1.482-4, 1.482-5, and 1.482-9, the first step of the residual profit split relies exclusively on external market benchmarks. As indicated in § 1.482-1(c)(2)(i), as the degree of comparability between the controlled and un controlled transactions increases, the relative weight accorded the analysis under this method will increase. In addition, to the extent the allocation of profits in the second step is not based on external market benchmarks, the reliability of the analysis will be decreased in relation to an analysis under a method that relies on market benchmarks. Finally, the reliability of the analysis under this method may be enhanced by the fact that all parties to the controlled transaction are evaluated under the residual profit split. However, the reliability of the results of an analysis based on information from all parties to a transaction is affected by the reliability of the data and the assumptions pertaining to each party to the controlled transaction. Thus, if the data and assumptions are significantly more reliable with respect to one of the parties than with respect to the others, a different method, focusing solely on the results of that party, may yield more reliable results.

(iii) *Example.* The provisions of this paragraph (c)(3) are illustrated by the following example.

EXAMPLE – APPLICATION OF RESIDUAL PROFIT SPLIT.

(i) XYZ is a U.S. corporation that develops, manufactures and markets a line of products for police use in the United States. XYZ's research unit developed a bulletproof material for use in protective clothing and headgear (Nulon). XYZ obtains patent protection for the chemical formula for Nulon. Since its introduction in the U.S., Nulon has captured a substantial share of the U.S. market for bulletproof material.

(ii) XYZ licensed its European subsidiary, XYZ-Europe, to manufacture and market Nulon in Europe. XYZ-Europe is a well- established company that manufactures and markets XYZ products in Europe. XYZ-Europe has a research unit that adapts XYZ products for the defense market, as well as a well-developed marketing network that employs brand names that it developed.

(iii) XYZ-Europe's research unit alters Nulon to adapt it to military specifications and develops a high-intensity marketing campaign directed at the defense industry in several European countries. Beginning with the 1995 taxable year, XYZ-Europe manufactures and sells Nulon in Europe through its marketing network under one of its brand names.

(iv) For the 1995 taxable year, XYZ has no direct expenses associated with the license of Nulon to XYZ-Europe and incurs no expenses related to the marketing of Nulon in Europe. For the 1995 taxable year, XYZ-Europe's Nulon sales and pre-royalty expenses are $500 million and $300 million, respectively, resulting in net pre-royalty profit of $200 million related to the Nulon business. The operating assets employed in XYZ-Europe's Nulon business are $200 million. Given the facts and circumstances, the district director determines under the best method rule that a residual profit split will provide the most reliable measure of an arm's length result. Based on an examination of a sample of European companies performing functions similar to those of XYZ-Europe, the district director determines that an average market return on XYZ-Europe's operating assets in the Nulon business is 10 percent, resulting in a market return of $20 million (10% × $200 million) for XYZ- Europe's Nulon business, and a residual profit of $180 million.

(v) Since the first stage of the residual profit split allocated profits to XYZ-Europe's contributions other than those attributable to highly valuable intangible property, it is assumed that the residual profit of $180 million is attributable to the valuable intangibles related to Nulon, i.e., the European brand name for Nulon and the Nulon formula (including XYZ-Europe's modifications). To estimate the relative values of these intangibles, the district director compares the ratios of the capitalized value of expenditures as of 1995 on Nulon-related research and development and marketing over the 1995 sales related to such expenditures.

(vi) Because XYZ's protective product research and development expenses support the worldwide protective product sales of the XYZ group, it is necessary to allocate such expenses among the worldwide business activities to which they relate. The district director determines that it is reasonable to allocate the value of these expenses based on worldwide protective product sales. Using information on the average useful life of its investments in protective product research and development, the district director capitalizes and amortizes XYZ's protective product research and development expenses. This analysis indicates that the capitalized research and development expenditures have a value of $0.20 per dollar of global protective product sales in 1995.

(vii) XYZ-Europe's expenditures on Nulon research and development and marketing support only its sales in Europe. Using information on the average useful life of XYZ-Europe's investments in marketing and research and development, the district director capitalizes and amortizes XYZ-Europe's expenditures and determines that they have a value in 1995 of $0.40 per dollar of XYZ-Europe's Nulon sales.

(viii) Thus, XYZ and XYZ-Europe together contributed $0.60 in capitalized intangible development expenses for each dollar of XYZ-Europe's protective product sales for 1995, of which XYZ contributed one-third (or $0.20 per dollar of sales). Accordingly, the district director determines that an arm's length royalty for the Nulon license for the 1995 taxable year is $60 million, i.e., one-third of XYZ-Europe's $180 million in residual Nulon profit.

(d) *Effective/applicability date* -

(1) *In general.* The provisions of paragraphs (c)(2)(ii)(B)(1) and (D), (c)(3)(i)(A) and (B), and (c)(3)(ii)(D) of this section are generally applicable for taxable years beginning after July 31, 2009.

(2) *Election to apply regulation to earlier taxable years.* A person may elect to apply the provisions of paragraphs (c)(2)(ii)(B)(1) and (D), (c)(3)(i)(A) and (B), and (c)(3)(ii)(D) of this section to earlier taxable years in accordance with the rules set forth in § 1.482-9(n)(2).

[T.D. 8552, 59 FR 35025, July 8, 1994; 60 FR 16382, Mar. 30, 1995, as amended by T.D. 9278, 71 FR 44486, Aug. 4, 2006; T.D. 9456, 74 FR 38844, Aug. 4, 2009; 74 FR 46345, Sept. 9, 2009]

ANNEX 2 RELEVANT REGULATIONS AND CASE LAW

Decision in *Amazon.com, Inc. & Subsidiaries v. Comm'r*, 148 T.C. No. 8 (23 March 2017).

Guidant LLC et al. v. Commissioner, Nos. 5989-11, 5990-11, 10985-11, 26876-11, 5501-12, 5502-12, United States Tax Court (19 July 2016).

Part VI Digital Business Models and Digitalization of the Economy

CHAPTER 19

Cross-Border Allocation of MNEs Profits (Losses) in Light of the Digitalization of the Economy: An Assessment of Amount A & B

Vikram Chand

I INTRODUCTION

In February 2019, the Organisation for Economic Co-operation and Development (OECD) released a public consultation document[1] (PCD), and in May 2019, the OECD released its work programme to develop a consensus-based solution.[2] The foregoing two documents essentially discuss proposals that either address the allocation of taxing rights (Pillar I) or unresolved Base Erosion of Profit Shifting (BEPS) issues (Pillar II). Then, in October 2019, the OECD Secretariat released its proposal for a Unified Approach[3] to address the Pillar I debate. Subsequently, in a January 2020 statement, the OECD presented an outline of the architecture of the Unified Approach, in particular, Amount A and Amount B.[4] It should be noted that the Unified approach represents an important milestone in the work of the OECD as the proposal entails a significant departure - specifically as regards Amount A - from the consensus around

1. OECD, Addressing the Tax Challenges of the Digitalisation of the Economy - Public Consultation Document, OECD/G20 Base Erosion and Profit Shifting Project (OECD Publishing, 2019).
2. OECD, Programme of Work to Develop a Consensus Solution to the Tax Challenges Arising from the Digitalization of the Economy, OECD/G20 Base Erosion and Profit Shifting Project (OECD Publishing, 2019).
3. OECD, Secretariat Proposal for a 'Unified Approach' under Pillar One, OECD/G20 Base Erosion and Profit Shifting Project (OECD Publishing, October 2019).
4. OECD, Statement by the OECD/G20 Inclusive Framework on BEPS on the Two-Pillar Approach to Address the Tax Challenges Arising from the Digitalisation of the Economy - January 2020, OECD/G20 Inclusive Framework on BEPS (OECD 2020).

the arm's-length principle (ALP).[5] In other words, it moves away from the separate entity approach and considers the entire Multinational enterprise (MNE) Group as a single economic unit for Amount A.

The purpose of this contribution is to provide our perspective on the OECD's unified approach. In order to do so, the contribution is structured as follows. It starts with issues surrounding Amount A, viz. Scope (section 2), Nexus (section 3), Profit/Loss allocation (section 4), Revenue Sourcing Rules (section 5), rules to eliminate double taxation (section 6), dispute prevention mechanisms (section 7) and issues related to its implementation outlet (section 8). Then we express our opinion on Amount B and its implementation outlet (section 9). We then conclude (section 10). In September 2020, the blueprint of the Unified Approach was leaked (hereinafter 'leaked report'). Thereafter, in October 2020, the Blueprint of the Pillar I proposal was officially published by the OECD.[6] The analysis presented in this chapter was prepared in April 2020 and has been updated with the findings of the leaked report as well as the officially published blueprint.

II SCOPE

1 Preliminary Remarks

The PCD issued in February 2019 had put forward three proposals, viz. the significant economic presence (SEP) proposal, user participation (UP) proposal and the marketing intangibles (MI) proposal. On the one hand, it could be argued that the Unified approach goes beyond the value creation standard as it incorporates elements of all three proposals, especially using a formulary approach. On the other hand, it could be argued that out of these three proposals, from a conceptual perspective, the Unified Approach seems to be built on the MI proposal. That latter proposal was premised on the policy rationale that a traditional or digital MNE can be actively present in a Market Country on a remote basis (for instance, digitally) or through a local presence (local subsidiary or permanent establishment (PE)) to develop existing or new market-related intangibles, such as brands, trade names, customer data, customer lists, and customer relationships.[7] The MI proposal essentially argued that, if a non-resident supplier actively intervenes in a Market Country through its own efforts and develops market-related intangibles therein, then the latter State should have a right to tax the profits (at least a part of it) linked to the intangibles. This proposal is justified by the fact that an intrinsic functional link exists between the marketing-related intangibles and market jurisdiction.[8]

5. OECD, Transfer Pricing Guidelines for Multinational Enterprises and Tax Administrations 2017.
6. *See* OECD/G20, Tax Challenges Arising from Digitalization – Report on the Pillar One Blueprint, October 2020 (OECD Publishing, 2020). Also *see* OECD, Report on Pillar I Blueprint. The leaked report is available here: https://www.oecd.org/tax/beps/statement-by-the-oecd-g20-inclusive-framework-on-beps-january-2020.pdf.
7. OECD, *supra* n. 1, at para. 30.
8. OECD, *supra* n. 1, at paras 31–32.

From an intrinsic link perspective, some scholars have argued that the use of Intellectual Property (IP) and profits associated with it could be 'sourced' to the country whose laws provide legal protection for that property.[9] In particular, it has been argued that 'marketing intangibles like trademark and goodwill ... are inherently connected to the sales market', especially sales made in a business to consumer (B2C) context.[10] Other commentators share a similar opinion and state that, under existing principles, 'a strong argument can be made that the jurisdiction where the base of customers or a network exists is a natural source for goodwill and customer-based intangibles'.[11]

If this line of reasoning is correct, the question arises as to why Amount A of the Unified Approach would only apply to consumer-facing and user-facing businesses,[12] the latter being highly digitalized businesses (HDBs)? In our view, a possible justification is that the intrinsic functional link is stronger in consumer-facing or user-facing businesses as opposed to non-consumer- facing/user-facing businesses.[13] This said, some commentators on the digital project have argued that the scope should cover all MNEs.[14]

Assuming that a Market Country could be justified to exercise its taxing right over the profits linked to these intangibles, the profits that could be taxed by this country should not be excessive and should remain in proportion to the 'benefits' provided by that State. In other words, an excessive reallocation of profits to the Market countries should not be made under Amount A. This is because the production countries (especially countries wherein trade intangibles are created) need to be compensated for generating profits.[15]

Further, it should be noted that any solution that targets consumer-facing businesses/user-facing businesses should be built on well-established tax policy principles, such as those agreed in the context of the 'Ottawa' Framework.[16] For instance, any solution should be as neutral as possible in the sense that it should apply to all consumer-facing businesses / user-facing businesses unless certain exceptions

9. L. Lokken, The Sources of Income From International Uses and Dispositions of Intellectual Property, 36 Tax L. Rev. 233, 242 (1981); M.A. Kane, A Defense of Source Rules in International Taxation, 32 Yale J. Reg. 311, 341–342 (2015); R. Vann, Reflections on Business Profits and the Arm's-Length Principle, in The Taxation of Business Profits under Tax Treaties, 145–146 (B.J. Arnold, J. Sasseville & E. M. Zolt eds, Canadian Tax Foundation, 2003).
10. R. Vann, Taxing International Business Income: Hard Boiled Wonderland and the End of the World, 2(3) WTJ, 337 (2010) Journals IBFD.
11. P. Oosterhuis & A. Parsons, Destination Based Income Taxation: Neither Principled Nor Practical?, 71 Tax L. Rev. 515, 522–524 (2018).
12. OECD, Public Consultation Document, *supra* n. 1, at para. 19 (and footnote 7).
13. V. Chand, Allocation of Taxing Rights in the Digitalized Economy: Assessment of Potential Policy Solutions and Recommendation for a Simplified Residual Profit Split Method, 47(12) Intertax, 2019, s. 5.3.
14. Public Comments, Procter and Gamble, p. 7; Public Comments, Nestle, p. 3; Public Comments, Maisto E Associati, p. 4.
15. OECD, Public Consultation Document, *supra* n. 1, at para. 57.
16. OECD, Electronic Commerce: Taxation Framework Conditions, Report by the Committee on Fiscal Affairs (OECD Publishing, 1998), at para. 9 (Box 2); Also *see* OECD, Addressing the Tax Challenges of the Digital Economy, Action 1 – 2015 Final Report, OECD/G20 Base Erosion and Profit Shifting Project, (OECD Publishing, October 2015), paras 10–13.

can be justified. Second, the solution should pursue the path of certainty and simplicity, especially with respect to profit allocation. Third, a solution should be efficient in that the compliance costs should be low for both tax administrations and taxpayers. Fourth, the solution should be effective in the sense that taxes can be easily collected by the tax administration and fair so that opportunities for tax avoidance are minimized. In the next section, we will discuss which businesses should be within or outside the scope of the Unified Approach.

2 Businesses in Scope and Out of Scope Based on Activities

A Consumer-Facing Businesses

Starting with consumer-facing businesses, we believe that a business should be carved in to the extent it's focal point is to create a brand or trade name that resonates in the minds of potential individual consumers.[17] Moreover, seen from the perspective of the MNE business, the objective of the enterprise should be to create a final product or provide a service for an individual consumer. In this sense, a difference should not be made as to whether the product/service is sold in a B2C or Business to Business (B2B) context. The controlling criteria is – for whom does the business develop the product/service? If the business makes the product/service primarily for consumption by an individual, then it should be carved in.

For example, an MNE, which is in the business of making branded chocolates, should be carved in. It should not matter whether the MNE sells branded chocolates directly to an individual (through its own store) or to another business (retailers), which then sells it to the individual. By contrast, businesses that do not create products or provide services targeted at individual consumers should not be carved in. This said, it remains challenging to develop a definition of what constitutes a consumer-facing business.[18]

Ideally, a reference needs to be made towards certain international benchmarks/information available in the public domain to understand what constitutes a consumer-facing business.

With respect to defining consumer-facing businesses (consumers being individuals), one possibility would be to refer to certain international benchmarks, such as the Industrial Classification Benchmark[19] or Global Industry Standard Classification[20] benchmark or other benchmarks.[21] Based on these benchmarks, the following businesses may fall within the scope of this proposal (non-exhaustive list).

17. OECD, *supra* n. 1, at para. 31.
18. Public Comments, Zalando, p. 2; Public Comments, Nestle, p. 4; Public Comments, Johnson and Johnson, p. 5; Public Comments, PwC, pp. 5–6.
19. Available on https://research.ftserussell.com/products/downloads/ICB_Rules.pdf.
20. Available on https://www.spglobal.com/marketintelligence/en/documents/112727-gics-mapbook_2018_v3_letter_digitalspreads.pdf.
21. For example, *see* International Standard of Industrial Classification available on https://unstats.un.org/unsd/publication/seriesm/seriesm_4rev4e.pdf. Also *see*, Statistical Classification of Economic Activities in the European Community available on https://ec.europa.eu/eurostat/

Consumer Goods Business, such as:

- food & beverages business (examples – food products, soft drinks, alcoholic beverages);
- personal goods business (examples – luxury goods, fashionable goods, consumer electronics, hygiene/healthcare goods, tobacco);
- household goods business (examples, household furnishing products or household appliances or cleaning products);
- automobiles and automobile component businesses (examples – cars, motorcycles, bikes);
- pharmaceutical business (examples – medical devices/medicines that are made for individual consumption);
- businesses whose core business is wholesaling or retailing goods (foods, drugs, clothes, etc.) can also fall within this category.

Consumer Services Business, such as:

- media business (examples – broadcasting through television or radio, publishing, entertainment business, such as motion pictures);
- travel and leisure businesses (examples – passenger airlines or cruises) or brick and mortar business that sell travel or leisure packages;
- telecommunication businesses (examples – mobile phone operators);
- financial services (examples – consumer finance services, such as credit cards, private banking, private insurance or investment advisory services) and so on.

Franchising / Licensing businesses that are often seen in either consumer goods or consumer services space, such as:

- businesses that franchise fast food restaurant concepts;
- businesses that franchise fashion concepts;
- businesses that franchise hotel concepts.

In fact, the blueprint indicates that the aforementioned businesses will be covered under the scope of Amount A.[22]

Furthermore, within this category, special attention should also be given to branded businesses that sell branded products to other businesses, which in turn use them for their own goods. For example, a branded tyre manufacturer (MNE M) could sell tyres to a branded car manufacturer (MNE W). MNE W installs those tyres in its cars and sells them to individual consumers. While MNE W will be within the scope of the proposal, the question arises as to whether MNE M will fall within the scope of this proposal. Arguably, they should as they can be classified under the automobile components business. The leaked report and the blueprint confirm this viewpoint and

statistics-explained/index.php/Glossary:Statistical_classification_of_economic_activities_in_the_European_Community_(NACE).

22. OECD, Blueprint on Pillar I, *supra* n. 6, at pp. 38-48; OECD, Leaked report, *supra* n. 6, at pp. 36-46.

indicate that such businesses will be covered under the scope of Amount A.[23] On this point, it is obvious that more work needs to be done vis-à-vis borderline cases.[24]

B User-Facing Businesses or Highly Digital Businesses

With respect to user-facing businesses, sufficient work has already been done by policymaking organizations/tax administrations.[25] For instance, businesses that develop a large user base for monetization purposes include, for example, businesses engaged in selling user data, online advertising, social media platforms, search engines and online market places/intermediation platforms.[26]

On the other hand, there are some businesses in which UP is less relevant. For example, HDBs such as online content providers (online streaming of music and videos) or businesses engaged in online gaming (at least, some segments) or online teaching or cloud computing businesses. On the one hand, it could be argued that such businesses are not user-facing/user-dependent, and thus, they should be outside the scope. On the other hand, as stated by the Indian and UK tax administration,[27] although UP by individuals plays a limited role in such businesses, it is nonetheless relevant.[28] Thus, such businesses could be within the scope of the proposal. In this regard, it should be noted that such businesses (along with other HDBs) were within the scope of the EU Directive on Significant Digital Presence.[29] Also, some commentators have explicitly argued for such businesses to be carved in (especially cloud computing businesses).[30] At this stage, E-retailers (that purchase / create physical products for reselling) could be within scope either under the user-facing category or the consumer-facing category.

In fact, the leaked report and the blueprint indicate that the aforementioned businesses, which are classified as automated digital service (ADS) related businesses, will be covered under the scope of Amount A under a positive list.[31]

---

23. OECD, Blueprint on Pillar I, *supra* n. 6, at pp. 47-48; OECD, Leaked report, *supra* n. 6, at pp. 46-47.
24. For other examples of border line cases, *see* Public Comments, Booking.com, pp. 7–8; Public Comments, Johnson and Johnson, p. 6.
25. European Commission, Proposal for a Council Directive on the Common System of a Digital Services Tax on Revenues Resulting from the Provision of Certain Digital Services, COM(2018) 148 final, 2018/0073(CNS), (21 March 2018); Also *see* Central Board of Direct Taxes, Income department – Government of India, Proposal for Amendment of Rules for Profit Attribution to Permanent Establishment (CBDT, 2019); UK: HM Treasury, Corporate tax and the Digital Economy: Position Paper Update (2018).
26. European Commission, *supra* n. 25, at pp. 7–9; Central Board of Direct Taxes, *supra* n. 25, para. 175; UK: HM Treasury, *supra* n. 25, para. 2.45 (2018).
27. Central Board of Direct Taxes, *supra* n. 25, para. 175; UK: HM Treasury, *supra* n. 25, para. 2.45 (2018).
28. Central Board of Direct Taxes, *supra* n. 25, para. 175; UK: HM Treasury, *supra* n. 25, paras 2.47–2.48 (2018).
29. *See* European Commission, Proposal for a Council Directive laying down rules relating to the Corporate Taxation of a Significant Digital Presence, (21 March 2018), pp. 1–19.
30. Public Comments, Procter and Gamble, pp. 2–3 and pp. 6–7.
31. OECD, Blueprint on Pillar I, *supra* n. 6, at pp. 22-38; OECD, Leaked report, *supra* n. 6, at pp. 22-30.

C Businesses Outside the Scope of Amount A

If the proposal applies to consumer- or user-facing businesses, then certain businesses will need to be carved out from the scope of the Unified Approach.

The first possible exclusion relates to businesses engaged in the extractive sector[32] such as businesses engaged in mining (examples – metals, minerals, coal and so on); or businesses engaged in the extraction of petroleum and natural gas or other renewable energy products; or businesses that sell renewable products (agricultural, fishery or forestry products and so on) including materials that are used in other businesses (examples – commodities, chemical material, construction material, forest products like paper, etc.). Another reason could be used to justify the carve-out for these kinds of businesses. For instance, when a non-resident extractive business operates in another State, that business will typically trigger a PE therein under Article 5. For example, Article 5(2)(f) provides that a PE includes a '*mine, an oil or gas well, a quarry or any other place of extraction of natural resources*'.[33] However, special attention should be given to oil and gas MNEs. This industry is usually divided into upstream, midstream and downstream businesses.[34] Arguably, some parts of downstream businesses are consumer-facing (e.g., selling petrol through petrol pumps to ultimate consumers). Thus, further consideration should be given to whether such businesses are to be carved in or carved out.

A second exclusion pertains to construction businesses. For instance, when a non-resident construction business operates in another State to build local infrastructure (houses, roads, ports etc.), that business will typically trigger a PE therein under Article 5(3).

The third example relates to shipping and airline businesses as special rules apply to them under the current framework. Cross-border taxation of such businesses is covered under Article 8 OECD MC.[35] The Article provides that, in many situations, the profits of such businesses are taxed in one State alone.[36] That country could be the State where the enterprise has its place of effective management or its place of residence. In other words, other countries in which the consumers reside (which could be Market countries) are not allowed to tax such profits. The main policy reasons for adopting this approach relate to either preventing overtaxation of such enterprises or practical difficulties that could arise with respect to the determination and allocation of taxable profit to market countries.[37] Thus, such businesses may be carved out from the

32. OECD, Public Consultation Document, *supra* n. 1, at para. 20.
33. Moreover, *see* A. Auerbach, M. Devereux, M. Keen & J. Vella, *Destination-Based Cash Flow Taxation*, Saïd Business School Working Paper 2017/09 (2017), pp. 37–38. These authors also argue that the extractive industry should be carved out from the scope of their proposal because the State in which a product is extracted always has the right to tax the profits derived from the extraction of the product (national resources and immovable property).
34. *See* UN, Taxation of the Extractive Industries by Developing Countries, pp. 11–16.
35. *See* Art. 8 OECD Model Tax Convention (2017).
36. OECD Model Tax Convention (2017): Commentary on Art. 8, para. 1
37. *UN Model Tax Convention (2017): Commentary on* Art. 8, paras 2–3. Also *see* Guglielmo Maisto. The History of Art. 8 of the OECD Model Treaty on Taxation of Shipping and Air Transport. 31(6) Intertax (2003): 232–244; Also *see* Public Comments, Maisto E Associati, p. 4.

scope of the proposal (Amount A) as, under the current framework, they are not taxed in the market countries even if they operate with a physical presence in those States.

The fourth example pertains to consumer financial services. In many situations, businesses, such as banks[38] and insurance[39] companies operate with a substantial presence in the Market countries (branches or subsidiaries) and carry out core commercial activities therein. This is mainly because of local market regulations. Moreover, some financial services businesses, when they operate on a cross-border basis, could be subject to high withholding taxes on a gross basis. For instance, banks, which are engaged in providing cross-border loans, could be subject to high withholding taxes on under Article 11 OECD MC.[40] Similarly, widely held investment funds or other funds (such as private equity funds) that invest in other countries (equity or debt instruments) could be subject to high withholding taxes under Article 10 OECD MC or Article 11 OECD MC. Moreover, if the investment is targeted at real estate (through real estate investment funds), then the State of the situs of the property has a right to tax the income generated by that property, either under Article 6 OECD MC or Article 13 OECD MC.[41] Thus, further analysis would be required to ascertain whether such businesses should be carved out from the scope of the proposal (Amount A) as under the current framework, they either operate with presence in market countries or they may be subject to high Market Country taxation on a gross basis.[42]

In fact, the leaked report and the blueprint make a discussion on these four aforementioned categories and indicate that some or all parts of such businesses will be excluded.[43]

3 Further Criteria: Turnover Thresholds

At the outset, it is desirable that the new rules should apply only to in-scope MNE Groups that exceed a certain consolidated revenue threshold. From an efficiency perspective (compliance costs), this would make sense. The secretariats proposal indicates that the threshold could be EUR 750 Million,[44] which is similar to the threshold set in the Country-by-Country Reporting (CBCR) standard.[45] This threshold, although used in a different context, is also found in proposals with respect to digital

38. *See*: OECD, 2010 Report on the Attribution of Profits to Permanent Establishments (OECD Publishing, 2010), Part II, para. 4.
39. *See*: OECD, 2010 Report on the Attribution of Profits to Permanent Establishments (OECD Publishing, 2010), Part IV, para. 2.
40. *See* Art. 11 OECD Model Tax Convention (2017). *See also* OECD Model Tax Convention (2017): Commentary on Art. 11, para. 7.7.
41. *See* Art. 6(1) OECD Model Tax Convention (2017); Also *see* Arts 13(1) and 13(4) OECD Model Tax Convention (2017).
42. Public Comments, KPMG, p. 5; Public Comments, EY, p. 7; Public Comments, Deloitte, p. 4.
43. OECD, Blueprint on Pillar I, *supra* n. 6, at pp. 49-61; OECD, Leaked report, *supra* n. 6, at pp. 47-65.
44. OECD, Public Consultation Document, *supra* n. 1, at para. 20.
45. OECD, Transfer Pricing Documentation and Country-by-Country Reporting, Action 13 – 2015 Final Report, OECD/G20 Base Erosion and Profit Shifting Project (OECD Publishing, October 2015).

service taxes (DSTs) proposed either by policymaking organizations (EU[46] or OECD[47]) or national governments of some countries, such as Austria,[48] Spain,[49] France,[50] Italy[51] and New Zealand.[52] Also, the UK[53] uses a comparable threshold of GBP 500 Million. It should be noted that some commentators prefer this turnover threshold,[54] whereas others do not,[55] and some have argued for higher thresholds, at least during the first few years of the proposal.[56] In our opinion, as a start, this threshold should be used, and after a few years, the amounts mentioned in the threshold should be reduced. The leaked report and blueprint highlight this viewpoint.[57]

Moreover, if a profit allocation solution is built on the basis of an MNE Business Line approach, then a relevant MNE Business Line Turnover Threshold should also be built in the potential solution.[58] From an efficiency perspective, this threshold also needs to be high in order to ensure that small revenue-generating business lines of an MNE are carved out from the scope of the proposal.

Another threshold that could be contemplated is the foreign/offshore activities revenue threshold. Consider the following situation, MNE Group X is headquartered in Country R. Its revenues from the Country R market amount to EUR 700 Million, and ten different offshore markets amount to EUR 50 million. While the MNE will be within scope, it may not make sense, from an efficiency perspective, to undertake an Amount A exercise in this scenario. The leaked report and blueprint indicate that this approach could be followed.[59]

III NEXUS

1 Preliminary Remarks

As a starting point, we agree that a new nexus should not be built into the existing PE definition but should rather be structured as an independent distributive rule (in fact, Amount A should be implemented through a new Multilateral Convention – *see* section

46. European Commission, *supra* n. 25.
47. OECD, Interim Report, para. 454.
48. Austria: Digitalsteuergesetz 2020 (132/ME), Art. 1, para. 2.
49. Spain: Proyecto de Ley del Impuesto sobre Determinados Servicios Digitales, Art. 8.
50. France: LOI n° 2019-759 du 24 juillet 2019 portant création d'une taxe sur les services numériques et modification de la trajectoire de baisse de l'impôt sur les sociétés, *ad Art. 299*, §III.
51. Italy: Bilancio di previsione dello Stato per l'anno finanziario 2019 e bilancio pluriennale per il triennio 2019–2021, n. 36, p. 8.
52. NZ: New Zealand Government, Options for Taxing the Digital Economy – a Government Discussion Document, (June 2019).
53. UK: Draft Legislation on the New Digital Services Tax, p. 4.
54. Public Comments, Uber, p. 10; Public Comments, Digital Economy Group, p. 6.
55. Public Comments, Nestle, p. 6.
56. Public Comments, Maisto E Associati, p. 5.
57. OECD, Blueprint on Pillar I, *supra* n. 6, at pp. 61-63; OECD, Leaked report, supra n. 6, at pp. 66-68.
58. Public Comments, Booking.com, p. 7; Public Comments, EY, p. 7.
59. OECD, Blueprint on Pillar I, *supra* n. 6, at pp. 63-64; OECD, Leaked report, *supra* n. 6, at pp. 68-70.

8). By doing so, unnecessary spillover effects that could arise with other existing treaty distributive rules that use the PE concept, for example, the PE concept used in Articles 10, 11, 12, 13, 15, 21 and 24 OECD MC could be avoided. Moreover, frictions could arise with existing profit attribution rules contained in Article 7 OECD MC. It should also be noted that such a new nexus should be built only for the purpose of Amount A and should not lead to any issues under other taxes (such as indirect taxes).

2 Nexus Built on an MNE Group Basis

If a profit allocation solution for Amount A is built on an MNE basis, then the nexus rule should, naturally, also be built on an MNE Group basis. The objective would be to ascertain the entire MNE Group's involvement in a market jurisdiction. Accordingly, the initial question that would arise is how you define an MNE Group for the purpose of this proposal.

A first possibility would be to refer to various accounting standards to derive a definition. One possible approach to derive a definition involves referring to consolidated financial statements that have been prepared in accordance with the rules mandated by the jurisdiction of the Ultimate Parent Company of the MNE Group. These statements, which could be based on local Generally Accepted Accounting Principles (GAAP) or International Financial Reporting Standards (IFRS), could be considered as a starting point for the analysis (in particular, IFRS 10). A second option would be to refer to the concept of associated enterprises under Article 9 OECD MC. Another option would be to resort to Article 5(8) OECD MC, which deals with the concept of closely related enterprises.

A common feature of the aforementioned provisions/guidance is their reference to control (either direct or indirect or through common control). Accordingly, by referring to the aforementioned provisions, in particular, the concept of 'control', the definition of an MNE Group could be developed.

3 Focus on Local Revenue

Several scholars, even prior to the BEPS project, have supported using local market turnover thresholds to develop a new nexus. Such a quantitative threshold, in addition to the MNE Group Revenue threshold, is also found in proposals with respect to DSTs proposed either by policymaking organizations, such as the EU (EUR 50 Million) or national governments of some countries, such as the UK (GBP 25 Million), Austria (EUR 25 Million), Spain (EUR 3 Million), France (EUR 25 Million), Italy (EUR 5 Million) and New Zealand (NZD 3.5 Million). We agree with the approach that nexus rules should predominantly be based on sales linked to a market. The leaked report and the blueprint indicate that this approach will be followed. In particular, it is stated that nexus for ADS businesses will be determined by resorting to a local market turnover threshold, whereas additional factors will apply for consumer-facing businesses.[60]

For the latter, qualitative factors could be considered. For instance, qualitative factors were considered in the context of the SEP proposal, such as user factors (for instance, collection of data from users), digital factors (for instance, maintaining a website in the local language and payment options in the local currency) or factors, such as responsibility for the final delivery of goods to customers, or the provision by the enterprise of other support services or sustained advertising, marketing and promotional activities. However, if this path were to be followed, it should be borne in mind that such factors could lead to rather subjective/imprecise outcomes, which, in turn, could lead to differences in interpretation and, ultimately, disputes. Thus, we do not recommend the use of such factors.

This said, the leaked report and the blueprint indicate that consumer-facing businesses would be subject to one or several 'plus' factors such as a local establishment (subsidiary or PE) that helps the MNE to do business (make sales) in that market jurisdiction.[61] As stated previously, these factors could lead to rather subjective/imprecise outcomes, which, in turn, could lead to differences in interpretation and, ultimately, disputes. Thus, we do not recommend the use of such factors unless and until they are objective in nature.

4 Degree of Permanence Requirements

We also believe that the nexus rule will need a temporal requirement to be built into it to show 'sustained and significant involvement' in the market jurisdiction. This will also ensure that isolated/one-off transactions are not caught by this provision.

One option to demonstrate this requirement is to resort to subjective factors found in the existing PE definition, such as the degree of permanence requirement. However, such a test could lead to tax uncertainty as the analysis would depend on the facts and circumstances of each taxpayer.

An alternative approach could be contemplated, which essentially states that the MNE would be considered to have a taxable nexus with a country if it exceeds the revenue thresholds in each year over the past three or five years.

5 Setting the Local Revenue Threshold

At the outset, the question arises as to whether the amount reflected in this threshold should be the sovereign choice of each State or should a threshold be suggested? Our analysis of various DSTs (as discussed above) indicates that countries contemplate different local revenue thresholds. Thus, we are inclined to say that each country should be free to set its own threshold. This said, we would like to highlight that a

60. OECD, Blueprint on Pillar I, *supra* n. 6, at pp. 66-70; OECD, Leaked report, *supra* n. 6, at pp. 71-72.
61. OECD, Blueprint on Pillar I, *supra* n. 6, at pp. 38-48; OECD, Leaked report, *supra* n. 6, at pp. 68-70.

minimum threshold should also be proposed. If countries start adopting low thresholds (for instance, INR 100,000 for the Indian equalization levy, which is approximately USD 1,400), then the costs of compliance with respect to administering this proposal become high. Thus, a minimum revenue threshold, which is substantially high, needs to be proposed. This would imply that a country cannot go below the proposed minimum threshold.

The minimum revenue threshold would also need to be expressed in a certain common currency. One possible option is to link it to a globally accepted currency, for instance, USD or Euro. However, issues could then arise with respect to converting USD/Euro into local currencies. Another option, which is found in the context of Article 17 OECD MC, is to refer to the International Monetary Fund (IMF) Special Drawing Rights (SDR). That standard provides the possibility to avoid referring to any local currency. Moreover, as outlined in the BEPS Action 1 report, the threshold should be set, taking into consideration the size of a countries market (for instance, by referring to the Gross Domestic Product (GDP) of a country for a particular year or a combination of a few years). Another important issue pertains to the determination of the country in which the revenue arises for an in-scope MNE (consumer or user country). This issue is discussed subsequently (*see* section 5).

IV PROFIT (LOSS) ALLOCATION: AMOUNT A

1 Overview of the Method

A Introductory Comments

In order to apply this method, this approach requires:[62]

- Step 1: Identification of the total profits of the MNE Group Business Line, for example, the overall profit margin (Z%).[63]
- Step 2: Calculate deemed routine profits margin (X%). This margin will then be deducted from the overall profit margin in order to arrive at a non-routine profit margin (Y%).[64]
- Step 3: The non-routine profit margin (Y%) will be split between a profit margin allocable to production activities, such as trade intangibles (V%) and profit allocable to market-related activities, such as a market-related margin (W%).[65]
- Step 4: The profit allocable to a market-related margin (W%) will then be allocated to the Market Country on the basis of an allocation key, such as sales.[66]

62. OECD, Public Consultation Document, *supra* n. 1, at paras 51–61.
63. OECD, Public Consultation Document, *supra* n. 1, at para. 53.
64. OECD, Public Consultation Document, *supra* n. 1, at paras 54–56.
65. OECD, Public Consultation Document, *supra* n. 1, at paras 57–59.
66. OECD, Public Consultation Document, *supra* n. 1, at paras 60–61.

B *Step 1: Calculation of MNE Group Profits or MNE Group Profit Margin*

At the outset,[67] the question arises whether the proposal applies to the whole MNE group (if it has more than one business line) or the relevant business line within an MNE.[68] Arguably, devising a potential solution with respect to a consolidated group (consolidated business lines) seems simpler and more predictable. However, such an approach may not provide accurate results as different businesses could be mixed with each other. Accordingly, a relevant MNE business line approach should be followed in order to have more accurate results.[69]

If an MNE Business Line approach is followed, an initial question that arises is, what is an MNE Business Line? Some MNEs may operate with a centralized business line, that is, through a centralized entrepreneur in one country. Others may have decentralized business lines with local entrepreneurs in many countries. Some other MNEs may report a particular business line on a regional basis (USA, Europe, Asia Pacific and so on). Thus, it would be difficult to provide hard guidance with respect to the definition of a business line.

Another issue pertains to the extent to which an MNE could go granular with respect to its business line information. Consider the following example:

- Level A: If an MNE (X) is engaged in selling food products and automobiles, then what are the business lines? In this situation, it is easy to state that the MNE has two different businesses.
- Level B: What happens if the food business of MNE X is divided between food for humans and food for pets? Will the pet food and human food constitute two different business lines, or are they a part of the same business line?
- Level C: Within the pet food business, food products could be developed for dogs and cats. Are the dog food or cat food business two different business lines or the same business line?
- Level D: Within the dog food business, the operating margins could be different for the USA market in comparison with the European market. In this regard, should the dog food business line be further segmented into a regional business line?

The next issue relates to the determination of consolidated profits (losses) of the MNE business line. As discussed previously, one could refer to consolidated financial statements that have been prepared in accordance with the rules mandated by the jurisdiction of the Ultimate Parent Company of the MNE Group.[70] These statements

67. For a similar discussion in the following sections, *see*, V. Chand, A. Turina & L. Ballivet, Profit Allocation Within MNEs in Light of the Ongoing Digital Debate on Pillar I – A '2020 Compromise'? From Using a Facts and Circumstances Analysis or Allocation Keys to Predetermined Allocation Approaches, 3 World Tax J. (July 2020), s. 5.1.
68. OECD, Public Consultation Document, *supra* n. 1, at para. 32.
69. OECD, Public Consultation Document, *supra* n. 1, at paras 30, 51, 53; Public Comments, Booking.com, p. 6.
70. OECD, Public Consultation Document, *supra* n. 1, at para. 53.

could be considered as a starting point for the analysis (local GAAP or IFRS).[71] This said, although consolidated statements provide a good overview of the MNE, they may not contain detailed information about an MNE Business Line. Thus, this information needs to be gathered perhaps by looking into internal data, such as managerial accounting records. However, the information from such records is less regulated than financial accounting information that is prepared for external stakeholders. Thus, the information obtained from such managerial records will need to be cross-checked with the consolidated financial statements to ensure consistency with the numbers that are being reported.

At this stage, we would like to submit that further work needs to be done in this area of MNE Business Lines. One possibility that could be considered to develop segmentation guidance on this matter is to resort to IFRS 8, which deals with reporting operating segments.[72] Another possibility is to give the MNE taxpayer the option to report MNE Business Line information, which could then be audited by an independent auditor.[73]

Several questions also arise with respect to determining the overall profit (loss) margin as contemplated under this step.

First, should gross or net profits (operating profits) be considered? As the objective of the proposal is to allocate profits to market countries, we believe that net profit information should be considered.

Second, if net profits, should these profits be based on Earnings Before Taxation (EBT), Earning Before Interest and Taxation (EBIT) or Earnings Before Interest Taxation Depreciation and Amortization (EBITDA) figures? In other words, what is the numerator for determining the overall profit margin? In this regard, it should be noted that in BEPS Action 4, it seems that the OECD gave preference to using EBITDA as it reflects an objective measure of economic activity.[74] Also, India, in the context of discussing the fractional apportionment method, showed a preference towards EBITDA.[75] On the other hand, EBIT figures are commonly used in a transfer pricing analysis.[76] While there are pros and cons towards using the foregoing two indicators, we believe that consideration should also be given to EBT[77] as it is the most appropriate

71. OECD/G20, Limiting Base Erosion Involving Interest Deductions and Other Financial Payments, Action 4: 2015 Final Report (OECD/G20 Base Erosion and Profit Shifting Project, 2015), paras 121–126.
72. *See* https://www.iasplus.com/en/standards/ifrs/ifrs8.
73. Public Comments, Procter and Gamble, p. 4; Public Comments, Spotify, p. 9; Public Comments, Nestle, p. 10; Public Comments, Booking.com, p. 11.
74. OECD/G20, Action 4: 2015 Final Report, *supra* n. 71, para. 141.
75. Central Board of Direct Taxes, *supra* n. 25, para. 159.
76. To calculate net profits (although in a separate entity context), *see* OECD Transfer Pricing Guidelines for Multinational Enterprises and Tax Administrations 2017, paras 2.83–2.91 (with an emphasis on para. 2.86). The UK also seems to prefer using this indicator in order to determine the operating margin. *See* UK: HM Treasury, Digital Services Tax Draft Guidance (2019), pp. 47–48.
77. Public Comments, Nestle, p. 10; Public Comments, Booking.com, p. 10; Public Comments, PwC, pp. 13–16; Public Comments, EY, p. 9; Public Comments, Deloitte, p. 5.

indicator to determine the true profitability of a business.[78] This said, we do acknowledge that it could be challenging to obtain MNE Business Line EBT details. Specifically, issues could arise with respect to splitting common costs,[79] especially when some businesses of an MNE are outside the scope of Amount A.[80] Moreover, certain adjustments will be required for exceptional or extraordinary income/expenses (e.g., gains/expenditure connected with acquisitions or dividends from shares and so on).[81]

Third, what should the numerator be weighed against in order to obtain a profit margin? As the objective of this new taxing right is to reallocate profits to the market jurisdiction on the basis of sales, an appropriate denominator would be sales of the relevant business line.[82]

However, if the levels of details that are required for applying an MNE Business line approach get extremely cumbersome, then the consolidated business line approach should be considered[83] as a safe harbour for Amount A in the sense that the consolidated profit margin will be used as a proxy for an in-scope MNE Business.[84] Moreover, another idea would be to allow only selected MNEs that exceed a certain turnover threshold to the segment.

The leaked report and the blueprint confirm that the OECD has recognized the above issues to determine the MNE taxable base and is moving its work in this direction.[85]

C Step 2: Calculation of Routine and Non-routine Operating Profit Margin

For the purpose of the rest of this document, we will assume that EBT/Sales is used as a profitability indicator.

Under this step, a certain percentage of the overall EBT margin is deemed to be a routine return margin. For example, if an MNE Group has an overall EBT margin of 40%, then a certain percentage (e.g., 10% of that margin) will be considered to be a deemed routine EBT margin, and the balance (30%) will be deemed to be non-routine EBT margin. This would imply that if an MNE Group has an EBT margin of less than 10%, then it will fall outside the scope of this proposal. Consequently, no profits will be allocated under Amount A.

78. V. Chand, Allocation of Taxing Rights, *supra* n. 13, s. 6.3. Also *see* Public Comments, Procter and Gamble, p. 11.
79. UK: HM Treasury, Digital Services Tax Draft Guidance (2019), pp. 49–50. Also *see* Public Comments, Skadden, p. 9.
80. Public Comments, Uber, pp. 3–4.
81. UK: HM Treasury, Digital Services Tax Draft Guidance (2019), p. 48; Public Comments, Unilever, p. 10; Public Comments, Amazon, p. 6; Public Comments, Skadden, p. 8.
82. Also, *see* OECD Transfer Pricing Guidelines for Multinational Enterprises and Tax Administrations 2017, paras 2.96–2.97.
83. Public Comments, Uber, p. 3.
84. V. Chand, Allocation of Taxing Rights, *supra* n. 13, s. 6.3.
85. OECD, Blueprint on Pillar I, *supra* n. 6, at pp. 103-115; OECD, Leaked report, *supra* n. 6, at pp. 110-126.

D Step 3: Splitting the Non-routine Margin

Continuing with the above, countries may agree upon a predetermined split. For example, an 80%–20% split, which divides the non-routine margin between production-related activities (for instance, trade intangibles) and market-related activities (for instance, MI). For example, if an MNE Group has a non-routine EBT margin of 30% (as in this example), then 80% of that is allocated to production-related activities, whereas 20% is allocated to market-related activities. This would imply that 6% of the overall EBT margin will be allocated to market-related activities.

E Step 4: Allocation to Market (Sales) Countries

Under this step, 6% of the MNEs in scope Business Lines revenue will be considered to be allocable to the sales/market countries. The allocation can be made on the basis of sales made in the respective jurisdiction. A key question that arises is with respect to the determination of the sales location. This is discussed later on (*see* section 5).

2 Profit Allocation: High-Level Illustration of This Method

To understand the application of this approach, consider the following example. SF Group, which has its listed ultimate parent entity in Country R (Company R), sells branded product X in several countries (this is the only business). According to its consolidated financial statements for the year 2021, SF Group has: (A) consolidated group operating revenue = USD 1 billion and (B) consolidated expenses = USD 600 million. Therefore, the Group profits (C) amount to USD 400 million. This amount (C) represents the Groups Earning Before Taxation. Let us assume that the Group generates 10% of its global revenue from Country S (USD 100 million) and 20% of its global revenue from Country S1 (USD 200 million). Under the current transfer pricing rules, all of SF Group's residual or non-routine profit is returned in Country R as the parent entity is the owner of the relevant trade and market-related intangibles. In order to allocate profits to Country S or Country S1, the method would apply as follows:

> **Step 1**: The Group EBT amounts to USD 400 million, and the EBT margin amounts to 40% (EBT/operating revenues).
> **Step 2**: The deemed routine EBT margin is 10%, and thus, 30% will be deemed to be a non-routine EBT margin.
> **Step 3**: The non-routine EBT margin of 30% is split between production activities (80%) and market activities (20%). Essentially, 6% of the EBT margin will be allocated to market-related activities.
> **Step 4**: MS Group's market-related profits are determined to be 6% of the overall revenues, which amounts to USD 60 million (USD 1 billion * 6%). The reallocation will work as follows. Country S: As 10% of the global sales are derived from Country S, it will be allocated USD 6 million (60 * 100/1,000 = 6) of that profit. Country S1: As 20% of the global sales are derived from

Country S1, it will be allocated USD 12 Million (60 * 200/1,000 = 12) of that profit. Country S and Country S1 will tax this profit at its ordinary corporate tax rate, regardless of whether the MNE Group has a physical presence in those countries.

The leaked and the blueprint report confirms that a similar approach will be followed with respect to profit allocation.[86]

3 Dealing with Losses and Loss Allocation

Amount A should also consist of a mechanism that provides relief for losses.[87] As a starting point, carry forward of losses for set-off against future profits should be considered as opposed to a carry-back system as the latter approach raises several administrative issues. Moreover, carry-back systems could raise budgetary concerns for governments.[88] Consider the following case, which builds on the aforementioned case that deals with SF Group.

SF Group, which has its listed ultimate parent entity in Country R (Company R), sells branded product X in several countries (this is the only business). According to its consolidated financial statements for the year 2020, SF Group has: (A) consolidated group operating revenue = USD 1 billion and (B) consolidated expenses = USD 1.2 billion. Therefore, the Group loss (C) amount to USD 200 million. This amount (C) represents the Groups Earning (loss) Before Taxation. In order to deal with losses, the method would apply as follows:

Step 1: The Group EBT amounts to negative USD 200 million, and the negative EBT margin amounts to approximately 20%.
Step 2: The deemed routine EBT margin is 10%. This margin will equally apply to losses. This would imply that if an MNE Group has a negative EBT margin, then this fixed deemed routine percentage will be added to the loss margin. This would amount to 20% + 10% = 30% and it will represent the non-routine margin.
Step 3: If the MNE has a non-routine margin of 30% (as in this example), then 80% of that is allocated to production-related activities, whereas 20% is allocated to market-related activities. Essentially, 6% of the overall loss margin will be allocated to market-related activities.
Step 4: SF Group's market-related loss is determined to be 6% of the overall revenues, which amounts to USD 60 Million (USD 1 billion * 6%). This loss will be carried forward for set-off against profits for future years. Thereafter,

86. OECD, Blueprint on Pillar I, *supra* n. 6, at pp. 126-129; OECD, Leaked report, *supra* n. 6, at pp. 139-143.
87. OECD, Public Consultation Document, *supra* n. 1, at paras 29, 37 & 51.
88. *See* OECD, Corporate Loss Utilisation through Aggressive Tax Planning, (OECD Publishing, August 2011); V. Chand, Allocation of Taxing Rights, *supra* n. 13, s. 6.3; Public Comments, Maisto E Associati, p. 11.

the profit (after taking into consideration the losses) will be reallocated to the market jurisdiction.

To illustrate, in the year 2021 (*see* the previous section), applying the four-step approach will lead to the conclusion that the market-related intangibles profits amount to USD 60 Million. This amount will be reduced by the 2020 loss of USD 60 Million, thus amounting to a profit to be reallocated of zero.[89]

The above example represents a situation wherein losses are earned within the Amount A regime, and the use of profit shortfalls are deployed (*see* Step 2 wherein the deemed routine return margin was added to the loss margin to ensure neutrality).

Special consideration should also be given to pre-existing losses that need to be brought into the Amount A regime, i.e., before that regime becomes operational.[90] For example, SF Group could be making losses at a consolidated level before entering into the Amount A regime, such as in the past four years, such as 2016 (USD 50 Million), 2017 (USD 40 Million), 2018 (USD 30 Million) and 2019 (USD 20 Million). One possible simple approach to deal with such losses is to simply state that the loss carry forward available to SF Group before entering into the regime amounts to the sum total of losses incurred in the past four years (*Uber* prefers this to be for ten years).[91] This would amount to USD 140 Million. This loss amount can then be carried forward on an unlimited basis for set-off against profits for future years. Thereafter, the profit (after taking into consideration the losses) will be reallocated to the market jurisdiction.

The leaked report and the blueprint confirm that the OECD has recognized the above issues to deal with losses and is moving its work in this direction.[92]

4 Selected Issue: The Issue of Double Counting in a Decentralized Setup

In many situations, local entrepreneurial entities (full-fledged distributors (FFD) or licensed manufacturers) could also be booking residual profits under the existing transfer pricing rules. Thus, there could be an overlap between local residual profits and Amount A, which also seeks to reallocate a part of the residual profits to the market countries. Consider the following example.

Co G, a tax resident of Country G (EU State), is the parent entity of an MNE Group that is active in several countries. Co G has developed its products in Country G and sells in that market and in other markets. In Country Y, the products are sold through a related distributor (FFD), Co Y, which reports an arm's-length operating margin of 10% on sales (this amount could be based on a comparability study or could have been

89. In this regard, also *see* Public Comments, Skadden, pp. 10–11.
90. Public Comments, Spotify, pp. 4–5; Public Comments, Amazon, p. 6; Public Comments, Digital Economy Group, p. 10; Public Comments, Maisto E Associati, p. 11.
91. Public Comments, Uber, p. 6.
92. OECD, Blueprint on Pillar I, *supra* n. 6, at pp. 116-122; OECD, Leaked report, *supra* n. 6, at pp. 127-134.

agreed in an Advance Pricing Agreement). Financial information: The overall consolidated operating revenue of the Group is USD 1,000, and the overall EBT is USD 400. The sales to end customers in Country Y amount to USD 300.

Amount A: In order to calculate this amount, the overall profit margin of the Group is 40%. The routine profit margin deemed to be is 10%. Accordingly, the residual profit margin is 30%. One-fifth of that margin is attributable to market-related profits that are linked to the Market countries. This would lead to the conclusion that the profit attributable to the Market countries is 6% of the overall revenues, which amounts to USD 60 (USD 1,000 * 6%). Country Y will be allocated USD 18 (60 * 300/1,000 = 18) of that profit under Amount A.

Existing Transfer Pricing rules: Co Y (FFD) is reporting an arm's-length margin of 10% on local sales. This amounts to USD (300 * 10/100 = 30).

To a certain extent, there is an overlap between Amount A and profit allocation under existing rules. Thus, in order to reduce this overlap, one possibility is to reduce the entire Amount C from Amount A liability. This would thus lead to the conclusion that the MNE Group does not pay any taxes in the Market Country under Amount A.

Another option, which is more nuanced, is to reduce from Amount A, an amount that is linked to non-routine margins. Assume that routine remuneration for low-risk distribution/marketing functions in Country Y amount to 4% on sales (Amount B). Thus, the amount that will be reduced from Amount A will be linked to the non-routine margin, that is, 6% on Country Y sales, which amounts to USD 18 (300 * 6/100 = 18). Thus, the taxable amount under Amount A in Country Y amounts to USD 18 – 18 = USD 0.[93]

Another possibility is to design a non-rebuttable safe harbour, which would say that if the local entity reports an X% (4%) of operating profits in the local market, then an Amount A allocation would not take place. Alternatively, if the local entity is in a loss-making situation or if its margin is less than 4%, then an Amount A allocation can take place.[94]

V SOURCING RULES: DETERMINATION OF LOCATION OF SALES AND PROFIT ALLOCATION

1 Developing Sourcing Rules

The new nexus, as well as the new profit allocation rule (Amount A), require the determination of the Market Country to whom the taxing rights will be reallocated.[95]

In order to determine this, one possible solution would be to refer to direct tax legislation/guidance of certain countries that allocate unitary corporate business profits based on several factors, such as the United States. Historically, several US

93. Also *see* Public Comments, Skadden, p. 4.
94. OECD, Blueprint on Pillar I, *supra* n. 6, at pp. 132–136; OECD, Leaked report, *supra* n. 6, at pp. 137-139.
95. *See* I. Grinberg, *Stabilizing 'Pillar One': Corporate Profit Reallocation in an Uncertain Environment*, Georgetown University Working Paper (2019), p. 41 retrievable on the SSRN Portal.

states have used the so-called Massachusetts formula. That formula allocates the income of a Multi-State corporation operating in the US among the US states by assigning equal weight to factors, such as payroll, assets and sales.[96] However, several US states have moved away from a three-factor formula to a single factor formula, that is, sales.[97] Naturally, the question arises as to how do you determine the state of sales for a Multi-State corporation. In this regard, the Multi-State Tax Commission[98] has developed/proposed a common set of rules, in particular, with respect to the receipts (sales) factor. Specifically, rules have been put forward to determine the location of sales of tangible property,[99] and market-based sourcing rules have been developed with respect to transactions that deal with services and intangibles (including franchising). These rules determine the location of sales by using certain approximations.[100]

Another possible solution would be to refer to value added tax (VAT) principles[101] that use proxies to determine the jurisdiction in which the final consumption occurs.[102] VAT legislations contain place of supply or place of taxation rules for B2B or B2C transactions with respect to goods, services and intangibles. For instance, a reference could be made to the work already done by the OECD in the context of its International Value Added Tax (VAT) /Goods and Services Tax (GST) guidelines.[103]

Moreover, for certain HDBs, a reference could be made to the work done by the European Commission[104] or national governments (such as the UK)[105] in the context of DSTs.

Several commonalities emerge from the above. The first commonality pertains to the use of approximations or proxies to determine the location of sale. Second, the rules focus on the customer (user) or/and the use/consumption by that customer (user). It should be noted that use/consumption could have different meanings in different business models. Therefore, for the purpose of developing sourcing rules, we suggest that proxies/approximations be considered, which could range, for example, from the location of the purchaser (customer location) or the final place of use/consumption (consumer use or consumer consumption location).[106]

---

96. Similar but different system also exists in Canada, in particular, its provinces. *See* European Commission: Taxation Papers, Formulary Apportionment and Group Taxation in the European Union: Insights from the United States and Canada, Woking Paper No. 8 / 2005, pp. 10–15. Also *see* R. Avi-Yonah, K. Clausing & M.Durst, *Allocating Business Profits for Tax Purposes: A Proposal to Adopt Formulary Profit Split,* December 2008, Michigan Law Working Paper, pp. 54–55.
97. *See* State Apportionment of Corporate Income available on https://www.taxadmin.org/assets/docs/Research/Rates/apport.pdf.
98. For instance, *see* Model General Allocation & Apportionment Regulations With Amendments Submitted for Adoption by the Commission 24 February 2017.
99. *Id.*, pp. 50–52.
100. *Id.*, pp. 52–100.
101. Public Comments, Amazon, pp. 4 and 9.
102. *See* W. Hellerstein & A Hitchhiker's Guide to the OECD's International VAT/GST Guidelines, 18 FLA. Tax Rev. 589, 598 (2016).
103. OECD, International VAT/GST Guidelines, (OECD Publishing, April 2017).
104. European Commission, *supra* n. 25, Art. 5.
105. UK: HM Treasury, Digital Services Tax Draft Guidance (2019).
106. M. Devereux, R. Feria, Designing and Implementing a Destination Based Corporate Tax, Oxford University Center for Business Taxation, WP 14/07, (2014), pp. 14–18; A. Auerbach, M.

2 Consumer Product or Consumer Service or Franchising Businesses

A Revenues from Consumer Products

At the outset, if Amount A is based on an MNE Business Line approach, then the focus should be placed on the core commercial activity of that business line. For example, if an MNE (headquartered in Country R) is in the business of making and selling branded chocolates, then the focus should be on ascertaining the location in which the branded chocolates are sold to unrelated customers. Consequently, inter-company transactions among related entities will need to be looked through.[107]

With respect to determining the sales location of unrelated customers, as a starting point, the location of the unrelated third-party purchaser (customer location) could be considered as a reasonable proxy.[108] For instance, if Company R of State R, which belongs to an MNE R Group, sells goods to an unrelated business (A) or a private customer (Mrs B) in State S, then the sales location is State S (assuming the goods are shipped to State S). This would be the case even if Company R sells to A or Mrs B through related parties.

An issue could arise, for example, when A (who is in State S) purchases the goods from Company R for its various establishments, for instance, its PEs or subsidiaries in Country S1, S2, S3 and so on. In other words, the goods will be shipped and consumed in these latter States. In this case, the question arises as to whether the consumption location proxy should be preferred over the customer location proxy? Ideally, this should be the case. However, from the MNE R Group's perspective (who will be subject to Amount A), an issue arises when A receives the goods in State S and then ships them on its own account to other countries. In this situation, MNE R Group may not have the information that the products have been shipped by A for consumption to various other locations. In this scenario, where it is impossible for MNE to obtain the information, it would be reasonable to say that Amount A should be allocated to State S.[109]

Also, in some situations (mostly B2B), the MNE R Group may wish to avoid taxes by taking advantage of the customer location proxy.[110] For example, there could be situations where an MNE group engaged in selling products could engage in tax planning or tax avoidance strategies, such as routing sales through an independent distributor, which is established in a no tax or low tax jurisdiction. In such a case, a specific anti-avoidance rule could be developed (SAAR). For instance, such a rule could

Devereux, M. Keen & J. Vella, *Destination-Based Cash Flow Taxation*, Saïd Business School Working Paper 2017/09 (2017), pp. 80–82; M. Devereux, A. Auerbach, M. Keen, P. Oosterhuis, W. Schön & J. Vella, *Residual Profit Allocation by Income*, Saïd Business School Working Paper 19/01, (2019), pp. 86–90.

107. Public Comments, Amazon, p. 4.
108. Public Comments, Procter and Gamble, p. 9; Public Comments, Amazon, p. 4.
109. OECD, Blueprint on Pillar I, *supra* n. 6, at pp. 93-95; OECD, Leaked report, *supra* n. 6, at pp. 103-104.
110. J.C Fleming, RJ. Peroni & S. Shay, Formulary Apportionment in the US International Tax System: Putting Lipstick on a Pig?, 36 Mich. J. Int'l L. 1 (2015), pp. 39–46 (2014).

deem the unrelated enterprise (the independent distributor) to be closely related if it substantially depends economically on the MNE.[111]

B Revenues from Consumer Services

With respect to determining the sales location of consumer services (without any online component), the place where the service is enjoyed/used could be considered as a reasonable proxy. For instance, if Company R of State R, which belongs to an MNE R Group, provides services (hotels or restaurant services) to an unrelated business (A) or a private customer (Mrs B) in State S, then the sales location is State S.[112]

C Revenues from Franchising Businesses

Franchising businesses usually franchise consumer goods or consumer services related concepts. Accordingly, the analysis made above with respect to determining the sales location of consumer goods/services would equally apply to Franchising businesses.[113]

3 Highly Digitalized Businesses

A Revenue from Online Advertising

The first example pertains to online advertisers that engage in targeted advertising. Consider the following triangular situation. Company F, which belongs to Group F, is a tax resident in Country R for its European operations and the users that maintain their profiles on the online platform live in Country U. Essentially, Company F gives its users the right to maintain their profiles on the platform and, in return, users contribute their personal data. Thereafter, the employees in Country R process that raw data and sell targeted advertising services to clients (Company B) in Country B. The service pertains to displaying Company B's product/services to Country U users. The contract stipulates that Company B will pay advertisement fees to Company F based on the number of times a user clicks on the advertisement. In this situation, the payor of the advertisement fee is in Country B (customer location), and the users are in Country U (viewing location).

The question arises as to whom should the taxing right on Amount A be allocated, i.e., to Country U and or Country B? In our view, the income should be allocated to Country U as these businesses create and exploit user networks. Thus, one

111. Some commentators have argued that they will not engage in such strategies as the cost of transporting products becomes more expensive. *See* Public Comments, Procter and Gamble, p. 9.
112. OECD, Blueprint on Pillar I, *supra* n. 6, at pp. 94-95; OECD, Leaked report, *supra* n. 6, at pp. 104-105.
113. OECD, Blueprint on Pillar I, *supra* n. 6, at pp. 95-96; OECD, Leaked report, *supra* n. 6, at pp. 105-106.

possible approach to determine Country U's relevant revenues is to ascertain whether the advertising is intended to be viewed by a Country U user.[114] In the above example, all the revenue is linked to Country U as it is intended to be displayed only for Country U users.[115]

B Revenue from Sale of User Data

The second example pertains to online search engines that could derive online advertising revenue and revenue from the sale of user data. For the former revenue source, *see* above, and for the latter, consider the following triangular situation. Company G, which belongs to Group G, is a tax resident in Country R for its global operations. The Company owns a famous search engine. The search engine (and the website on which it operates) collects data from users from Country U whenever they access the online search platform. The data collected is sold to Company B in Country B. In this situation, the payor is in Country B (customer location), and the users are in Country U (viewing location).

The question arises as to whom should the taxing right on Amount A be allocated, i.e., to Country U and or Country B? In our view, the income should, once again, be allocated to Country U as these businesses create and exploit user networks/user data.[116]

C Commission Revenues from Intermediation Services

The third example pertains to online marketplaces. Such marketplaces could connect users (sellers and purchasers) with each other for a wide range of underlying activities, such as a tangible service, sale of goods or intangibles (apps) and so on. If the seller and purchaser are in the same country, then the revenues will be sourced only to that country. However, issues could arise in triangular situations. Consider the following illustrations.

The first situation – Company A, which belongs to Group A, is headquartered in Country A, and it runs an online marketplace platform that connects accommodation seekers to accommodation providers. Accommodation providers (users) from Country C (owners of apartments) list their real estate property on the platform. At the same time, Mr B from Country B maintains his profile on the platform. Mr B books an apartment in Country C through the Country A platform. Mr B uses his credit card for the transaction, which amounts to USD 100. Company A retains a commission of USD

114. European Commission, *supra* n. 25, Art. 5. Also *see* European Commission, Impact Assessment Accompanying the document Proposal for a Council Directive laying down rules relating to the Corporate Taxation of a Significant Digital Presence and Proposal for a Council Directive on the Common System of a Digital Services Tax on Revenues Resulting from the Provision of Certain Digital Services, 81 final/2, 2018/ (21 March 2018), Annexure 12, pp. 150–153.
115. OECD, Blueprint on Pillar I, *supra* n. 6, at pp. 74-75; OECD, Leaked report, *supra* n. 6, at pp. 97-98.
116. OECD, Blueprint on Pillar I, *supra* n. 6, at pp. 75-76; OECD, Leaked report, *supra* n. 6, at pp. 98-99.

10 and passes on the balance to the accommodation provider in Country C. The question that now arises is which country is the location of sale for the new nexus and profit allocation rule from the Group A's perspective. Is it Country B or Country C, or both?[117]

The second situation - Company A, which belongs to Group A, is headquartered in Country A, and it runs an online marketplace platform that connects buyers and sellers of goods. Essentially, sellers of goods from Country C list their products on the platform. At the same time, Mr B from Country B maintains his profile on the platform. Mr B orders the products through the Country A platform. Mr B uses his credit card for the transaction, which amounts to USD 100. Company A retains a commission of USD 10 and passes on the balance to the seller in Country C. The question that now arises is which country is the location of sale for the new nexus and profit allocation rule from Group A's perspective. Is it Country B or Country C, or both?

The third situation - Company A, which belongs to Group A, is headquartered in Country A, and it runs an online application platform (apps) that connects developers of apps and purchasers of apps. Essentially, developers from Country C list their apps on the platform. At the same time, Mr B from Country B downloads the app from the platform onto his mobile device. Mr B uses his credit card for the transaction, which amounts to USD 100. Company A retains a commission of USD 20 and passes on the balance to the developer in Country C. The question that now arises is which country is the location of sale for the new nexus and profit allocation rule from the Group A's perspective. Is it Country B or Country C, or both?

The EU Commission, in the context of DSTs, considers that taxing rights could be allocated to both 'user' locations in the above cases.[118] We agree with this line of reasoning and suggest an equal split.[119]

However, with respect to the intermediation of tangible services, we have only one remark. The UK Her Majesty Revenues and Customs (HMRC) states that a special rule applies with respect to the property (land) in the UK, even if the owner of the property is outside the UK, and a non-UK user utilizes that property.[120] In such a case, the revenue is sourced to the UK. Thus, we believe that further consideration should be given to transactions that involve the use of property in the sense that the revenues associated with such transactions could be sourced only to the country where the property is situated and used (which, by default, could be the consumption location from the perspective of the consumer who is availing the service on the platform).

D Digital Content Services

The fourth example pertains to online streaming businesses. Such businesses derive revenue from streaming movies, music and so on. Consider the following situation.

117. Public Comments, Booking.com, p. 9.
118. European Commission, Impact Assessment, *supra* n. 114, pp. 153–155.
119. OECD, Blueprint on Pillar I, *supra* n. 6, at pp. 75-79; OECD, Leaked report, *supra* n. 6, at pp. 100-101.
120. UK: HM Treasury, Digital Services Tax Draft Guidance (2019), p. 38.

Company N, which belongs to Group N, is a tax resident in Country R for its global operations. The Company provides stream movies online to customers/users in Country U for a monthly membership fee. The users use their credit cards to pay for such services. In this situation, the payor is in Country U, who happens to also be the customer. In this situation, the revenue will be sourced to Country U as the payor is a resident therein.[121]

E Cloud Services

The fifth example pertains to cloud services. Such businesses could provide services directly to individuals or directly to businesses.

With respect to determining the sales location, as a starting point, the location of the unrelated third-party purchaser (customer location) could be considered as a reasonable proxy.[122] For instance, if Company M of State R, which belongs to an MNE M Group, sells cloud services to an unrelated business (A) or a private customer (Mrs B) in State S, then the sales location is State S (assuming the services are used therein).

An issue could arise, for example, when A (who is in State S) purchases the services from Company R for its various establishments, for instance, its PEs or subsidiaries in Country S1, S2, S3 and so on. In other words, the services will be delivered and used in these latter States. In this case, the consumption location proxy should be preferred over the customer location proxy.[123]

VI ELIMINATION OF DOUBLE TAXATION: SURRENDER JURISDICTION

1 Identification of Paying Entities

The first issue pertains to the identification of the relevant taxable person who would provide relief for the taxes paid in the market countries. As the objective of Amount A is to reallocate a part of the residual profits to the market countries, we believe that the relevant taxpayer(s) to whom the Amount A liability should be allocated is/are the entities in the MNE Group that book residual profits.

MNE Businesses operate with a variety of structures, for instance, centralized or decentralized structures or a combination of them.[124]

In a centralized structure, it could well be possible that the centralized principal is the one who is making key decisions associated with MNEs' activities and the one which is booking residual profits. In this case, that entity would be identified as the paying entity. For example, consider the situation of MNE R, which is in the business of

121. OECD, Blueprint on Pillar I, *supra* n. 6, at pp. 79-80; OECD, Leaked report, *supra* n. 6, at pp. 100-101.
122. Public Comments, Procter and Gamble, p. 9; Public Comments, Amazon, p. 4.
123. OECD, Blueprint on Pillar I, *supra* n. 6, at pp. 80-81; OECD, Leaked report, *supra* n. 6, at pp. 102-103.
124. *See* Public Comments, Nestle, p. 2.

making and selling branded clothes. It has its ultimate parent, viz. Company R in Country R. Company R operates as a centralized principal entity. The company sells its clothes, which are produced in Country R, in twenty different markets. The clothes are sold through low-risk distributors. If an Amount A tax liability arises in the twenty different markets, then it is clear that Company R could be identified as the relevant taxpayer as it has made substantial decisions associated with its value chain. In other words, we would deploy to a transfer pricing analysis to determine which entity within the Group is booking residual profits. By doing so, we are looking into the activities of the various entities as well as their profitability thresholds.[125]

Of course, several issues arise when multiple entities within an MNE group make substantial contributions / perform substantial activities and could be considered to be the owner of non-routine or deemed residual profits. For example, consider the situation of Company R in Country R that has developed all intangibles. Company R sells its products in the State R market. Further, for its overseas operations, Company R establishes a centralized business model (Company P – a principal entity) in Country P. Company P employs the intangibles for its operations and derives business income on a remote basis from several countries (including State S) and pays an arm's-length amount of royalties to Company R. If a tax liability arises in State S for the MNE Group under Amount A, then the question arises as to who is the taxpayer to whom the tax liability could be attributed, i.e., is it Company R or Company P? In this case, as Company P is engaged with the Country S market, it should be considered, as a start, to be the relevant taxpayer.[126]

On the other hand, when Company P cannot bear the entire Amount A liability, then both entities (who are characterized as entrepreneurs for transfer pricing purposes) could be identified as the relevant taxpayers. This would imply that both Country R (Company R) and Country P (Company P) could provide relief. The relief could be divided into a predetermined proportion, for instance, based on the entities operating revenues.[127]

The analysis may get even more complicated when you are dealing with a fully decentralized MNE. For example, consider the situation of MNE P, which is headquartered in Country P through Company P. That entity owns all trade and MI of the Group with respect to Product X. Company P sets up a licensed manufacturer is Country R (Company R) to which all intangibles are licensed. Company R makes and sells products in Country R. Company R pays an arm's-length royalty to Company P.[128] If a tax liability arises for MNE P under Amount A in Country R, then as a start, the relevant taxpayer would be Company R as it sells in the State R market. However, if the entity is a loss-making entity, then the relevant taxpayer could be Company P. This said, a large MNE (Unilever) has argued that Amount A should not apply to licensed

125. OECD, Blueprint on Pillar I, *supra* n. 6, at pp. 144-149; OECD, Leaked report, *supra* n. 6, at pp. 170-178.
126. OECD, Blueprint on Pillar I, *supra* n. 6, at pp. 149-151; OECD, Leaked report, *supra* n. 6, at pp. 176-180.
127. OECD, Blueprint on Pillar I, *supra* n. 6, at pp. 151-153; OECD, Leaked report, *supra* n. 6, at pp. 180-181.
128. For a similar operating model, *see* Public Comments, Unilever, p. 5.

manufacturers.[129] Another MNE (Johnson & Johnson), as well as other commentators, have argued that Amount A should not be applicable to FFD.[130] Moreover, some commentators have argued that if the royalty paid by Company R is subject to a withholding tax on a gross basis by Country R, then that amount should be reduced from the Amount A allocation with respect to Country R. This is because the withholding tax captures a part of the IP profit at source. As an alternate, the withholding tax could also be credited against the Amount A tax liability.[131]

2 Relief Mechanisms

The next question pertains to which method should be used to alleviate double taxation. Currently, countries follow either the credit method or exemption method depending on whether they favour a policy based on capital-import or capital-export neutrality. Article 23 A and B OECD MC mirrors this policy difference. On the other hand, to alleviate double economic taxation in a transfer pricing context, countries resort to tax base corrections, that is, corresponding adjustments.[132] At this stage, we believe that the manner in which double taxation is alleviated should remain the sovereign choice of each State, viz. the credit or exemption system,[133] although it seems that some commentators prefer a corresponding adjustment system.[134]

VII DISPUTE PREVENTION MECHANISMS AND TAX CERTAINTY

Several disputes could arise within the context of Amount A with respect to the aforementioned points. Thus, detailed guidance (commentary) will need to be developed to minimize differences in interpretation. Moreover, it would be appropriate to focus on obtaining consensus via multilateral competent authority agreements on areas that are prone to maximum litigation. In other words, the focus should be on dispute prevention and obtaining upfront tax certainty.[135] The work of the OECD moves in this direction wherein a panel mechanism is proposed to ensure tax certainty and smooth implementation of Amount A.[136]

---

129. Public Comments, Unilever, p. 3.
130. Public Comments, Johnson and Johnson, p. 5; *See* Public Comments, Skadden, p. 4.
131. Public Comments, Digital Economy Group, pp. 9–10; Public Comments, Maisto E Associati, pp. 6–7.
132. *See* Art. 9(2) OECD Model Tax Convention (2017).
133. OECD, Blueprint on Pillar I, *supra* n. 6, at pp. 154-158; OECD, Leaked report, *supra* n. 6, at pp. 183-189.
134. Public Comments, Uber, p. 10; Public Comments, Amazon, p. 8; Public Comments, Nestle, p. 12; Public Comments, Skadden, p. 6; Public Comments, Digital Economy Group, p. 5; Public Comments, KPMG, p. 13; Public Comments, EY, p. 13.
135. V. Chand, Allocation of Taxing Rights, *supra* n. 13, s. 6.5; Public Comments, Johnson and Johnson, p. 8.
136. OECD, Blueprint on Pillar I, *supra* n. 6, at pp. 176-197; OECD, Leaked report, *supra* n. 6, at pp. 212-229.

VIII IMPLEMENTATION OF AMOUNT A

1 Information Exchange for Amount A

In order to implement the new method, the aforementioned information (e.g., MNE Business Line profits or losses as well as the location of sales) will need to be reported. An appropriate documentation package will need to be developed and then be exchanged among tax administrations. Substantial work has already been done in relation to CBCR. Accordingly, one possibility would be to modify the current version of CBCR documentation in such a way that it would facilitate the implementation of the new taxing right.[137] If this path is followed, then the automatic information exchange framework would need to be amended too.

2 Collection of Taxes by Market Countries

Assuming an Amount A liability arises for the MNE Group, a question arises with respect to how market countries can collect taxes for Amount A. One possible answer is to give the MNE the option to nominate a constituent entity (as discussed in the EU DST[138]) or a responsible member,[139] as discussed in the UK DST. This entity will be liable with other entities of the MNE (to the extent they are there) in the market jurisdiction to remit taxes to the local government (similar to a one-stop-shop system).[140] Where Amount A applies in the absence of a physical presence in the Market Country, another possibility would, of course, be for this country to impose a withholding tax. The problem with this latter approach, however, is that taxes would then be collected on a gross and not on a net basis. It is questionable whether such a policy would be consistent with the rationale pursued by the allocation of non-routine profits under Amount A. Further, while applicable to dividends, interest and royalties under the OECD MC, this policy is switched off where such items are connected to a PE situated in the state of source.[141] Conceptually, therefore, it would seem inconsistent to switch to gross basis taxation under Amount A.[142] Thus, a simplified one-stop-shop type of system will need to be developed.[143]

3 New Multilateral Convention

Several alternatives could be contemplated to implement the solutions on a multilateral basis. With respect to the MNE Group approach and Amount A, one possibility is to

137. Public Comments, Zalando, p. 2.
138. European Commission, Impact Assessment, *supra* n. 114, p. 156.
139. UK: HM Treasury, Digital Services Tax Draft Guidance (2019), p. 52.
140. Public Comments, Unilever, p. 4; Public Comments, Digital Economy Group, p. 8.
141. Articles 10(4), 11(4) and 12(3) OECD MC.
142. Concurring: Public Comments, Spotify, pp. 8–9; Public Comments, Uber, p. 12; Public Comments, Unilever, p. 8; Public Comments, Amazon, p. 8; Public Comments, Digital Economy Group, p. 7; Public Comments, KPMG, p. 10.
143. OECD, Blueprint on Pillar I, at Chapter 10; OECD, Leaked report, *supra* n. 6, at Chapter 10.

modify the existing Multilateral Instrument (MLI). However, the MLI only modifies existing tax treaties.[144] Thus, this approach may not be suitable to implement the Amount A approach. Another possibility is to develop a new standalone Multilateral Convention dealing with substantive matters (scope, nexus, profit (loss) allocation, relief and so on). We believe that this approach should be adopted, and consideration should be given to a new Multilateral Convention.[145]

IX PROFIT ALLOCATION: AMOUNTS B

Unlike Amount A, Amount B is intended to remain within the range of the ALP. With respect to it,[146] first, the question arises as to whether it applies to all businesses or whether it is applicable to consumer-facing or ADS businesses? From a neutrality standpoint, we would find it prima facie difficult to justify the application of this amount only to consumer/ADS businesses.

Second, Amount B should only be applicable to taxpayers (local PE or a separate related entity) that mainly do marketing or distribution activities or a combination of them.[147]

Third, the question arises as to whether this amount is a minimum profit allocation regime or a safe harbour that could be rebutted[148] (as understood in the transfer pricing context). Although discussed in a slightly different context, a minimum profit allocation regime had already been advocated by India in the context of the SEP proposal. Essentially, the Central Board of Direct Taxes had proposed that the taxable base in India for a non-residents SEP should, at a minimum, be equal to 2% of Indian revenues even if the non-resident is making losses.[149] In our opinion, such an approach would be very difficult to reconcile with the 'principles of economic capacity and net basis taxation',[150] in particular, the ability to pay principle. Moreover, we fail to see the justification for such an approach from a proportionality standpoint. Consequently, we

144. *See* thereupon R. Danon & H. Salomé, The BEPS Multilateral Instrument: General Overview and Focus on Treaty abuse, IFF Forum für Steuerrecht 2017, pp. 197 et seq.
145. OECD, Blueprint on Pillar I, at Chapter 10; OECD, Leaked report, *supra* n. 6, at Chapter 10.
146. OECD, Public Consultation Document, *supra* n. 1, at paras 62–65.
147. Public Comments, Johnson and Johnson, p. 7.
148. For a discussion on safe harbours or presumptions, *see* OECD, OECD Transfer Pricing Guidelines for Multinational Enterprises and Tax Administrations 2017, paras 4.95–4.133; A. Turina, Back To Grass Roots: The Arm's Length Standard, Comparability and Transparency: Some Perspectives From The Emerging World, 10 World Tax J. 2, pp. 332–336 (2018); S. Picciotto, *Problems of Transfer Pricing and Possibilities for Simplification,* ICTD Working Paper 86, (Box 4) (November 2018), p. 29.
149. Central Board of Direct Taxes, *supra* n. 25, paras 161–163.
150. *See* OECD, Corporate Loss Utilisation, *supra* n. 88. *See also* under Swiss law Danon R, Com. ad Arts 57–58 N 177 et seq. in: Noël Y/Aubry-Girardin F. (eds) Impôt fédéral direct: Commentaire de la loi sur l'impôt fédéral direct, 2017.

do not favour the application of a minimum profit allocation regime for marketing/distribution/sales activities.[151]

This said, if the minimum profit allocation regime is designed on the basis of margins based on the ALP, then we would support this approach. We agree that the existing transfer pricing system, in general, could trigger several disputes among taxpayers and tax administrations.[152] Thus, in order to achieve certainty, such a regime could be contemplated.[153] The regime, as a start, could be applied to low-risk marketing/distribution functions[154] (this is already contemplated in the OECD Transfer Pricing Guidelines).[155]

In fact, such an approach is already followed by the tax administration in Israel.[156] Their guidance states that a 3%–4% (return on sales) profitability margin applies for distributions activities and a 10%–12% (return on costs) margin for marketing activities. Moreover, their guidance contains a detailed discussion of low-risk distribution and marketing activities. Thus, references could be made to their guidance to derive a definition of distribution/marketing activities that could be within the scope of this proposal. It should be noted that these activities should not amount to: (i) 'unique and valuable contributions', especially activities that create valuable local intangibles; (ii) be classified as 'highly integrated' operations, or (iii) lead to 'shared assumption of economically significant risks' or 'separate assumption of closely related risks'.[157] If they do, then the activities need to be analysed under the existing ALP profit allocation system.

While, in some situations, MNEs could distinguish between distribution and marketing activities, we do acknowledge that, in many situations, such activities could

151. Concurring: Public Comments, Spotify, p. 7; Public Comments, Amazon, p. 5; Public Comments, Digital Economy Group, p. 12; Public Comments, Maisto E. Associati, p. 12; Public Comments, KPMG, p. 11; Public Comments, Deloitte, p. 8.
152. *See* J. Andrus & P. Oosterhuis, Transfer Pricing After BEPS: Where Are We and Where Should We Be Going, 95 Taxes the Tax Magazine 89, 104 (March 2017). Also, *see* V. Chand, Achieving Certainty in an Uncertain Profit Allocation Environment (Editorial), 47(12) Intertax (2019).
153. R. Collier & J. Andrus, Transfer Pricing and the Arm's Length Principle (Oxford University Press, 2017), at 269–270. Also *see* Public Comments, Booking.com, p. 13; Public Comments, Skadden, p. 6.
154. Thereafter, they could be broadened to other areas, such as contract research and development, low-risk procurement operations and contract and toll manufacturing. However, some commentators argue that Amount B should already tackle these transactions. *See* Public Comments, Skadden, p. 2.
155. OECD Transfer Pricing Guidelines for Multinational Enterprises and Tax Administrations 2017, pp. 459–463.
156. For more details, *see* Circular 11/2018, available at https://home.kpmg/content/dam/kpmg/xx/pdf/2018/10/tnf-israel-11-oct9-2018.pdf (unofficial translation) and Circular 12/2018, available at https://home.kpmg/content/dam/kpmg/xx/pdf/2018/10/tnf-israel-12-oct9-2018.pdf (unofficial translation). Also *see*, Israel's OECD, Transfer Pricing Country Profile, Updated May 2019, question 24, available at https://www.oecd.org/tax/transfer-pricing/transfer-pricing-country-profile-israel.pdf.
157. OECD, Revised Guidance on the Application of the Transactional Profit Split Method, OECD/G20 Base Erosion and Profit Shifting Project (OECD 4 June 2018). Also *see* EU Commission – EU Joint Transfer Pricing Forum (EUJTPF), The Application of the Profit Split Method within the EU, Doc JTPF/002/2019 (March 2019).

be intertwined with each other.[158] For instance, see the various decisions rendered by Indian Courts on Advertising, Marketing and Sales promotion expenses.[159]

Also, contrary to the approach followed in Israel, we are of the opinion that the different margins need to be proposed for different businesses. In our experience, the margins applied for low-risk distribution/marketing activities differ from industry to industry from country to country. Thus, a range of margins will need to be proposed.[160]

With respect to rules that will deal with Amount B, we foresee an amendment of the OECD Transfer Pricing Guidelines Multilateral Memorandum of Understanding that could be attached to the new multilateral convention.[161]

X CONCLUSION

While the OECD is still discussing and debating the details of the new solution, unilateral measures are on the rise. These measures, depending on the jurisdiction, could apply to 'all MNE enterprises' (such as diverted profit taxes) or could be targeted only at 'digital MNE enterprises' (such as DSTs). Thus, in order to stabilize the international tax system without creating substantial chaos, countries should not adopt unilateral changes but should work towards developing a consensus-based solution. In fact, if the OECD goes forward with the unified approach, then unilateral measures should indeed be abolished.[162] This said, as outlined in this contribution, substantial work needs to be done on that approach as it goes beyond the ALP framework, and at the same time, it seeks to simplify the transfer pricing system. It could be difficult to obtain consensus on all matters related to the unified approach by the end of this year. However, it could well be possible that countries arrive at an agreement in the year 2021 as the Pillar I blueprint puts forward a strong foundation from which a consensus could be derived.

SELECTED BIBLIOGRAPHY

International Organisations Guidance

EU Commission – EU Joint Transfer Pricing Forum (EUJTPF), The Application of the Profit Split Method within the EU, Doc JTPF/002/2019, 2019.

European Commission, Impact Assessment accompanying the document Proposal for a Council Directive laying down rules relating to the Corporate Taxation of a Significant Digital Presence and Proposal for a Council Directive on the Common

158. For instance, *see* the watch example. *See* OECD Transfer Pricing Guidelines for Multinational Enterprises and Tax Administrations 2017, Annex to Chapter VI: Examples on Intangibles, Example 8, pp. 570–572.
159. *See Maruti Suzuki India Ltd. v. Addl. CIT TPO* [2010]; *LG Electronics India (P.) Ltd. v. Asstt. CIT* [2013]; *Sony Ericsson Mobile Communications India (P.) Ltd. v. CIT* [2015] 3; *Bausch & Lomb Eyecare India (P.) Ltd. v. Addl. CIT* [2016]; *CIT-LTU v. Whirlpool of India Ltd.* [2016].
160. Public Comments, PwC, pp. 27–30.
161. All these matters are discussed in the OECDs blueprint. OECD, Blueprint on Pillar I, at Chapter 8; *See* OECD, Leaked report, *supra* n. 6, at Chapter 8.
162. Also *see* Public Comments, EY, p. 2.

System of a Digital Services Tax on Revenues Resulting from the Provision of Certain Digital Services, SWD/2018/082 final - 2018/072 (CNS), 2018.

European Commission, Proposal for a Council Directive on the Common System of a Digital Services Tax on Revenues Resulting from the Provision of Certain Digital Services, COM/2018/0148 final - 2018/0073(CNS), 2018.

European Commission, Proposal for a Council Directive laying down rules relating to the Corporate Taxation of a Significant Digital Presence, COM/2018/0147 final - 2018/072(CNS), 2018.

European Commission: Taxation Papers, Formulary Apportionment and Group Taxation In the European Union: Insights From the United States and Canada, Woking Paper No. 8 / 2005.

OECD, Addressing the Tax Challenges of the Digitalisation of the Economy - Public Consultation Document, OECD/G20 Base Erosion and Profit Shifting Project, OECD Publishing, Paris 2019.

OECD, Addressing the Tax Challenges of the Digital Economy, Action 1 - 2015 Final Report, OECD/G20 Base Erosion and Profit Shifting Project, OECD Publishing, Paris 2015.

OECD, Corporate Loss Utilisation through Aggressive Tax Planning, OECD Publishing, Paris 2011.

OECD, Electronic Commerce: Taxation Framework Conditions, Report by the Committee on Fiscal Affairs, OECD Publishing, Paris 1998.

OECD, International Compliance Assurance Programme Pilot Handbook, OECD publishing, Paris 2018.

OECD, International Compliance Assurance Programme Pilot Handbook 2.0, OECD Publishing, Paris 2019.

OECD, International VAT/GST Guidelines, OECD Publishing, Paris 2017.

OECD/G20, Limiting Base Erosion Involving Interest Deductions and Other Financial Payments, Action 4: 2015 Final Report, OECD/G20 Base Erosion and Profit Shifting Project, OECD Publishing, Paris 2015.

OECD, Model Tax Convention on Income and on Capital 2017 (Full Version), OECD Publishing, Paris 2017.

OECD, OECD Transfer Pricing Guidelines for Multinational Enterprises and Tax Administrations 2017, OECD Publishing, Paris 2017.

OECD/G20, Tax Challenges Arising from Digitalization - Report on the Pillar One Blueprint, October 2020, OECD Publishing, Paris 2020.

OECD, Report on the Attribution of Profits to Permanent Establishments 2010, OECD Publishing, Paris 2010.

OECD, Revised Guidance on the Application of the Transactional Profit Split Method, OECD/G20 Base Erosion and Profit Shifting Project, OECD Publishing, Paris 2018.

OECD, Secretariat Proposal for a 'Unified Approach' under Pillar One, OECD/G20 Base Erosion and Profit Shifting Project, OECD Publishing, Paris 2019.

OECD (2020), Statement by the OECD/G20 Inclusive Framework on BEPS on the Two-Pillar Approach to Address the Tax Challenges Arising from the Digitalisation of the Economy - January 2020, OECD/G20 Inclusive Framework on BEPS, OECD, Paris.

OECD, Tax Challenges Arising from Digitalisation - Interim Report 2018: Inclusive Framework on BEPS, OECD/G20 Base Erosion and Profit Shifting Project, OECD Publishing, Paris 2018.

OECD, Transfer Pricing Documentation and Country-by-Country Reporting, Action 13 - 2015 Final Report, OECD/G20 Base Erosion and Profit Shifting Project, OECD Publishing, Paris 2015.

UN, United Nations Model Double Taxation Convention between Developed and Developing Countries, UN, New York 2017.

UN, United Nations Handbook on Selected Issues for the Taxation of the Extractive Industries by Developing States, UN, New York 2019.

National Law Guidance

Austria: Der Nationalrat, Digitalsteuergesetz 2020 (132/ME), 2019.

France: Gouvernement de la République française, LOI n° 2019-759 du 24 juillet 2019 portant création d'une taxe sur les services numériques et modification de la trajectoire de baisse de l'impôt sur les sociétés, 2019.

India: Central Board of Direct Taxes, Income department - Government of India, Proposal for Amendment of Rules for Profit Attribution to Permanent Establishment (CBDT), 2019.

Italy: Governo italiano, Bilancio di previsione dello Stato per l'anno finanziario 2019 e bilancio pluriennale per il triennio 2019–2021, 2019.

New Zealand: New Zealand Government, Options for Taxing the Digital Economy - a Government Discussion Document, 2019.

Spain: Gobierno de España, Proyecto de Ley del Impuesto sobre Determinados Servicios Digitales, 2019.

United Kingdom: HM Treasury, Corporate tax and the Digital Economy: Position Paper Update, 2018.

United Kingdom: HM Revenue & Customs, Draft Legislation on the New Digital Services Tax, 2019.

United States: Multi-State Tax Commission (MTC), Model General Allocation & Apportionment Regulations With Amendments Submitted for Adoption by the Commission February 24, 2017.

Scholarly Books & Articles (Non-exhaustive List)

J. Andrus & P. Oosterhuis, Transfer Pricing After BEPS: Where Are We and Where Should We Be Going, 95 Taxes The Tax Magazine, p. 89, 2017.

B. Arnold, Threshold Requirements for Taxing Business Profits under Tax Treaties, 57 Bull. Int'l Tax'n 10, p. 476, 2003.

A. Auerbach, M. Devereux, M. Keen & J. Vella, Destination-Based Cash Flow Taxation, Saïd Business School Working Paper 2017/09, 2017.

R. Avi-Yonah, & O. Halabi, A Model Treaty for the Age of BEPS, Law & Economics Working Papers, Paper 103, p. 15, 2014.

R. Avi-Yonah, Designing a 21st Century Taxing Threshold: Some International Implications of South Dakota vs. Wayfair, Public law and Legal Theory Research Paper No. 611, 2018.

R. Avi-Yonah, K. Clausing & M. Durst, Allocating Business Profits for Tax Purposes: A Proposal to Adopt Formulary Profit Split, Michigan Law Working Paper, 2008.

A.J. Cockfield, Balancing National Interests in the Taxation of Electronic Commerce Business Profits, 74 Tulane L. Rev., p. 133, 1999.

R. Collier & J. Andrus, Transfer Pricing and the Arm's Length Principle, Oxford University Press, Oxford 2017.

V. Chand, Achieving Certainty in an Uncertain Profit Allocation Environment (Editorial), 47(12) Intertax, 2019.

V. Chand, Allocation of Taxing Rights in the Digitalized Economy: Assessment of Potential Policy Solutions and Recommendation for a Simplified Profit Split Method, 47(12) Intertax, 2019.

V. Chand, A. Turina & L. Ballivet, Profit Allocation Within MNEs in Light of the Ongoing Digital Debate on Pillar I – A '2020 Compromise'? From Using A Facts and Circumstances Analysis or Allocation Keys to Predetermined Allocation Approaches, 3 World Tax Journal 2020, July 2020 (published online).

R. Danon, Can Tax Treaty Policy Save Us? The Case of the Digital Economy, in B. Arnold (ed), Tax Treaties After the BEPS Project: A Tribute to Jacques Sasseville, Canadian Tax Foundation, 2018, pp. 75 et seq.

R. Danon & H. Salomé, The BEPS Multilateral Instrument: General Overview and Focus on Treaty Abuse, IFF Forum für Steuerrecht 2017, pp. 197 et seq.

R. Danon & V. Chand, Public Comments on Addressing the Tax Challenges of the Digitalisation of the Economy – Public Consultation Document, OECD/G20 Base Erosion and Profit Shifting Project, OECD Publishing, 2019, available on https://www.dropbox.com/s/hou6dvuckmahoft/OECD-Comments-Received-Digital-March-2019.zip?dl = 0.

M. Devereux & R. de la Feria, Designing and Implementing a Destination Based Corporate Tax, Oxford University Center for Business Taxation, WP 14/07, 2014.

M. Devereux, A. Auerbach, M. Keen, P. Oosterhuis, W. Schön & J. Vella, Residual Profit Allocation by Income, Saïd Business School Working Paper 19/01, 2019.

J.C Fleming, RJ. Peroni & S. Shay, Formulary Apportionment in the US International Tax System: Putting Lipstick on a Pig?, 36 Mich. J. Int'l L. 1, 2015.

I. Grinberg, Stabilizing 'Pillar One': Corporate Profit Reallocation in an Uncertain Environment, Georgetown University Working Paper, 2019.

W. Hellerstein, A Hitchhiker's Guide to the OECD's International VAT/GST Guidelines, 18 FLA. Tax Rev., p. 589, 2016.

M.A. Kane, A Defense of Source Rules in International Taxation, 32 Yale J. on Regulation, p. 311, 2015.

L. Lokken, The Sources of Income From International Uses and Dispositions of Intellectual Property, 36 Tax Law Rev., p. 233, 1981.

G. Maisto, The History of Article 8 of the OECD Model Treaty on Taxation of Shipping and Air Transport, Intertax 31.6, p. 232, 2003.

P. Oosterhuis & A. Parsons, Destination Based Income Taxation: Neither Principled Nor Practical?, 71 Tax Law Rev., p. 515, 2018.

S. Picciotto, Problems of Transfer Pricing and Possibilities for Simplification, ICTD Working Paper 86, 2018.

W. Schön, Ten Questions about Why and How to Tax the Digitalized Economy, Max Planck Institute for Tax Law and Public Finance, Working Paper 2017-11, 22, 2018.

W. Schön, One Answer to Why and How to Tax the Digitalized Economy, Max Planck Institute for Tax Law and Public Finance, Working Paper 2010-10, 3-12, 2019.

L. Spinosa & V. Chand, A Long-Term Solution for Taxing Digitalized Business Models: Should the Permanent Establishment Definition Be Modified to Resolve the Issue or Should the Focus be on a Shared Taxing Rights Mechanism?, 46 (6/7) Intertax, p. 476, 2018.

A. Turina, Back To Grass Roots: The Arm's Length Standard, Comparability and Transparency - Some Perspectives From The Emerging World, 10 World Tax J. 2, p. 295, 2018.

R. Vann, Reflections on Business Profits and the Arm's-Length Principle, in The Taxation of Business Profits under Tax Treaties, B.J. Arnold, J. Sasseville & E.M. Zolt eds, Canadian Tax Foundation, p. 133, 2003.

R. Vann, Taxing International Business Income: Hard Boiled Wonderland and the End of the World, 2 WTJ 3, Journals IBFD, p. 291, 2010.

Public Comments on the Unified approach by the following commentators which are available on: Amazon, Booking.com, Digital Economy Group, Deloitte, Ernst & Young, Johnson and Johnson, KPMG, Procter and Gamble, Netflix, Maisto E Associati, Nestle, PwC, Skadden, Spotify, Uber, Unilever, Zalando.

CHAPTER 20

Application of the Profit Split Method to Digital Business Models and to the Digitalization of the Economy

Vikram Chand

I INTRODUCTION

Under the current international corporate tax framework, business income is 'sourced'[1] in the State where an enterprise through its 'origin'[2] or '*supply*'[3] or 'value creation'[4] factors (such as employees) carries on business or economic activities. Therefore, if an enterprise (Company R), through its employees, produces in one State (Country R, the State in which it is a tax resident) and sells on a remote basis in another State (Country S) then corporate tax on that business income or profit is only paid/payable in the former State (Country R).

On the other hand, from an international corporate tax perspective, when Company R from Country R carries on business in Country S through 'origin' or

1. V. Chand, Allocation of Taxing Rights in the Digitalized Economy: Assessment of Potential Policy Solutions and Recommendation for a Simplified Residual Profit Split Method, 47(12) Intertax 1023–1026 (2019); K. Vogel, Worldwide vs. Source Taxation of Income: A Review and Re-evaluation of Arguments (Part II), 16 (10) Intertax 310, 320 (1988); *id.*, Part III, 16 (11) Intertax 393, 398 (1988); M. Devereux, Taxation of Outbound Direct Investment: Economic Principles and Tax Policy Considerations, 24 (4) Oxford Rev. Econ. Policy 698, 712–715 (2008).
2. E. Kemmeren, Source of Income in Globalizing Economies: Overview of the Issues and a Plea for an Origin-Based Approach, 60 (11) Bull. Intl. Taxn. 430, 433–437 (2006).
3. A. Schafer & C. Spengel, ICT and International Taxation: Tax Attributes and Scope of Taxation, Discussion Paper, 02-81 Centre for European Economic Research 11, 11–12 (2002).
4. W. Schön, Ten Questions about Why and How to Tax the Digitalized Economy, Max Planck Institute for Tax Law and Public Finance, Working paper, 2017-11, 22 (2017); J. Becker & J. Englisch, Taxing Where Value Is Created: What's 'User Involvement' Got to Do with It?, 47 (2) Intertax 161, 163–164 (2019).

'supply' or 'value creation' factors therein (such as its employees) then the latter State usually taxes that business income. From a taxable nexus perspective, the value creation factors (such as employees) in Country S could either be a part of a separate related entity (related company) or the same enterprise, i.e., a permanent establishment (PE).[5] From a profit allocation perspective, transfer pricing rules, which are based on the arm's-length principle (ALP),[6] are typically used to allocate profits to the separate related entity[7] or to the PE.[8] These rules usually allocate profits to the taxable nexus based on the functions, assets and risks associated with that nexus.[9]

The (Base erosion and profit shifting) BEPS Action Plan, in particular, BEPS Actions 8–10 and BEPS Action 7[10] have provided further guidance on the application of the ALP to related entities or PEs. These changes apply to all enterprises and are not specifically targeted at highly digitalized businesses (HDBs), such as online advertisers, online market places, online resellers and so on. However, the guidance does contain several examples that could impact HDBs. Accordingly, the purpose of this contribution is to initially assess the impact of those changes, in particular, the application of the transactional profit split method (TPSM)[11] to selected digital business models. Specifically, in section II, the author discusses the application of the TPSM for transactions that take place among separate related entities and in section III, the author discusses the application of those changes for transactions that take place between head office and PEs.

In section IV, the author summarizes his key findings from the previous two sections. Thereafter, in section V, the author discusses his opinion on the application of the profit split method (PSM) in the context of the international corporate tax debate triggered by the digitalization of the economy[12] with respect to multinational enterprises (MNEs). Finally, he concludes in section VI.

5. OECD, Model Tax Convention on Income and on Capital: Condensed Version 2017 (OECD, 2017). *See* Art. 5 OECD Model (2017).
6. OECD, Transfer Pricing Guidelines for Multinationals Enterprises and Tax Administrations 2017 (OECD 2017).
7. *See* Art. 9(1) OECD Model (2017).
8. *See* Art. 7(2) OECD Model (2017). *See also* OECD, 2010 Report on the Attribution of Profits to Permanent Establishments (OECD 2010). This report provides detailed guidance the interpretation of Art. 7(2) of the OECD Model Convention. *See* OECD Model: Commentary on Art. 7, paras 8–9 (2017).
9. However, with respect to PEs we would like to highlight that, depending on the actual tax treaty and State practices, formulary approaches may also be used. *See* Art. 7(4) OECD Model (2008).
10. OECD, BEPS Action 7: Additional Guidance on the Attribution of Profits to Permanent Establishments (OECD March 2018).
11. OECD, Revised Guidance on the Application of the Transactional Profit Split Method, OECD/G20 Base Erosion and Profit Shifting Project (OECD 4 June 2018). *See also* EU Commission-EU Joint Transfer Pricing Forum (EUJTPF), The Application of the Profit Split Method within the EU, Doc JTPF/002/2019 (March, 2019).
12. *See* OECD, Addressing the Tax Challenges of the Digital Economy – Action 1: 2015 Final Report, OECD/G20 Base Erosion and Profit Shifting Project (OECD Publishing 2015), at 11; OECD, Tax Challenges Arising from Digitalization – Interim Report 2018: Inclusive Framework on BEPS, OECD/G20 Base Erosion and Profit Shifting Project (OECD Publishing 2018).

II PROFIT ALLOCATION AMONG SEPARATE LEGAL ENTITIES WITHIN AN MNE

1 Post-BEPS Transfer Pricing Guidance

A Accurate Delineation of the Transaction

Article 9 of the OECD Model endorses the ALP for pricing transactions between associated enterprises.[13] The updated Transfer Pricing Guidelines, which aligns taxation outcomes with 'value creation',[14] state that the application of the ALP requires a comparison of the related-party transaction with comparable uncontrolled transactions. The two steps of this analysis are to: (i) identify the commercial or financial terms between related parties and the economically relevant aspects attached to such terms in order to properly delineate the related-party transaction (which is done through a detailed functional analysis); and (ii) undertake a comparability analysis to compare the controlled transaction with uncontrolled transactions.[15]

In the context of accurately delineating the transaction, the updated OECD Guidelines makes several key changes (a discussion of all changes is outside the scope of this contribution). First, it states that returns will be allocated to an entity if that entity controls and has the financial capacity to bear the economically significant risks.[16]

Control over risk[17] exists when the entity has: (1) the capability to make decisions to take on, lay off or decline a risk-bearing opportunity, together with the actual

13. For a similar discussion in this section, see V. Chand & A. Baez Moreno, 'Solving the Allocation of Taxing Rights Debate for the Digitalized Economy: Shortcomings of the Digital PE Proposal and Reconsideration of the Base Eroding Payments Proposal' in: Pistone, Weber (eds), Taxing the Digital Economy 2019, pp. 126–130.
14. For a critical analysis of the value creation concept, *see*: J. Hey, 'Taxation Where Value is Created' and the OECD/G20 Base Erosion and Profit Shifting Initiative, 72 (4/5) Bull. Int'l Taxation (2018); S.C. Morse, Value Creation: A Standard in Search of a Process, 72 (4/5) Bull. Int'l Taxation (2018); Krister Andersson, Should We Use Value Creation or Destination as a Basis for Taxing Digital Businesses? – Krister Andersson's Comments on the 2018 Klaus Vogel Lecture Given by Professor Michael Devereux, 72 (12) Bull. Int'l Taxn. (2018).
15. OECD, Transfer Pricing Guidelines, para. 1.33.
16. OECD, Transfer Pricing Guidelines, para. 1.60.
17. The 'control' over risk requirement has received a great deal of criticism. First, it is argued that this particular requirement can easily be met by having the right people doing the right job. This could lead to the shifting of taxable bases from high tax states to low tax states. Thus, the arm's-length principle promotes tax competition. Second, the guidelines state that in situations where multiple associated enterprises control the risks, the risk should be allocated to the associated enterprise that demonstrates 'most control'. The demonstration of this requirement could indeed be challenging from a practical perspective, especially in MNEs where management boards are similar/spread across various entities and where consensus-based decision-making takes place. Third, a few commentators have argued that the control test goes beyond the boundaries of the arm's-length standard. It is stated that several situations exist among independent enterprises where the incidence of risk is separate from the control over risk requirement. In other words, enterprises bear risks that they do not control. Accordingly, courts may deviate from the control requirement if this is proven. Fourth, it is argued that the level of factual detail that is required to understand which party controls the risks is substantially high. Consequently, it could be burdensome for the taxpayers and the tax administrations to

performance of that decision-making function; and (2) the capability to make decisions on whether and how to respond to the risks associated with the opportunity, together with the actual performance of that decision-making function. Specifically, the guidance states that: (3) 'the capability to mitigate risk, that is the capability to take measures that affect risk outcomes, together with the actual performance of such risk mitigation'[18] is not necessary in order to have control over the risks.[19] Moreover, an entity could be considered to have the financial means when it has the appropriate access to the funding to take on or to lay off the risk, to pay for the risk mitigation functions and to bear the consequences of the risk if it materializes.[20]

Second, with respect to ownership of intangibles,[21] the updated guidance states that an entity will be allocated intangible-related returns (e.g., royalties or capital gains) if that taxpayer carries out control-related functions[22] and bears control-related risks,[23] as well as provides all assets (including funding)[24] associated with development or acquisition, enhancement, maintenance, protection and exploitation of intangibles[25] (DEMPE activities).[26] Importantly, the guidance also states that if another related entity contributes to the control over key intangible-related risks then that enterprise could be entitled to a 'profit-sharing element'.[27]

---

undertake this analysis. Fifth, there is no clarity as regards whether the concept of control over risk for the purpose of Art. 9 and the significant people functions with respect to risk assumption under Art. 7 are similar or different. The OECD does not provide an answer to this issue. Accordingly, the approach adopted in an Art. 9 and an Art. 7 analysis could be different. *See* V. Chand & B. Malek, The Relevant Economic Activity Test and its Impact on International Corporate Tax Policy, 3 British Tax Rev. 421 (2019). *See also* R. Collier & J.L. Andrus, Transfer Pricing and the Arm's Length Principle (Oxford: OUP, 2017), at 230–247.

18. OECD, Transfer Pricing Guidelines, para. 1.61.
19. OECD, Transfer Pricing Guidelines, para. 1.65.
20. OECD, Transfer Pricing Guidelines, para. 1.64.
21. The updated guidance defines intangibles as 'something which is not a physical asset or a financial asset, which is capable of being owned or controlled for use in commercial activities, and whose use or transfer would be compensated had it occurred in a transaction between independent parties in comparable circumstances'. Specifically, a marketing intangible has broadly been defined as 'An intangible that relates to marketing activities, aids in the commercial exploitation of a product or service and/or has an important promotional value for the product concerned. Depending on the context, marketing intangibles may include, for example, trademarks, trade names, customer lists, customer relationships, and proprietary market and customer data that is used or aids in marketing and selling goods or services to customers'. On the other hand, trade intangible has been defined as 'An intangible other than a marketing intangible'. For instance, such intangibles include patents, know-how and trade secrets and so on'. OECD, Transfer Pricing Guidelines, para. 6.6 and OECD, Transfer Pricing Guidelines, paras 6.18–6.20.
22. OECD, Transfer Pricing Guidelines, paras 6.50–6.58.
23. OECD, Transfer Pricing Guidelines, paras 6.65–6.68.
24. OECD, Transfer Pricing Guidelines, paras 6.59–6.64.
25. OECD, Transfer Pricing Guidelines, para. 6.71.
26. In several examples, the guidelines illustrate that royalty income (or capital gains) would be reallocated from the legal owner to the entity that controlled the DEMPE risks. *See* Examples 1, 2, 3, 15 and 17 in Annex to Chapter VI, OECD, Transfer Pricing Guidelines; Furthermore, *see* Collier & Andrus, Transfer Pricing and the Arm's Length Principle, at 214–215; For a detailed analysis of the ownership requirement of the intangibles *see* S. Wilkie, The Definition and Ownership of Intangibles: Inside the Box? Outside the Box? What is the Box?, 4(3) World Tax J. 222 (2012).
27. OECD, Transfer Pricing Guidelines, para. 6.72.

B *The Transactional Profit Split Method*

In the context of the second step that deals with determining the ALP, the updated guidance expands on the application of the TPSM.[28] This method aims at splitting the combined profits (or losses) arising from controlled transactions between associated enterprises on an economically valid basis, which approximates the division of profits that would have been anticipated and reflected in an agreement made at arm's-length. The method is applicable in the following three situations.[29]

First, when the associated enterprises make unique and valuable contributions (especially in the form of unique and valuable intangibles). It is stated that 'contributions (for instance functions performed, or assets used or contributed) will be "unique and valuable" in cases where: (i) they are not comparable to contributions made by uncontrolled parties in comparable circumstances; and (ii) they represent a key source of actual or potential economic benefits in the business operations'.[30] Although Examples 1, 2, 3 and 5[31] shed light on this concept, at this stage, it is rather unclear what is precisely meant by unique and valuable.[32] This said, one aspect is certain. In order for this indicator to apply, a contribution should be 'unique' as well as 'valuable'.[33]

Second, when the associated enterprises are engaged in highly integrated activities. It is stated that 'a high degree of integration means that the way in which one party to the transaction performs functions, uses assets and assumes risks is interlinked with, and cannot reliably be evaluated in isolation from, the way in which another party to the transaction performs functions, uses assets and assumes risks'.[34] From an analysis of the various examples,[35] it seems that the concept applies to both parallel-integrated activities (Examples 6–7) as well as sequential integrated activities (Example 9). This said, several commentators have commented that the concept needs to be defined in a clearer manner as its definition is relatively broad and openly formulated with no clear threshold.[36] The EU Commission report provides further guidance on this concept by stating:

> In practical terms, the operations would be 'highly integrated' when two or more legal entities share and/ or combine functions, assets and risks, while jointly achieve a common objective (e.g. a project whereby the parties jointly contribute

---

28. For a similar discussion in this section, see V. Chand & A. Baez Moreno, 'Solving the Allocation of Taxing Rights Debate for the Digitalized Economy: Shortcomings of the Digital PE Proposal and Reconsideration of the Base Eroding Payments Proposal' in: Pistone, Weber (eds), Taxing the Digital Economy 2019, pp. 130–136.
29. EUJTPF, The Application of the Profit Split Method, at. 5.
30. OECD, Profit Split Method, paras 2.130–2.132; EUJTPF, The Application of the Profit Split Method, at. 7–8.
31. OECD, Profit Split Method, Examples 1, 2, 3 and 5 of the report.
32. L.Stähli, The Use of the Profit Split Method in Highly Integrated Transactions, 25 Int'l Transfer Pricing J.), at 283 (2018).
33. EUJTPF, The Application of the Profit Split Method, at. 7–8.
34. OECD, Profit Split Method, paras 2.133–2.138; EUJTPF, The Application of the Profit Split Method, at. 8–12.
35. OECD, Profit Split Method, Examples 6, 7 and 9 of the report.
36. For instance, *see* L. Stähli, The Use of the Profit Split Method, at 283 and 288.

> to each part of the process towards a common outcome). 'Highly integrated' does not necessarily mean using the same resources or service provider. Rather, there needs to exist a common objective and a combination of joint contributions. Additionally, it should be sustained that it would not be possible to materialize such a jointly achieved objective without the participation of the other party in the transaction.[37]

Lastly, when the associated enterprises either: (i) share assumption of economically significant risks, that is, when both parties 'control' an important risk; or (ii) separately assume closely related risks, that is, when each party 'controls' an interrelated or interlinked risk to the transaction.[38] Although Example 10[39] is used to shed light on the latter indicator (ii), the contributions made by the associated enterprises in that example could also be considered to be unique and valuable or highly integrated. Moreover, the example does not seem helpful in understanding these terms.

If one of the above three indicators exists, the use of the TPSM is considered to be appropriate. This said, in many situations, there could be an overlap among these three indicators. On the other hand, the PSM should not apply when one party performs only simple functions. Moreover, it may well be possible that the PSM does not apply in a situation when the accurately delineated transaction can be benchmarked with independent comparables. For instance, *see* examples 4 and 8 which deal with a limited functional distributor and contract manufacturer respectively. Even though a certain degree of integration exists in these examples, the entities do not make any unique and valuable contribution and neither do they share economically significant risks.

However, the mere lack of comparables does not automatically justify the application of the PSM. In situations where exact comparables do not exist, a more pragmatic approach needs to be adopted. A possibility is to allow taxpayers to broaden their comparable search criteria by looking at: (i) independent enterprises with slightly different business strategies or business models; (ii) independent enterprises which could be a situation in different markets; or (iii) independent enterprises engaged in different industries but situated in the same market.[40]

With respect to the division of the profit (or loss) to be split, the OECD Guidelines suggest two approaches, namely the contribution profit split analysis[41] and the residual profit split analysis[42] (RPS), by accepting that such approaches are neither exhaustive nor mutually exclusive. Under both approaches, the relative contributions of the associated enterprises generating the profit need to be ascertained.[43] Depending on the situation, external market data, internal data,[44] bargaining theory models, discounted cash flow analysis or survey approaches could be used. Thereafter, the crucial question

37. EUJTPF, The Application of the Profit Split Method, at. 11.
38. OECD, Profit Split Method, paras 2.139–2.140; EUJTPF, The Application of the Profit Split Method, at. 12–13.
39. OECD, Profit Split Method, Example 10 of the report.
40. EUJTPF, The Application of the Profit Split Method, at. 5 and Annex 1, at. 16.
41. OECD, Profit Split Method, paras 2.150–2.151.
42. OECD, Profit Split Method, paras 2.152–2.153 and Examples 11–12 of the report.
43. EUJTPF, The Application of the Profit Split Method, at. 4–5.
44. OECD, Profit Split Method, paras 2.166–2.168; EUJTPF, The Application of the Profit Split Method, at. 13.

concerns how to translate the relative contributions into a ratio for splitting the profit. Based on the approach that has been utilized, 'facts and circumstances' allocation keys need to be ascertained to split anticipated or actual profits (or losses).[45] These keys, depending on the situation could relate to asset-based factors,[46] cost-based factors,[47] people-based factors, sales-based factors and so on.[48]

2 Application to Selected Digital Business Models

Two examples found in the TPSM report are relevant to digital business models. Example 5 deals with a situation where WebCo has developed a software code for a web crawler (a trade intangible). The crawler scans online web pages to collect pricing data. Thereafter, WebCo licenses the intangible to its associated enterprise viz., ScaleCo. Under the terms of the licence, ScaleCo is responsible for scaling up the web crawler and deciding on the crawling strategy. Specifically, ScaleCo is responsible for designing add-ons for the web crawler and in customizing the product to address gaps in the local market. On the other hand, WebCo continues to develop the underlying crawler technology. The functional analysis indicates that the key risk of the business pertains to the development risk and based on the new 'control over risk' framework, the risk is assumed by both parties. Accordingly, as both parties control the key risk, the PSM applies to determine the arm's-length remuneration of the licence fees.[49]

Example 3 deals with a scenario where electronic appliances are produced for sale to consumers by two members of a group. Specifically, Company A performs all functions in relation to research and development and manufacturing using its valuable know-how. On the other hand, Company B performs all activities related to marketing activities which result in a valuable trademark. Specifically, the activities are related to designing the marketing strategy, deciding on the level of marketing expenditure and validating the impact of the marketing campaigns on a monthly basis. Also, Company B performs activities in relation to the global distribution of products. In this regard, Company B develops a unique algorithm to get feedback from customers. Accordingly, as both parties make unique and valuable contributions, the PSM applies to determine the arm's-length remuneration of the sale of goods transaction from Company A to Company B.[50]

In the interim report, the OECD discusses several case studies, which highlight that HDBs typically operate with related local entities in the market jurisdiction, for instance, HDBs, such as a social network business model,[51] a digital re-seller[52] or a business engaged in ride for hire activities.[53] The local entities usually perform

45. OECD, Profit Split Method, paras 2.154–2.165. *See also* Examples 13–14 of the report.
46. OECD, Profit Split Method, paras 2.179–2.180. *See also* Example 15 of the report.
47. OECD, Profit Split Method, paras 2.181–2.183. *See also* Example 16 of the report.
48. EUJTPF, The Application of the Profit Split Method, at 13–15 and Annex 2 and 3, at. 17–21.
49. OECD, Profit Split Method, Example 5 of the report.
50. OECD, Profit Split Method, Example 5 of the report.
51. OECD, 2018 Interim Report, paras 100–129.
52. OECD, 2018 Interim Report, paras 162–189.
53. OECD, 2018 Interim Report, paras 190–220.

activities that are either software-related, such as local platform configuration, partial software development and customer support, or are marketing-related, such as local marketing and sales.

Arguably, based on the examples contained in the revised report, it can be argued that the TPSM should be applicable when a local entity in the market jurisdiction carries out:

- software-related activities, such as providing suggestions and assisting on adapting algorithms/technologies to cater to the local market requirements and on introducing new features that would be attractive to users in that market (which could be similar to those carried out by ScaleCo in Example 5); and/or
- marketing/sales activities, such as advertising, promoting the use of online services, translating the services in the local language, tailoring them to the local cultural tastes, technical consulting to users, adhering to local regulatory requirements, negotiating sales with potential customers and so on (which could be similar to those carried out by Company B in Example 3).

This is because the activities of the local entity make unique and valuable contributions. Put differently, the local entities' activities represent a key source of economic benefits. Alternatively, it could be argued that the activities of the local entity are highly integrated with those of the non-resident entity. This is because both entities combine functions, assets and risks, to achieve a common commercial objective. Some commentators[54] support this position and argue that the OECD Transfer Pricing Guidelines need to be clarified. Essentially, they propose that a proper functional analysis needs to be carried out to understand the roles and responsibilities of all the entities in a highly digitalized MNE, especially an MNE which creates value out of data (e.g., a search engine or social network business model). In particular, they stress that when the staff of the related local entity carries out core value-adding functions for the digital MNE (data mining, software- or sales-related functions), those functions cannot be considered to be routine in nature. Consequently, the TPSM should be applied to split the profits between the non-resident entity and local entity. Thus, the taxpayer in the market jurisdiction should be compensated appropriately for the 'true' value it creates/adds to the digital business model.[55] In other words, more profits (losses) should be allocated to the market jurisdiction. This said, the application of the TPSM would indeed depend on an accurate delineation of the transaction. If the delineation indicates that the local entity merely assists in collecting data or executes its software- or sales-related activities under the supervision of the non-resident entity or the activities are non-core activities, then a one-sided transfer pricing method, viz. the

54. For instance, *see* M. Olbert & C. Spengel, International Taxation in the Digital Economy: Challenge Accepted?, 9 (1) World Tax J., 3, at 38–42 (2017).
55. A. Martín Jimenez, BEPS, the Digitalized Economy and the Taxation of Services and Royalties, 46 (8/9) Intertax, at 629 (2018).

transaction net margin method (TNMM)[56] could be used to determine the taxable profit of the local entity.

III PROFIT ALLOCATION AMONG HEAD OFFICE AND PEs WITHIN AN MNE

1 Post-BEPS Profit Attribution Framework

Under Article 7(1) of the OECD Model, business profits of a non-resident enterprise (NRE) are taxable in the market jurisdiction only when a PE is constituted therein.[57] In the Action 7 Final Report, it was argued that taxpayers could circumvent the creation of a PE: (i) by relying on the specific activity exceptions listed in Article 5(4);[58] and (ii) through the use of commissionaires or other arrangements by relying on the literal wording of Article 5(5) and (6).[59] Thus, the rationale of BEPS Action 7 was to modify Article 5 of the OECD Model. These amendments, which do not represent minimum standards, have been adopted by a selected number of States pursuant to Articles 12 and 13 of the Multilateral Instrument,[60] respectively. OECD statistics indicate that the new provisions on Article 5(4) are estimated to apply only to 277 bilateral tax agreements whereas the new provisions on Article 5(5) are estimated to apply only to 206 bilateral tax agreements.[61] Therefore, their rate of adoption has been rather low.

Under Article 7(2) of the OECD Model (2010/2014/2017 versions), the profits attributable to the PE are those that the PE would have earned acting on an arm's-length basis.[62] Specifically, a two-step approach, also known as the authorized OECD approach (AOA or full AOA), is provided to determine the profits attributable to a PE.[63] The steps are similar to an Article 9 analysis discussed previously and some States have adopted it (such as Germany, Japan and Hong Kong).[64]

The first step involves carrying out a functional and factual analysis to hypothesize the PE. In other words, this step entails understanding the activities carried out by the PE considering its significant people functions (SPF), assets and risks and its dealings with associated enterprises, including the head office (an accurate delineation

56. OECD, Transfer Pricing Guidelines, paras 2.64–2.105.
57. OECD Model (2017), Art. 7(1).
58. OECD, Action 7 Final Report, paras 10–15. *See also* OECD Model: Commentary on Art. 5, paras 58–78.
59. OECD, Action 7 Final Report, paras 5–9. *See also* OECD Model: Commentary on Art. 5, paras 82–101 & 102–114.
60. OECD, Multilateral Convention to Implement Tax Treaty Related Measures to Prevent Base Erosion and Profit Shifting (Multilateral Convention 2016) (24 November 2016).
61. OECD, 2018 Interim Report, para. 272.
62. OECD, 2010 Report on the Attribution of Profits to Permanent Establishments, at 12–13, para. 8.
63. OECD, 2010 Report on the Attribution of Profits to Permanent Establishments, at 13, para. 10.
64. R. Collier & J. Vella, Five Core Problems in the Attribution of Profits to Permanent Establishments, World Tax J., at 165–167 (May 2019).

of a dealing).[65] The second step involves pricing the dealing with the associated enterprise(s) by reference to transfer pricing principles (pricing the dealing).[66]

On the other hand, even though the Commentary on Article 7(2) of the OECD Model (2008) endorsed the AOA, differences did exist between both versions.[67] The major difference relates to the recognition of internal dealings between the head office and PE, such as internal royalties and interest. Also, the 2008 version included provisions that were considered not to be consistent with the ALP, that is, Article 7(4) which provided that States can allocate profits to a PE using an apportionment method (a formulary approach) up to the extent it was customary in that State. Also, Article 7(5)[68] provided that profits could not be attributed to a PE that performed purchasing functions for the head office. Provisions similar to Article 7 of the OECD Model (2008) are also found in Article 7 of the UN Model (2011 and 2017 versions with certain exceptions).[69] However, the Committee of Experts on international taxation has rejected the application of the AOA to interpret the business profits provision of the UN Model.[70]

States typically conclude tax treaties with each other by using either the OECD Model (various versions) or the UN Model. Accordingly, the attribution of profits to a PE depends on the exact wording contained in the tax treaty. Essentially, States can follow the AOA approach (based on the ALP) and non-AOA approach (formulary approaches).

2 Application to Selected Digital Business Models

Two examples found in BEPS Action 7 profit attribution report are relevant to the discussion here. The examples will be discussed assuming that the relevant tax treaty follows the AOA. [71]

The first example[72] deals with an OnlineCo (Country R resident), which is engaged in the business of selling goods in Country S through its website. Essentially, customers in Country S order the product on the website. Thereafter, Online Co ensures

65. For a detailed analysis of this step, *see* OECD, 2010 Report on the Attribution of Profits to Permanent Establishments, at 24–49, paras 57–182.
66. For a detailed analysis of this step *see* OECD, 2010 Report on the Attribution of Profits to Permanent Establishments, at 49–57, paras 183–223.
67. For a comparison of the two versions, *see* e.g., A. Wintsch, Attribution of Profits to Permanent Establishments: The 2008 Art. 7 Versus the 2010 Art. 7 of the OECD Model, 24 (5) Intl. Transfer Pricing J. (2017).
68. Wintsch, Attribution of Profits to Permanent Establishments, para. 2.4.3.
69. United Nations Model Double Taxation Convention between Developed and Developing Countries (2011); United Nations Model Double Taxation Convention between Developed and Developing Countries (2017).
70. UN Model, Art. 7.
71. For a similar discussion in this section, see V. Chand & A. Baez Moreno, 'Solving the Allocation of Taxing Rights Debate for the Digitalized Economy: Shortcomings of the Digital PE Proposal and Reconsideration of the Base Eroding Payments Proposal' in: Pistone, Weber (eds), Taxing the Digital Economy 2019, pp. 132–135.
72. OECD, Additional Guidance on the Attribution of Profits to Permanent Establishments, paras 11–25.

that the product is delivered to the customer from a warehouse that OnlineCo operates directly in State S. The functional analysis indicates that employees of R Co deal with the purchase and sale of products. On the other hand, the warehouse, which is operated by twenty-five employees, is used only for the purposes of storing and delivering goods to customers. Specifically, the employees handle the receipt of shipments from suppliers, the stocking of the goods, and the execution of deliveries to customers in Country S, using independent delivery service providers (such as courier services).

Under the new wording of Article 5, that is reflected in Article 13(2) as well as 13(4) of the MLI, such activity carried out at the warehouse will trigger a PE. Under the first step of the AOA, the question arises as to whether the storage and delivery activity carried out at the warehouse is a routine activity or an activity which makes unique and valuable contributions/or which is highly integrated.

If it is argued that the activity is a routine activity then, under the second step, a one-sided transfer pricing method, viz. the TNMM could be used to determine the taxable profit of the PE (net cost plus method). This could be the case when the warehouse only carries out limited functions, such as picking and packing, storage as well as delivery/dispatch[73] under the control and supervision of the head office. On the other hand, if it is argued that the warehousing activity represents a high value-added activity that involves making unique and valuable contributions or a highly integrated activity then, under the second step, the TPSM could be applied. This could be the case when the warehouse carries out the previously mentioned functions on an independent basis (i.e., SPF with respect to risk assumption) and additional functions, such as: (i) receiving Country S's customer orders simultaneously with Online Co; (ii) analysing data related to Country S's customers; (iii) website/portal site maintenance with reference to Country S; (iv) stock analysis, management and replenishment; and (v) reviewing Country B's marketing strategy, such as advertising and potential price changes, based on Country B's specific data analysis.[74] Accordingly, the PE could be entitled to a larger share of the profits. Thus, a proper functional analysis will need to be carried out, in light of OnlineCo's digital business model, to determine the degree of importance of the storage and delivery activities.

The second example deals with an online advertiser.[75] SiteCo, a company resident in State R, provides targeted online advertising services to its clients on its social network website. SellCo, an associated enterprise that is a resident in State S, enters into an exclusive service contract with SiteCo for sales/marketing services. Pursuant to this agreement, SellCo markets the online advertising services of SiteCo to potential clients. Essentially, the employees of SellCo play an active role to convince prospective clients to acquire SiteCo's online advertising services. Also, the personnel are responsible for deciding on the appropriate amount, type and form of advertising.

73. J.F. Dutriez, Attribution of Profits to a Permanent Establishment of a Company Engaged in Online Sales of Goods through a Local Warehouse, 25(3) Intl. Transfer Pricing J., s. 4.1 (2018).
74. *Id.*, s. 4.2.
75. OECD, Additional Guidance on the Attribution of Profits to Permanent Establishments, paras 59–69.

The clients enter directly into a contract with SiteCo. For its services, SellCo is remunerated on a fixed percentage basis (a percentage of the sales it generates).

Under the old wording of Article 5(5), it is argued that SellCo did not have a PE in State S as SellCo (through its employees) did not have the authority to conclude contracts in the name of SiteCo. However, under the new wording that is reflected in Article 12(1) of the MLI, SiteCo would trigger a PE in State S. In this case, SellCo is a dependant agent enterprise and the PE of SiteCo is a dependant agent PE (DAPE). Consequently, Article 9 of the OECD Model would apply to test whether or not the conditions/prices between SellCo and SiteCo are at arm's-length whereas Article 7 would apply to the transactions between the SiteCo (head office) and the DAPE.[76]

In order to determine the arm's-length remuneration of SellCo under Article 9, the question arises as to whether the marketing/sales activity carried out by its personnel is a routine activity or an activity which is highly integrated or which makes unique and valuable contributions. If it argued that the activity is a routine activity then the TNMM could be used to determine the taxable profit of the SellCo (for instance, by using a net cost plus return or a net return on sales approach). This would typically be the case when an accurate delineation of the transaction indicates that the sales/marketing risks are 'controlled' by SiteCo's personnel in the sense that they set the sales strategy for Country S, they supervise the personnel working in SellCo, they are responsible for setting the pricing policy in respect to the advertising services and tailoring that policy for the local market and so on. In this situation, SellCo will be characterized as a taxpayer that provides routine marketing services. Consequently, it will be treated as the tested party for undertaking a transfer pricing analysis due to its least complex profile.[77] On the other hand, if it is argued that the activities of SellCo represent a high value-added activity that involves making unique and valuable contributions or a highly integrated activity then the TPSM could be applied. This would be the case when an accurate delineation of the transaction indicates that the sales/marketing risks are 'controlled' by SellCo's personnel or SellCo's personnel contribute actively towards managing those risks. Thus, a proper functional analysis will need to be carried out, in light of SiteCo's digital business model, to determine the degree of importance of the sales/marketing activities.

The two-step approach of the AOA will apply to determine the profits attributable to the DAPE. To reiterate, the first step involves carrying out a functional and factual analysis in order to hypothesize the PE, i.e., to understand the activities carried out by the PE in light of its SPF, assets and risks, and to understand its dealings (transactions) with associated enterprises (including the head office). It could be argued that, under this step, the DAPE does not perform any SPF relevant to the assumption of risks. The SPF relevant to economically significant risks (such as risks associated to sales/marketing), as accurately delineated under Article 9, are performed by personnel either working in State R for SiteCo or personnel working in State S for SellCo. Thus, as the DAPE does not carry out any SPF on its own, it does not contribute to the 'value creation' process. As a result, it should not be attributed to any risks, and consequently

76. *Id.*, paras 62–63.
77. OECD, Transfer Pricing Guidelines, paras 3.18–3.19.

no profits.[78] Therefore, it could be argued that once SellCo has been compensated on an arm's-length basis, there would not be further income attribution to the DAPE as the DAPE did not perform any activity on its own.[79]

However, if one applies the approach followed by the BEPS Action 7 profit attribution report different results could arise. The report argues that under the first step, the functions performed by personnel of SellCo should be attributed to the DAPE. Accordingly, the risks associated with those functions should be attributed to the DAPE. Essentially, the report provides that the profits attributable to the DAPE are equal to sales to third-party customers, as reduced by: (i) the amount that SiteCo would have received from the DAPE for selling the advertising space (an internal dealing); (ii) an arm's-length remuneration of SellCo; and (iii) other expenses related to the PE.[80] If this approach were to be followed, then arguably, the profits attributable to the DAPE would need to be computed and they could be either 'positive, nil or negative'.

In situations where the sales/marketing risks are 'controlled' by SellCo, the report recognizes that 'the profits attributable to the PE could be minimal or even zero'.[81] However, the question then arises as to whether additional profits could be attributed to the PE when the sales/marketing risks are 'controlled' by SiteCo whereas the day-to-day selling and marketing functions are performed by SellCo. To reiterate, assumption of risks by a PE depends on the SPF carried out by the PE's personnel at the PE location.[82] SPF relevant to risk assumption 'are those which require active decision-making with regard to the acceptance and/or management (subsequent to the transfer) of those risks'.[83] The question arises as to whether the risk allocation framework for the purpose of Article 9 and Article 7 of the OECD Model is similar. The OECD's updated report on profit attribution (2018) states, 'While there may be functions that would be considered both significant people functions for the attribution of risk for the purposes of the AOA and risk control functions for the purposes of Article 9, the conclusion cannot be drawn that these two concepts are aligned or can be used interchangeably for purposes of Article 7 and Article 9.'[84] Specifically, the key question that arises is whether active decision-making with regard to risk acceptance and management in the context of the AOA includes the elements (1) and (2) only or elements (1), (2) as well as (3) which have been discussed in the context of the updated OECD TPG on risk allocation (*see* section III 1). In other words, do SPF include day-to-day risk mitigation functions?

78. OECD, 2010 Report on the Attribution of Profits to Permanent Establishments, paras 233–244.
79. *See* P. Baker & R. Collier, The Attribution of Profits to a Permanent Establishment, (91b) General Report IFA Cahiers 2006, at 21 (2006); P. Drobnik, The Attribution of Profits to a Dependent Agent PE – If the Dependent Agent Is a Commissionaire (Wholly Owned Subsidiary) of the Principal, Intl. Transfer Pricing J., 197, at 202 (May/June 2018); R. Collier & J. Vella, *Five Core Problems*, at 176–181.
80. OECD, Additional Guidance on the Attribution of Profits to Permanent Establishments, paras 64–69.
81. *Id.*, para. 42.
82. OECD, 2010 Report on the Attribution of Profits to Permanent Establishments, paras. 15 and 68.
83. *Id.*, para. 22.
84. OECD, Additional Guidance on the Attribution of Profits to Permanent Establishments, para. 40.

We are of the opinion that that allocation of risks and returns for the purpose of Article 7 and Article 9 should be similar.[85] This would imply that if the sales/marketing risks are '*controlled*' by SiteCos personnel then they should only be attributed to the head office and not to the DAPE even though the day-to-day functions are performed by SellCo. Thus, there should not be any further income attribution to the DAPE. However, at the same time, we do recognize that this is an area that could lead to tax uncertainty as tax administrations could argue that: (i) the functions performed by SellCo, such as day-to-day sales and marketing, which would constitute SPF, should be attributed to the DAPE; and (ii) consequently, all risks associated with those functions should be attributed to the DAPE, irrespective of the place where they are performed. If this approach is to be followed, the functions performed at the level of the head office and the associated risks (marketing- or sales-related risks) could be attributed to the DAPE. This would, thus, enhance the profits attributable to the DAPE as it could be argued that the DAPE should be benchmarked against a local distributor of advertising services. There is no doubt that this position is disputable.

IV THE CURRENT STATUS OF THE EXISTING PROFIT ALLOCATION FRAMEWORK

In general, BEPS Actions 8–10 and Action 7 have introduced several subjective concepts to interpret the application of the ALP. Specifically, the TPSM is applicable to situations involving unique and valuable contributions or highly integrated activities or when parties share economically significant risks. These indicators, along with their examples, are subjective and could lead to different interpretations. Also, in the context of several business models (including digital business models), it is clear that the tax administrations of market jurisdictions will argue for the application of this method, especially, when the taxpayer in their jurisdiction contributes to the DEMPE activities associated with the intangible. For instance, software research and development for trade-related intangibles (such as algorithms) or sales-related activities for marketing-related intangibles (such as trademarks or trade names). Thus, Actions 8–10 create an uncertain profit allocation environment. From a policy perspective, it would be appreciated if the OECD could continue its work on the TPSM and provide additional guidance on the subjective concepts discussed therein, in particular, their application to digital business models.

Several issues also arise with respect to the changes made by BEPS Action 7, in particular, the changes made towards allocating profits to PEs. As a starting point, profit allocation under the AOA depends on the SPF, assets employed and risks assumed. If the activity carried out by the PE involves making unique and valuable contributions or if its activity is highly integrated with that of its head office, then arguably the TPSM could be applied to remunerate the PE. This being said, a tension arises between the nexus and profit allocation concepts when the PE does not carry out

85. For a similar position, *see* R. Petruzzi & R. Holzinger, Profit Attribution to Dependent Agent Permanent Establishment in a Post-BEPS Era, 9 (2) World Tax J., 263, at 294 (2017).

any 'value creation' activities. This is typically the case when a DAPE gets triggered due to the activities of a related local entity. Arguably, as the DAPE does not carry out any activities (no functions, assets and risks) its remuneration should be zero. However, in light of the guidance issued on profit allocation to such PEs, market jurisdictions will argue for additional profit attribution to PEs. Consequently, BEPS Action 7, similar to BEPS Actions 8–10, creates an uncertain profit allocation environment,[86] the outcome of which would lead to higher compliance-related costs for businesses.[87]

Furthermore, in order to avoid the creation of a DAPE pursuant to BEPS Action 7, several MNE groups have restructured their operations. For instance, principal entities in several industries have restructured their operations from a commissionaire to a local risk distributor (LRD) in the Market State. Similarly, several digital businesses, which have operated on a remote basis through centralized structures, have changed their business models and have created the so-called resellers.[88] As a result, the entity in the Market State (LRD or reseller) reports taxable income (profit or losses). However, as these related local entities assume limited risks, under the current ALP framework substantial profits can continue to be shifted outside the market jurisdiction (especially to entities that bear substantial risks). Also, several businesses, including digital businesses, continue to operate on a remote basis (without any tangible presence in the Market States). The question then arises as to how can the Market Country tax the income of NREs? This matter is discussed in the next section and it focuses mostly on the profit allocation issue.

V PROFIT ALLOCATION AND THE DIGITALIZATION OF THE ECONOMY: A LEAD INTO THE DEBATE

1 The Profit Allocation Issue

With the rise of digitalization, there is the growing concern that MNEs, especially HDBs, can centralize operations and sell their products/services on a remote basis (especially over the internet) and derive substantial business income from other countries (Market Country or Market State or Market jurisdiction) without any physical presence of personnel or with minimal presence therein. Moreover, some businesses can use digital technologies to collect data from users of a platform or end consumers with the ultimate objective to enhance and commercialize their own product/service offering. Arguably, operating without/with a less physical presence and collecting data is also possible due to the fact that, in the digital age, companies rely extensively on intangibles.[89] Taking into consideration these features, from a tax policy standpoint, the question arises as to how can the Market Country tax the business income of a NRE

86. Also see V. Chand, 'Achieving Certainty in an Uncertain Profit Allocation Environment' in: Intertax, 2019 (Vol. 47), No. 12, pp. 1000–1002.
87. R. Collier & J. Vella, *Five Core Problems*, at 180–181.
88. OECD, 2018 Interim Report, para 262.
89. OECD, Interim Report 2018, para. 34.

which operates without any physical presence or with minimal presence therein? [90] The answer to this question would essentially entail the development of new nexus as well as profit allocation rules (also depending on the precise solution, new rules that resolve issues relating to relief from double taxation as well as dispute prevention/resolution). While designing new nexus rules to deal with this issue is a challenging task, the most important piece of the puzzle relates to the design of new profit (loss) allocation rules.

In February 2019, the OECD released a public consultation document[91] (PCD) which addresses the tax challenges raised by the digitalization of the economy. The PCD essentially discusses proposals that either address the allocation of taxing rights (Pillar I) or unresolved Base Erosion of Profit Shifting (BEPS) issues (Pillar II). Thereafter, in May 2019, the OECD/G20 inclusive framework released its programme of work to develop a consensus-based solution for both issues.[92]

Essentially, the PCD put forward the following three solutions that are to be analysed on a 'without prejudice' basis: the user participation, the significant economic presence (SEP) and the marketing intangibles approach. Furthermore, to resolve the profit allocation issue under Pillar I, the programme of work contemplates the following three approaches, viz. the Modified Residual Profit Split Method (MRPS), the Fractional Apportionment Method as well as a Distribution-based approach. [93]

As discussed previously, under the current framework, profit allocation to related entities or PEs depends on the ALP. The ALP allocates profits to a taxable nexus based on the value created by that nexus. In other words, profit allocation to the nexus does not depend on the profits created by the entire MNE group as a whole. However, the profit allocation mechanisms that are being contemplated under all these proposals follow, in one way or another, a 'global approach to determination of profit'[94] that needs to be reallocated to a new nexus.

2 The Profit Allocation Solutions

A The Modified Residual Profit Split Method

This method seems to be linked to the market-related intangibles proposal,[95] which arguably applies to a broad set of businesses (although its precise scope of applicability

90. On this matter, also see V. Chand, 'Allocation of Taxing Rights in the Digitalized Economy', pp. 1026–1027.
91. OECD, Addressing the Tax Challenges of the Digitalisation of the Economy – Public Consultation Document (OECD/G20 Base Erosion and Profit Shifting Project, 2019).
92. OECD/G20, Programme of Work to Develop a Consensus Solution to the Tax Challenges Arising from the Digitalization of the Economy (OECD/G20 Base Erosion and Profit Shifting Project, 2019).
93. For a recent detailed discussion on these three approaches, see V. Chand, A. Turina & L. Ballivet, 'Profit Allocation Within MNEs in Light of the Ongoing Digital Debate on Pillar I – A "2020 Compromise"? From Using A Facts and Circumstances Analysis or Allocation Keys to Predetermined Allocation Approaches', World Tax J., July 2020 (published online), section 4.
94. OECD, Public Consultation Document, at para. 56.
95. OECD, Public Consultation Document, at para. 47. The proposal will also cover HDBs.

is not yet certain). The MRPS follows a 'top-down' methodology. Under this approach,[96] first, the total profits of the MNE group will need to be determined. Second, routine profits allocable to all MNE group members will need to be calculated. This could be ascertained either by resorting to a transfer pricing analysis or using a mechanical approach (simplified conventions). Then the routine profits will be deducted from the overall profits in order to arrive at the residual profit. Third, the residual profit will then be split between profit allocable to trade intangibles and profit allocable to market-related intangibles. In order to evaluate the contribution of market-related intangibles to the residual profit, several approaches could be used, such as using cost-based methods or predetermined formulas (simplified conventions). Fourth, the profit allocable to market-related intangibles would then be reallocated to the Market Country on the basis of an allocation key, such as sales or depending on the business model, users of a platform.

To understand the application of this approach, consider the following example that has been inspired by a PCD that was issued by the New Zealand government.[97] SF Group, which has its listed parent entity in New Zealand (NZ), is engaged in the business of selling high end branded clothes, bags and footwear. According to its consolidated financial statements for the year 2019, SF Group has: (A) consolidated group revenue = NZD 1 billion and (B) consolidated operating expenses = NZD 800 million. These expenses comprise of NZD 300 million in cost of goods sold, NZD 250 million in research and development costs, NZD 150 million in marketing and sales costs and NZD 100 million in overheads and administration. Therefore, the Group operating profits (C) amount to NZD 200 million.

Let us assume that the Group generates 10% of its global revenue from Country B (NZD 100 million). It has a subsidiary in Country B which is classified as an LRD. All of SF Group's residual profit is returned in NZ under the current transfer pricing rules as the parent entity is the owner of the relevant intangibles. In order to allocate profits to Country B, the MRPS would apply as follows:

- Step 1: The Group Profit amounts to NZD 200 Million.
- Step 2: A routine return is calculated on all functions performed. This return could be calculated on the basis of an arm's-length analysis or a predetermined approach (as safe harbour). For the purpose of the example, let us assume that the routine return on all activities (research, marketing and administration) is assumed to be 10% of all expenses, other than the cost of goods sold. This means the routine return is calculated as NZD 500 million expenses × 10% = NZD 50 million. The residual return would thus amount to NZD 200 million – NZD 50 million = 150 million.
- Step 3: We need to determine the proportion of residual profit attributable to market-related intangibles. Once again, this could be determined by using an arm's-length analysis (or a capital expenditure analysis) or a predetermined

96. OECD, Programme of Work, at para. 28.
97. *See* New Zealand Government, Options for Taxing the Digital Economy – a Government Discussion Document, at. 36 (June 2019).

approach (as a safe harbour). For the purpose of the example, we will use a predetermined formula. The formula divides the residual profit between trade intangibles and marketing intangibles. It does this by comparing the consolidated costs incurred by SF Group, that is, it compares SF Group's research and development (R&D) costs with its marketing and sales (M&S) costs. The R&D costs amount NZD 250 million whereas M&S costs amount to NZD 150 million. Thus, the residual profit allocable to market-related intangibles will amount to NZD 150 million (residual profit) × NZD 150 (M&S costs) / NZD 400 (R&D costs + M&S costs) = NZD 56.25 million.

- Step 4: SF Group's marketing intangibles profit is allocated between its market countries in proportion to SF Group's revenue from each country. Country B contributes 10% of SF Group's total revenue, so Country B will be allocated 10% of SF Group's marketing intangibles profit. This means that Country B will be allocated 10% × NZD 56.25 Million = NZD 5.625 million profit. Country B will tax this profit at its ordinary corporate tax rate, regardless of whether SF Group has a physical presence in Country B. Country NZ will give SF Group a credit or exemption for this tax.

B Fractional Apportionment Method

This method seems to be linked to the SEP concept,[98] which seems to apply only to HDBs. Thus, it could amount to a ring-fenced solution. While the details of the profit allocation mechanism are not yet out,[99] a reference could be made to a recent draft report of the Indian tax administration to understand the application of this approach (although their approach was discussed in the context of attributing profits to PEs that arise under current treaty rules, such as a fixed place or agency PE rules).

First, the profit derived from the Market Country needs to be determined. The proposal contemplates that this could be calculated by applying the global profit rate of the MNE group to the revenues generated in a particular jurisdiction. For example, let us assume that Company R from Country R, which is in the cloud computing business, sells remotely in India and derives gross revenue of USD 100. Also, let us assume that the MNE group to which Company R belongs makes a consolidated operating profit margin based on its consolidated financial accounts of 30% (consolidated operating profit/consolidated sales). Thus, under the first step, the profits derived from India would amount to USD 30 (30% of USD 100).[100]

Second, the profits will be split on the basis of predetermined formulas (allocation keys). For example, the draft report contemplates giving equal weight to employees, assets and sales.[101] Moreover, India also argues that 'users' can be regarded as

98. OECD, Public Consultation Document, at para. 52.
99. OECD, Programme of Work, at paras 30–31.
100. Central Board of Direct taxes, Income department – Government of India, Proposal for Amendment of Rules for Profit Attribution to Permanent Establishment, at para. 159 (CBDT, 2019).
101. *Id.*, at paras 152–158.

value creation factors. Thus, in the context of certain digitalized businesses where user participation plays an important role, the Indian proposal also contemplates allocating a certain weight to users based in India. Essentially, it is contemplated that sales will be allocated a weightage of 30%, users 10%-20% (depending on whether they are passive or active users) and the balance will be allocated to assets and employees.[102] As users are passive contributors to a cloud computing business, the weight of 10% will apply.

This would imply that 60% of the profit out of the total profit determined under first step will be allocated to Country R (due to the presence of employees and assets) and 40% will be allocated to India (on the basis of sales and users). Thus, approximately 40% USD 30, i.e., USD 12 will be the profit of the SEP on which corporate taxes will have to be paid in India.

Interestingly, with respect to the first step, the Indian tax administration is of the view that profits should be allocated to India, even if, the MNE Group makes a loss at the global level. All facts remaining the same, assume that the MNE Groups consolidated operating profit margin is negative (-5%). Even in such situations, the proposal states that the taxable base in India should, at a minimum, be equal to 2% of Indian revenues. Thus, profits derived from India will amount to USD 2 and one-third of those profits (USD) 0.66 will then be allocated to the SEP in India on which corporate taxes will have to be paid

C Distribution-Based Approach

Lastly, a distribution-based approach is being contemplated. This approach is based on a proposal made by Johnson & Johnson.[103] At this point, it is not clear whether the proposal is linked to the market-related intangibles or SEP proposal. This proposal, which applies to a broad set of businesses (although its precise scope of applicability is not yet certain), follows a 'bottom-up' methodology. To understand this approach, a difference needs to be made between two situations. First, when an NRE operates with a local taxable presence in the Market Country, that is, through a separate entity or a PE that could be characterized as a distributor (LRD or a full-fledged distributor). Second, when an NRE operates in the Market Country on a remote basis.

With respect to the first situation, the proposal contemplates that a baseline profit (or a routine return) could be allocated to the local taxable presence for its marketing or distribution or user-related activities. This baseline return could be a predetermined fixed percentage (e.g., 3% on sales made in that country) or could be based on industry or market-related margins. Thereafter, the baseline profit could be increased based on MNE groups' overall profitability. In this way, a portion of the residual return could also be reallocated. In relation to the second situation, the proposal also contemplates allocating a baseline and residual return to the market jurisdiction. However, the

102. *Id.*, at paras 176-178.
103. *See* Public Comments by Johnson&Johnson to the OECD PCD, at, 1-5.

question arises as to whether the baseline return/residual returns, under both approaches, operate as a safe harbour or a final return allocation.[104] There is no clarity on this.

3 High-Level Policy Assessment

There are two broad approaches that could be used to allocate profits to separate legal entities or PEs that exist within an MNE. At one end of the spectrum, countries can resort to using the ALP. At the other end of the spectrum, countries can resort to the 'enterprise doctrine'. This doctrine considers an MNE group as a single unit for tax purposes. The group's *aggregated profit* constitutes its tax base. It is then divided between various establishments by predetermined allocation keys. Under the current international corporate tax framework, the ALP is used to allocate profits in a vast majority of cases.

The MRPS can be considered to be a hybrid profit allocation method. Although it follows an MNE group approach, the ALP is still retained in determining the profit to be allocable to market-related intangibles. For instance, the ALP could be used to calculate routine returns (step 2) or to calculate residual returns allocable to marketing intangibles (step 3). However, the analysis could be rather subjective. Thus, the use of safe harbours (or simplified conventions) could be considered in its various steps to obtain certainty.

The fractional apportionment method moves away completely from the ALP and allocates profits based on predetermined formulas. The approach seems to respect the separate entity philosophy, in the sense, that the profit linked to the sales of an NRE (a single entity) is captured in the market jurisdiction. However, the profits to be allocated to the market are linked to MNE group results. This said, this approach also seems to allocate profits to the new presence even if the MNE as a whole is making losses at the consolidated level (minimum profits). The adoption of this framework, at this stage, seems rather unlikely as it represents a significant shift from the current transfer pricing framework. However, the method could possibility infiltrate and coexist with the existing rules if a ring-fenced solution is developed which targets only HDBs.

Similar to the previous approach, the distribution-based approach also seems to allocate minimum profits to the market jurisdiction. If an NRE has an LRD in the market then that entity will be allocated a baseline profit (3 % on sales). The proponents of this approach contend that such an approach would reduce transfer pricing disputes linked to distribution structures. On the other hand, when the NRE sells on a remote basis, the approach would also allocate a minimum profit to the market. In both situations, these profits could be adjusted upwards if the MNE groups operating profit margins exceed a certain percentage. While writing this contribution, it is difficult to ascertain as to whether this method will operate within the ALP framework (through the use of safe harbours) or will it move away completely from the ALP and allocate profits based on predetermined formulas.

---

104. *See also* OECD, Programme of Work, at paras 32-35.

The three different profit allocation regimes do not appear mutually exclusive and may be combined to reflect a two-tiered 'unified' approach along a continuum, with formulaic approaches being of suitable adoption in those situations where they represent a more efficient alternative or in all those situations where the comparability analysis cannot be conducted in a suitable way for intrinsic or extrinsic reasons. In fact, this is the direction that the OECD has adopted with respect to the so called 'unified approach' which is the subject matter of discussion in another chapter in this book.

VI CONCLUSION

Prior to the BEPS Project, the application of the ALP was already considered to be a highly subjective exercise. BEPS Actions 8–10 and BEPS Action 7 have enhanced this subjectivity by introducing new concepts, providing unclear guidance on existing concepts or remaining silent with respect to concepts that overlap in an Article 9 and Article 7 context. Specifically, the three indicators used in the context of the TPSM, are open-ended with no clear thresholds. Thus, there is no doubt that transfer pricing disputes will proliferate as tax administrations will start applying the TPSM to many situations (especially in the context of business models operated by HDBs). Thus, rather than providing tax certainty on open-ended concepts, policymakers are currently focusing their efforts on developing new profit allocation mechanisms to resolve the tax challenges raised in the context of Pillar I. This is understandable given the political interest on this topic and the need to arrive at a consensus-based solution. The approaches that are being considered, in one way or another, involve the use of a PSM (albeit, a new version that is linked to MNE group profits and not to a separate entities profits). The new PSM, up to the extent it incorporates the ALP, will also increase tax uncertainty (this could, however, be reduced by incorporating safe harbours or simplified conventions). Nonetheless, one thing is certain – the PSM will continue to dominate the discussion on profit allocation within an MNE for the years to come, especially, for centralized and decentralized business models.

SELECTED BIBLIOGRAPHY

Books and Articles

K. Andersson, 'Should We Use Value Creation or Destination as a Basis for Taxing Digital Businesses? – Krister Andersson's Comments on the 2018 Klaus Vogel Lecture Given by Professor Michael Devereux' in: Bulletin for International Taxation, 2018 (Vol. 72), No. 12, pp. 684–689.

P. Baker & R. Collier, 'The Attribution of Profits to a Permanent Establishment', General Report, in: IFA Cahiers, 2006 (Vol. 91b). pp. 21–67.

J. Becker & J. Englisch, 'Taxing Where Value Is Created: What's "User Involvement" Got to Do with It?', in: Intertax, 2019 (Vol. 47), No. 2, pp. 161–171.

V. CHAND & B. MALEK, 'The Relevant Economic Activity Test and its Impact on International Corporate Tax Policy', in: British Tax Review 3, 2019, No. 3, pp. 394–424.

V. CHAND & A. BAEZ MORENO, 'Solving the Allocation of Taxing Rights Debate for the Digitalized Economy: Shortcomings of the Digital PE Proposal and Reconsideration of the Base Eroding Payments Proposal' in: Pistone, Weber (eds), Taxing the Digital Economy 2019, pp. 119–158.

V. CHAND, 'Allocation of Taxing Rights in the Digitalized Economy: Assessment of Potential Policy Solutions and Recommendation for a Simplified Residual Profit Split Method' in: Intertax, 2019 (Vol. 47), No. 12, pp. 1023–1041.

V. CHAND, 'Achieving Certainty in an Uncertain Profit Allocation Environment' in: Intertax, 2019 (Vol. 47), No. 12, pp. 1000–1002

V. CHAND, A. TURINA & L. BALLIVET 'Profit Allocation Within MNEs in Light of the Ongoing Digital Debate on Pillar I – A "2020 Compromise"? From Using A Facts and Circumstances Analysis or Allocation Keys to Predetermined Allocation Approaches' in: World Tax Journal, July 2020 (published online).

R. COLLIER & J. VELLA, 'Five Core Problems in the Attribution of Profits to Permanent Establishments' in: World Tax Journal, May 2019, pp. 159–187.

R. COLLIER & J.L. ANDRUS, Transfer Pricing and the Arm's Length Principle, Oxford: OUP, 2017.

M. DEVEREUX, 'Taxation of Outbound Direct Investment: Economic Principles and Tax Policy Considerations', in: Oxford Review of Economic Policy, 2008 (Vol. 24), No. 4, pp. 698–719.

P. DROBNIK, 'The Attribution of Profits to a Dependent Agent PE – If the Dependent Agent Is a Commissionaire (Wholly Owned Subsidiary) of the Principal' in: International Transfer Pricing Journal, May/June 2018, pp. 197–207.

J.F. DUTRIEZ, 'Attribution of Profits to a Permanent Establishment of a Company Engaged in Online Sales of Goods through a Local Warehouse', in: International Transfer Pricing Journal, 2018 (Vol. 25), No. 3, pp. 185–196.

J. HEY, 'Taxation Where Value is Created and the OECD/G20 Base Erosion and Profit Shifting Initiative', in: Bulletin for International Taxation, 2018 (Vol. 72), No. 4/5, pp. 203–208.

C.B. ILHAN, 'The Use of Value Chain Analysis in a Profit Split' in: International Transfer Pricing Journal, July/August 2018, pp. 273–279.

E. KEMMEREN, 'Source of Income in Globalizing Economies: Overview of the Issues and a Plea for an Origin-Based Approach', in: Bulletin for International Taxation, 2006 (Vol. 60), No. 11 pp. 430–452.

A. MARTÍN JIMENEZ, 'BEPS, the Digitalized Economy and the Taxation of Services and Royalties', in: Intertax, 2018 (Vol. 46), No. 8/9, pp. 620–638.

S.C. MORSE, 'Value Creation: A Standard in Search of a Process' in: Bulletin for International Taxation, 2018 (Vol. 72), No. 4/5, pp. 196–202.

M. OLBERT & C. SPENGEL, 'International Taxation in the Digital Economy: Challenge Accepted?', in: World Tax Journal, 2017 (Vol. 9), No. 1, pp. 3–46.

R. PETRUZZI & R. HOLZINGER, 'Profit Attribution to Dependent Agent Permanent Establishment in a Post-BEPS Era', in: World Tax Journal, 2017 (Vol. 9), No. 2, pp. 263-300.

A. SCHAFER & C. SPENGEL, 'ICT and International Taxation: Tax Attributes and Scope of Taxation', Discussion Paper, Centre for European Economic Research, 2002 No. 02-81 pp. 1-42.

W. SCHÖN, 'Ten Questions about Why and How to Tax the Digitalized Economy', Max Planck Institute for Tax Law and Public Finance, Working paper, 2017 No. 2017-11, pp. 1-31.

T. SCHWÄRZLER, 'Using the Capital Allocation Approach to Permanent Establishment', in: International Transfer Pricing Journal, 2017 (Vol. 24), No. 2, pp. 97-110.

L. SPINOSA & V. CHAND, 'A Long-Term Solution for Taxing Digitalized Business Models: Should the Permanent Establishment Definition Be Modified to Resolve the Issue or Should the Focus Be on a Shared Taxing Rights Mechanism?' in: Intertax, 2018 (Vol. 46), Nos 6 and 7, pp. 476-494.

L. STÄHLI, 'The Use of the Profit Split Method in Highly Integrated Transactions' in: International Transfer Pricing Journal, 2018 (Vol. 25), No. 4, pp. 280-288.

K. VOGEL, 'Worldwide vs. Source Taxation of Income: A Review and Re-evaluation of Arguments' Part II), in: Intertax, 1988 (Vol. 16), No. 10, pp. 310-320.

K. Vogel, 'Worldwide vs. Source Taxation of Income: A Review and Re-evaluation of Arguments' (Part III), in: Intertax, 1988 (Vol. 16), No. 11, pp. 393-402.

S. WILKIE, 'The Definition and Ownership of Intangibles: Inside the Box? Outside the Box? What is the Box?', in: World Tax Journal, 2012 (Vol. 4), No. 3, pp. 222-248.

A. WINTSCH, 'Attribution of Profits to Permanent Establishments: The 2008 Article 7 Versus the 2010 Article 7 of the OECD Model', in: International Transfer Pricing Journal, 2017 (Vol. 24), No. 5, pp. 342-350.

Documents of International Policy Making Organisations

OECD (2010): '*Report on the Attribution of Profits to Permanent Establishments*', 22 July 2010.

OECD (2015): '*Addressing the Tax Challenges of the Digital Economy – Action 1: 2015 Final Report*', OECD/G20 Base Erosion and Profit Shifting Project, 5 October 2015.

OECD (2017), '*Model Tax Convention on Income and on Capital*', 21 November 2017.

OECD (2017), '*Transfer Pricing Guidelines for Multinationals Enterprises and Tax Administrations*', 10 July 2017.

OECD (2017): '*Commentaries on the Articles of the Model Tax Convention*', 21 November 2017.

OECD (2018): '*BEPS Action 7: Additional Guidance on the Attribution of Profits to Permanent Establishments*', 22 March 2018.

OECD (2018): '*Revised Guidance on the Application of the Transactional Profit Split Method*', OECD/G20 Base Erosion and Profit Shifting Project, 21 June 2018.

OECD (2018): '*Tax Challenges Arising from Digitalization*' - Interim Report 2018: Inclusive Framework on BEPS, OECD/G20 Base Erosion and Profit Shifting Project, 16 March 2018.

OECD (2019): '*Addressing the Tax Challenges of the Digitalisation of the Economy*', Public Consultation Document, OECD/G20 Base Erosion and Profit Shifting Project, 13 February 2019.

OECD/G20 (2019): '*Programme of Work to Develop a Consensus Solution to the Tax Challenges Arising from the Digitalization of the Economy*', OECD/G20 Base Erosion and Profit Shifting Project, 31 May 2019.

UN (2011): '*Model Double Taxation Convention between Developed and Developing Countries*', 2011.

UN (2017): '*Model Double Taxation Convention between Developed and Developing Countries*', 2017.

Central Board of Direct Taxes, Income department - Government of India, Proposal for Amendment of Rules for Profit Attribution to Permanent Establishment, at para. 159, 2019.

EU Commission-EU Joint Transfer Pricing Forum (EUJTPF) (2019): '*EU Joint Transfer Pricing Forum the Application of the Profit Split Method Within the EU*', DOC: JTPF/002/2019/EN, March 2019.

New Zealand Government (2019): '*Options for Taxing the Digital Economy*', A Government Discussion document, June 2019.

PART VII Selected Industry Experiences

CHAPTER 21

Selected Industry Experiences and Theoretical Approaches

*Emmanuel Llinares & Amanda Pletz**

I INTRODUCTION

The profit split method has been applied for many years in a wide range of situations and industries. The objective of these case studies is to present how the profit split method can be applied.

The case studies presented in this chapter are inspired from actual situations. They have been modified and adapted to preserve confidentiality and for simplification purposes. These cases pre-date the issuance of the revised Organisation for Economic Co-operation and Development (OECD) guidance. However, they were selected as they are consistent with the new guidance. Where appropriate, we indicate the parts of the revised guidance that the cases address. The intention is to provide a significant amount of detail on the context of the transactions and the functional profile of the transacting parties so that the case studies are as realistic as possible. In each of these case studies, numerical examples are included to demonstrate the application of the method.

The first case relates to the financial services industry. In this case study, the profit split method is applied across the entire business being evaluated. Hence, in this case, the method is not applied to set or test a transfer price for a specific transaction but is applied to test globally the overall coherence of the transfer pricing policy. This is not the standard way of applying the method to date, but it may nevertheless be informative. This is the reason why it has been selected here.

* The authors would like to thank Jacques Potin, Principal at NERA Economic Consulting for his contribution to this chapter.

The second case study relates to the software industry. The fact pattern and the types of issues being addressed can also be applied to online companies, provided they also have significant investment in IT and related areas. In this case study, the method is applied (in this case, on an *ex ante* profit basis) to set transfer prices for a given transaction, namely the value of the trademark. In this business, technology plays a very important role. The key feature of the application of the profit split method in this case study is that it, in fact, provides a price to the trademark as well as an implied value of the technology.

The third case study relates to the determination of a brand royalty in the cosmetics industry. Its application relates to a situation where there are licensing agreements with third-party licensors that can be relied upon.

To some extent, these relationships with third licensors may relate to brands that are not originally active in the cosmetics industry and where a brand owner/licensor asked a licensee active in the cosmetics industry to develop and market cosmetics products. It offers an illustration of the application of the contribution analysis in a profit split analysis.

II APPLICATION OF THE PROFIT SPLIT METHOD IN THE FINANCIAL SERVICES INDUSTRY

1 Introduction

This case study relates to a multinational enterprise in the asset management industry.[1] The enterprise operates in various European countries through subsidiaries. This case study illustrates the application of the residual profit split method across the entire value chain using compensation of key person as the split factor.[2] In line with the revised guidance on the application of the transactional profit split method, this method first identifies the profits to be split from the controlled transaction and then splits the relevant profits using an economically valid basis. In other words, the profit split method, namely the residual profit split method, in this case, is applied to all the entities to split the entire profit of the multinational enterprise. The remainder of this case study includes:

- a presentation of the facts of the case;
- the economic analysis describing the application of the profit split method; and
- concluding remarks.

1. The asset management industry has become an increasingly global and integrated industry with functions across the value chain spread globally, potentially contributing to intangibles. The OECD Revised Guidance on the Application of the Transactional Profit Split Method (June 2018) highlights the relevance of the use of profit split methodology in these types of conditions. It is further illustrated in the highly simplified Example 6 provided in the guidance. The recognition of this would likely lead to an increasing use of profits splits in this sector.
2. OECD, Revised Guidance on the Application of the Transactional Profit Split Method (June 2018), para. 2.114 and para. 2.166.

2 Facts of the Case

We provide below a brief overview of the key roles and responsibilities of the entities involved in the value creation process as well as a summary of the value chain analysis for this asset management group.

A Summary of Function and Related-Party Transactions

There are in total seven entities in this asset management company. These entities and the cross-border transactions between them are:

- A Luxembourg asset management company. This entity collects management and administration fees from third-party investors and it also hosts some administrative functions.
- A UK entity and an Irish entity host portfolio management functions (including investment research functions). The UK and Irish entities receive portfolio management fees from the Luxembourg asset management company.
- The UK entity is involved in distribution activities and also hosts marketing functions as well as some fund design functions. The distribution and marketing activities are remunerated through a distribution fee received from the Luxembourg asset management company. The fund design functions are remunerated through the portfolio management fees received from the Luxembourg asset management company.
- Entities in Germany, France, Switzerland and Italy are only involved in distribution activities.

The Figure 21.1 shows the cross-border transactions between the above-mentioned entities.

Figure 21.1 Overview of Cross-Border Transaction Between Related Parties[3]

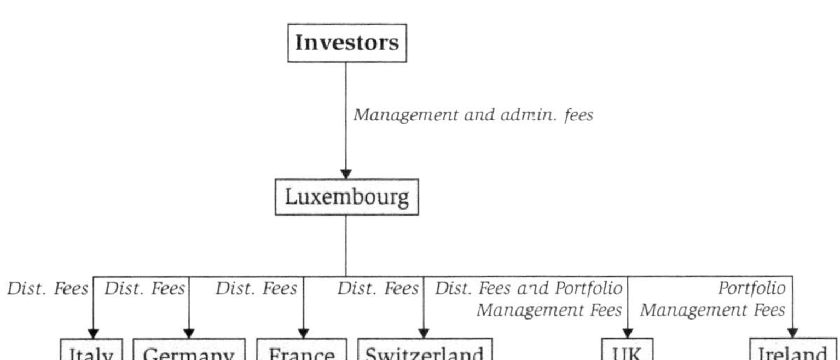

3. In this figure, 'Dist. Fees' refers to distribution fees and 'Admin. Fees' refers to administration fees.

B *Summary Value Chain and Functional Assets and Risks Analysis*

The value chain analysis of this multinational enterprise has led to the identification of four main value drivers:

- Fund design and marketing, which, in the case at hand, includes fund design activities, fund registration and advertising and marketing. The functions relating to this value driver are performed by the entities in Luxembourg and the UK. The total costs of these functions for the multinational enterprise as a whole are 80.
- Distribution and fund-raising, which includes the activities relating to fund-raising and sales of the fund. These activities rely, in part, on the reputation of the multinational enterprise, its performance record and its trade name. The functions relating to this value driver are performed in the UK, Germany, France, Switzerland and Italy. Total costs of these functions for the multinational enterprise as a whole are 400.
- Investment management includes investment research activities (e.g., research on equity investment being considered), trading risk control activities and the investment advisory activity per se. The functions relating to this value driver are performed in the UK and Ireland. Total costs of these functions for the multinational enterprise as a whole are 240.
- Fund administration encompasses the reporting activities (including customer services), performance measurement, regulatory compliance and accounting and safekeeping. The functions relating to this value driver are performed by the entities in Luxembourg and the UK. The total costs of these functions for the multinational enterprise as a whole are 80.

In addition to these functions, there are strategic management functions and support functions (e.g., human resources, information technology) which play a role across the whole value chain. The multinational enterprise also relies on a number of intangibles. In the total costs provided above, the costs of these functions and the costs of developing, enhancing, maintaining, protecting and exploiting the intangibles have already been accounted for.

The figure below provides a graphical summary of the value chain analysis. It includes both the functions of the entities, their assets as well as the total costs incurred by the entities for each value driver.[4]

4. In practice, based on experience, such information may be particularly difficult to obtain. In this example, the data may be obtained because there are a limited number of legal entities and all the entities are involved in the same related activities. In other words, there are no other activities (such as traditional banking activities, for example) that some of these entities would be involved in and not others).

Figure 21.2 Summary of Value Chain Analysis: Functions, Assets and Costs of Entities

Value Drivers	**FUND DESIGN & MARKETING**	**DISTRIBUTION & FUND RAISING**	**INVESTMENT MANAGEMENT**	**FUND ADMINISTRATION**
Summary of Functions Assets (and Risks), mapped to each value driver	• Fund design • Registration • Advertising and marketing	• Fund raising & selling • Trade name • Reputation • Performance record	• Research • Trading Risk control • Investment advice	• Reporting (and customer service) • Performance measurement • Regulatory compliance • Accounting and safekeeping
	STRATEGIC MANAGEMENT			
	INTELLECTUAL PROPERTY			
	OTHER SUPPORT FUNCTIONS			
Total Annual Costs	Costs = 80	Costs = 400	Costs = 240	Costs = 80
Entities involved	Luxembourg UK	UK, Germany, France, Switzerland, Italy	UK, Ireland	Luxembourg, UK

C A Note on Method Selection

It is common practice in the asset management industry to apply the comparable uncontrolled price (CUP)[5] method to price-related party transactions. In particular, we expect that the CUP method can be used for pricing administration fees, distribution fees (including marketing) and investment management fees (including fund design). The CUP method can be applied using internal comparable transactions if the multinational enterprise has relationships with third-party providers. This can be the case for distribution in countries where the enterprise does not have an entity and relies on third-party providers to distribute its products. This can also be the case in investment management, for example, for products that the enterprise would sell but would not manage on its own (e.g., specialized investment areas for which the enterprise does not have the capabilities). In addition, there are external comparable data that may be available to price-related party transactions on distribution, investment management and fund administration.

In this case, there are no internal comparable transactions data that can be relied upon. There are external comparable data and these have been relied upon as the primary approach. The profit split method is applied as a corroborative approach. The profit split method is applicable for the following reasons:

- There are intangibles across the whole value chain. Several entities contribute to developing those intangibles. This is the case primarily for investment

5. *See* OECD Transfer Pricing Guidelines for Multinational Enterprises and Tax Administrations 2017, Part II, p. 101 (hereinafter: '2017 OECD TPG'), Part II, p. 101.

management but also in the case at hand for fund design and distribution activities.

- There are a number of high value-adding activities that are performed by a number of entities that have a direct consequence on the financial performance of the multinational enterprise as a whole, notably with regards to the impact significant risks may have on financial performance. In particular, fund design and investment management functions relate to strategic and marketplace risk, distribution functions relate to marketplace risks and operational risks, and fund administration functions relate to operational risks. In this respect, we anticipate that the approach proposed in this case study is consistent with paragraphs 2.139 to 2.141 of the Revised Guidance on the Application of the Transactional Profit Split Method.

3 Economic Analysis: Application of the Profit Split Method

A *Step 1: Identification of Costs by Function and by Value Driver*

The first step in the analysis is the identification of cost data by function for each of the entities in the value chain.

The Table 21.1 provides a breakdown of the costs for each of the entities by value driver. In this table, the costs have also been broken down by function, each column being a function. In addition, for each entity, we provide the breakdown of the costs into costs corresponding to the higher value-added contribution and costs of the part of the function that deserves a routine remuneration.

In the table below 'important' refers explicitly to the total compensation-related costs of the 'important' people in the organization. Total compensation-related costs include not only the salary and wages paid to the employee but all the employer-related costs directly associated with the employment (e.g., including employer social security charges). In this case, no adjustment to compensation was made to reflect, for example, differences in costs of living. Such adjustments may need to be considered if there are important differences in such costs. Note that given the way the residual profit split method is applied here such adjustments could lead to allocating an additional remuneration to the entity that benefits from lower costs of living. Such adjustment, therefore, leads to having local entities retain the benefits from having access to lower labour costs. It is not certain that such an assumption is systematically accurate.

The level of hierarchical seniority completed with discussion with management was relied upon to identify these important people within the organization.

Table 21.1 Breakdown of Costs by Functions

	Nature of Function	*Fund Design & Marketing*		*Distribution & Fund Raising*	*Investment Management*	*Fund Admin.*	*Total*
		Fund Design	Marketing				
Lux	Support					20	**20**
	Important	10					
UK	Support		40	80	60	60	**240**
	Important	10	20	40	120		
Ireland	Support				20		**20**
	Important				40		
Germany	Support			50			**50**
	Important			30			
France	Support			50			**50**
	Important			30			
Italy	Support			60			**60**
	Important			40			
Switzerland	Support			10			**10**
	Important			10			
Total Costs	Total Costs	**20**	**60**	**400**	**240**	**80**	**800**

	Nature of Function	*Fund Design & Marketing*		*Distribution & Fund Raising*	*Investment Management*	*Fund Admin.*	*Total*
		Fund Design	Marketing				
Important	20	20	150	160	0	0	350
Support	0	0	40	250	80	80	450
Revenues							**1,000**
Total Profits							**200**

B Step 2: Routine Remuneration

In the next step of the application of the profit split method, the support functions are remunerated using the transactional net margin method (TNMM). In this case, a markup on the cost of 10% is applied. In practice, it is possible to apply a range of returns rather than just a point estimate. The Table 21.2 shows the allocation of routine profits by an entity using a markup on costs of 10%.

Table 21.2 Breakdown of Routine Remuneration by Entity

	Fund Design & Marketing		*Distribution & Fund-Raising*	*Investment Management*	*Fund Admin.*	*Total*
Revenues	Fund Design	Marketing (C + 10)	(C + 10)	(C + 10)	(C + 10)	
Lux		0	0	0	22	**22**
UK		44	88	66	66	**264**
Ireland		0	0	22	0	**22**
Germany		0	55	0	0	**55**
France		0	55	0	0	**55**
Italy		0	66	0	0	**66**
Switzerland		0	11	0	0	**11**
Total Routine Remuneration	**0**	**44**	**275**	**88**	**88**	**495**
Routine Profits	**0**	**4**	**25**	**8**	**8**	**45**
Total Residual Profits						**155**

C Step 3: Discussion on Residual Profit Split Factor

In this case, compensation of key personnel is used as the residual profit split factor. In practice, other factors could have been considered. These factors may include the total labour cost of each entity, total operating costs of each entity or the assets under management (hereinafter: 'AUM') that each entity can be held responsible for.

Nevertheless, these factors present numerous drawbacks. First, the use of total labour cost is likely to overcompensate the entities that host a number of support or low value-added functions. The use of total operating costs would essentially correspond to a cost-plus methodology where the markup is the group markup spread in proportion to operating cost.[6] This split factor would work if there were a correlation in the industry between costs incurred and value creation. However, in practice, such a mechanism also suffers from the fact that operating costs are not necessarily a good

6. *See* 2017 OECD TPG, Part III, p. 117.

proxy for value creation. Namely, there are a number of functions the costs of which would be included in the split factor and that would not be entitled to a residual remuneration. Hence, this approach is likely to be inconsistent with the way value is being created. Finally, the main difficulty with the use of AUM in the case at hand is that several entities can be held jointly responsible for the same level of AUM. For example, the entity in charge of distribution may distribute AUM managed by one of the investment management entities and the administrative functions of which are handled by a third entity. Hence, the use of AUM, in this case, does not enable to reflect the differences in the nature of the functions.

As regards compensation of key personnel, there are a number of academic publications on the link between compensation and performance.[7] These studies generally support the relationship between performance and compensation, with some caveats. In summary, the rationale for using compensation as a split factor, in this case, is based on the following considerations:

- compensation of employees can generally be characterized as arm's-length;
- objective evidence for arm's-length compensation is available;
- empirical evidence associates human capital with an impact on a firm's productivity separate from other forms of capital;[8]
- there is a positive relationship between both base and variable compensation and the level of human capital and job responsibility; and
- within a given organization, variable compensation for management may be a good indicator not only of performance but also of relative contribution to value creation, especially for business units with knowledge and authority to make managerial decisions.

However, it is important to stress that annual compensation, in particular, may fail to properly account for long-term risk-taking and historical intangibles.

In the case at hand, neither long-term risk-taking nor historical intangibles are explicitly reflected in the model. This may be suitable if the compensation structure (and particularly the base and variable compensation mechanism) naturally reflects these two factors or if these two factors do not play a major role in the value creation process.

If properly executed, the analysis should be consistent with paragraph 2.147 of the Revised Guidance on the Application of the Transactional Profit Split Method, which notably stipulates that the determination of the profit splitting factor should be consistent with the functional analysis and be capable of being measured in a reliable manner.

In this case, the split factor is based on total compensation. The reason why this is the case is that we are trying to measure the relative contribution to the value creation of key functions within the organization. In other circumstances, the use of contingent compensation may be appropriate.

7. Some of the literature on this topic includes: GERHART/MILKOVICH, pp. 663–691; JENSEN/MURPHY, pp. 138–153; and ROTH/O'DONNELL, pp. 678–703.
8. JORDAN, pp. 402–420.

We provide below the breakdown of the total compensation-related costs of the important people within the organization for each category of function.

Table 21.3 Compensation-Based Split Factor by Function

	Fund Design & Marketing		*Distribution & Fund-Raising*	*Investment Management*	*Fund Admin.*	*Total*
	Fund Design	Marketing				
Split factor Compensation-based Estimate of contribution	20	20	150	160	-	350
Compensation-based split factor (in % of residual profits)	6%	6%	43%	45%		100%
Residual Profit	9	9	66	71	-	155
Routine Remuneration	-	44	275	88	88	
Implied Revenues (routine + residual)	**29**	**73**	**491**	**319**	**88**	**1 000**

The analysis above is performed to determine the remuneration of each core function. In this example, it is possible to show the remuneration of each entity, however.

D Checking Consistency with Application of Other Methods

In this case, we would expect, at least for price-setting purposes, to have to price each transaction one by one using the transactional net margin or CUP method, for example. The question that arises is therefore whether the results of the price-setting approach are consistent with those of the profit split approach.

Let's assume that the CUP method is applied to price the administration fees, the distribution fees (including marketing) and the investment management fees (including fund design). The results of the CUP approach are:

- administration fee remuneration = 0.20% of AUM;
- investment management fees = 0.70% of AUM; and
- distribution fees (weighted average) = 1.10% of AUM.

If we now consider consolidated AUM for the multinational enterprise of 50,000, we can estimate the remuneration for each of the above functions. We would then end up with the remuneration shown in Table 21.4. For each function, we also show in this table the implied revenues that were obtained from the application of the residual profit split method.

Table 21.4 Remuneration of Function: Comparison of CUP and Profit Split Methods

	Distribution, Fund-Raising and Marketing	*Investment Management and Fund Design*	*Fund Admin.*	*Total*
CUP-Based Remuneration	550	350	100	1,000
Implied Revenues from Residual Profit Split	564	348	88	1,000

In this case, the results of the CUP and profit split method are broadly consistent. This may not always be the case.

When properly applied and in theory, the CUP method provides a reliable market outcome and should be broadly consistent with a profit split. However, large deviations may reveal data availability or comparability issues.

4 Concluding Remarks

The profit split aims at replicating the market outcome. For price-setting purposes, the profit split method can be difficult to manage. In this profit split example, compensation of key functions is only observed *ex post* and the pricing of transactions is therefore indirect. If the remuneration mechanism of key employees of the multinational enterprise is known ahead of time, the profit split method may also be applied in a price-setting mechanism, provided that there is not much discretion in the determination of the compensation.

At any rate, when using compensation as a split factor, labour market, as well as longer-term considerations, may cause deviations between the performance of functions and compensation. Finally, compensation may not always reflect risk exposure.

III APPLICATION OF THE PROFIT SPLIT METHOD IN THE TECHNOLOGY INDUSTRY

1 Introduction

This case study focuses on a multinational group in the software industry. The group distributes various software solutions which are developed by different IP owners within the group. A group central entity develops a common 'umbrella' brand to conduct cross-solutions marketing. The central entity grants to each IP owner a licence to use the 'umbrella' brand.

In this case study, we apply the profit split method (with cost capitalization) to determine the arm's-length level of the royalties paid by the IP owners to the central entity. The next section presents the facts of the case and explains why the profit split method is appropriate in the case at hand. The following section contains the economic analysis, with an application of the residual profit split method. Finally, we conclude by highlighting the merits of the approach used to implement the profit split method.

2 Facts of the Case and Method Selection

This section first provides a brief overview of the key roles and responsibilities of the entities involved in the value creation process of the software group and presents a summary value chain analysis. Then, on the basis of this analysis, we explain why we selected the profit split method to determine the royalties paid by the IP owners to the central entity.

A Summary of Functions and Related-Party Transactions

The software group is composed of three types of entities:

- The group has five IP owners. Entities A and B are located in the US. Entities C, D and E are located in European countries. Each IP owner is responsible for a brand, for which it conducts software development activities and marketing activities.
- The group's central entity, located in the US, is in charge of the marketing activities conducted at the group level in relation to an 'umbrella' brand used for cross-product marketing. The group central entity also provides support services to the other group entities.
- In a number of countries, the distribution entities sell the various software products to final clients, value-added distributors and other resellers.

The main transactions involving the group entities are as follows:

- the revenue earned by an IP owner is the revenue generated by the sales of the products sold under its brand;
- each IP owner pays to the central entity a royalty for the use of the 'umbrella' brand, as well as management fees; and
- each IP owner also remunerates the distribution entities selling its products to third-party clients.

The Figure 21.3 shows the main intra-group transactions.

Figure 21.3 Overview of the Main Intra-Group Transactions Within the Software Group

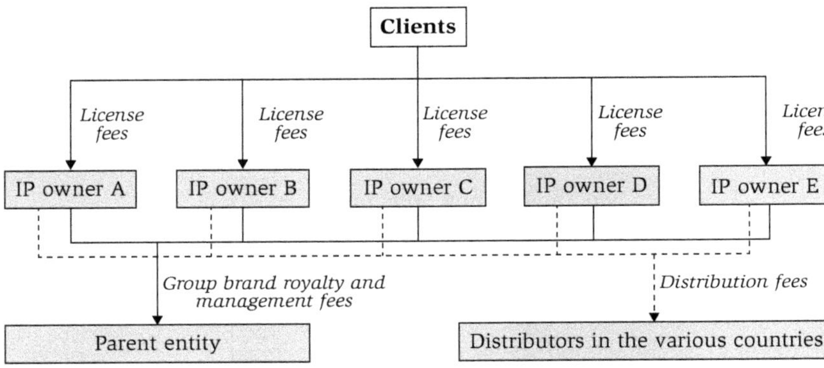

B Summary Value Chain Analysis

The value chain analysis of this multinational group has led to the identification of three main value drivers:

- Strategic marketing and innovation: This value driver relates to the development of software solutions for the clients:
  - The first function involved is strategic marketing: its goal is to understand the needs of the clients and to imagine the product portfolio that is the best for them. This function is performed by the marketing department of the central entity and the marketing departments of the IP owners, with the former focusing on the group-level initiatives and on the complementarities between the various products.
  - The other function relating to this value driver is the R&D function performed by the various IP owners. They employ a large number of highly qualified researchers and engineers.
  - By performing those functions, the central entity and the IP owners develop valuable marketing and technology intangibles.
- Operational marketing: This value driver is important since the solutions proposed by the group are highly diverse and usually complex. To communicate with the clients, the value proposition of the group, substantial marketing activities are required:
  - the central entity conducts marketing campaigns relating to the group 'umbrella' brand and to cross-product selling initiatives;
  - each IP owner focuses on communication relating to its own brand; and
  - the operational marketing activities, conducted by the central entity and the IP owners, contribute to the value of the marketing intangibles.

- Distribution: Distribution activities consist of pre-sales activities (e.g., relationships with resellers and value-added distributors, identification of potential clients and software demonstration), sales activities (client meetings, sales administration) and post-sales activities (after-sales services). Those functions are performed by the distribution entities of the group.

The figure summarizes the value chain analysis. It includes the functions of the entities, the assets they develop and the main risks associated with the various functions and assets. Notably, it shows that the main risks include the strategic and marketplace risks, assumed by both the central entity (developing the 'umbrella' brand) and the IP owners (developing its own brand-specific intangibles).

Figure 21.4 Summary of Value Chain Analysis: Functions, Assets and Associated Risks

Value Drivers	**STRATEGIC MARKETING AND INNOVATION**	**OPERATIONAL MARKETING**	**DISTRIBUTION**
Summary of Functions, Assets and Risks, mapped to each value driver	• Functions: strategic marketing ("umbrella" brand, product brands), R&D • Assets: development of technology and marketing intangibles • Risks; strategic and marketplace risks	• Functions: operational marketing • Assets: development of marketing intangibles • Risks: strategic and marketplace risks	• Functions: distribution • Assets: not significant • Risks: operational risks
		SUPPORT FUNCTIONS	
Entities involved	• Parent entity ("umbrella" brand marketing) • IP owners (R&D, product brand marketing)	• Parent entity ("umbrella" brand marketing) • IP owners (R&D, product brand marketing)	Distribution entities

C A Note on Method Selection

For determining the arm's-length level of the 'umbrella' brand royalty, there are two main candidates for selection as the most appropriate method: the CUP method and the profit split method. In fact, the OECD indicates that '[t]he transfer pricing methods most likely to prove useful in matters involving transfers [or the licensing] of one or more intangibles are the CUP method and the transactional profit split method'.[9]

We first considered whether the application of the CUP method is appropriate in the case at hand. First, we found that the group does not license its 'umbrella' brand to

9. 2017 OECD TPG, para. 6.145.

any third party; hence, no internal comparable data is available. Second, we conducted a search for agreements comparable to the 'umbrella' brand licensing agreements. No sufficiently comparable agreement could be identified. As a consequence, we concluded that the CUP method cannot be applied reliably to determine the arm's-length level of the 'umbrella' brand royalty.

We then considered the application of the profit split model and found that it is a solution for sharing profits between the IP owners and the central entity:

- the parties make unique and valuable contributions; and
- reliable data on profits and expenses are available within the software group, which makes possible the application of the profit split model.

More specifically, since the contributions of the various entities include activities that can be valued by reference to a one-sided method and benchmarked using comparables, the residual profit split model was used. It was applied to the actual consolidated profits segmented for each product brand. The profits are split into two main stages:

(1) First stage: The entities are remunerated for their non-unique contributions:
   - for the provision of support services, the central entity is remunerated via management fees determined on a cost-plus basis (with an appropriate allocation between the IP owners);
   - for the provision of general and administrative services, the IP owners are remunerated on a cost-plus basis; and
   - the distribution entities are remunerated with an appropriate return on sales.

(2) Second stage: The residual profit made on each product brand is split between the entities contributing to unique intangibles. For a given brand, these are the brand IP owners, developing technology intangibles and its product brand, and the central entity, developing the 'umbrella' brand.

As mentioned above, the 'umbrella' brand royalty depends on the actual profits, not on the profits anticipated before the realization of the economically significant risks. We made this choice following the OECD Guidelines,[10] which indicate that when the parties assume the same economically significant risks, actual profits should be used. In the case of the software group, the IP owners and the central entity notably assume the strategic and marketplace risks.

3 Economic Analysis: Application of the Profit Split Method

The residual profit split model was applied at the brand level. In fact, as shown below, the profitability varies between the various brands developed and distributed by the

10. *See* OECD, Revised Guidance on the Application of the Transactional Profit Split Method (June 2018), para. 2.159.

group. The profits to be split between the IP owner and the central entity, therefore, vary from one brand to the other. Given the fact that the relative contribution of the IP owner and the central entity is similar for the various products, an arm's-length bilateral bargaining between the central entity and the various IP owners would lead to a lower remuneration of the central entity for the less profitable brands. This is why the profit split model has to be applied at the brand level.

A Stage 1: Determination of the Routine Remuneration

In the first stage of the analysis, the entities are remunerated for their non-unique contributions:

- For the provision of support services, the central entity is remunerated via management fees determined on a cost-plus basis (with an appropriate allocation between the IP owners). The markup applied to the internal costs is 5% and no markup is applied to the external costs. The brand turnover is used as the key to allocating the recharged costs between the various IP owners.
- For the provision of general and administrative (hereinafter: 'G&A') services, the IP owners are remunerated on a cost-plus basis. The markup applied to the internal costs (i.e., 50% of G&A costs in this case) is 5% and no markup is applied to the external costs. This markup is meant to be in line with the markup on low value-adding services specified in paragraph 7.61 of the OECD Transfer Pricing Guidelines for Multinational Enterprises and Tax Administrations 2017 (hereinafter: '2017 OECD TPG').
- For their distribution services, the distribution entities are remunerated with an appropriate return on sales. The return on sales paid by the IP owners to the distribution entities is 2.5%. This return on sales is the median return of the set of software distribution companies identified. The approach applied here is, therefore, the TNMM.

The IP owners pay management fees to the central entity and distribution fees to the distribution entities. The corresponding amounts appear in the profit and loss statements (hereinafter: 'P&Ls') of the IP owners.

Table 21.5 shows the P&Ls of the IP owners (before payment of the 'umbrella' brand fees) and the remuneration of the routine function (G&A) they performed.

Table 21.5 P&Ls of the IP Owners and Routine Remuneration

	Formula	*IP Owner A*	*IP Owner B*	*IP Owner C*	*IP Owner D*	*IP Owner E*
Revenue (software revenue)	(a)	65.00	20.00	25.00	35.00	13.00
Costs						
Entrepreneurial costs						
R&D	(b)	55.00	4.00	5.00	6.00	3.00
Marketing (IP owner)	(c)	4.00	1.00	2.00	1.00	2.00
Cost of routine functions						
Cost of software	(d)	7.00	0.50	3.00	5.00	1.00
General & administration (G&A) costs	(e)	3.00	1.50	4.00	1.00	2.00
Management fees (paid to Central Entity, includes markup on costs)	(f)	4.00	1.00	1.00	2.00	1.00
Distribution costs (paid to distributors, includes return on sales)	(g)	5.00	8.00	2.00	6.00	2.00
Operating profits	(h) = (a)-(b)-(c)-(d)-(e)-(f)-(g)	-13.00	4.00	8.00	14.00	2.00
Operating margin, % of revenues	(i) = (h)/(a)	*-20%*	*20%*	*32%*	*40%*	*15%*

	Formula	*IP Owner A*	*IP Owner B*	*IP Owner C*	*IP Owner D*	*IP Owner E*
Remuneration of routine function (IP Owner)						
Markup on G&A costs	(j) = (e) x 50% x 2.5%	0.08	0.04	0.10	0.03	0.05

In Table 21.5, it can be noted that IP owners B, C, D and E have a significantly positive operating margin. On the other hand, IP owner A makes an operating loss in the year of interest. This is due to the exceptionally large R&D expenses it made in that year.

B *Stage 2: Split of the Residual Profits*

In the second stage of the analysis, the residual profits made on each product brand are split between the entities contributing unique intangibles. As explained earlier, each IP owner contributes by developing technology intangibles and its product brand. The central entity contributes by developing the 'umbrella' brand.

Note that once the routine remunerations have been subtracted from the operating profits, two more steps are required to compute the residual profit or 'Residual economic operating profits'[11] made in relation to the software products of each IP Owner:

- First, the entrepreneurial costs incurred by the IP owner must be eliminated (*see* (k) in Table 21.6). In fact, the entrepreneurial costs incurred in the year of interest may not be fully attributed to the year of interest but may also have an impact on later years. As a result, the entrepreneurial costs incurred by the IP owner are added to the operating profit (after remuneration of the routine functions). The amount obtained after those entrepreneurial costs have been added back is the 'net revenue' that can be allocated to the entrepreneurs (the IP owner and the central entity).[12]
- Second, the residual profits can be obtained by subtracting the amortization amounts for the share of entrepreneurial capital (*see* (l) and (m) in Table 21.6).[13] Those amortization amounts can be considered as the 'consumption' of entrepreneurial capital in the year of interest. The amortization amounts are computed as part of the cost capitalization model.

11. By using the term 'Residual economic operating profits', we follow HIGINBOTHAM, The Profit split method: Effective Application for Precision and Administrability.
12. Note that so far in the analysis, the entrepreneurial marketing costs incurred by the central entity have not been subtracted, hence they do not have to be eliminated. An alternative approach is to consider that the entrepreneurial costs incurred by the central entity should be taken into account to compute the 'consolidated profits' jointly made by an IP owner and the central entity. In this alternative approach, the entrepreneurial marketing costs incurred by the central entity should be eliminated when computing the residual profits.
13. For each share of entrepreneurial capital, the amortization amount in a given year depends on the past investments and the useful life of those investments. In fact, the amortization amount is the sum of the amortization amounts corresponding to each of the past investments that are not fully depreciated at the beginning of the year. Note that the amortization amounts in Table 6 (*see* (l) and (m)) cannot be computed with the information provided in this case study (since we do not provide information on the past investments). Therefore, the reader should take those amortization amounts as given.

After discussions with the firm's management, including managers of the R&D and marketing departments, the following 'gestation lags' and 'economic life' were considered as part of the cost capitalization model:

- For R&D, one year is required between the moment an investment is incurred and the first time the investment can have an impact. Hence, the 'gestation lag' for R&D is one year. For R&D, we also estimate that the useful life of an investment is, on average, ten years. This estimate can be supported by industry evidence and input from experts within the industry.
- For marketing, similar evidence suggests that there is no gestation lag and that its useful life is on average two years.

Based on those considerations, we can compute the share of entrepreneurial capital available in any given year as well as the amortization amounts for any given year.

The remuneration of an entrepreneur (here, an IP owner or the central entity) in a given year is computed as the sum of:

- the amortization of the entrepreneur's entrepreneurial capital in the year of interest; and
- a share of the residual profits. The share of residual profits allocated to an entrepreneur for its entrepreneurial investments is computed as the ratio between the entrepreneur's share of entrepreneurial capital and the total share of entrepreneurial capital.

More fundamentally, the profit split approach presented here aims at equalizing overall returns on investments by the parties.[14] In the case at hand, it is consistent with the outcome of an arm's-length bargaining process between the central entity and each IP owner.

Table 21.6 illustrates the application of those principles to the software group. We focus on the revenues attributable to the central entity for the development of the 'umbrella' brand. As explained in the introduction, determining the arm's-length level of the trademark royalty is the main objective of the analysis.

Table 21.6 Computation and Split of the Residual Profits

	Formula	*IP Owner A*	*IP Owner B*	*IP Owner C*	*IP Owner D*	*IP Owner E*
Elimination of R&D and marketing by IP Owner	(k) = (b) + (c) in Table 21.5	59.00	5.00	7.00	7.00	5.00

14. *See* HIGINBOTHAM.

	Formula	*IP Owner A*	*IP Owner B*	*IP Owner C*	*IP Owner D*	*IP Owner E*
Allocation Amort. R&D and marketing by IP Owner	(l)	35.00	4.00	8.00	8.00	4.00
Allocation Amortization Central Marketing	(m)	1.50	0.50	0.50	1.00	0.50
Residual Profits	(n) = (h)-(j) + (k)-(l)-(m), with (h) and (j) in Table 21.1	9.43	4.46	6.40	11.98	2.45
Residual profits, % of revenues	(o) = (n)/(a), with (a) in Table 21.5	*15%*	*22%*	*26%*	*34%*	*19%*
Entrepreneurial capital shares						
R&D by IP Owner	(p)	96.00%	90.00%	93.00%	97.00%	85.00%
Marketing by IP Owner	(q)	3.00%	7.00%	5.00%	0.05%	13.00%
Marketing by Central Entity	(r)	1.00%	3.00%	2.00%	2.95%	2.00%
Royalty paid to Central Entity ('umbrella' brand)	(s) = (m) + (r)/[(p) + (q) + (r)] x (n)	1.59	0.63	0.63	1.35	0.55
Royalty paid to Central Entity ('umbrella' brand), % of revenue	(t) = (s)/(a), with (a) in Table 21.5	***2.45%***	***3.17%***	***2.51%***	***3.87%***	***4.22%***

Table 21.6 first shows that for IP owner A, whose operating profits is negative (*see* Table 21.5), the residual profit is positive. This is due to the fact that once it is recognized that the exceptionally large R&D investment made in the year of interest should be allocated to the many years over which the related intangibles will be used (given its useful life), the actual R&D expenses attributable to the year of interest are relatively small (35 as opposed to 59).

The last line of Table 21.6 indicates that the arm's-length royalty rates vary from one IP owner to another. They are in the range of 2.45%–4.22%. One can note that the highest royalty rate is the one determined for IP owner E despite the fact that this IP owner has a relatively small residual profit (when expressed as a percentage of revenue). This is explained by the relatively large amortization amount for central marketing, the first component of the royalty paid to the central entity for the development of the 'umbrella' brand.

4 Concluding Remarks

The approach described above can be relied upon in a number of industries where investments to develop significantly valuable intangibles are important. It enables, as illustrated in the example above, to take into account various types of intangibles. One of its main features is that it tends to equalize returns on entrepreneurial capital, a nice feature, consistent with arm's-length behaviour in many circumstances.

IV APPLICATION OF THE PROFIT SPLIT METHOD IN THE FASHION INDUSTRY

1 Introduction

This case study relates to the application of the profit split method to value a brand royalty in the cosmetics industry. The objective of this case study is to provide an economic analysis to determine the royalty rates remunerated to brand owners in the context of their intra-group trademark licensing. To do this, the analysis relies on a number of arrangements within a multinational enterprise related to dealings with third-party licensors, which have or are licensing their brands to the multinational enterprise. The multinational enterprise is then responsible for developing a range of products, promoting the products and distributing them.

In practice, this analysis is conducted based on financial data obtained from relationships between the multinational enterprise and the third-party licensors that could be used to assess arm's-length royalty rates. In this context, we relied upon data from a number of such relationships.

In this study, we provide a summary of the context of the analysis, outline the approach relied upon for the economic analysis and provide illustrative results.

The economic analysis described below enables a determination of the royalty rates remunerated to a brand owner for the brands for which they are responsible. Given the availability of relationships with third parties, this analysis relies upon an approach referred to as the comparable profit split method. The comparable profit split method was first introduced by Rozek and Koreko in their seminal article 'Transfer Prices for the Intangible Property Embodied in Products with Extraordinary Profit Potential.'[15] Under the 2017 OECD TPG, this analysis could be considered a contribution analysis as described in paragraph 2.150 of the OECD Revised Guidance on Profit

15. *See* ROZEK/KOREKO.

Splits (hereinafter: Revised Guidance).[16] This case study is also intended to be consistent with the suggestions in paragraph 2.167 of the Revised Guidance.

Notably, the Revised Guidance states that:

- Under a contribution analysis, the relevant profits, which are the total profits from the controlled transactions under examination, are divided between the associated enterprises in order to arrive at a reasonable approximation of the division that independent enterprises would have achieved from engaging in comparable transactions. This division can be supported by comparables data where available.[17]
- One possible approach is to split the relevant profits based on the division of profits that actually is observed in comparable uncontrolled transactions. Examples of possible sources of information on uncontrolled transactions that might usefully assist the determination of criteria to split the profits, depending on the facts and circumstances of the case, include joint-venture arrangements between independent parties under which profits are shared, such as development projects in the oil and gas industry; pharmaceutical collaborations, co-marketing or co-promotion agreements; arrangements between independent music record labels and music artists; uncontrolled arrangements in the financial services sector, etc.[18]
- the overriding objective [of the profit split method] should be to approximate as closely as possible the split of profits that would have been realized had the parties been independent enterprises.[19]

2 Facts of the Case

Company A belongs to Multinational Enterprise AA, active in the cosmetics industry. Multinational Enterprise AA is a diversified cosmetics company operating a number of brands, most of which are brands it owns. But Multinational Enterprise AA, through some of its affiliates, is also a licensee of brands owned by third parties. These third parties have licensed out their brands to Multinational Enterprise AA because they do not have the capacities to develop and market a range of cosmetics products (their brands originally being known in other industries, such as fashion, music or film, for example).

Within Multinational Enterprise AA, Company A licenses out trademarks it legally owns to related parties (the Related-Party Distributors). In the context of these

16. OECD, Revised Guidance on the Application of the Transactional Profit Split Method: Inclusive Framework on BEPS: Action 10, OECD/G20 Base Erosion and Profit Shifting Project (June 2018) OECD Paris. www.oecd.org/tax/beps/revised-guidance-on-the-application-of-the-transactional-profit-split-method-beps-action-10.pdf.
17. *Id.* para. 2.150.
18. *Id.* para. 2.167.
19. *Id.* para. 2.146.

related-party transactions, Company A conducts a number of development, enhancement maintenance and protection functions in relation to the trademarks. The Related-Party Distributors are performing distribution functions, as well as key value-added marketing activities in relation to the markets or territories for which they are responsible. The Related-Party Distributors are also responsible for some maintenance and protection functions for the trademark owned by Company A, and they are exploiting the trademarks owned by Company A. In addition, the Related-Party Distributors are also directly or indirectly contracting with related-parties' developers and suppliers to obtain the products they need. For the sake of simplicity, we assume the transactions related to suppliers and developers are priced at arm's-length.

Within Multinational Enterprise AA, there are a number of arrangements with third-party licensors. In the context of these relationships, entities within Multinational Enterprise AA are licensing in the trademark owned by third parties. These Multinational Enterprise AA entities are responsible for some maintenance and protection functions for trademarks owned by the third-party licensors. In these dealings, the functions performed, assets used and risks assumed by the entities in Multinational Enterprise AA are similar to the functions performed, assets used and risks assumed by the Related-Party Distributors in the context of the related-party transactions.

3 Application of the Profit Split Method

A A Note on Method Selection

In this case, there are relationships with third parties that may be relied upon to perform the analysis. In addition, profit-level data from both the licensee and the licensor are available in the context of the third-party transactions.

In this respect, paragraph 6.116 of the 2017 OECD TPG states:

> [W]here the CUP method is considered to be the most appropriate transfer pricing method, but also has importance in applying other methods that rely on comparables. In the case of a transfer of an intangible or rights in an intangible that provides the enterprise with a unique competitive advantage in the market, purportedly comparable intangibles or transactions should be carefully scrutinised. It is critical to assess whether potential comparables in fact exhibit similar profit potential.

This tends to be particularly difficult to assess with the CUP method. The profit split method, as it is applied in this case, enables one to take the profit potential into account.

In the case at hand, following the Revised Guidance, an analysis of these potential internal comparables is performed to confirm that application of the profit split method is more reliable than the application of the CUP method, in line with paragraph 2.143.[20]

20. Paragraph 2.143 states: 'In general, it will tend to be the case that the presence of factors indicating that a transactional profit split is the most appropriate method will correspond to an

Therefore, while CUP may be applied (with the profit potential limitation mentioned above), the use of profit data may enable one to take into account differences between the tested transactions and the comparable transactions that could influence the royalty rate, particularly with regard to profit potential.

In essence, the basis for using such data is that in open market transactions, we would expect transacting parties to agree to a royalty level that enables the licensor and the licensee to obtain an arm's-length share of the profits in relation to the use of the intangible being licensed. In particular, the application of this method should enable one to take into account some factors that may influence the profit potential.[21] Furthermore, application of this approach is expected to be consistent with paragraph 2.170 of the Revised Guidance in that it is based on 'evidence of a similar split achieved between independent parties in comparable transactions'.

The use of profit data may then be relied upon to determine intra-group royalty rates. In the context of this approach, the related-party royalty rates can be set as a per cent of sales, for example, but the rates are determined based on the observed split of profits between licensors and licensees in the context of third-party transactions. The profit split ratio (i.e., sharing of the total profits of both the licensee and the licensor in the context of their relationship) in the context of the uncontrolled transaction should be considered as a direct reflection of the bargaining power of both parties and of their respective contribution to value creation.

B Description of Approach

The comparable profit split method estimates arm's-length royalty rates based on the split of observed historical profits between third-party licensors and licensees.

In practice, the comparable profit split method enables the use of the internal comparable uncontrolled transactions to estimate the royalty rate for a controlled transaction in situations where profits would vary.

Indeed, if the entities entering the comparable uncontrolled transactions (i.e., third-party licensors and Multinational Enterprise AA in the present case) have experience in negotiating licences, a consistent pattern in the split of total profit should be observed.

If such a pattern is observed, the profit split ratio can be used to estimate an arm's-length royalty rate. This royalty rate would be set so that it enables the sharing of expected profits based on the ratio observed in third-party transactions.

The Figure 21.5 illustrates the basic functioning of this approach.

---

absence of factors indicating that an alternative transfer pricing method—one which relies entirely on comparables—is the most appropriate method, determined in accordance with paragraph 2.2 of these Guidelines. Put another way, if information on reliable comparable uncontrolled transactions is available to price the transaction in its entirety, it is less likely that the transactional profit split method will be the most appropriate method.'

21. In line with s. D.2.1.7 expectations of future benefits in Chapter VI of the 2017 OECD TPG.

Figure 21.5 Summary of the Approach Adopted

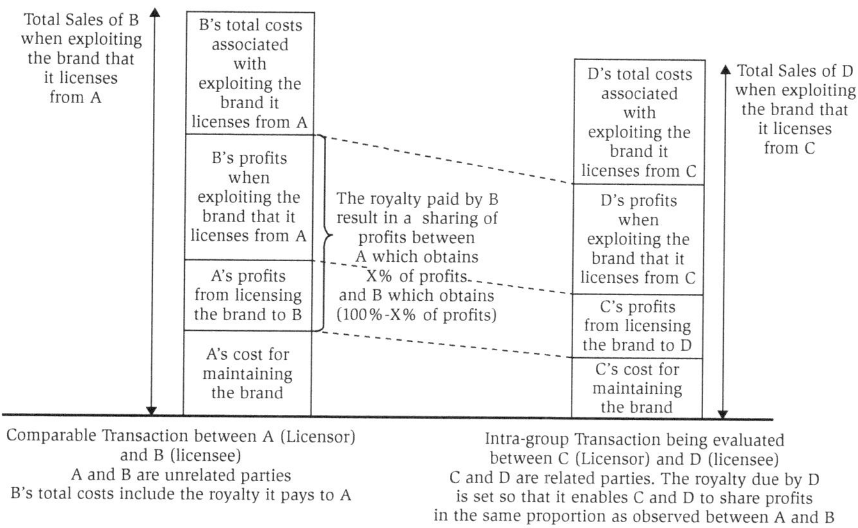

C Data Relied Upon

In practice, in order to apply this method, annual data is needed from the following relationships entered into by entities that are part of Multinational Enterprise AA. Namely, entities B, C, D, E, F, G, H, I, J, K, and L – all part of Multinational Enterprise AA – have entered into agreements with third-party licensors or third-party licensees. Data on these relationships from both the licensee and the licensors, including revenues, costs and profit data, are available over several years.

The data relied upon is provided below. Note that in this analysis, to avoid relying on years that may reflect a start-up situation and may not be representative of the situation in which the controlled transactions take place, we have combined data for each of the comparable relationships from four years after the relationships began. The reasons for not taking the first four years into account are:

- The fact that within the first four years, the relationship may not yet be considered long-term, as Multinational Enterprise AA has the possibility to discontinue the relationship. Therefore, in this case, these first few years of data were not factored in.
- The objective of the analysis is to determine intra-group royalties, which relate to brands that have been long-established within the group. The use of the first years of data from the comparable may not be reflective of the conditions the entities face in the context of their intra-group brand licensing.

Table 21.7 shows the relied-upon data and the years over which the data were made available. The data shown are net present value data over the entire observation period, using the weighted average cost of capital (hereinafter: WACC) as a discount factor and discounting back to the first year of the observation period. The observation period excludes the first four years of data for each comparable. It also varies from one comparable to the other since some transactions were entered into at an earlier date than others. The last two lines in the table show the breakdown of the profit share of the licensor and the licensee over the entire period of observation.

Table 21.7 Summary of the Data

	Comparable Relationships (NPV Data over the Period of Observation)									
	B	*C*	*D*	*E*	*F*	*H*	*I*	*J*	*K*	*L*
Observation Period	2005–2017	2009–2017	2000–2017	1995–2017	2011–2017	1992–2017	2003–2017	2008–2017	2001–2017	1990–2017
Licensor's Profits	30	10	250	100	15	80	15	15	40	250
Licensee's Profits	270	40	750	200	25	240	85	15	60	350
Total Profits	300	50	1,000	300	40	320	100	30	100	600
Share of Licensor's Profits	10.0%	20.0%	25.0%	33.3%	37.5%	25.0%	15.0%	50.0%	40.0%	41.7%
Share of Licensee's Profits	90.0%	80.0%	75.0%	66.7%	62.5%	75.0%	85.0%	50.0%	60.0%	58.3%

We calculated the range of share of licensees' profits from the comparable relationships listed above. The interquartile range of these shares is provided in Table 21.8.

Table 21.8 Interquartile Range

	Interquartile Range of Licensee's Share of Profits
Quartile 1	60.6%
Median	70.8%
Quartile 3	78.8%

4 Concluding Remarks

This analysis suggests that in the context of the relationship between third parties, the licensee's share of the net present value of profits ranges from approximately 60% to 80%. This means that in the context of intra-group transactions, the royalty rates should be set so that the licensee earns the same share of profits.

This approach can be used *ex post* to test the arm's-length nature of royalties or *ex ante* on a budget basis to determine the budget royalty rates. From an implementation perspective, it would probably be important to consider reviewing the split of profits periodically to ensure the observed split of profit between licensee and licensor that results from the application of the royalty rates is not too different from what was initially anticipated.

The comparable profit split method could be implemented in the case at hand, in the cosmetics industry, because of the availability of comparable uncontrolled transactions with third-party licensors. When applicable, the comparable profit split can be a powerful and accurate technique. It is notably applied in the pharmaceutical industry, where licensing of high-value intangibles between third parties is common, offering a range of uncontrolled transactions to possibly leverage.

SELECTED BIBLIOGRAPHY

GERHART BARRY / MILKOVICH GEORGE T., Organizational Differences in Managerial Compensation and Financial Performance, in: Academy of Management Journal, 30 November 2017, 33/4.

HIGINBOTHAM HARLOW, The Profit split method: Effective Application for Precision and Administrability, in: BNA Tax Management Transfer Pricing Special Report, 1996, 5/11.

JENSEN MICHAEL C / MURPHY KEVIN J., CEO Incentives – It's Not How Much You Pay, But How, in: Harvard Business Review, May-June 1990, 68/3.

JORDAN JENNIFER M., Salary and Decision Making: Relationship Between Pay and Focus on Financial Profitability and Pro-sociality in an Organizational Context, in: Journal of Applied Social Psychology, February 2010, 40/2.

ROTH KENDALL / O'DONNELL SHARON, Foreign Subsidiary Compensation Strategy: An Agency Theory Perspective, in: Academy of Management Journal, 1996, 39/3.

ROZEK RICHARD / KOREKO GEORGE, Transfer Prices for the Intangible Property Embodied in Products with Extraordinary Profit Potential, in: Tax Notes International, 18 October 1999.

Index

V

www.ingramcontent.com/pod-product-compliance
Ingram Content Group UK Ltd.
Pitfield, Milton Keynes, MK11 3LW, UK
UKHW020233290926
15470UKWH00002B/506

9 789403 524